D1600825

"In this fine book Tom Schwanda lets us in on something that has regrettably been kept a secret in recent years: that the Puritans have much to teach us about a genuinely Christian—yes, and even a profoundly Calvinist!—mysticism. Isaac Ambrose here offers us profound guidance from the seventeenth century, about matters that are of crucial importance for the present-day quest for godliness."

—**Richard Mouw,** President and Professor of Christian Philosophy, Fuller Theological Seminary

"As Tom Schwanda shows in this fascinating study of Isaac Ambrose's spiritual delight in the ravishing beauty of Christ, such a piety is typically Puritan and also of enormous value for our day. Forgetfulness, nay rejection, of the way the Puritans read texts like the Song of Solomon has hindered contemporary appreciation of their piety and its exegetical basis. May a renewed appreciation of their exegesis lead to an ever-deepening recognition of the importance of Puritan piety!"

—**Michael A .G. Haykin,** Professor of Church History and Biblical Spirituality, Southern Baptist Theological Seminary

"While mystical ideas must always be sifted with biblical discernment, it is undeniable that the Reformed and Puritan tradition contains a richly experiential emphasis on delighting in God through Christ. Tom Schwanda has done us a great service in probing that tradition in this study of Isaac Ambrose in his historical context. He offers a nuanced explanation of Ambrose's view of being ravished with Christ, the Bridegroom of the church. He . . . encourages evangelicals to return to our Reformed roots in order to grow in authentic spirituality."

—**Joel R. Beeke,** President of Puritan Reformed Theological Seminary, Grand Rapids

"Schwanda's study of the 'contemplative-mystical piety' of seventeenth-century English Puritan Isaac Ambrose exhibits the best kind of Christian scholarship. This deeply researched book by an accomplished historian also explores the relevance of Ambrose's sense of intimacy with Christ for spiritual practice today. Schwanda renders a great service to the academy and church alike by bringing the writings and spiritual life of this key figure in the Puritan movement to light."

—**Charles Hambrick-Stowe,** Pastor, First Congregational Church of Ridgefield, Connecticut

"Puritans are often depicted as legalistic disciplinarians who agonized over predestination. This richly researched book offers an important corrective. Isaac Ambrose was a Puritan pastor devoted to contemplative piety, a man who long before Thoreau enjoyed month-long annual retreats in the woods. Schwanda situates his subject within a variety of broader contexts and makes a compelling case for 'Puritan mysticism' . . . a valuable addition to the literature on Reformed spirituality."

—**John Coffey,** Professor of Early Modern History, University of Leicester

Soul Recreation

Soul Recreation

The Contemplative-Mystical Piety
of Puritanism

Tom Schwanda

Foreword by J. I. Packer

PICKWICK *Publications* · Eugene, Oregon

SOUL RECREATION
The Contemplative-Mystical Piety of Puritanism

Pickwick Publications
An Imprint of Wipf and Stock Publishers
199 W. 8th Ave., Suite 3
Eugene, OR 97401

www.wipfandstock.com

Grateful appreciation is given to San Francisco Theological Seminary, San Anselmo, California, for the use of the Spiritual Movement Matrix in chapter 3.

All quotations of Scripture are from the *Authorized Version* (*Kings James Version*) of 1611.

ISBN 13: 978-1-61097-455-4

Cataloging-in-Publication data:

Schwanda, Tom.

  Soul recreation : the contemplative-mystical piety of Puritanism / Tom Schwanda, with a foreword by J. I. Packer.

  xx + 292 p. ; 23 cm. Includes bibliographical references and index.

  ISBN 13: 978-1-61097-455-4

  1. Ambrose, Isaac, 1604–1664. 2. Christian life—Puritan authors. 3. Spirituality—Puritans—History. 4. Dissenters, Religious—England. I. Packer, J. I. (James Innell). II. Title.

BV4509.5 S357 2012

Manufactured in the U.S.A.

For Grace, my beloved wife,

*with whom I am privileged to share a godly marriage
(as the Puritans called it).*

Contents

Illustrations

Foreword

We live in a buzzword society, or rather in a complex of interlocking buzzword societies, each of which develops technical or semi-technical terms that become buzzwords among its own initiates. One such, currently fashionable in the professional world of theologians and church historians, is *retrieval*. This term signifies something that many individual scholars have been trying to do for half a century and more, namely feeding wisdom from the past into present discussions to produce insight, depth, stability, and overall enrichment. The rationale of retrieval is recognition that the Holy Spirit has been active as the church's teacher since Pentecost, directing God's people to focus attention on this and that in light of the Word of God, and so bequeathing a legacy of tested and lived-out truth for the benefit of those who come after, who will need these resources for encountering—and, when necessary, countering—cultural, theological, attitudinal, and behavioral challenges.

Dr. Schwanda's book is cast as a call to retrieval, from a particular Puritan source, for a particular Reformed and evangelical purpose. He wades into the sometimes choppy waters of present-day Puritan studies in order to analyze in a fully disciplined way the devotional theology, experience, and directives of pastor Isaac Ambrose, who in his own day was a much appreciated master in the field of affective spirituality. His goal is to recommend Ambrose's mapping of the believer's inner life as meriting discerning retrieval today. Dr. Schwanda believes that such retrieval, leading to a renewal of contemplative prayer as a pathway to invigorating delight in God, would make a solid contribution to healthy evangelical spirituality in our time, and in this I think he is right. So I commend this excellent work on Isaac Ambrose with enthusiasm.

J. I. Packer
Professor of Theology, Regent College, Vancouver

Acknowledgments

The creation of a book requires a journey that involves many people. While it is impossible to recognize every individual that has contributed to this research and writing there are many significant people that I want to acknowledge. I am most grateful for my wife, Grace Schwanda, who faithfully supported and consistently encouraged me during the many years of gestation of this book, even though they often reduced our time together. I also thank my family and friends for their support. I acknowledge Philip Sheldrake who has wisely guided my research. This is a modified revision and updating of my Ph.D. thesis at Durham University. Professor Sheldrake has always provided a depth of knowledge and insight and valuable questions and feedback that have expanded my understanding and greatly improved the quality of this work. However, any errors that remain are my responsibility. Further, I am also grateful for Alec Ryrie and David Cornick, my examiners, who encouraged me to publish this work. Books do not get published without wise and patient editors and I have greatly benefitted from working with Robin Parry and other members of Wipf & Stock Publishers.

Further, I express my deep appreciation to Ben C. Johnson, who first challenged me to begin my Ph.D. and as treasurer of the Griffith Theological Research Foundation encouraged me to apply for this scholarship. This was made possible by Dean and Lois Griffith, whose generosity created the Griffith Theological Research Foundation scholarship at Columbia Theological Seminary (Decatur, GA). I must also mention my former colleague and friend, Benjamin J. Boerkoel, Sr. who granted me first choice of his massive library of Puritan sources when his move into a retirement home required him to radically reduce the size of his library.

Many of the sources used in this research were the gift of Benjamin's generosity. Sadly Benjamin died before this research was completed.

Researching the English Puritans gave me the opportunity to visit their homeland many times. Over the years I was fortunate to engage in conversation, whether in person or through email, with numerous scholars and who have challenged and sharpened my thinking on Puritan piety. I gratefully acknowledge my new English and Dutch friends: David Appleby, Julia Beelen, Elizabeth Clarke, John Coffey, Arie de Reuver, David Field, Ann Hughes, Tony Lane, Susan Hardman Moore, Willem Op't Hof, Roger Pooley, Herman Selderhuis, and Alan Sell. On the "other side of the pond," I was also privileged to have the support and insightful conversations of fellow North American scholars including: Joel Beeke, John Bolt, Mark Burrows, Steven Chase, Ron Frost, Ron Gleason, Richard Godbeer, Charles Hambrick-Stowe, Jim Houston, Evan Howard, Kelly Kapic, Belden Lane, Richard Muller, Scoti Old, Jim Packer, Gary Sattler, Stephen Spencer, Dennis Tamburello, John Visser, Diane Willen, and John Witvliet. Additionally I offer my deep appreciation to Jim Packer for writing the foreword to this book.

Finally, I am grateful for my Wheaton College community, including my dean, Jill Peláez Baumgaertner, and my colleagues: Kathleen Cruse, Roger Lundin, Leland Ryken, Dan Treier, Kevin Vanhoozer, Jim Wilhoit and other members of the Christian Formation and Ministry department. I also express my deep appreciation to Andrew Pride, Michael Rade, Liz Harbers, and Kirsten Hitchcock as my student research assistants during both my Ph.D. studies and the completion of this book. In particular, I acknowledge Jim Wilhoit and Kathleen Cruse who carefully read the entire final manuscript of this work. Thank you to all who contributed to bringing this work to life.

Abbreviations

CD   Karl Barth, *Church Dogmatics*. Translated by G. W. Bromiley and T. F. Torrance. 13 vols. Edinburgh: T. & T. Clark, 1936–75.

DNB   *Dictionary of National Biography*. Edited by Leslie Stephen and Sidney Lee. 21 vols. London: Oxford University Press, 1917

ODNB   *Oxford Dictionary of National Biography*. Edited by H. C. G. Matthew and Brian Harrison. 60 vols. Oxford: Oxford University Press, 2004.

OED   *Oxford English Dictionary*. 2nd ed. Prepared by J. A. Simpson and E. S. C. Weiner. 20 vols. Oxford: Clarendon, 1989.

SCC   Bernard of Clairvaux, *Sermo super cantica canticorum* (Sermons on the Song of Songs). 4 vols. Vols. 1 and 2, translated by Kilian Walsh; vol. 3, translated by Kilian Walsh and Irene M. Edmonds; vol. 4 translated by Irene M. Edmonds. Kalamazoo, MI: Cistercian, 1971–80.

Introduction

The questions that first prompted this book originally arose out of Christian ministry when I was a pastor. At that time, it was common for Protestants who became interested in the spiritual life to seek the guidance of Roman Catholic writers or spiritual directors. In fact, I did that myself over thirty years ago. I visited my Roman Catholic pastor friend and expressed my spiritual hunger and desire to grow deeper in God. I have never forgotten his wise counsel. He confirmed that although he had been formed in the life of prayer during his seminary training, he now was so overwhelmed by the demands of his large parish that he had no time to practice what he had learned. Surprisingly, he encouraged me to discover the roots of my own spiritual tradition. Therefore, the reason why I became interested in Reformed spirituality and the study of the Puritans was due to my Roman Catholic pastor friend.

As I received training and became a spiritual director myself, fellow clergy and laity often spoke to me of their frustration of the lack of spiritual resources within the Protestant tradition. When I offered them the same counsel that I had received, I discovered that many were not interested or equipped to search for the treasures of their respective Protestant tradition. Instead, they gravitated towards the more readily accessible resources of Roman Catholic spirituality. This book will strongly affirm the validity of other streams of Christian spirituality, nonetheless, it is also imperative for those who are interested in ecumenical dialogue, or even ministry in the contemporary world, to have a significant background in their own Christian tradition. If a person is unaware of his or her own spiritual roots, it is likely to create a vacuum and even frustration that there are no significant representatives or spiritual practices within that tradition. A conviction that has long inspired my own study in the history of Christian spirituality is that if you examine any tradition in detail you will discover the representative strengths and weaknesses of the broader history of the church. Therefore, the historical question of what can the Reformed and Evangelical traditions contribute to the study of Christian spirituality became the basis for this research.

Since those early days I have become a professor and now have the opportunity of training students for Christian ministry. This combines the importance of discovering the context and wisdom of the past as well as seeking to enable contemporary pilgrims to learn from the Communion of Saints. While the majority of this research is historical and theological, it concludes in the final chapter by asking the pastoral question, how can the forgotten and neglected treasures of Puritan piety speak to the contemporary church, and, in particular, those of the Reformed and Evangelical traditions? Historical amnesia and outdated caricatures of the Puritans may cause some readers to wonder if there is any relevance to the Puritans for today. However, I confess my deep appreciation and indebtedness to these seventeenth-century spiritual giants who developed a vibrant personal and communal piety that was radically God-centered and because of their deep enjoyment of the Triune God often focused on contemplation and heavenly meditation to deepen their intense desires for God.

Therefore, this book raises two important questions: Was Isaac Ambrose a Puritan mystic and can contemporary Reformed and Evangelical Christians retrieve any wisdom from his writings to guide their piety? The first chapter of this book acknowledges the difficulty of defining mysticism. Clearly, over its long history within the Christian church there have been vivid illustrations of the strengths and potential dangers of mysticism. Rather than rejecting mysticism, Bernard McGinn offers a broader construct that provides greater clarity than other approaches and reduces the distorted perceptions of many. It further expands the possibility of recognizing the presence of God and the importance of the mystical element more widely in the history of Christian spirituality. This chapter substitutes the language of contemplative-mystical piety for McGinn's mystical element since, the former is more reflective and consistent with the Protestant tradition. Additionally, Isaac Ambrose is introduced as the primary focus of this book.

Chapter 2 will explore the critical theme of the biblical-theological foundation of union with Christ, often called spiritual marriage. A historical survey will indicate that spiritual marriage played a significant role in Bernard of Clairvaux, John Calvin, and the Puritans. Unlike Calvin, who eschewed the allegorical reading of the Song of Songs, the Puritans more closely resembled Bernard in their reading of this exceptional text of biblical mysticism. Just as the Puritans spoke freely of the intimacy and joys of spiritual marriage with Jesus, as the divine Bridegroom, they equally believed in celebrating the intimacy and joys of godly or earthly marriage. This background enables a careful consideration of Isaac Ambrose's usage of spiritual marriage. Central to Ambrose's understanding of spiritual marriage is both the person's union with Christ as well as the deepening experience of communion with Christ. The third chapter creates a contemplative biography of Isaac Ambrose. He understood contemplation as gazing at God in love out of gratitude. While much of Ambrose's diary was lost, the available evidence produces a vivid description of his contemplative attitude, personal and communal spiritual practices, and experiences that emerge from his spiritual marriage with Jesus. The most unique feature about Ambrose was his annual month-long retreats in May, in which he retired into the woods to more intentionally cultivate his relationship with God and renew himself for his public ministry with others.

Chapter 4 examines the broader Christian understanding of meditation and contemplation and the specific manner in which Ambrose both taught and practiced these disciplines. A survey of Ambrose and other seventeenth-century Puritan writings reveal their familiarity with Bernard of Clairvaux as well as other Western Catholic spiritual writers. This chapter culminates in a detailed examination of Ambrose's use of contemplation as well as its benefits and effects. The next chapter presents the most distinctive aspect of this book. While numerous scholars have explored various dimensions of the contemplative-mystical piety of the Puritans, no one to my knowledge has devoted sustained research to the Puritan usage of the erotic language of Song of Songs expressed in ravishment. Further, ravishment was a primary term to express the Puritan delight and enjoyment of God in spiritual marriage. This chapter will also summarize Ambrose's teaching on the benefits and effects of ravishment on the soul. The final chapter marks a critical transition and moves from the historical theological focus of the contemplative-mystical piety of Isaac Ambrose to the practical matter of retrieval. However, before retrieving Ambrose's piety for contemporary Reformed and Evangelical Christians, the question must be asked what happened to the contemplative tradition within Puritanism. This will necessitate an inquiry into the areas of resistance and suspicion of contemplation and mysticism of Karl Barth. However, Barth is not representative of the entire Reformed tradition, and Herman Bavinck will offer a contrasting position that is more receptive to contemplative piety. The critical issue of retrieval will be examined to determine how we can recover both Ambrose's piety and his sources. Additionally, the chapter will conclude with the retrieval of seven specific themes and principles from Ambrose's contemplative-mystical piety for the contemporary Protestant church.

This work relies heavily upon the documents from the seventeenth century. Spelling had not yet been standardized, and it was often common to italicize various phrases or entire sentences. I have retained all spellings as they appeared in the original documents. Therefore, any italicized words in primary and secondary sources appeared in the originals.

Unless otherwise indicated, all quotations from the Bible are from the *Authorized Version* (1611).

ISAAC AMBROSE

J.Miller.Preston.

Rev. Isaac Ambrose.

xix

Chapter One

Introduction to Puritan Mysticism

Isaac Ambrose was "[o]f a retiring disposition, his mind of the
contemplative order, he was in true sense a religious mystic."
—Benjamin Nightingale[1]

Was **Isaac Ambrose** a Puritan mystic and can the contemporary
church retrieve any wisdom from his writings?[2] These two questions will shape the substance and structure of this work. Ambrose was
a moderate seventeenth-century Lancashire Puritan minister whom
Benjamin Nightingale called a "religious mystic." Therefore, the primary
question is whether it is legitimate to call Isaac Ambrose a Puritan mystic.
This will necessitate a study of the nature of Puritan mysticism, examining both the theological foundation as well as historical antecedents for
it. Many readers may find the juxtaposition of the terms Puritanism and
mysticism not only paradoxical but also improbable. All too often the
perception of many regarding the Puritans is that they were hardheaded
and cold hearted. They are seen as spiritually cold, legalistic, eschewing
all forms of fun, sexually-pinched, and devoid of passion. While much
scholarship has defended this mistaken position, more recently some

1. Nightingale, *Isaac Ambrose, Religious Mystic*, 20.

2. For an overview of Isaac Ambrose's life and ministry see the chronology at the
back of this book.

writers have begun to correct these distortions. Jean Williams' research has been most significant in reclaiming the legitimacy of Puritan mysticism. This chapter will examine her conclusions in greater detail, but for now it is important to summarize her findings. Unlike some previous researchers who acknowledged the possibility of mysticism on the fringes or as an oddity within mainstream Puritanism, Williams argues persuasively "that mystics and mystically-inclined individuals naturally grew out of the soil of moderate Puritanism: they were not hybrid offshoots, but expected outgrowths of mainstream Puritan theology and devotion which itself had many mystical elements."[3]

The secondary question of this book is the practical issue of retrieval that lies behind the historical-theological question. Does Isaac Ambrose have any wisdom to teach the contemporary Protestant church about piety and growing in deeper union and communion with God? In that sense, this study is an exercise in practical theology as much as it is in historical theology. This book will often use the categories of Protestants, Reformed, and Evangelical interchangeably. Clearly all Reformed and Evangelical Christians were Protestant, but obviously not all Protestants were Reformed or Evangelical. I am employing the term Reformed to describe the theology of many mainstream Puritans who were the descendants of John Calvin, rather than limiting it to any cluster of specific denominations. I will also frequently combine the term Reformed with the term Evangelical to signify those from outside Reformed churches who practiced a Reformed theology and spiritual life. Further, I am aware of the debate that still persists in defining the origin of Evangelicals. While David Bebbington and many others favor the eighteenth century, other scholars push the date back to the Puritans[4] Whether one acknowledges the Puritans as Evangelicals or antecedents to them, there are many parallels between the seventeenth-century Puritans and today's Evangelicals.

In recent years numerous Protestant Christians who were formed by a strong cognitive emphasis have been leaving their churches and searching for deeper and more experiential relationships of faith. The reality is that the Evangelical and Reformed traditions have much to learn from their earlier Catholic roots, even as the Roman Catholic Church

3. Williams, "Puritan Enjoyment of God," 9.

4. See for example, Haykin and Stewart, *Advent of Evangelicalism*, esp. 146–68, 252–77.

can equally learn from the Protestant church. In the following chapters it will become evident that many Reformed writers of the sixteenth and seventeenth centuries willingly embraced and even strongly endorsed medieval sources from the Western Catholic Church, not limited to but especially those of Bernard of Clairvaux.

It is appropriate to say a few words about the selection of Isaac Ambrose as the subject of this book. First, and most importantly, from a research perspective, no one has examined his life or theology in a sustained way or devoted a book to him. Therefore, his writings provide a very fertile ground for examination. Further, he is representative of the moderate stream of Puritanism and displays a balanced and integrative dynamic of both the intellect and affect. This critical combination seems lacking today in many Reformed and Evangelical churches. A third compelling factor is that while many of the writings of prominent Puritans of the seventeenth century have been forgotten or are no longer being republished, Ambrose's writings are.[5] The fact that he has stood the test of time warrants a closer examination of his theology and piety. To orient us to this chapter and to construct a common vocabulary, I will first examine the three critical words of "mysticism," "Puritanism," and "Puritan mysticism." This will be followed by a review of the most salient writings on Puritan mysticism and Isaac Ambrose. Since one of the primary goals of this study is whether or not Puritan piety can be retrieved for the contemporary church, the hermeneutical process of reading Puritan and other texts must be considered.

DEFINING MYSTICISM

The problematic nature of mysticism has occupied scholars for generations yielding little clarity and consensus.[6] Further, embarking upon this pilgrimage it must be asserted that Isaac Ambrose and his fellow Puritans of the seventeenth century would not have employed this term nor had the ability to understand the nature of it. However, that is no different for Western and Roman Catholic mystics who would more readily warrant

5. Ambrose, *Looking Unto Jesus.* Sprinkle Publications, 1986 and Ambrose, *The Christian Warrior* (contemporary title for *War with Devils*). Soli Deo Gloria Publications, 1997.

6. For a helpful introduction to mysticism see Wiseman, "Mysticism"; McGinn, "Mysticism"; Turner, "Mysticism"; Perrin, "Mysticism," *Blackwell Companion*; and Tamburello, *Ordinary Mysticism.*

this label. Bernard McGinn remarks, "[n]o mystics (at least before the present century) believed in or practiced mysticism. They believed in and practiced Christianity."[7] According to Michel de Certeau, "mysticism" as a noun first appeared in early seventeenth-century France.[8] Even further, the word "mysticism" did not enter the English language until the eighteenth century.[9] A review of four popular seventeenth-century dictionaries confirms this; however, the word "mystery" and "mystical" were already in common usage.[10] Indeed the language of "mystical" and "mystically" was introduced by Clement of Alexandria (ca. 150–ca. 215) already in the early third century.[11]

William Inge concludes his study of mysticism with a sample of twenty-six definitions of "mysticism" and "mystical theology" and acknowledges that the list could have been greatly expanded.[12] The difficulty of defining the nature of mysticism can be further illustrated by the assessment of the spiritual life of St. Thérèse of Lisieux by two prominent Roman Catholic theologians of the last century. On the one hand, Louis Bouyer asserts that she was a mystic, while, on the other, Hans Urs von Balthasar maintains that she was not because she possessed no acquaintance with or desired the typical experiences associated with mysticism.[13] Therefore, Heiko Oberman's reminder about the necessity for clarity is appropriate, as he warns that an inaccurate understanding tends to "block access to mysticism." This is especially true of Protestants whose distorted categories have produced an "understanding of mysticism [that] has also been prejudiced."[14] Perhaps the most

7. McGinn, *Foundations of Mysticism*, 266–67. For a summary of the development of the term "mysticism" see Bouyer, "Mysticism: Essay of the Word." For a succinct survey of the history of spirituality that is strongly focused on mysticism see Sheldrake, *Spirituality & History*, 40–64.

8. De Certeau, *Mystic Fable*, 107; cf. 94–112; cf. Harmless, *Mystics*, 261–62.

9. The first entry for mysticism appears in 1736. *OED*, 10:176. However, the term mystical appeared as early as 1500 and mystic in 1382. *OED*, 10:175. Further the term mystery appeared in 1315. *OED*, 10:173. Of these terms, mystery was the only term that would have been used in Scripture (e.g. Rom 16:25; 1 Cor 15:51; Eph 5:32; Col 1:26; 1 Tim 3:16).

10. See Cawdrey, *Table Alphabetical*; Wilson, *Christian Dictionary*; Cockeram, *English Dictionarie*; Phillips, *New World of English Words*.

11. McGinn, *Foundations of Mysticism*, 102.

12. Inge, *Christian Mysticism*, 335–48.

13. Wiseman, "Mysticism," 682.

14. Oberman, "Meaning of Mysticism," 80.

common misconception people associate with mysticism is that voiced by Dennis Tamburello: "[t]he problem in these discussions is that mysticism is assumed to mean a pantheistic absorption into God or merging of identities between the believer and God."[15] Unfortunately, this perception of mysticism is difficult to shed, and many writers who address this from within Protestantism raise this as a primary concern. Friedrich Heiler, a convert from Roman Catholicism, is one person responsible for creating this distortion of a union of absorption.[16] Significantly for the purposes of this book, McGinn reminds his readers that if a "union of absorption" is used to define mysticism, then there "are actually so few mystics in the history of Christianity that one wonders why Christians used the qualifier 'mystical' so often."[17] Oberman further articulates another common Protestant concern that mysticism is too closely associated with Roman Catholicism and marginalizes the usage of Scripture.[18] However, Oberman clearly reveals his own position in concluding, "without Christian mysticism, there is no faithful and living Church to withstand the Hell of the Last Days."[19]

The combination of distorted perceptions among Protestants and Roman Catholics alike and the inability to find a consensus definition among scholars has raised the question of the validity of this term. Alister McGrath argues, "[t]he difficulty in using the term 'mysticism' to refer to what is now more widely known as 'spirituality' is that the term has so many unhelpful associations and misleading overtones that its continued use is problematic."[20] While McGrath is correct to recognize the problematic nature of the word mysticism, his solution of collapsing the term into spirituality continues to advance a similar misconception by implying that all expressions of spirituality are synonymous with mysticism. What McGrath fails to recognize is that typically mysticism

---

15. Tamburello, "John Calvin's Mysticism," 504; cf. Tamburello, *Union with Christ*, 21–22, 103.

16. Wakefield, *Puritan Devotion*, 89; cf. Heiler, *Prayer*, 136 for actual quote.

17. McGinn, *Foundations of Mysticism*, xvi; cf. 83. McGinn clarifies the difference between the "union of identity" or "union of indistinction" that is partaking of the actual essence of God found in Meister Eckhart and some of the Beguines and the older teaching of the "loving union of wills" (1 Cor 6:17) found in Bernard. "Mysticism," 3:119.

18. Oberman, "Meaning of Mysticism," 80; cf. Nuttall, "Puritans and Quaker Mysticism," 522 for additional Protestant suspicions of mysticism.

19. Ibid., 90.

20. McGrath, *Christian Spirituality*, 6.

is a more distinctive and carefully defined component of the more general term spirituality. Many expressions of spirituality do not reflect the depth of intimacy suggested by mysticism. Thus there has been an attempt to retrieve the term and its validity for use in speaking of one's experience of God. Denys Turner also raises questions about the usage of mysticism; however, he affirms the positive value for "historical reconstruction" of the term.[21] Accepting this premise, this study seeks to explore the validity of a "historical reconstruction" of mysticism within seventeenth-century Puritan piety.

Further, some scholars differentiate between two broad traditions of Christian mysticism. As with all generalizations, there is a danger in pressing these distinctions too far, however, history has revealed a christocentric affective love mysticism that gives prominence to the *via positiva* which has its biblical foundation in St. Paul. This kataphatic approach is in stark contrast to the *via negativa* or apophatic way that tends to focus on the intellect and has its biblical origin in St. John.[22] However, the history of mysticism is far too complex and fluid to neatly correspond with these tidy categories, and it is important to remember the elasticity of these approaches to mysticism. John of the Cross, though strongly apophatic, had a deep appreciation for the more kataphatic Bernard of Clairvaux and his sermons on the Song of Songs. Further, while Pseudo-Dionysius is frequently mentioned as the founder of the apophatic school he also emphasized the kataphatic.[23] Harvey Egan reminds readers that "any genuine Christian mysticism must contain apophatic as well as kataphatic elements."[24] Therefore, while the Puritans displayed a strong affinity for Bernard, that does not negate the reality of apophatic expressions of mysticism as Jean Williams' research has demonstrated.[25]

Among the most recent efforts towards a revised understanding of mysticism is the research of Bernard McGinn. While his magisterial study has not yet reached the seventeenth century, he provides an extremely valuable heuristic model for the study of Puritan mysticism.[26]

21. Turner "Mysticism," 460–61.

22. Ibid. Cf. Oberman, "Meaning of Mysticism," 81–85. Steven Ozment makes the same distinction but acknowledges it is a "gross contrast." *Age of Reform*, 115–16.

23. McGinn, *Foundations of Mysticism*, 159.

24. Harvey Egan, "Christian Apophatic and Kataphatic Mysticisms," 405.

25. Williams, "Puritan Enjoyment of God," 267–70, 393. See for example, Barker, *Jesus Christ the Great Wonder*.

26. McGinn is preparing a six volume series entitled *The Presence of God: A History*

Indeed McGinn provides great encouragement to Protestants and no doubt many others, as he summarizes two distinctive forms of mysticism. The first involves "some form of union of identity with God through purely contemplative practice, especially one that bypasses the mediatorial role of Christ and the place of scripture and the community." McGinn quickly critiques this aberrant form and asserts that this type of mysticism rarely existed in Christianity. The second form of "mysticism is [the] broader and more flexible sense argued for in this volume" that reflects "the existence of a mystical element."[27] Therefore, rather than attempting to delineate a concise definition, McGinn prefers to speak in broader terms. He draws upon Baron von Hügel's research that parsed religion into the three dimensions of the institutional, intellectual, and mystical.[28] Significantly, von Hügel stressed that these three elements must be kept in balance.[29] McGinn maintains, "the mystical element in Christianity is that part of its belief and practices that concerns the preparation for, the consciousness of, and the reaction to what can be described as the immediate or direct presence of God."[30] Michael Downey agrees, "[t]he governing category for viewing the tradition of mysticism need not be solely that of union with God as is often assumed . . . Indeed, there is much to suggest that 'presence' rather than 'union' is the more appropriate category in interpreting the traditions of Christian spirituality."[31]

McGinn's broad definition includes three main areas of concern, the mystical element of Christianity, the mystical process or way of life, and the mystical experience.[32] In his third volume he restates his understanding of mysticism, "[t]he mystical element within Christianity, as I have argued throughout this history, centers on a form of immediate encounter with God whose essential purpose is to convey a loving knowledge (even a negative one) that transforms the mystic's mind and

---

of Western Christian Mysticism. To date the first four volumes, reaching the mid-fifteenth century, have been released.

27. McGinn, *Foundations of Mysticism*, 65–66.

28. Von Hügel, *Mystical Element of Religion*, 1:9, 60–61.

29. Ibid., 2:68–69, 387–92.

30. McGinn, *Foundations of Mysticism*, xvii.

31. Downey, *Understanding Christian Spirituality*, 67.

32. McGinn, *Foundations of Mysticism*, xvi–xvii.

whole way of life."[33] McGinn's understanding of mysticism is obviously more expansive than this and includes a nuanced perspective on the role of experience that has been frequently seen by scholars in the past as a central feature of mysticism. That treatment which fits more directly with the contemplative biography of Isaac Ambrose will be examined in chapter 3. McGinn has provided a great service to the church in expanding the horizons for both Roman Catholic and Protestant scholars, thereby creating the framework for discovering the broader richness of the "mystical element" within Christianity. Therefore, by adapting McGinn's schema, the goal of this book is not to prove whether or not mysticism existed in Puritanism, since that would be anachronistic, but rather whether there was a "mystical element" in Puritanism. Further, by employing other categories of McGinn's treatment of mysticism did the Puritans in general, and Isaac Ambrose in particular, employ a mystical language or vocabulary, mystical theology, write mystical texts, and record mystical experiences?

DEFINING PURITANISM

Puritanism, like mysticism, is another challenging term to define.[34] John Coffey provides a succinct and excellent summary of the nature of this long running debate, including the significant scholars and issues surrounding the word "Puritan."[35] Patrick Collinson accurately reminds readers that the word "[p]uritan was never a term of ecclesiological or confessional precision."[36] More accurately, it was a pejorative word of slander or rebuke, and, since the Puritans' agenda emphasized godly living, they often preferred the term "the godly."[37] John Coffey and Paul

---

33. McGinn, *Flowering of Mysticism*, 26.

34. The literature surrounding this debate is massive. The best writings for tracing this are: Coffey, "Puritanism, Evangelicalism and Protestant Tradition," 255–61; Coffey and Lim, *Cambridge Companion to Puritanism*, 1–7; Kapic and Gleason, *Devoted Life*, 16–18; Spurr, *English Puritanism*, 3–8; Durston and Eales, *Culture of English Puritanism*, 1–31; Collinson, "Puritans," 3:364–70; Lake, "Defining Puritanism—again?"; David Hall, "Narrating Puritanism"; and Como, *Blown by the Spirit*, 1–32. Older but still valuable is Finlayson, "Puritanism and Puritans," 201–23.

35. Coffey, "Puritanism, Evangelicalism and Protestant Tradition," 255–61.

36. Collinson, "Puritans," 3:364.

37. Haigh, *Plain Man's Pathways to Heaven*, 46, 47, 104, 122–23, 128; Collinson, *Godly People*, 1–17; Tom Webster, *Godly Clergy*, esp. 3, 4, 95–121; and Ann Hughes, "Frustrations of Godly."

Lim introduce their study of Puritanism by using five themes to explore this term more fully. They maintain that Puritans were descendants of the Reformation, with Calvinistic roots, who originated within the Church of England, who eventually proved to be divisive, and that their influence quickly overflowed into the European context.[38]

This specific study is focused primarily on Puritan piety and affirms that at the heart of it "Puritanism was a devotional movement, rooted in religious experience."[39] However, piety does not function in isolation from theology or ecclesiology, and Stephen Yuille helpfully expands the discussion of Puritanism as an ecclesiastical, political, theological, and spiritual movement.[40] Therefore, while scholars continue to wrestle and wrangle over definitions,[41] this blurring of boundaries has caused some researchers to assert that it is more accurate to speak in terms of "Puritanisms."[42]

This is further reinforced by the practice of some scholars to classify Puritans more specifically into different categories. According to Jerald Brauer, Puritans can be divided into four different streams of piety: legalist (that Brauer names nomism), evangelical, rationalist, and mystical.[43] Brauer maintains that this classification is helpful because "[t]ypology is a heuristic tool that enables a historian to account for obvious differences and to distinguish between figures in the same movement."[44] Janice Knight has simplified this by reducing it to two categories: "Intellectual Fathers" who were represented by Thomas Hooker, Thomas Shepard, William Perkins, and William Ames and the "Spiritual Brethren" who included Richard Sibbes, John Preston, and John Cotton.[45] While she acknowledges the danger of "oversimplif[ying] the complex ideas in question," she continues this approach.[46] Norman Pettit criticizes Knight

38. Coffey and Lim, *Cambridge Companion to Puritanism*, 2–7. The final point of expansion will be evident in later discussions involving the Dutch *Nadere Reformatie*.

39. Hambrick-Stowe, *Practice of Piety*, vii; cf. 23, 38, 53, 113; cf. Packer, *Quest for Godliness*, 28; Dewey Wallace, *Spirituality of Later Puritans*, xi; and Haller, *Rise of Puritanism*, 9.

40. Yuille, *Puritan Spirituality*, 5–17.

41. Clary, "Taxonomy of English Puritanism."

42. Coffey, "Puritanism, Evangelicalism and Protestant Tradition," 261.

43. Brauer, "Types of Puritan Piety," 42, 44–58.

44. Ibid., 42.

45. Knight, *Orthodoxies in Massachusetts*, 2–3, 31.

46. Ibid., 131.

10

for this very reason of attempting to force Puritans into overly rigid categories.[47] Further, as with many typologies, a person might equally fit in more than one category. This is clearly evident by Brauer's placement of Samuel Rutherford in the nomist category, whereas Jean Williams believes he "was also a mystic."[48] Additionally, Brauer positions Sibbes in the evangelical stream in part because of his numerous sermons on the Song of Songs yet this specific identification reveals the strong mystical flavor in his writings.[49]

Philip Sheldrake comments on the benefits of "types of spirituality." However, he also cautiously asserts, "[t]here is a danger that, if applied too rigidly or exclusively, these distinctions will force historical personalities into preconceived models which do damage to their complexity."[50] Clearly this demonstrates the difficulty of classification. Therefore, employing Yuille's language of Puritanism as an ecclesiastical movement would include Sibbes, Baxter, and Owen as well as the Church of England bishops Bayly, Hall, and Reynolds. One possible solution that still allows for distinctions within Puritanism is Finlayson's suggestion that envisions Puritans living along a "spectrum" or continuum rather than being forced into rigid categories of demarcation.[51] Therefore, narrow categories of differentiation are as likely to conceal insights, as they are to reveal them. This danger will be shortly illustrated in Simon Chan's categories that ultimately distort his reading of Isaac Ambrose. Further, even when examining Puritan mysticism and the distinctions between the moderate Puritans and their more radical descendants such as the Quakers and Ranters, it is helpful to remember Coffey's admonition that "all these sects had emerged from *within* the Puritan subculture."[52]

One additional complexity that must be recognized in defining Puritanism is that of polemics. Seventeenth-century England was certainly not unique in this, but the battle lines were often drawn and redrawn with vociferous attacks both in print and in public. Those who

47. Pettit, review of *Orthodoxies in Massachusetts*, 145–50.

48. Compare Brauer, "Types of Puritan Piety," 46n19 with Williams, "Puritan Enjoyment of God," 9n37.

49. Brauer, "Types of Puritan Piety," 48.

50. Sheldrake, *Spirituality & History*, 209; cf. 196, 217–18 for the benefits of using typologies.

51. Finlayson, "Puritanism and Puritans," 208, 211, 223.

52. Coffey, "Puritanism, Evangelicalism and Protestant Tradition," 260.

found themselves embroiled in controversies tended to define the categories far more precisely than we would today. Tobias Crisp provides
a helpful illustration. While many moderate Puritans, including Isaac
Ambrose, attacked Crisp for his antinomian tendencies, he is still considered a Puritan by contemporary scholars.[53] This blurring of boundaries signals the importance of flexibility in demarcation and supports the
claim of a varied genealogy of seventeenth-century Puritanisms.[54]

DEFINING PURITAN MYSTICISM

The combination of the two previous key terms of mysticism and
Puritanism are now joined to ask if mysticism existed within Puritanism?[55]
For many, the idea of Puritan mysticism is atypical and incongruous.
However, numerous scholars have emerged since Geoffrey Nuttall de-
clared over sixty years ago, "Puritan mysticism is a field still almost en-
tirely unexplored."[56] Broadly speaking, I envision Puritan mysticism as
the grateful and loving beholding of God through God's mighty acts and
Scripture, in which one experiences union and deepening communion

53. Beeke and Pederson, *Meet the Puritans*, 164–68.

54. The situation in Ireland was as complex if not more so than in England.
Crawford Gribben's *God's Irishmen* provides an illuminating study of this especially in
the Cromwell period, replete with it various divisions and counter divisions.

55. The best-published sources for tracing Puritan mysticism are Winthrop
Hudson, "Mystical Religion in Puritan Commonwealth"; Brauer, "Puritan Mysticism
and Liberalism"; Brauer, "Types of Puritan Piety"; Maclear, "Heart of New England
Rent"; Wakefield, *Puritan Devotion*, esp. 101–8; Wakefield, "Mysticism and its Puritan
Types"; Nuttall, "Puritan and Quaker Mysticism"; Nuttall, *Holy Spirit in Puritan
Faith*; Stoeffler, *Rise of Evangelical Pietism*; Rupp, "Rapture of Devotion in English
Puritans"; Lovelace, *American Pietism of Cotton Mather*; Hambrick-Stowe, *Practice of
Piety*, Hambrick-Stowe, *Early New England Meditative Poetry*; B. R. White, "Echoes of
Medieval Christendom"; Dewey Wallace, *Spirituality of Later Puritans*; Dewey Wallace,
Shapers of English Calvinism, esp. 51–85; King, "Affective Spirituality of John Owen";
Williams, "Puritanism: Piety of Joy"; van den Berg, "English Puritan Francis Rous";
Belden Lane, "Two Schools of Desire"; Dever, *Richard Sibbes*; Schwanda, "Gazing at
God"; and de Reuver, *Sweet Communion*. Outdated and less helpful is Bronkema,
Essence of Puritanism. Dissertations focusing on Puritan mysticism include: Brauer,
"Francis Rous, Puritan Mystic"; Chan, "Puritan Meditative Tradition" and Williams,
"Puritan Enjoyment of God." Ronald Frost devotes one chapter to Richard Sibbes' un-
derstanding of mystical marriage, "Richard Sibbes' Theology of Grace." Further two
other dissertations explore the possibility of Puritan mysticism: Won, "Communion
with Christ" and Yeoman, "Heart-Work."

56. Nuttall, *Holy Spirit in Puritan Faith*, 146.

with Jesus Christ through the power and guidance of the Holy Spirit. While there has been no critical study on Puritan mysticism, a handful of articles and dissertations have begun the much-needed examination of this significant topic. Nonetheless, some skeptics might raise the question "Why should such a scorned and misunderstood topic as Puritan mysticism be explored when it is fraught with such little clarity?" Further, why perpetuate the confusion by asking whether there could be a legitimate expression of Puritan mysticism?

However, there are at least three valid reasons for examining this question of Puritan mysticism. First, a careful examination into the theological foundation of Puritan spiritual practices and the resulting spiritual texts and experiences will assist in revealing a more accurate picture of a frequently denigrated and grossly misconstrued tradition. This rehabilitation would provide a more accurate and balanced under-standing of a significant movement of the sixteenth and seventeenth-centuries. Second, to include Puritanism within the conversation with other Christian traditions regarding mysticism elevates the validity and authenticity of Puritan piety. There are those within the Protestant tradition who are apologetic or even embarrassed when discussing the topic of spirituality. Due to historical amnesia, many contemporary Evangelical and Reformed Christians are unaware of the richness of their spiritual roots. The greater the attention of scholars to Puritan piety the more these forgotten but valued principles can be reclaimed. Third, an awareness of the distinctions of Puritan mysticism can expand the conversation within the larger study of Christian mysticism. What were the roots, challenges, unique spiritual practices, and writings of Puritan piety, and how can their distinctive emphases contribute to the study of Christian mysticism?

Jerald Brauer was the first to heed Nuttall's invitation and in 1948 wrote a dissertation on Francis Rous, the British Member of Parliament and devotional writer.[57] Brauer defines a "Christian mystic, then, [as] a person who has had an extremely intimate experience of being person-ally united with God and who follows the threefold mystic path that he might repeat such an experience and exhibit the results of the union in his daily life."[58] Rous' writings, especially on *The Mysticall Marriage*, frequently employ the union with Christ or spiritual marriage metaphor.

57. Brauer, "Francis Rous, Puritan Mystic."
58. Ibid., 13.

However, according to Brauer, the presence of a "mystical element" does not make one a mystic.[59] One must also have "mystical experience" and employ "mystical theology."[60] He further cautions readers not to be too hasty in using the term mystic with the Puritans: "[t]he fact of a heavy mystical emphasis does not mean that any of these Puritans became mystics or practiced the mystical life."[61] Nonetheless, Brauer maintains that there were numerous themes within Puritanism that prepared them for mysticism, including a strong doctrine of the Holy Spirit, immediacy of faith, and a disciplined moral life that emphasized asceticism that was an outgrowth of spiritual marriage.[62]

Brauer offers a number of significant conclusions that must be briefly mentioned. His claim that Puritan mysticism developed from within Puritanism itself as they read "Augustine, Gregory and Bernard" rather than any direct "contemporary Continental" influence appears accurate.[63] However, his contention that Rous was the first Puritan mystic[64] is inconsistent with the Puritan themes and tendencies just mentioned. Further, his narrow definition of mysticism prevents him from noticing the mystical element in writers such as Sibbes, whom he specifically denies was a mystic.[65] This restriction in defining Puritan mysticism leads to Brauer's surprising claim that there were only six to eight Puritan mystics.[66] His list of Puritan "mystics in the fullest sense of the term" includes John Everard, Giles Randall, Peter Sterry, and perhaps Morgan Llwyd, and Walter Cradock."[67] Most of these individuals reflect the more radical stream of Puritanism. Clearly this small number reflects his definition that relies upon the Dionysian mysticism of the threefold way. While Brauer concedes that Rous never used the three-fold way of purgation, illumination, and union in his writings, he still insists that they can reflect those insights.[68] The most questionable conclusion

59. Ibid., 14.
60. Ibid., 127; cf. 147.
61. Ibid., 49; cf. 14.
62. Ibid., 33–41; cf. 323.
63. Ibid., 33; cf. 279, 323, 329.
64. Ibid., 44, 184, 231, 287, 329.
65. Ibid., 291.
66. Ibid., 293.
67. Ibid., 289.
68. Ibid., 131.

reached by Brauer asserts that those Puritans who were mystics eventually moved away from Puritanism.[69] While this reveals some degree of accuracy related to the Quakers and other Spirit enthusiasts, these individuals are usually not representative of a healthy Christian mysticism. Rous himself never left Puritanism, and Brauer ultimately tempers those remarks regarding him, who "emerged directly from his Puritanism and remained closely related to it."[70] Brauer published a number of articles since his thesis, the most recently in 1987. However, there has been no significant expansion in his position, and Rous is still the only moderate Puritan listed among his candidates for Puritan mysticism.[71] Further, Brauer misreads Wakefield in asserting he denied the possibility of mysticism within Puritanism.[72]

More helpful for the broader study of Puritan mysticism is the pioneering research of Geoffrey Nuttall. His earlier and still seminal work on *The Holy Spirit in Puritan Faith and Experience* surveys the spectrum of seventeenth-century English piety, examining the writings of Puritans, Quakers, and other more radical expressions alike. In a more recent article, Nuttall has focused more exclusively on the prospect of mysticism within moderate Puritanism.[73] A significant difference between Brauer and Nuttall is the latter's broader definition that eschews the traditional three-fold manner of defining mysticism. Nuttall helpfully illustrates the reality of mystical writings in Puritans using John Preston, Rous, Rowland Stedman, and Edward Polhill. Significantly, all four writers employ the allegorical reading of the Song of Songs.[74]

Brauer and Nuttall are not alone in their assessment that there is some expression of mysticism within Puritanism. Moreover the seventeenth century was a fertile period for the development of renewed spirituality and "affective devotion" in both Protestant and Roman Catholic churches.[75] The Protestant expressions included the Puritans as well as Pietism on the Continent, while within Roman Catholicism this was manifested in Jansenism, Quietism, and devotion to the sacred heart of

69. Ibid., 289.

70. Ibid., 329.

71. Brauer, "Types of Puritan Piety," 53–58.

72. Ibid., 40n6.

73. Nuttall, "Puritan and Quaker Mysticism."

74. Ibid., 521.

75. Hambrick-Stowe, *Practice of Piety*, 23.

Jesus.[76] However, there are some scholars who appear to be overly generous in their assessment. Richard Lovelace declares: "that the Puritans implicitly assumed that every Christian was to be a mystic."[77] Additionally, some scholars in their enthusiasm to affirm Puritan mysticism fail to adequately define their use of language. Lovelace mentions the "Puritan mysticism" of Jonathan Edwards without any indication of the nature or meaning of this word.[78] Unfortunately, this lack of precision can be harmful, increasing the fear of more cautious scholars that leads them to quickly reject the concept of "mysticism" due to its more dubious history. Conversely, some writers dilute the definition of "mysticism" to such an extent that it no longer has any value since virtually anyone can qualify.[79]

Not surprisingly, there are others who object to the prospect of Puritan mysticism. Mark Dever is reticent in applying the term mysticism to Sibbes' spirituality and prefers the more conducive word "affectionate."[80] John Coffey registers a similar concern in applying the term mystic to Samuel Rutherford. He concedes that "[p]erhaps we would be wise to follow Mark Dever's suggestion that instead of describing Puritans as 'mystics' (which implies a rather vague and undogmatic spirituality), we would do better to follow their own terms and call them 'affectionate theologians.'"[81] Paul Cook draws the distinction more forcefully, with Thomas Goodwin asserting that mysticism is incompatible with biblical Christianity.[82] Further, Cook maintains, "[t]he true mystic is unconcerned with doctrine. He worships in a richly symbolic atmosphere, whereas the Puritan rejected such symbolism as dishonouring to God."[83]

These conflicting views of resistance prompt the question why some scholars find mysticism incompatible with Puritanism. The primary motivation for this rejection is a distorted perception of mysticism. Arie de Reuver, describing the sixteenth century, provides a helpful commentary that was still accurate in the next century for the Puritans. He insists, "the

76. Campbell, *Religion of the Heart*, 2.

77. Lovelace, *American Pietism of Cotton Mather*, 105–6.

78. Lovelace, "Afterword, Puritans and Spiritual Renewal," 308.

79. Coffey, *Theology and British Revolutions*, 83n5.

80. Dever, *Richard Sibbes*, 137.

81. Coffey, *Theology and British Revolutions*, 95.

82. Cook, "Thomas Goodwin—Mystic?" 46.

83. Ibid., 48.

rejection of mysticism by the reformers involved only a certain form of it." The type of mysticism rejected can be summarized as one that sought a union of absorption or indistinction, "practices as a meritorious precondition for salvation that ignored grace," restricted to the monastery, and "upset the balance between faith and love at the expense of faith."[84] Additional concerns of some contemporary Puritan scholars regarding mysticism include the diminishment of Christ's role in the believer's life and undervaluing of Scripture.[85] Gordon Mursell's qualifications of Puritan mysticism provides a valuable summary on this topic. He writes,

> This kind of spirituality may be termed "mysticism" if by that is implied a direct and unmediated experience of God that is vouchsafed to the individual Christian, provided we remember three things: first, that this experience happens within the context of a personal intimacy, for which marriage is the natural analogy. . . ; secondly, that . . . there is no suggestion of an ontological union, a mutual absorption of the soul into the Godhead; and, thirdly, that the natural context for the development of this intimacy is not . . . in the monastic life, but precisely in the midst of the Christian community, and supremely in its worship.[86]

Readers will recognize the strong similarity between Mursell's summary and McGinn's previous description of the two forms of mysticism. Further and significantly, Roman Catholics did not welcome all types of mysticism indiscriminately, acknowledging that there could be unhealthy expressions of it and experienced similar fears regarding it at various stages of their history.[87] Due to this ongoing lack of clarity regarding the term, some scholars today are hesitant to use the word mysticism in connection with Puritan piety. These are legitimate concerns since we must acknowledge that mysticism has had an uneven history over the centuries and has both collected many excesses and pushed the boundaries of theological orthodoxy beyond the acceptable limits for some in the church.[88]

---

84. De Reuver, *Sweet Communion*, 22; cf. Hambrick-Stowe, *Early New England Meditative Poetry*, 10; and Hartley Hall, "Shape of Reformed Piety," 213.

85. Andrew Davies, "Holy Spirit in Puritan Experience," 29.

86. Mursell, *English Spirituality: From Earliest Times*, 369.

87. See for example McGinn, "Mysticism," 3:120; Mursell, *Story of Christian Spirituality*, 212, 234–35; and von Balthasar, *Prayer*, 117–18, 121–22.

88. For example Pope John XXII pronounced Meister Eckhart's teaching as heretical due to his emphasis upon the union of absorption or indistinction. McGinn,

The significance of McGinn's revised framework that employs the mystical element rather than mysticism should not be minimized. Indeed, one of my primary desires for this research on the potential of Puritan mysticism in Isaac Ambrose that builds upon McGinn is that it will adequately respond to these reasonable criticisms of Puritan scholars and also encourage the greatly needed research in this largely unexamined reservoir of Puritan literature. Moreover, it is helpful to recognize that some scholars who were initially reticent to speak of mysticism within Puritanism are now able to embrace the possibility of the mystical element in Puritanism when it is understood in a biblical or historically balanced manner.[89] Therefore, I strongly affirm Wakefield's conclusion when he asserts, "we are not wrong to speak of Mysticism" in the Puritans and further "that the Mysticism of the English Puritans is in need of extended research."[90]

At another level, we must realize that there were Puritan scholars prior to McGinn who employed the language of "mystical element"[91] or "mystical piety"[92] or "deeply mystical tone"[93] or "mystical material" and "mystical tendencies"[94] that today reflect McGinn's scholarship. Nevertheless, no one has intentionally employed McGinn's broader understanding of "mysticism" in a consistent and sustained manner in studying the Puritans. Therefore, by employing McGinn's description, it can now be asked whether there was a "mystical element," or what this book will call the "contemplative-mystical piety" within Puritanism?

There are a number of reasons for making this substitution. While the broader term mystical element is a helpful improvement over the confusion-riddled language of mysticism, there is no doubt numer-

---

"Mysticism," 3:119. However, Tamburello reminds readers of Eckhart's contemporary rehabilitation. *Ordinary Mysticism*, 115–18.

89. Coffey, *Theology and British Revolutions*, 95; Dever, *Richard Sibbes*, 158; Cook, "Thomas Goodwin—Mystic?" 47, 48; Andrew Davies, "Holy Spirit in Puritan Experience," 29.

90. Wakefield, "Mysticism and Its Puritan Types," 44; cf. Wakefield, *Puritan Devotion*, 108.

91. Brauer, "Francis Rous, Puritan Mystic," 14, 281, 288, 299; Stoeffler, *Rise of Evangelical Pietism*, 131; Dewey Wallace, *Spirituality of Later Puritans*, xvii; and Williams, "Puritan Enjoyment of God," 2.

92. McGiffert, *God's Plot*, 29; cf. 26–27.

93. Stoeffler, *Rise of Evangelical Pietism*, 84.

94. Nuttall, "Puritan and Quaker Mysticism," 527.

ous vestiges of Reformed and Evangelical suspicion are still lingering. Moreover, this is a study about Isaac Ambrose, and certainly he would be alarmed to be called a mystic even though he frequently spoke of contemplation. The term "contemplation" has had a better history within many parts of the Protestant tradition, and therefore serves as a gentler introduction to the mystical element. Wakefield suggests that the word contemplation is "a more satisfactory term to apply" than mystical,[95] and de Certeau notes that contemplation was the word of choice for most of the history of Christian spirituality.[96] More specifically, contemplative denotes the attitude and awareness in which a person approaches life. It is based on the grammar of gazing on the Triune God. Additionally, it communicates a devotional intensity that reflects the deep desire to live in conscious union and communion with God. The word mystical used in combination with contemplative seeks to express the outcome or the subjective experience of being in union with Christ. These experiences are always a gift of God and not the result of a person's efforts, though those efforts may prepare the person for God's presence. Piety is used instead of the more common contemporary term spirituality for two reasons. Spirituality has become so broadly based today that it has lost much of its meaning without some descriptive adjective placed before it, such as Reformed spirituality or Cistercian spirituality. Second, piety was the preferred word for Reformed believers of the sixteenth and seventeenth century and included a broader arena in which the spiritual life was lived, unlike the contemporary usage that frequently privileges the individual.

Jean Williams has produced the most comprehensive research on the topic of Puritan mysticism. Her vast and far ranging study focuses upon both clergy and laity, including the often-neglected study of women, and thereby addresses one of the most under researched areas in Puritan studies. She reverses the commonly held opinion that if anything resembling mysticism existed within Puritanism that it was abnormal rather than a common experience.[97] Not only is she comfortable in recognizing and affirming the reality of Puritan mystics, but her primary assertion is that mysticism is not only present in the radical Puritans but firmly

95. Wakefield, *Puritan Devotion*, 90.

96. De Certeau, *Mystic Fable*, 94–95; cf. Harmless, *Mystics*, 261.

97. Williams, "Puritan Enjoyment of God," 8–9; cf. Williams, "Puritanism: Piety of Joy," 4–14 for a brief summary of her conclusions.

established among the moderate Puritans including Sibbes and Owen.[98] This is all the more convincing since Williams began her research with the strong bias "that Puritanism is not supposed to be characterized by mysticism."[99] Further, and central to her conclusion is that Puritan mysticism, while conscious of the medieval roots, is not directly derived from Roman Catholic mysticism but rather is an indigenous expression fashioned within the uniqueness of Puritan theology and, instead of being a rare occurrence, was common throughout Puritanism.[100] This also corrects Brauer's perception that Rous was the first Puritan mystic. Williams' assessment that mysticism was at odds with the Reformed theological and spiritual roots of Puritanism has been most recently validated by the research of Dewey Wallace. He asserts that Peter Sterry was a "Calvinist mystic" and after persuasively arguing this point he concludes: "But Sterry was not a mystic in spite of his Puritan commitments and Calvinistic theology, nor even someone mystical by inclination, who, coming of age in Puritan and Calvinist England, pushed his Puritanism and Calvinism in as mystical a direction as they could go, but was a mystic also because, like others before him, he drew out the mystical potential of Calvinist theology and Puritan spirituality."[101]

Further, in returning to Williams, she reveals an awareness of McGinn's broader definition of mysticism,[102] and her research is divided into the four categories of theology, vocabulary, devotion, and enactment or records of spiritual experience. Nonetheless, she continues to employ the terminology of Puritan mysticism rather than McGinn's broader language of the mystical element of Puritanism.[103] She does not indicate her reason for this choice, though perhaps her motivation is dependent upon her desire to recover the legitimacy of Puritan mysticism. It still appears problematic, however, due to the confusion of many regarding the nature and heritage of Christian mysticism. In fact, Williams herself rejects the similarity of Puritan mysticism with "classic Christian mysticism" since many associate the latter with the absorption of humanity

98. Ibid., 11, 21.

99. Ibid., ix.

100. Ibid., 15, 102n267, 226, 392.

101. Dewey Wallace, *Shapers of English Calvinism*, 85.

102. Williams, "Puritan Enjoyment of God," 17n62, 18n64.

103. Ibid., 25–26, 140, 394–99, etc. These references are merely illustrative of her almost universal practice throughout her dissertation.

into the Godhead.[104] Another significant feature of her research is that, while she recognizes the necessity for the specific theological character of Puritanism,[105] she continues to employ the language of union with God, which is more typically Roman Catholic, than the Puritan preference of union with Christ. For the Puritans this created a stronger parallel between union with Christ and Jesus as the divine Bridegroom in spiritual marriage. Further, in light of this it is noteworthy to trace her criticism of Charles Hambrick-Stowe, whom she insists employs a Roman Catholic understanding of union as the culmination rather than the origin of the spiritual life.[106] However, upon closer examination, the specific references she cites reveals her misreading of Hambrick-Stowe. Clearly he recognizes, as chapter 2 will argue, that the Puritans understood union with Christ as the beginning of spiritual marriage and "that they [i.e. the Puritans] would not attain full salvation until the soul was perfectly united with Christ after death."[107] One limitation of this otherwise outstanding study of Puritan mysticism is that Williams did not dialogue with any dissertations, including Brauer and the soon to be examined research of Simon Chan.

There is one gap, however, that remains underdeveloped in this extensive survey. In Williams' investigation of the nature and practice of contemplation she devotes much of her energy to the examination of the apophatic nature of it. This is extremely valuable since this dimension is frequently ignored or even denied in Puritan studies. However, what is missing is an equal sensitivity to the recognition of and appreciation for the importance of heavenly meditation as an expression of Puritan contemplation. Closely related to this is the minimal treatment of the *visio Dei* and the significance of gazing on or beholding God. Additionally, while recognizing the prevalence of ravishment as an expression of Puritan enjoyment of God, Williams does not engage in any great depth with the theology of this critical term. Therefore, these missing or underdeveloped themes will figure more prominently in this present study.

---

104. Compare Williams, "Puritan Enjoyment of God," ix, with Williams, "Puritanism: Piety of Joy," 8.

105. Williams, "Puritan Enjoyment of God," 11–12.

106. Ibid., 11–12, 66.

107. Hambrick-Stowe, *Practice of Piety*, 19, 197; cf. 60, 79, 286. Williams misses Hambrick-Stowe's emphasis upon "full" union.

EVIDENCE OF THE CONTEMPLATIVE-MYSTICAL
PIETY WITHIN PURITANISM

In Brauer's pioneering research he distinguished between two forms of Puritan mysticism that he named "classical Christian mystics" and "Christian Spirit mystics."[108] Francis Rous illustrated the first category while John Saltmarsh, William Dell, William Erbery, Thomas Collier, Walter Craddock, and George Fox characterized the second.[109] Previously, Brauer had asserted that John Everard, Giles Randall, Peter Sterry, and perhaps Morgan Llwyd "appear to be mystics in the fullest sense of the term."[110] What is striking about these names is that, apart from Rous and Sterry, many of these individuals typically represent the more radical stream of Puritanism. David Como's research clarifies the reason why some were called radical: "in their own day, the ideas and practices in question were regarded by most contemporaries (both Puritan and non-Puritan) as excessive and disruptive of the right notions of orthodoxy or order."[111] Therefore, since this book focuses on Isaac Ambrose, it will only consider the contemplative-mystical piety within the moderate stream of Puritanism unless directly impacted by its radical relatives.[112] Further, this reflects the approach of Ambrose and other likeminded Puritans who were careful to distance themselves from the radical mystics who typically discounted the mediatorial role of Jesus Christ and elevated a person's subjective experience above that of Scripture to determine the validity of that experience. One additional reason for limiting this study to the contemplative-mystical piety of moderate Puritanism is that it parallels the wisdom of Ernest Stoeffler's study of Pietism: "[i]f Pietism is to be seen truly it, like other historical movements, must be seen with reference to its center, not its circumference."[113] Further, as will soon become clear, there is impressive evidence for the contemplative-mystical piety within moderate Puritanism, including mystical language and

---

108. Brauer, "Types of Puritan Piety," 53; cf. "Francis Rous, Puritan Mystic," 23–29.

109. Ibid., 53–56. Compare with 14n71. Brauer spells Crad[d]ock both ways.

110. Brauer, "Francis Rous, Puritan Mystic," 289.

111. Como, "Radical Puritanism," 242.

112. For an examination of the radical or spirit mysticism within Puritanism see: Nuttall, *Holy Spirit in Puritan Faith*; George Johnson, "From Seeker to Finder"; Maclear, "Heart of New England Rent"; Welch, "Quakers, Ranters and Puritan Mystics"; Mack, *Visionary Women*; and Como, *Blown By the Spirit*, esp. 219–65.

113. Stoeffler, *Rise of Evangelical Pietism*, 12.

vocabulary, mystical theology, and even mystical experience. Richard Sibbes, Francis Rous, Thomas Goodwin, Samuel Rutherford, Richard Baxter, John Owen, Peter Sterry, and Cotton Mather are most frequently mentioned as reflective of this contemplative-mystical piety.[114] While it would be easy to compile a lengthy list of other Puritans, some of the more familiar names that reflect the contemplative-mystical piety include Joseph Hall,[115] John Preston,[116] Robert Bolton,[117] Thomas Shepard,[118] and John Flavel.[119]

RESEARCH RELATED TO ISAAC AMBROSE

Isaac Ambrose has attracted only sporadic interest from scholars, thereby making this present book distinct. Robert Halley (1796–1876), a nonconformist minister, is perhaps best remembered today for his religious history of Lancashire.[120] Halley was the first scholar to give any serious recognition to Ambrose, and his broad sweeping treatment of Lancashire history provides a valuable context for understanding the religious setting of the seventeenth century in which Ambrose lived. He summarizes the details of Ambrose's life and ministry, including a few

114. The best sources for exploring the contemplative–mystical piety in moderate Puritanism are Nuttall, *Holy Spirit in Puritan Faith*; Nuttall, "Puritan and Quaker Mysticism"; Chan, "Puritan Meditative Tradition"; and Williams, "Puritan Enjoyment of God." More specifically for Sibbes see Dever, *Richard Sibbes*, esp. 135–60 and Frost, "Richard Sibbes' Theology of Grace," 97–121. For Francis Rous see Brauer, "Francis Rous, Puritan Mystic"; Wakefield, *Puritan Devotion*, 103–6; and van den Berg, "English Puritan Francis Rous." For Thomas Goodwin see Watkin, *Poets and Mystics*, 56–69 and Cook, "Thomas Goodwin—Mystic?" For Rutherford see Coffey, *Theology and British Revolutions*, esp. 82–113 and Coffey, "Letters by Samuel Rutherford." For Richard Baxter see Stoeffler, *Rise of Evangelical Pietism*, 88–96; Nuttall, "Puritan and Quaker Mysticism," 525–27; and Chan, *Spiritual Theology*, 99–100. For John Owen see Packer, *Quest for Godliness*, esp. 191–218; King, "Affective Spirituality of John Owen"; and Kapic, *Communion with God*, 147–205. For Sterry see Dewey Wallace, *Shapers of English Calvinism*, 51–85. For Cotton Mather see Lovelace, *American Pietism of Cotton Mather*, esp. 110–97 and Hambrick-Stowe, *Practice of Piety*, esp. 278–87.

115. Stoeffler, *Rise of Evangelical Pietism*, 83–85, and Chan, *Spiritual Theology*, 99–100.

116. Wakefield, "Mysticism and Puritan Type," 40 and Nuttall, "Puritan and Quaker Mysticism," 520.

117. Rupp, "Devotion of Rapture," 120–21.

118. McGiffert, *God's Plot*, esp. 26–29.

119. Yuille, *Inner Sanctum of Puritan Piety*, 85–94.

120. Halley, *Lancashire: Puritanism and Nonconformity*.

selections from Ambrose's diary preserved in *Media* that explores the importance of sanctification through the use of spiritual practices. As a result of Ambrose's spiritual disciplines, for example, from his annual month-long May retreats in the woods, Halley asserts that Ambrose was the "most meditative Puritan of Lancashire."[121] Additionally, he asserts, "Isaac Ambrose is better known as a practical writer than any other."[122] What is lacking in Halley is any theological reflection on Ambrose's writings or spiritual practices.

Benjamin Nightingale (1854–1928), another nonconformist pastor who, like Ambrose, served in the town of Preston, displayed a special appreciation for Ambrose. Nightingale was strongly dependent upon Halley for much of his material, but he did expand the historical details of both church politics and Ambrose's family background. His assessment regarding Ambrose's piety also parallels that of Halley, declaring that he was '[o]f a retiring disposition, his mind of the contemplative order, he was in true sense a religious mystic."[123] Additionally, Nightingale provides one example of the continued interest in Ambrose's writings in the latter portion of the seventeenth century.[124] But similar to Halley, Nightingale does not study the theology or the dynamics of the spiritual practices of Ambrose. Gordon Wakefield in his significant study, *Puritan Devotion* was the first scholar to pay attention to Ambrose's style of meditation.[125] However, his treatment is brief and focuses more on the background and structure of *Looking Unto Jesus* than it does to the experiential piety that might result from this approach. Wakefield reiterates the conclusion of both Halley and Nightingale, describing Ambrose as a "Lancashire Nonconformist of contemplative disposition."[126]

Milo Kaufmann introduces a significant transition, being the first literary critic to display an interest in Ambrose.[127] Kaufmann traces the development of Puritan meditation according to two streams, one more formal approach reflected by Bishop Joseph Hall and the second more imaginative focused on the heavenly meditation of Richard Sibbes.

---

121. Ibid., 2:195.
122. Ibid., 2:202; cf. 194.
123. Nightingale, *Isaac Ambrose, Religious Mystic*, 20.
124. Ibid., 26–27.
125. Wakefield, *Puritan Devotion*, 88, 96–98.
126. Ibid., xiii.
127. Kaufmann, *Pilgrim's Progress and Puritan Meditation*.

Kaufmann places Ambrose in the meditative tradition of Hall yet oddly cites him as an example of heavenly meditation.[128] Indeed, there are numerous places where Kaufmann appears to misread Ambrose, but since they are directly related to the development of Ambrose's understanding and practice of meditation and contemplation they will be discussed in chapter 4. However, Kaufmann does not appear to appreciate the fullness of Ambrose's method of meditation nor the importance of imagination for him in this process. Barbara Lewalski is another literary critic who includes Ambrose in her study, though to a much lesser extent than Kaufmann.[129] Her primary goal is to redress the strongly Roman Catholic focus of Louis Martz's study of meditation. Lewalski makes two significant contributions in relation to Kaufmann: a more balanced treatment of Puritan meditation and the liberation of Ambrose from the restrictive status of a lifeless clone of Hall. Erica Longfellow is the most recent literary critic to include Ambrose in her study.[130] Once again, there is little interaction with Ambrose's piety. The primary focus of Kaufmann, Lewalski, and Longfellow has been on Ambrose's style of meditation. In reality, their treatment reflects more of the mechanics of meditation. In every case, *Media* was the only source examined with little appreciation for the theological or experiential dimensions of Ambrose's piety. Therefore, while in varying degrees these sources engage the nature of Puritan meditation, Ambrose is not the primary figure of any of them. Additionally, none of these works have included Ambrose's magnum opus *Looking Unto Jesus* which provides a vivid christological kaleidoscope of Puritan meditation through a theological foundation of union with Christ. This assessment further reveals the value of a careful and detailed study of the contemplative-mystical piety of Isaac Ambrose.

Before examining the unpublished research that specifically address Ambrose, there is one dissertation that provides a broader framework for examining him. Jonathan Won explored the degree of continuity and discontinuity between Calvin and the seventeenth-century Puritans in their understanding of union and communion with Christ.[131] He concluded that there was both significant commonality as well as divergence

128. Ibid., 134.
129. Lewalski, *Protestant Poetics*.
130. Longfellow, *Women and Religious Writing*.
131. Won, "Communion with Christ."

between Calvin and the English Puritans. Interestingly, in some categories the Puritans reflected greater affinity for Bernard of Clairvaux than
Calvin. This was particularly true in the Puritan allegorical reading of
Song of Songs and the more experiential nature derived from it.[132] Won
also rightly concludes that the Puritans displayed a greater proclivity
towards the "mystical tradition" than Calvin.[133] Further, while I would
agree with his assessment than Calvin emphasized union with Christ
more than communion, I take exception to the idea that the Puritans
emphasized communion with Christ more than union.[134] One must remember that Calvin is one person, and the Puritans obviously provide
a much broader cross section of writing, where it is not uncommon to
find a balanced emphasis upon both union and communion with Christ.

Simon Chan has written the only significant dissertation that takes
into account Isaac Ambrose.[135] Unlike previous literary scholars who only
read Ambrose's *Media*, Chan also read *Prima, Ultima, Looking Unto Jesus*,
and *Communion with Angels*. *Media* and *Looking Unto Jesus* have already
been introduced. *Prima* is Ambrose's work on the new birth and regeneration and *Ultima* is devoted to death, judgment, the terrors of hell, and
preparing for heaven. *Communion with Angels* explores how a person
might cultivate a greater awareness of angels and how they minister to a
person during the various periods of life from birth to death. The great
strength of Chan's research is his extensive reading among the primary
sources on Puritan practices of meditation. He also recognizes the significance of heavenly meditation[136] for the Puritans, thus correcting the
oversight of Williams' dissertation. However, far less helpful is the manner in which Chan understands mysticism resembling Brauer though not
as narrowly focused on the *triplex via* or three-fold way.[137] Chan believes
the Puritan emphasis upon preparation can be "the puritan equivalent to

132. Ibid., 294, 334, 340–41, 344, 356.

133. Ibid., 353.

134. Ibid., 351.

135. I am aware of two additional doctoral studies that mention Isaac Ambrose.
John Martone, a student of Lewalski, briefly comments on Ambrose's method of meditation and journal writing. Martone, "Map of Heaven," 9, 93–95, 166. Joanne Jung has
referenced some of Ambrose's practices of conferences or group spiritual direction.
Jung, "Conference: Communal Tradition of Puritan Piety," 112, 123, 126, 128, 130.

136. Chan, "Puritan Meditative Tradition," esp. 122–41.

137. Ibid., 118.

the purgative way."[138] Another limitation that restricts Chan's ability to see greater evidence of mysticism within Puritanism is his use of the traditional language of "infused contemplation" as a determinate for mysticism.[139] Therefore, not surprisingly, he concludes, "it seems strange that, given the puritans' intellectual acceptance of mysticism as noted at the beginning of this chapter, the experience was not as extensively cultivated nor as actively encouraged as would be expected."[140] Since Chan wrote his study before McGinn's usage of a broader definition for mysticism, he can hardly be faulted for this. However, this does restrict his ability to discover a fuller expression of the mystical element or what I am calling the contemplative-mystical piety of Puritanism. One additional limitation that affects Chan's potential for locating the contemplative-mystical piety within Puritanism is his neglect of some of the significant secondary literature that has explored this question. This leads him to assert that Gordon Wakefield denied the possibility of Puritan mysticism.[141] However, Wakefield later revised his assessment affirming, "we are not wrong to speak of Mysticism" in relation to the Puritans.[142]

More significantly, Chan locates two distinctive streams of Puritan piety, one that he calls the ascetic stream that includes Joseph Hall, Richard Baxter, Thomas Hooker, and Isaac Ambrose. These individuals are characterized by their intensity of spiritual practices "in which heavenly meditation"[143] was the result, and, further, they gave "scant attention [to the Holy Spirit] in their exposition of the devotional life.[144] One significant discrepancy is that while Hall was not known for his use of imagination both Ambrose and Baxter were.[145] The other category of the enthusiast stream or Spirit mystics includes Richard Sibbes, John Cotton, Francis Rous, and John Owen. Chan delineates that the "meditative technique" for these Spirit mystics has "become a duty stripped of much of its ascetical precision." Further, "the intense feeling and ec-

---

138. Ibid., 71–72; cf. 216. In fact, Chan arranges three of his chapters to follow the pattern of purgation, illumination, and union.

139. Ibid., 130.

140. Ibid., 143; cf. 122.

141. Ibid., 117–18.

142. Wakefield, "Mysticism and Its Puritan Types," 44.

143. Chan, "Puritan Meditative Tradition," 120.

144. Ibid., 188; cf. 191.

145. Ibid., compare 182 with 186.

static language" so common among the ascetic stream is "conspicuously absent"[146] while there is a strong dependency upon the direct operation or inner testimony of the Spirit.[147] Surprisingly, Chan employs the suspect term "enthusiasts" to describe the second stream of Puritan meditation when he himself declares, "[p]art of the failure to deal adequately with the question may be due to the fact that attempts at understanding puritan mysticism have been based largely on the wrong sources—on those who should be called "enthusiasts" rather than "mystics.""[148]

Sheldrake previously asserted the strengths and weaknesses of typologies, and in Chan's usage they appear mostly negative. There are three reasons for this. First, and most importantly, Chan's distinction places Ambrose in the ascetical stream that specifically implies that he and others of this category had a weak or insignificant understanding of the inner testimony of the Spirit. However, a more accurate reading of Ambrose reveals a very strong reliance upon the direct operation or inner witness of the Spirit's work in meditation and contemplation. While it may be accurate to maintain the priority of the Spirit's role in Sibbes, it is nonetheless inaccurate to minimize or ignore it in Ambrose.[149] Therefore, Chan's structure and use of classification drives a wedge in Ambrose's theology and leads him to underestimate the role of the Spirit in Ambrose's piety. Second, the ascetical school anchored in Hall was not known for its imagination. This is hardly accurate for Ambrose or Baxter. Third, Chan's usage of the terminology "enthusiastic" is unhelpful since Brauer, among others, uses this language to describe the radical Puritans of the Quakers, Seekers, and Ranters.[150]

More specifically, in Chan's examination of Isaac Ambrose he explores Bishop Joseph Hall's influence on the development of meditation in Ambrose. He devotes seven pages to analyzing Ambrose's pattern of piety in *Looking Unto Jesus*. Chan is mistaken in his interpretation of Ambrose's nine-fold way of looking at Jesus. Since this figures more prominently in Ambrose's development of meditation and contemplation, this will be examined in chapter 4. Further, my reading of

146. Ibid., 200.

147. Ibid., 191, 194, 196, 197, 210, 216.

148. Ibid., 120.

149. Yuille concludes identically in his evaluation of Chan's assessment of George Swinnock. Yuille, *Puritan Spirituality*, 211–12.

150. Brauer, "Types of Puritan Piety," 56–58.

Ambrose's method of meditation finds less dependency upon Ignatius of Loyola than Chan.

Perhaps what is most significant as we summarize the state of research on the contemplative-mystical piety in Puritanism is the lack of a common voice on this topic. Scholarship is still in its infancy and rarely has one scholar interacted with another except for a brief comment. The most extensive and recent work remains Williams' "The Puritan Quest for Enjoyment of God." Therefore, there are three strands of research that have emerged. The oldest school defines mysticism narrowly according to the traditional *triplex via* and, except for Rous, locates mysticism in the radical groups of the Quakers and Ranters.[151] A second stream typically comprised of more confessional Reformed theologians is fearful of the narrow definition for mysticism. However, when a broader definition resembling McGinn's mystical element is used, most of these scholars are willing to concede that a contemplative-mystical piety does indeed exist within Puritanism.[152] The third school of thought, which I personally affirm, is the emerging collection of scholars who believe that contemplative-mystical piety is fully present across the mainstream of Puritanism.[153] Once again it must be reiterated that there has been minimal conversation between any of the above writers on this topic.

WRITINGS OF ISAAC AMBROSE

Ambrose was a fairly productive writer for his day, though he can hardly compare with the prolific pens of Richard Baxter and John Owen. Both *Prima* and *Ultima* were published in 1640. *Prima* had the sub-title, *The First Things or Regeneration Sermons*,[154] and *Ultima*, *The Last Things or Meditation Sermons*, which as we have already seen dealt with death and

---

151. See 11n55, 21n112, 22n114 for Brauer, Maclear, and Watkin.

152. See 16n85, 21n112, 22n114 for Andrew Davies, Welch, Coffey, and Cook. Dever also reflects this position but it is difficult to assess if he would accept the principles of a contemplative–mystical piety.

153. See 11n55 above for Nuttall, Stoeffler, Dewey Wallace, Belden Lane, and de Reuver. Though Williams misreads Wakefield, he would fit in this category as well as Williams herself. Though Chan insists on employing the narrow definition of mysticism his research validates the reality of contemplative-mystic piety in moderate Puritanism.

154. Ambrose, *Prima* (1640), t.p. The 1650 printing revised the title to *The Doctrine of Regeneration, the New Birth, the Very Beginning of a Godly Life*.

preparation for heaven.[155] While these two works were issued only in a first edition, there were minor changes that appeared in subsequent printings. These variations will be noted throughout this book when they are relevant to the discussion. *Media*, which was first issued in 1650, was subtitled, *The Means, Duties, Ordinances, both Secret, Private and Publike, for Continuance and Increase of a Godly Life, (once begun,) Till We Come to Heaven.*[156] This was Ambrose's only work that was designated by specific editions; the second revised edition was released in 1652 followed by the third revision in 1657. Two major changes from the first to the second editions involved the addition of another spiritual practice that Ambrose called "the saints' suffering" and replacing assorted retreat experiences from numerous years with a series of entries from a single year. There were additional minor variations between the second and third editions. Further, *Prima, Media, & Ultima* were issued in a single volume in 1650, 1654, and 1659. *Looking Unto Jesus* and *Redeeming the Time* were both published in 1658. *Looking Unto Jesus*, Ambrose's largest and most popular work, was sub-titled, *A View of the Everlasting Gospel, or, the Souls Eying or Jesus, as Carrying on the Great Work of Mans Salvation from First to Last.*[157] *Redeeming the Time* was the funeral sermon for Lady Margaret Houghton, Ambrose's primary patron while in Preston. *Looking Unto Jesus* was later combined without any alteration of the text with *War with Devils* and *Ministration of, and Communion with Angels* as *The Three Great Ordinances of Jesus Christ* in 1662.[158] *War with Devils*, Ambrose's work on spiritual battle, traces both Satan's assaults and the duties a Christian should employ to resist these attacks; *Ministration of, and Communion with Angels* explores the ways in which a Christian can receive the guidance of God's heavenly messengers throughout the various stages of a person's life. The first edition of *The Compleat Works of Isaac Ambrose* was published in 1674, ten years after his death.

The specific references throughout this work will vary, depending upon the particular need or theme to illustrate. However, since the

---

155. Ambrose, *Ultima* (1640), t.p. The 1650 printing expanded the title to *Certain Meditations on Life, Death, Judgment, Hell, Right Purgatory, and Heaven.*

156. Ambrose, *Media* (1650), t.p.

157. Ambrose, *Looking Unto Jesus*, t.p.

158. Ambrose, *Three Great Ordinances of Jesus Christ*, t.p. There were no subtitles for any of these books in this edition.

standard edition of *Looking Unto Jesus* is 1658 and *Redeeming the Time*, *War with Devils* and *Communion with Angels* were printed in only one edition, no dates will be given in footnote references for these sources. Ambrose also wrote two dedications for Henry Newcome's works.[159] Additionally, there are a few surviving manuscripts of letters of Isaac Ambrose that have been printed in various histories of Lancashire.

THE HERMENEUTICAL PROCESS

As previously indicated, most early modern or Puritan historians give little attention to the subject of hermeneutics. Two exceptions to this both point to Quentin Skinner.[160] However, his primary focus is political thought, and my research will draw upon the more appropriate field of hermeneutical theory that is consistent with the discipline of Christian spirituality.[161] Since this is a historical theological study of seventeenth-century Puritanism, history is of the utmost importance. Philip Sheldrake reminds readers of the critical importance of how we think about the past and the broader issue of historical consciousness.[162] Therefore, one must approach this subject carefully, aware of the potential dangers of oversimplifying the complexity of any person or movement of spirituality, sensitive to the continuity and discontinuity between sources of different traditions and time periods, and presentism.[163] Further, Sheldrake asserts that the study of history requires that certain choices must be made, in particular those pertaining to specific time period, geographical boundaries, and what themes will be examined.[164] For this study, Isaac Ambrose, a seventeenth-century Lancashire Puritan, and his sources frame the time period and geography. Since this is an examination of the contemplative-mystical piety of the Puritans, those themes as well as the theological foundations of that piety will be the

159. Newcome, *Sinners Hope* and *Usurpation Defeated*.

160. Coffey, *Theology and British Revolutions*, 25–26 and Trueman, "Puritan Theology as Historical Event," esp. 257–60.

161. See for example Sheldrake, *Spirituality & History*, esp. 91–112, 171–95; Sheldrake, "Interpretation." in *Blackwell Companion*; Sheldrake, "Spirituality and Its Critical Methodology"; and Dreyer and Burrows, *Minding the Spirit*.

162. Sheldrake, "Spirituality and Its Critical Methodology," 17.

163. Sheldrake, *Spirituality & History*, esp. 17–39, 65–90 and Sheldrake, *Explorations in Spirituality*, 31–36.

164. Ibid., 101–5.

primary focus. Closely related is the importance of context and culture. Reading Ambrose within his context requires sensitivity to the political tensions of nonconformity and recognition of the heavy concentration of Roman Catholics in Lancashire. Additionally, the theological dynamics exert a great influence as will shortly be illustrated in the motivation behind Ambrose's work *Media*. Further, it has become appropriate to stress the role of contemplation not only methodologically but also more fully as a hermeneutical method in the study of Christian spirituality.[165] Significantly, this reinforces and validates the focus of this present study.

While many writers have contributed to the development of hermeneutics I will follow David Tracy,[166] who created his method by interacting with Gadamer and Ricoeur. Tracy's approach is grounded in interpreting the "classic" text and possesses at least three assumptions: "First, there exists a qualitative difference between a classic and a period piece; second, there exists an assumption that a classic, by definition, will always be in need of further interpretation in view of its need for renewed application to a particular situation: third, a classic, again by definition, is assumed to be any text that always has the power to transform the horizon of the interpreter and thereby disclose new meaning and experiential possibilities."[167] Further, Tracy contends that the Scripture of the Old and New Testament "serve for the Christian as the classic judging and transforming all other classics."[168] This is particularly important for this research since the Bible was the primary focus of Ambrose's writings. Tracy emphasizes another significant aspect of a classic text in quoting Hans-Georg Gadamer's famous assertion that there is an "excess of meaning" in these texts.[169] A positive outcome of following Tracy's emphasis upon the classic text challenges readers to engage the primary texts and not blindly accept the typical uneven perceptions of some secondary sources. There are four steps to Tracy's hermeneutical process: preunderstanding, provocation, dialogical conversation, and the community of readers.[170]

165. Sheldrake, "Spirituality and Its Critical Methodology," 26–29.

166. Tracy, *Analogical Imagination*, 99–153.

167. Tracy, *On Naming the Present*, 115.

168. Ibid., 117.

169. Tracy, *Analogical Imagination*, 102. Tracy's reference is to Gadamer, *Truth and Method*, 253–58. However, those pages relate to the nature of a "classic text." For Gadamer on "excess of meaning" see *Truth and Method*, esp. 263–64; cf. 70.

170. Ibid., 118–21; cf. 130–31.

While these steps have a logical order, they are not necessarily sequential but dynamically reflect the hermeneutical circle.

The first step of preunderstanding recognizes that no one approaches a classic text completely objectively. The accumulated history of effects surrounds the reader with expectations, fears, and questions for the text. Many readers who have approached the Puritans have not received them well. This negative perception makes it difficult to be receptive to them in general and even more suspect to any idea of contemplative piety. In reality, this may be due to a selective reading of the primary sources. These fears may also revolve around the themes of sexuality and marriage and are related to the term "ravishment" that is often perceived by some as an indicator of sexual repression or violence. Therefore, it is essential that readers listen carefully to the text in context and not become sidetracked by critics.

Provocation is the second step of the interpretive process. Classic texts have the ability to provoke, vex, challenge, unsettle, and transform readers. Clearly the reader is not in full control of the experience since the reading of the text demands a response. Therefore, it is vital that the reader remain open to the text. This openness will likely provoke and reveal the reader's initial preunderstanding. For example, some readers are surprised to discover the Puritan usage of spiritual marriage as a metaphor for union with Christ. Others might be more shocked to recognize the Puritan perception of Jesus as divine Bridegroom. This could be especially unsettling for some males. Perhaps others might react even more strongly to the Puritan usage of "ravishment" as an expression of delight and enjoyment of God. These examples vividly illuminate a "hermeneutic of suspicion" that require readers to wrestle more deeply with the issues provoked within them by the text. In other words, the horizon of the text unsettles the horizon of the reader. Further, it is likely that some of these examples could vex the very legitimate feminist concerns of patriarchy and violence. As they arise, it is important to listen carefully but not necessarily take them so far that the reader is unable to listen to and learn from the Puritans. This demonstrates that multiple forms of provocation may occur. Closely related is Elizabeth Dreyer's warning of the danger of anachronistic and other forms of misusing and abusing medieval mystical texts. Her guidelines of not imposing the contemporary context on the original context or discounting the original setting are equally valuable for reading the seventeenth-century Puritans.[171]

Third, Tracy emphasizes the need for dialogical conversation with the text.[172] Originally Gadamer and Tracy conceptualized this as a "back-and-forth movement" between the horizon of the text and the horizon of the reader.[173] However, in recent years the imagery of an interactive game has been replaced by the more engaging imagery of performing a musical composition.[174] This is suggestive of the performative nature of the dynamic conversation that can be created between reader and text. It requires sensitivity to the text that is able to both welcome and respond to the themes that are elicited. Charles Cohen reminds readers that the best approach for studying the Puritans is to allow them to speak for themselves.[175] This necessitates awareness to the clues embedded within the text. Therefore, in following Ambrose's embedded guidance, he reveals the motivation for writing *Media* was to address the decreased interest in spiritual duties due to the antinomian backlash. Further, *Looking Unto Jesus* was penned out of gratitude to Jesus for his recovery from a severe illness. Both of these themes will figure prominently in chapter 3 and 4. Further, Sheldrake comments upon the importance of a text's structure as a guide to the dynamic at work within a text.[176] In *Media*, Ambrose quotes Bernard of Clairvaux's teaching that contemplation is of two kinds, the intellect and affect. Significantly, this two-fold structure becomes the foundation upon which *Looking Unto Jesus* is built. These examples illustrate that inherent within a classic text are questions that the reader needs to notice and negotiate. Mary Frohlich recognizes the importance of questions in Bernard Lonergan and comments that the "proper question" stimulates insight and that "Lonergan's almost child-like yet incredibly productive question was, 'what are we doing when we are knowing?'"[177] McGinn was deeply influenced by Lonergan, and

171. Dreyer, "Whose Story Is It?" 151–72.

172. For an expansion on the dynamic nature of conversation in Tracy see *Plurality and Ambiguity*, 18–27.

173. Tracy, *Analogical Imagination*, 120; cf. Tracy, "Theological Method," 41.

174. See for example Lash, *Theology on Way to Emmaus*, 40–46.

175. Cohen, *God's Caress*, 20.

176. Sheldrake, *Spirituality & History*, 178.

177. Frohlich, "Spiritual Discipline, Discipline of Spirituality," 66; cf. Lonergan, *Method in Theology*, 261.

McGinn's questions what is the mystical element, mystical vocabulary, mystical theology, mystical consciousness, mystical path, and how do we read and interpret the mystical texts will exert a strong influence in this study on Isaac Ambrose. A significant challenge during this third step is to negotiate the conversation between the two horizons of the reader and text. Further, Sheldrake stresses the value of a contemplative approach to this reading.[178] This reinforces Frohlich's comments about the childlike nature of Lonergan's questions, since children's questions model a desire to understand and enjoy, not to analyze and control.

The importance of the community of readers is Tracy's fourth step. Reading is not done in isolation, and the insights of others either resonate and confirm understanding encouraging a hermeneutic of consent or further provoke and challenge the person to examine more deeply his or her own awareness and whether or not it was a possible interpretation of the text. McGinn's consistent usage of a broader definition of mysticism is ultimately a confirmation of the more isolated previous usages by Puritan scholars of the mystical element or its variations on that theme. While the resistance of many scholars to find evidence of Puritan mysticism causes numerous readers to be skittish about this possibility, the research of Jean Williams and Simon Chan assert the reality, not as a rarity but as a common feature of a healthy Puritan piety. I too join that community of readers in engaging this study. The next step that we must turn to is an exploration of Ambrose's theology and piety that created the foundation for his contemplative-mystical experiences of God and love for his neighbor.

---

178. Sheldrake, "Spirituality and Its Critical Methodology," 25–29.

Chapter Two

Biblical and Theological Foundations
of Spiritual Marriage

Is it thus, O my soul? hath the Lord Christ indeed discovered his
will, to thee for his Spouse? What, he that is so holy, to marry such
an impure wretch as thou art? O how should this but melt-thee into
a flame of *love?*. . . O my soul, henceforth cling to thy Savior, go out
of thy self, and creep to him, and affect not onely union, but very
unity with him; bathe thy self hereafter again and again, many and
many a time in those delicious intimacies of thy Spiritual marriage.

—Isaac Ambrose[1]

Christian spirituality records the long history of believers hungering
for God. The metaphor of union with Christ has occupied a cher-
ished place in that history since the New Testament. This language was
common in the patristic, monastic, and medieval periods as well as to
Ambrose and other Puritans and continues even into the present age.[2]
Alongside the development of mystical union in the Western Church,

1. Ambrose, *Media* (1657), 235 (incorrectly numbered 237)–36.
2. For a general orientation to spiritual marriage see McGinn, "Mystical Union in
Judaism, Christianity, and Islam" and Marcoulesco "Mystical Union." For a broader
theological perspective see Smedes, *Union with Christ*.

theosis or deification in the Eastern Church must also be recognized. While this topic has become increasingly more important in studies of mystical union, space prevents an examination of it in this work.[3] The specific focus of this chapter is on the biblical and theological foundation of union with Christ or spiritual marriage. To better appreciate the Puritan perspective on this we must understand how they read the pivotal book Song of Songs. Further, it is essential to grasp the Puritan understanding of godly marriage and enjoyment of sex before we can examine the Puritans in general and Isaac Ambrose in particular on their teaching of spiritual marriage.

BIBLICAL FOUNDATIONS OF SPIRITUAL MARRIAGE

Bernard McGinn stresses the foundational role of Scripture and maintains it was used as a "sacred text" in the early history of Christian mysticism.[4] Further, McGinn asserts exegesis was inseparable from mysticism at least through the twelfth century.[5]

According to A. A. Bialas the most frequently used Scriptures for spiritual marriage in the early church through the Roman Catholic Reformation were Hos 2:19; Matt 9:15; 2 Cor 11:2; Rev 21:2.[6] Additionally John 17:21; 1 Cor 6:17; 13; 1 John 4:1–19 would provide a similar inspiration.[7] Seventeenth-century Puritan preachers utilized many of the same texts in their sermons on spiritual marriage. Among the more popular Old Testament passages were Ps 45; Isa 62:4–5; Hos 2:19; and Mal 3:1.[8] Prominent New Testament Scriptures included Matt 25; John 17; Rom 6:5; 1 Cor 6:17; 2 Cor 11:2; Eph 5:32; 1 John 1:3 and Rev 3:20.[9]

---

3. One can detect echoes of deification in many of the writings of the Western Church; however, they are rarely as dominant as in Orthodox spirituality. For deification in Francis Rous see Brauer, "Francis Rous, Puritan Mystic," 178–82, 187. For a Reformed consideration see Billings, *Calvin, Participation, and the Gift.* More broadly see Christensen and Wittung, *Partakers of the Divine Nature* and Kärkkäinen, *One with God.*

4. McGinn, *Foundations of Mysticism,* 3; cf. 4, 345n1.

5. McGinn, *Growth of Mysticism,* xi, 26, 133; cf. McGinn, *Foundations of Mysticism,* 64, 86.

6. Bialas, "Mystical Marriage," 105.

7. McGinn, "Love, Knowledge and Unio Mystica," 60–62, 65.

8. For Ps 45:10–11 see Vincent, *Christ the Best Husband;* for Isa 62:4–5 see Edwards, *Church's Marriage to Her Son;* for Hosea see King, *Marriage of the Lambe* on Hos 2:20 and Baillie, *Spiritual Marriage* on Hos 2:19; for Mal see Hooker, *Soules Implantation,* 81–153.

9. For Matt 25 see Shepard, *Parable of Ten Virgins;* for John 17 see Burgess, *CXLV*

Western Catholics and Protestants alike turned to the Song of Songs as a favorite text for spiritual marriage.[10] This has been true at least since Origen in the third century. While this would surprise no one reading the monastic or medieval writers, it may seem totally out of character for the Puritans. Nonetheless, Puritan preachers including John Collinges, John Cotton, Richard Sibbes, Thomas Brightman, John Robotham, and James Durham produced detailed commentaries and lengthy sermon series on the Song of Songs. Others, such as Edward Taylor, would later employ the Song of Songs for his Saturday evening communion preparatory meditations.[11] Further, many writers drew heavily upon this text when communicating about spiritual marriage. This was true of Isaac Ambrose. It places him in the good company of John Owen, whose *Communion with God* and Samuel Rutherford whose *Letters* are both highly dependent upon the bridal imagery of the Song of Songs. Perhaps not unsurprisingly some critics have reacted strongly to the intensely erotic nature of Rutherford's *Letters*.[12] Until very recently there has been no Protestant counterpart to Ann Matter's study of the medieval usage of the Song of Songs.[13]

While Protestants and Western Catholics shared a dependence upon the same Scripture that should not imply that they always derived an identical meaning. George Scheper distinguishes between the monastic and Puritan usage that while similar in exegetical approach yielded a different metaphor.[14] Susan Hardman Moore suggests that a

---

Expository Sermons and Flavel, *Method of Grace*, 33–49 on John 17:23; for Rom 6:5 see Brinsley, *Mystical Implantation*; for 1 Cor 6:17 see Hooker, *Soules Exaltation*, 1–53 and Lye, *True Believers Union*; for 2 Cor 11:2 see Pearse, *Best Match*; for Eph 5:32 see Preston, *Churchs Marriage*; for 1 John 1:3 see Owen, *Communion with God*; and for Rev 3:20 see Flavel, *England's Duty*, 4:4–268.

10. Matter, *Voice of My Beloved*, 123; Hambrick-Stowe, *Practice of Piety*, 28–29; and Coffey, "Letters by Samuel Rutherford," 104.

11. The literature on Taylor's usage of the Song of Songs is vast. See for example Hambrick-Stowe, *Early New England Meditative Poetry*, 38–62, 129–264 and Hessel-Robinson, "Edward Taylor's Preparatory Meditations."

12. Coffey, *Theology and the British Revolutions*, 108–9. Rutherford also used Song 2:14–17 for his sermon, *Christ and the Doves*.

13. Matter, *Voice of My Beloved*. Another standard work on the medieval period is Astell, *Song of Songs in Middle Ages*. During the final stages of preparing this book I received Elizabeth Clarke's, *Politics, Religion and the Song of Songs*. This is an excellent and far ranging study of the Puritan usage of the Song of Songs and will fill a great need; cf. Scheper, "Reformation and Song of Songs" and Williams, "Puritan Enjoyment of God," 177–211.

14. Scheper, "Reformation and Song of Songs," 557–58.

significant distinction between the monastic and Puritan usage of Song
of Songs focuses on the increased practice of marriage in the Puritans.[15]
While the monastic and medieval church leaders were required to practice celibacy and extol virginity, many Puritan ministers were married.
This would lead to a differing awareness around gender and the soul.
Indeed, Puritans encouraged young couples to think in terms of "double
marriage," looking not only at the prospect of earthly marriage but also
considering the greater joy of heavenly marriage with Jesus.[16] We will
return to this theme in greater depth later in this chapter.

HISTORICAL ROOTS OF SPIRITUAL MARRIAGE

McGinn contends that until the twelfth century the language of union
with God was not particularly common. The increased usage of this
metaphor was related to a number of interacting features including the
Dionysian emphasis upon ascent and completion of the spiritual journey.[17] Further, this period has often been called the "Twelfth-Century
Renaissance" that among other things emphasized, "divine and human
love [that] was expressed in subjective mysticism and in courtly love."
Additionally a new awareness of the individual and interpersonal relationships, a growing appreciation of humanness, including the humanity of Christ, and new spiritual forms emerged.[18] Undoubtedly the most
significant person towering over the twelfth century was Bernard of
Clairvaux.

Both Isaac Ambrose and many other Puritans exhibited a great
fondness for Bernard of Clairvaux.[19] Bernard's eighty-six sermons from
the Song of Songs are massive and only a few illustrations can be offered.
In one particularly significant reference Bernard writes:

15. Moore, "Sexing the Soul," 179.

16. See Godbeer, *Sexual Revolution in Early America*, 74.

17. McGinn, "Love, Knowledge and Unio Mystica," 61–62.

18. Sheldrake, *Brief History of Spirituality*, 77; cf. McGinn, "Western Christianity,"
323–29.

19. The literature on Bernard is immense. Two general introductions are McGinn,
Growth of Mysticism, 158–224 and Tamburello, *Bernard of Clairvaux, Essential Writings*.
On Bernard's understanding of *unio mystica* see Tamburello, *Union with Christ*; Gilson,
Mystical Theology of Bernard; Casey, *Athirst for God*, esp. 191–208 and de Reuver, *Sweet
Communion*, 27–60.

"Arise my love, my bride, and come." The bridegroom draws attention to the greatness of his love by repeating words of love ... Never yet, as far as I recall, has he mentioned the bride openly in this whole work, except when she goes to the vineyards and draws near the wine of love. When she will have attained to it and become perfect she will celebrate a spiritual marriage; and they shall become two, not in one flesh but in one spirit, as the apostle says: "He who is united to the Lord becomes one spirit with him."[20]

Bernard alerts his readers to a number of key principles. God, the divine Bridegroom, takes the initiative in calling individuals into spiritual marriage. This is a reminder that grace was important for Bernard. Further, it is clear that this is a process; union is something that needs to be attained. This passage also employs 1 Cor 6:17 which was Bernard's favorite Scripture to represent union with God.[21] And, "[f]urthermore, 'he who is united to the Lord becomes one spirit with him,' his whole being somehow changed into a movement of divine love ... But God is love, and the deeper one's union with God, the more full one is of love."[22] Therefore, "[s]uch love, as I have said, is marriage, for a soul cannot love like this and not be beloved; complete and perfect marriage consists in the exchange of love."[23] These expressions are representative of the essential nature of love for Bernard in spiritual marriage.

Mystical union was also significant in John Calvin's theology. In recent years there has been considerable debate whether Calvin had a "central dogma." While older Calvin studies focused upon predestination, more recently the pendulum has swung to the centrality of union with Christ.[24] However, the best of contemporary research, while not minimizing the importance of *unio mystica*, asserts that Calvin was too complex to have a single "central dogma."[25] Although Calvin's writings are replete with abundant references to union with Christ, there are a few that specifically employ the language of spiritual marriage. Calvin asserts,

---

20. Bernard, *SCC* 61:1.

21. McGinn, *Growth of Mysticism*, 213, 215.

22. Bernard, *SCC* 26:5.

23. Ibid., 83.6.

24. Partee, "Calvin's Central Dogma Again," 191–99 and Hageman, "Reformed Spirituality," 60–61. For an opposing view see Wenger "New Perspective on Calvin."

25. Billings, *Calvin, Participation, and the Gift*, 19.

God very commonly takes on the character of a husband to us. Indeed, the union by which he binds us to himself when he receives us into the bosom of the church is like sacred wedlock, which must rest upon mutual faithfulness [Eph. 5:29–32]. As he performs all the duties of a true and faithful husband, of us in return he demands love and conjugal chastity. That is we are not to yield our souls to Satan, to lust, and to the filthy desires of the flesh, to be defiled by them.[26]

Calvin nicely expands the nature of sacred wedlock by addressing the importance of reciprocal expression of love and commitment as well as purity and devotion to God, as the divine husband. Calvin uses the same imagery later when he declares:

This union alone ensures that, as far as we are concerned, he has not unprofitably come with the name of Savior. The same purpose is served by that sacred wedlock through which we are made flesh of his flesh and bone of his bone [Eph. 5:30], and thus one with him. But he unites himself to us by the Spirit alone. By the grace and power of the same Spirit we are made his members, to keep us under himself and in turn to possess him.[27]

Significantly, contra Bernard, spiritual marriage for Calvin is more ecclesial and related to Eph 5. Additionally Calvin stresses the critical role of the Holy Spirit who serves as the initiator and bond of this mystical union.[28] Bernard's relational emphasis of love appears to be altered in Calvin to focus more on salvation and faith.

To summarize more broadly, there are a number of important continuities and discontinuities between Bernard and Calvin. The commonalities include the importance of grace in the union with Christ, the union is of the will and not of essence, and the centrality of Christ's humanity. Conversely, Bernard typically spoke of union with God rather than Christ, and this union focused more on love, emphasizing the Song of Songs. Calvin spoke most frequently of union with Christ and focused

---

26. Calvin, *Institutes*, 2.8.18. Calvin also employs Isa 62:4–5 and Hos 2:19–20 in this section to reinforce the importance of faithfulness to God. Engrafting is Calvin's favorite image when speaking of being joined with Christ. Tamburello, *Union with Christ*, 111

27. Calvin, *Institutes*, 3.1.3; cf. 2.12.7; 4.19.35. Calvin also uses the metaphor of "holy marriage" in his *Commentary on Hosea*, 2:21–22 and "spiritual marriage" in his *Commentary on Matthew* 22:2.

28. According to Tamburello, the Holy Spirit also serves an important function in Bernard of Clairvaux. *Union with Christ*, 44–45.

on faith, emphasizing the foundational role of the sacraments. Both reformers placed some restrictions on it. Bernard taught that the monastery was the primary place to experience it. Calvin's view was more inclusive of clergy and laity; however, it could be argued that he limited it to those who were among God's elect. Bernard's favorite text was 1 Cor 6:17, and Eph 5:30–32 was the corresponding counterpart for Calvin.[29] However, the most significant distinction, especially as it relates to this chapter, is that while Song of Songs was foundational and contemplation was highly desirable for Bernard's understanding, neither held the same significance for Calvin.[30] While it has become customary to summarize the distinctions between Bernard and Calvin in this manner, upon closer examination some of these distinctions fade. In reality, Bernard does seem to appreciate the importance of faith; likewise Calvin's understanding was not devoid of love.[31] More importantly, what appears lacking in this discussion is the appreciation of the dynamic nature of faith in Calvin's theology. While faith originates in the mind for Calvin it is sealed in the heart. Therefore, for Calvin faith includes a strong affective dimension and when combined with the Holy Spirit creates a robust sense of enjoyment of Christ. Calvin maintains,

> We also, in turn, are said to be "engrafted into him" [Rom 11:17], and to "put on Christ" [Gal 3:27]; for, as I have said, all that he possesses is nothing to us until we grow into one body with him. It is true that we obtain this by faith. Yet since we see that not all indiscriminately embrace that communion with Christ which is offered through the gospel, reason itself teaches us to climb higher and to examine into the secret energy of the Spirit, by which we come to enjoy Christ and all his benefits.[32]

29. Ibid., 90. For the significance of Eph 5:30–32 see Moore, "Sexing the Soul," 179n11.

30. Much of this is summarized from Tamburello, *Union with Christ*, 105–7; cf. Chin, "*Unio Mystica* and *Imitatio Christi*," 306. While Calvin gave minor attention to the Song of Songs, this was not true for Theodore Beza, his replacement. Long, *Eucharistic Theology*, 55–60.

31. De Reuver, *Sweet Communion*, 58. For the predominant emphasis of love in Bernard and faith in Calvin see Tamburello, *Union with Christ*, 85, 91, 103, 107. For a critique of Tamburello's method see Chin, "*Unio Mystica* and *Imitatio Christi*," 44–51. McGinn also appears to minimize the affective dimension of faith in Calvin. "Mysticism," 3:122. Tamburello concedes that faith was also important for Bernard and that love played a significant role for Calvin. *Union with Christ*, 144n47, 40, 105.

32. Calvin, *Institutes*, 3.1.1; cf. 3.2.7; 3.2.14; 3.2.36. Calvin connects faith to the "double grace" of justification and sanctification. *Institutes*, 3.11.1. Won also stresses the experiential nature of union with Christ for Calvin. "Communion with Christ," 33.

Additionally, it is vital to recognize that for Calvin spiritual marriage was intimately connected with the celebration of the Lord's Supper and contained a strong relational theme. Ronald Wallace accurately summarizes this crucial aspect of Calvin's theology: "[w]hen we have such communion with him by the Holy Spirit, Calvin explained, he is not only brought down to us on this earth, but our souls are also raised up to him so that we can participate here and now in his ascended life and glory."[33] This reveals another critical distinction between Bernard and Calvin that is not typically recognized. Bernard spoke of union with God while Calvin spoke of both union and communion with Christ.[34] The theological background for this can be traced to the differing perceptions regarding justification and sanctification. Indeed Bernard, as other medieval writers, did not distinguish as clearly as Calvin and the Protestant Reformers did on these two graces of God.[35] When the Puritan understanding of spiritual marriage is examined, it will be clear how communion significantly includes a strong relational theme.

PURITAN READING AND EXEGESIS OF SCRIPTURE

As previously mentioned, the Song of Songs was a favorite Puritan text for spiritual marriage, but how did they read this Scripture? Isaac Ambrose provides an illuminating insight in summarizing the purpose of Ps 45, which was often used as a compact version of the Song of Songs.[36] Ambrose declares, "*the spiritual marriage and love between Christ and his Church*, whereof *Solomons* marriage with *Pharaohs* daughter, was a figure and type and likewise to shew the perfect love that ought to be between the husband and the wife."[37] "Figure and type" clearly reveal a more dynamic engagement with the text and indicate that Ambrose was not limited to a literal reading of Scripture. At one level it was not uncommon to conflate these terms and many seventeenth-century dictionaries

33. Ronald Wallace, *Calvin, Geneva and the Reformation*, 198 and Ronald Wallace, *Calvin's Doctrine of the Word*, 206–7.

34. Tamburello speaks of the "twofold communion with Christ" and is one scholar who recognizes this major distinction. *Union with Christ*, 86.

35. Ibid., 107; cf. 41–63; cf. McGrath, "Justification" and Gründler, "Justification and Sanctification in Calvin and Bernard."

36. Bainton, "Bible in Reformation," 8 and Williams, "Puritan Enjoyment of God," 177n108.

37. Ambrose, *Media* (1657), 499–500.

defined "type" as a "figure, example, shadow of anything."[38] Yet at another level, a distinction could be drawn between them. William Perkins, who authored one of the primary preaching manuals in the early seventeenth century, demonstrates awareness to figures of speech when he includes metaphors, metonymies, and synecdoche in his work.[39] He also recognized the difference between "Analogical & plaine, or Crypticall and dark" passages.[40] Perkins cites 1 Cor 11:24 "[t]his is my body, which is broken for you." as an example and explains why this passage could not be taken literally.[41] Additionally, James Durham presents a helpful distinction between typology and allegory, "[t]ypes suppose still the verity of some history, as Jonah's casting in the sea, and being in the fish's belly three days and three nights, when it is applied to Christ in the New Testament, it supposeth such a thing once to have been: allegories again, have no such necessary supposition, but are as parables, proponed for some mystical end."[42] However, in practice, even the distinctions between typologies and allegories could blur.[43]

Further, the Puritans recognized that some passages were allegorical in nature, such as the Song of Songs. Durham distinguished between an "allegoric exposition of scripture, and an exposition of allegoric scripture: the first is that which many fathers and schoolmen fail in, that is, when they allegorize plain scriptures and histories, seeking to draw out some secret meaning, other than appeareth in the words; and so will fasten many senses upon one scripture."[44] Therefore, Durham maintains that the Song of Songs is to be read allegorically.[45] Most Puritans affirmed this

38. Cawdry, *Table Alphabetical*, n.p.; cf. Phillips, *New World*, n.p.; Cockeram, *English Dictionarie*, 2nd pt., n.p.; and Blount, *Glossographia*, n.p.; cf. Lowance, *Language of Canaan*, 19, 66.

39. Perkins, *Arte of Prophecying*, 54–57.

40. Ibid., 45, 46. Thomas Lea notes, "[t]his recognition moderated their emphasis on literalism so that they did not practice a wooden literalism that could lead to serious errors in interpretation." Lea, "Hermeneutics of the Puritans," 281.

41. Ibid., 47–49. For the use of figural language in the Puritans see Lowance, *Language of Canaan* and Lewalski, *Protestant Poetics*, esp. 31–146.

42. Durham, *Song of Solomon*, 30. Benjamin Keach authored one of the primary works of typology. *Tropologia: Key to Metaphors*. For an overview to typology see Lowance, *Language of Canaan*, esp. 16–27.

43. Schneiders, "Scripture and Spirituality," 17; cf. Williams, "Puritan Enjoyment of God," 182n117.

44. Durham, *Song of Solomon*, 43.

45. Ibid., 30–31.

assessment[46], though they also understood that Solomon was a "type" of Christ.[47]

The Puritan sensitivity to allegories, figures of speech, and typology unsettles the assumption that the Protestant Reformation fully embraced the literal sense of Scripture. Brevard Childs corrects this distorted thinking: "[i]n the post-Reformation period . . . both the orthodox Lutherans and Calvinists had almost immediate difficulty in maintaining the unity of the literal sense which increasingly was fragmented in different levels of meaning."[48] In reality the literal reading of Scripture had been emphasized by Hugh of St. Victor (1096–1141) long before Luther's resistance to allegorical reading.[49] Previously, Augustine had advanced a double literal reading of Scripture based on 2 Cor 3:6, "[t]he letter kills but the spirit makes alive" that sought both the literal and spiritual sense of a passage.[50] However, due to the often excessive interpretations that developed around allegorical reading, the Protestant Reformers rejected the *quadriga* or four-fold pattern of reading Scripture according to the literal, allegorical, tropological, and anagogical meaning and resorted to the literal practice.[51] Lisa Gordis is correct that polemics was certainly a major motivation behind the intense resistance to the *quadriga*.[52] Perkins continued the same trajectory opposing the *quadriga* stating, "*[t]here is one onelie sense, and the same is the literall.*"[53] However, this condemnation surprisingly evolves into an affirmation: "[a]n allegorie is onely a certaine manner of uttering the same sense. The Anagoge and

46. Williams, "Puritan Enjoyment of God," 183 and Knott, *Sword of Spirit*, 53.

47. Lowance, *Language of Canaan*, 46–47 and Williams, "Puritan Enjoyment of God," 181n114.

48. Childs, "Sensus Literalis of Scripture," 87.

49. Ibid., 83; cf. Schneiders, "Scripture and Spirituality," 15–16.

50. Steinmetz, "Superiority of Pre-Critical Exegesis," 28–29.

51. Gordis, *Opening Scripture*, 20; cf. 238n22. The seminal study on the *quadriga* is de Lubac, *Medieval Exegesis*. Other helpful resources include Schneiders, "Scripture and Spirituality," 9-19; Muller, *Dictionary of Theological Terms*, 254–55; and Wilson, *God Sense*. Muller asserts that the *quadriga* continued to exist following the Protestant Reformation. "Biblical Interpretation in the Reformation," 3–16 and *Post-Reformation Reformed Dogmatics*, 2:469–82.

52. Gordis, *Opening Scripture*, 20, 238n22; cf. Scheper, "Reformation and Song of Songs," 552.

53. Perkins, *Arte of Prophecying*, 31.

Tropologie are waies, whereby the sense may be applied."[54] Further, in his preaching manual Perkins provides specific directions on how to expound allegory and reminds his readers that the apostle Paul frequently employed them in his epistles.[55]

Consequently, this leads some contemporary scholars to contend that the Puritan allegorizing of the Song of Songs was due to their squeamishness regarding sex and attempt to minimize it.[56] However, others maintain the opposite and Williams declares: "[f]or the vast majority of Puritan writers interpreted Canticles as an allegory of the love between Christ and the individual believer. This hermeneutic was not chosen chiefly to de-eroticise the Song, but to increase its spiritual value, for it was the very sensuality of its language which made it such an apt descriptive tool for ecstatic enjoyment of God. Puritan mysticism was communicated using a profoundly sensual and even erotic love-language."[57] McGinn recognizes the same principle within the broader context of Christian spirituality and asserts that "erotic imagery of kisses and breasts, was one of the central scriptural foundations in the history of Christian mysticism."[58] Therefore, it is illuminating that the Puritans turned to Prov 31 as their favorite text for wedding sermons, not the Song of Songs.[59] Perhaps in their mind the Song of Songs had been elevated more exclusively for spiritual marriage rather than earthly marriage.

PURITAN CELEBRATION OF GODLY MARRIAGE AND SEX

The Puritans often referred to their earthly marriage as godly marriage.[60] While scholars debate whether the Puritans drew inspiration for their

54. Ibid. One of Perkins' examples of doctrine strongly resembles the four-fold method of reading. *Arte of Prophecying*, 126. Durham claims that the apostle Paul used the *quadriga* in Galatians 4. *Song of Solomon*, 30. Muller asserts that the *quadriga* continued in some form in Calvin. "Biblical Interpretation in the Reformation," 11–12.

55. Ibid., 75, 97. Durham provides five rules for expositing allegories. *Song of Solomon*, 46–48.

56. Scheper, "Reformation and Song of Songs," 558.

57. Williams, "Puritan Enjoyment of God," 194–95; cf. 184, 196.

58. McGinn, "Mysticism and Sexuality," 46; cf. McGinn, "Language of Love," 205.

59. See the four volumes of wedding sermons published as *Conjugal Duty: Delightful Wedding-Sermons* in the Dr Williams's Library.

60. The primary sources will be introduced throughout this section. The secondary literature on godly marriage is extensive. Some useful sources include: Haller and Haller, "Puritan Art of Love"; Frye, "Puritanism on Conjugal Love"; Leites, "Duty to

godly marriage from their experience with Christ in spiritual marriage
or vice versa,[61] Isaac Ambrose maintains that Christ and his spouse are
an example for the husband and wife in godly marriage because the
quality of Christ's love is far superior to that of human love.[62] This is a
clear message of Eph 5:25.[63] Samuel Rutherford's *Letters*, which are full
of vivid and erotic nuptial imagery, agrees with Ambrose's assessment
declaring, "[l]et her give Christ the love of her virginity and espousals,
and choose Him first as her Husband, and that match shall bless the
other."[64] Somewhat surprisingly, Erica Longfellow contends, "[w]ith
the exception of William Gouge, who attempts to literalise the mystical marriage metaphor, in most Puritan writers the mystery of mystical
marriage has very little connection to human marriage."[65]

Frequently readers who have not been exposed to a careful examination of the primary texts are prone to caricature individuals or
movements from history. Clearly the Puritans have been consistently
criticized and ridiculed for their teaching on marriage and sex. In fact
many writers employ the term puritanical as a repressive and pejorative
label.[66] However, once the Puritan marriage manuals have been read it
will be difficult to maintain that perception. The Puritan emphases can
be summarized as follows: the softening of the hierarchical understanding of marriage within a patriarchal society, the recognition of the benefit of marriage beyond procreation, and a greater celebration of intimacy
and sex within marriage.

Desire"; Ryken, *Worldly Saints*, 39–55; Todd, "Spiritualized Household"; Packer, *Quest for Godliness*, 259–73; Doriani, "Puritans, Sex, and Pleasure"; Fletcher, "Protestant Idea of Marriage"; Williams, "Puritan Enjoyment of God," 159–73; and Peters, *Patterns of Piety*.

61. For the primary influence of spiritual marriage see Godbeer, "Performing Patriarchy," 301; Godbeer, "Love Raptures," 53, 63–65, 70; and Godbeer, *Sexual Revolution in Early America*, 72; cf. Porterfield, *Feminine Spirituality in America*, 39. For the primary influence of godly marriage see Moore, Sexing the Soul," 176n5, 180, 182. For an appreciation of the reciprocal nature of the marriage metaphor see Godbeer, "Love Raptures," 54, 62, and Godbeer, *Sexual Revolution in Early America*, 72; cf. Williams, "Puritan Enjoyment of God," 176.

62. Ambrose, *Media* (1657), 323, 325.

63. Hieron, *Bridegroome*, 15.

64. Rutherford, *Letters*, 483.

65. Longfellow, *Women and Religious Writings*, 23.

66. Doriani, "Puritans, Sex, and Pleasure," 125; cf. Verduin, "Our Cursed Natures," 223.

No one denies that the seventeenth-century landscape was highly patriarchal continuing the practice that had existed for centuries. However, within Puritanism there was a softening of the rigidity and control that had marked previous generations. Robert Cleaver, writing in 1592, declares:

> A wise husband, and one that seeketh to live in quiet with his wife, must observe these three rules. Often to admonish; Seldome to reprove; and never to smite her . . . The husband is also to understand, that as God created the woman, not of the head, & so equall in authoritie with her husband; so also hee created her not of *Adams* foote, that she should be troden downe and despised, but he tooke her out of the ribbe, that shee might walke joyntly with him, under the conduct and government of her head.[67]

Thomas Gataker in a sermon preached almost forty years after Cleaver continues the same imagery and expands it, "[s]he was made for man, & given to man, not to be a *play-fellow*, or a *bed-fellow*, or a *table-mate*, onely with him (and yet to be all these too) but to bee a *yoke-fellow*, a *work-fellow*, a *fellow-labourer* with him, to be *an assistant* and *an helper* unto him, in the managing of such *domesticall and household affaires*."[68] Earlier Gataker reminds both husband and wife to recognize that their respective partner is a gift from God.[69] William Whately argues that a husband and wife "are indebted each to other in reciprocall debt."[70] However, the husband's higher position of authority also included greater responsibility and he was expected to provide a good example for his wife.[71] Puritan pastors were keenly aware of human nature, and Richard Steele in preaching on Eph 5:33 declares that the apostle Paul was observing the most frequent failings of couples, that "husbands too

67. Cleaver, *Godly Form of Householde Government*, 201. William Gouge follows the same principle and forbids the husband from beating his wife. *Domesticall Duties*, 394, 396. However, Whately maintains that under certain circumstances it may be necessary. *Brides-Bush* (1623), see esp. 107, 123, 125.

68. Gataker, *Certaine Sermons*, 128. The original source of this imagery was likely Chrysostom's homily on Ephesians. Steele, "Duties of Husbands and Wives?" 290; cf. Packer, *Quest for Godliness*, 262 and Longfellow, *Women and Religious Writing*, 120 for other variations. For John Donne's opposing view of Genesis 2 imagery see Todd, "Spiritualized Household," 113n72.

69. Gataker, *Good Wife Gods Gift*, 22–23.

70. Whately, *Bride-Bush* (1617), 1.

71. Ibid., 19.

commonly being defective in their love, and wives most defective in their reverence and subjection."[72]

William Gouge provides a striking illustration of the dynamics of hierarchy. The publication of his *Of Domesticall Duties* created an outcry among many of the women in his London congregation. By the third edition he acknowledged their criticism that he was overbearing and that his teaching was excessive. Significantly, these women felt the freedom to voice their concerns; equally important Gouge acknowledged them in print.[73] It is also noteworthy that his teaching on sex within marriage was reciprocal and that he was one of the most progressive Puritans on this subject. Christine Peters further clarifies both the dynamics within Gouge's congregation and the broader perspective of Puritan family hierarchy.[74] Therefore, while no one would deny that patriarchy was firmly ensconced within Puritan culture, there was greater flexibility and freedom for women than commonly assumed.[75] In fact, Diane Willen concludes that "godliness [among Puritan wives] tempered patriarchy" and that normal gender roles were more conditioned by specific structure or order in a given situation than by the gender of a person.[76] Further, Peters citing Gouge asserts that men could actually forfeit their authority as the head of the family due to drunkenness, card playing, or illicit sex.[77]

Isaac Ambrose follows a similar pattern in his teaching on godly marriage in his exploration of the roles of husband and wife in *Media*. He begins with a general summary of mutual responsibilities. Husbands and wives should offer "sweet, loving, and tender-hearted pouring out of their hearts, with much affectionate dearness into each others bosoms. This mutual-melting-heartedness, being preserved fresh and fruitful, will

72. Steele, "Duties of Husbands and Wives," 274.

73. Gouge, *Domesticall Duties*, 4. This does not appear in the 1627 second edition. All citations from Gouge in this book are from the 1634 third edition.

74. Peters, *Patterns of Piety*, 314–16; cf. Fletcher, "Protestant Idea of Marriage," 167–69.

75. Limitations of space prevent a more detailed treatment of this expanding study of patriarchy. For further exploration see Richardson, *Puritanism in North-West England*, 107–9; Lake, "Feminine Piety and Personal Potency"; Porterfield, "Women's Attraction to Puritanism"; Porterfield, *Feminine Spirituality in America*, esp. 3–39; Willen, "Godly Women in Early Modern England"; Willen, "Construction of the Feminine"; Godbeer, "Performing Patriarchy"; and Longfellow, *Women and Religious Writing*, esp. 1–41.

76. Willen, "Godly Women in Early Modern England," 580, and Godbeer, "Performing Patriarchy," 293.

77. Peters, *Patterns of Piety*, 317.

infinitely sweeten and beautifie the marriage state." Further, he encourages couples to "resemble and imitate . . . the compassionate and melting compellations which Christ and his Spouse exchange in the *Canticles*."[78] Therefore, according to Ambrose, spiritual marriage should guide godly marriage and takes its guidance from the Song of Songs. Next, he addresses the specific duties of husbands and wives. The husband is charged to "dearly love his Wife" and "wisely maintain and manage his authority over her." Husbands are warned that love based on "beauty, riches, lust, or any other slight grounds, is but a blaze, and soon vanisheth, but if grounded on these considerations, and especially on this union of marriage, it is lasting and true."[79] The wife in turn is to "be in submission to her husband" and "be an helper to him all her days."[80] Further, Ambrose affirms that the wife is to submit to her husband only if those things reflect Christ. In response to the question "[w]hat if her husband command things contrary to Christ? Must she therein be subject?" Ambrose declares "No."[81]

Second, the Puritans reversed the order for the purpose of marriage. To appreciate the radical shift, there is need for some awareness of the medieval context that the Protestant Reformation inherited. Marriage was prohibited for the clergy in the West and while the laity were permitted and even encouraged to marry, virginity had held an elevated status for over a millennium.[82] In most sections of the church the general perception was holiness was most likely to be attained through a life of virginity. Reflective of this strong mindset, the Protestant Reformers continued to speak of virginity and chasteness, but now redefined it according to the exclusiveness to one person as husband or wife.[83] Further, Article Thirty Two of the Church of England's *Thirty Nine Articles* explicitly approved of clergy marriage, though not making it obligatory.[84]

78. Ambrose, *Media* (1657), 323.

79. Ibid., 324.

80. Ibid., 327.

81. Ibid., 328.

82. McGinn, "Mysticism and Sexuality," 48–51, and McGinn, "Tropics of Desire," 134–35. For a summary of the status and restrictions of marriage within the Western Catholic Church at this time see Ryken, *Worldly Saints*, 40–42; Packer, *Quest for Godliness*, 260–61; and Doriani, "Puritans, Sex, and Pleasure," 142.

83. Calvin, *Institutes*, 4.12.28.

84. Young, "Origin of Newman's Celibacy," 16; cf. 18.

Indeed, most clergy of the Church of England were married, though there were a few rare exceptions as witnessed by the words of George Herbert: "[t]he Country Parson considering that virginity is a higher state than Matrimony, and that the Ministry requires the best and highest things, is rather unmarried, than married."[85]

Far more significant was the reversal of the order of the purposes for marriage. Throughout the history of the church the primary reason for marriage was procreation. This order still existed in the *Book of Common Prayer* (1549): 1. procreation of children, 2. remedy against sin and to avoid fornication, and 3. mutual society, help, and comfort.[86] While a cross section of the early Puritan sources reveal a variation in the order, by the time of the *Westminster Confession* in 1648 they are standardized that "[m]arriage was ordained for the mutual help of husband and wife, for the increase of mankind with a legitimate issue, and of the Church with an holy seed, and for preventing of uncleanness."[87] Fletcher observes, "[f]ollowing St Paul's precepts in 1 Corinthians, there is a notable lack of reference to intercourse being solely or primarily for the purpose of procreation."[88] With the clear reversal between the first and third reasons, mutual companionship became primary. Additionally the Puritans used the term "due benevolence" to capture this deepening sense of mutuality within marriage. Gouge asserted, "[d]ue benevolence is one of the most proper and essential acts or ends of marriage- it preserves chastity, it increases the legitimate brood in the world, and & it provides a means for the affection of the married couple." Further, due benevolence "must bee performed with good will and delight, willingly, readily, and cheerfully."[89] Perkins adds this description to due benevolence: "by an holy kind of rejoicing and solacing themselves each with other, in a mutuall declaration of the signes and tokens of love and kindness." Perkins employs both Prov

85. Herbert, *Country Parson*, ch. 9, 66. Herbert wrote this work in 1632; cf. Taylor, *Holy Living*, 82.

86. James Johnson, "Puritan Thought on Marriage," 429; cf. Ryken, *Worldly Saints*, 47–48.

87. *Westminster Confession*, XXIV:ii; cf. Packer, *Quest for Godliness*, 261–62.

88. Fletcher, "Protestant Idea of Marriage," 179. Gouge confirms this principle, "[f]or though procreation of children be one end of marriage, yet it is not the onely end." *Domesticall Duties*, 183.

89. Gouge, *Domesticall Duties*, 224.

5:18–19 and Gen 26:8 that figured prominently in the Puritan marriage manuals reflecting their understanding of the enjoyment of sex.[90]

Third, the Puritan teaching on marriage celebrates intimacy and the enjoyment of sex. Packer speaks of the "erotic agape of romantic marriage"[91] and asserts that the Puritans frequently made use of Prov 5:18–19 in their preaching on the joys of marriage: "[m]ay you rejoice in the wife of your youth. A loving doe, a graceful deer—may her breasts satisfy you always, may you ever be captivated by her love."[92] Thomas Gataker exegetes this text and declares that one of the duties of a husband was to take pleasure in his wife:

> "*Joy and delight in her. Drink,*" saith the wise man, "*the water of thine own cistern: Let thy fountain be blessed: . . . and rejoice in the wife of thy youth: let her bee unto thee as the loving Hind, and the pleasant Roe: Let her brests or her bosome content thee at all times: & delight continually*, or as the word there is, even *doate on the love of her.*" As if the holy Ghost did allow some such private daliance and behaviour to married persons betweene themselves as to others might seem dotage: such as may be *Isaacke* sporting with *Rebecka*.[93]

Employing the robust nature of the same verse, Gouge reminds couples of the delight within marriage: "[a]s the man must be satisfied at all times in his wife, and even ravisht with her love; so must the woman be satisfied at all times in her husband, and even ravisht with his love."[94] Later he returns to this same verse and instructs husbands to let their affection delight completely in their wives. He then amplifies the power of this lovemaking and reminds his readers that the hart and roe buck "are most enamored of their mate and even mad againe in their heat and desire after them."[95] He continues, "[a]n husbands affection to his wife

---

90. Perkins, *Christian Oeconomie*, 122.

91. Packer, *Quest for Godliness*, 263.

92. Ibid., 265–66.

93. Gataker, *Certaine Sermons*, 2:206; cf. Hilder, *Conjugall Counsell*, 39, and Daniel Cawdrey, *Family Reformation Promoted*, 114. The reference to Isaac sporting Rebekah is Gen 26:8; cf. Cleaver, *Godly Form of Household Government*, 175 and Smith, *Sermons*, 12 for sanctioning love play using Gen 26:8 and Frye, "Puritanism on Conjugal Love," 153 for the usage of Prov 5:18–19.

94. Gouge, *Domesticall Duties*, 219.

95. Ibid., 365. Previously Cleaver counsels couples to take mutual delight in each other since Prov 5:18–19 asserts, "so the wife should bee a delight unto her husband

cannot be too great, if it be kept within the bonds of honesty, sobriety and comelinesse."[96] Richard Baxter counsels couples to "[k]eep up your conjugal love in a constant heat and vigour."[97] Gouge also employs Gen 26:8, articulating that God does not expect husbands and wives to be like the Stoics without affection; rather, husbands should delight in their wives. Additionally he instructs couples to "[r]ead the Song of Songs, and in it you shall observe such affection manifested by Christ to his Spouse . . . A good patterne and precident for Husbands."[98] While it is difficult to know the actual marital practices of the Puritans, one brief glimpse is available in the study of three seventeenth-century Puritan couples. What surfaces, surely as no surprise, is that no two marriages or relationships are identical.[99]

Because the Puritans took marriage very seriously they also recognized the great importance of guarding it from temptations that could destroy or weaken it. First, they vigilantly emphasized the appropriateness of behavior within a given context. Intimacy and sexual expressions were not for the public eye. Gouge once again draws upon Gen 26:8 and comments that Isaac and Rebecca had enjoyed themselves in private and then adds, "[m]uch greater liberty is granted to man and wife when they are lone, then in company."[100] This relates also to his warning about the danger of excessive sex.[101] Similarly Perkins cautions couples that, "excesse in lusts is no better than plaine adulterie before God."[102] Finally, there was a constant warning against adultery and the importance of commitment to your partner. Gouge, who again appears to be the most progressive Puritan in addressing these matters, may once again be

---

and so in like manner, shee ought to take delight in him." *Godly Forme of Household Government*, 176.

96. Ibid., 366; cf. 365 Gouge also declares as long as the husband's desire does "exceed not the bonds of Christian modesty and decency, are very fit, and pertinent to the purpose."

97. Baxter, *Christian Directory*, 522.

98. Gouge, *Domesticall Duties*, 366.

99. Stevie Davies examines the lives of Ralph and Jane Josselin, Nehemiah and Grace Wallington, and Lucy and John Hutchinson. Stevie Davies, *Unbridled Spirits*; cf. Morgan, *Puritan Family*, 47–64.

100. Gouge, *Domesticall Duties*, 393; cf. 280.

101. Ibid., 224–25.

102. Perkins, *Christian Oeconomie*, 113; cf. Frye, "Puritanism on Conjugal Love," 150–52.

surprising. He argues that, while the Western Catholic Church placed the primary responsibility on the woman for avoiding adultery, he believes that biblically both couples are equally responsible, but then he adds that man should be punished more than the woman since he is required to set a higher example.[103] Gouge understood that one of the best ways to prevent adultery is "that husband and wife mutually delight each in other, and maintaine a pure and fervent love betwixt themselves, yielding that due benevolence one to another which is warranted and sanctified by Gods Word, and ordained of God for this particular end."[104] As a result, some critics upbraid the Puritans for their strict boundaries regarding sexuality. However, Belden Lane's perceptive comments resonate more accurately with the integrity of the Puritan understanding of marriage and sex. He writes, "[t]his is why the Puritans were necessarily so concerned about propriety and purity—not because they were innately prudish, but because their very piety lent itself to an excess of ardor."[105] Therefore, it is no surprise that the Puritans struggled with the temptations of pre-marital sex. Godbeer states, "roughly one-fifth of English brides in the late sixteenth and early seventeenth centuries were already pregnant by the time they were formally married."[106]

Not withstanding these claims, it would be inaccurate to assume that the Puritans had completely severed themselves from the medieval perception that sin was transmitted through sex.[107] Nonetheless, there was considerable freedom and advancement from previous generations. In fact, denying sex to your partner was a cause for public discipline in New England and at times could even constitute grounds for divorce.[108] That certainly does not reinforce the typical impression of "Puritanical love" as advanced by many contemporary voices. The Puritans mostly embraced a robust understanding of healthy sex within marriage. The joys and intimacy that they were able to share in their godly marriages mirrored and encouraged a similar intimacy with Jesus Christ in spiritual

---

103. Gouge, *Domesticall Duties*, 221; cf. Whately, *Bride-Bush* (1623), 30.

104. Ibid., 224.

105. Belden Lane, "Covenant and Desire in Puritan Spirituality," 77; cf. Belden Lane *Ravished By Beauty*, 24–25; cf. 99.

106. Godbeer, *Sexual Revolution in Early America*, 3; cf. 29, 345n25; cf. Masson, "Typology of the Female," 309.

107. Ibid., 61–62; cf. Doriani, "Puritans, Sex, and Pleasure," 138.

108. Ibid., 59–60.

marriage. However, as will soon be clear, the Puritans were always careful not to elevate their love for their partner above their love for Jesus.

SPIRITUAL MARRIAGE IN THE WRITINGS
OF THE PURITANS[109]

The Puritans followed the theological foundation of Calvin and understood union with Christ began at a person's conversion.[110] In fact, many Puritans referred to their conversion as their wedding or marriage day. Flavel declares, "[t]hat when Christ comes into the soul he will not come empty-handed. It is Christ's *marriage-day*, and he will make it a good day, a festival day."[111] While numerous images were used to describe this new relationship, they all communicated the message of unity with Christ.[112] Thomas Hooker used both the older language of Calvin's ingrafting as well as the language of being "knit" together.[113] Other Puritan divines used the imagery of a "marriage knot" or "love-knot."[114] Depending upon the specific writer, spiritual marriage was either between Jesus Christ and the church or the individual believer. John Preston declared, "[t]here is a match between Christ and the church: and consequently, betweene Christ and every particularman that is a member of the true body of Christ."[115] Benjamin King described this union as "that neere and

109. All of the sources used for this chapter were written by men. See Elizabeth Clarke, *Politics, Religion and the Song of Songs* and Longfellow, *Women and Religious Writings*, esp. 3–17, for female sources.

110. I am aware of the debate regarding preparationism as a prelude to conversion. Many scholars have refuted this distortion and correctly advanced the priority of God's initiative in the Puritan understanding of conversion as well as the connection between grace and duty in their spiritual practices. See for example Schaefer, "Spiritual Brotherhood," 168–78, 182–209 and Hambricke-Stowe, *Practice of Piety*, 21–22, 197–241.

111. Flavel, *England's Duty*, 214.

112. Flavel is representative of the Puritans when he speaks of the "four elegant and lively metaphors" that describes the union between Christ and the believer, "two pieces united by glue," "graff and stock," "conjugal union," and the "head and members." *Method of Grace*, 34–35.

113. Hooker, *Soules Exaltation*, 1–2, 4. Within Hooker's larger work of *Soules Implantation* was a smaller work entitled, *Soules Ingrafting*. For knitting imagery see Hooker, *Soules Exaltation*, 16, 18, 20, 24–25, 40.

114. See Shepard, *Parable of Ten Virgins*, 325; Flavel, *England's Duty*, 207; Vincent, *Christ the Best Husband*, 3; Pearse, *Best Match*, 41, 60, 61, 163, 227, 240, 275.

115. Preston, *Churches Marriage*, 1.

intimate conjunction, that is betwixt Christ and every beleeving soule, which is so great and intimate, that Christ and a beleever are sayd to bee one: Ephes. 5.32."[116] Some authors oscillated between both of these uses while others focused more on one than the other. To summarize, the Puritan understanding of union with Christ broadly resembled both Bernard and Calvin. They would all acknowledge that this union was spiritual, mystical, deep, real, and indissoluble.[117]

However, there is some variation regarding the origin and dynamics of growth in union with Christ. In the last chapter both Brauer and Chan sought to trace their respective Puritans through the *triplex via* while Williams adamantly asserted Hambrick-Stowe sought to overlay a Roman Catholic understanding of union as the conclusion rather than the origin of the Puritans' spiritual journey. This conundrum is best resolved by recognizing the more nuanced understanding of contemporary Roman Catholic scholarship. Sheldrake asserts, "[a]n over-emphasis on separate, successive stages, with universal application, conflicts with a sense of the uniqueness of each person's spiritual journey as well as with the freedom of God and unpredictability of grace." And further, "by focusing exclusively on union with God as the final stage, we may miss the point that union with God is not so much a stage above and beyond all others as the precondition of all spiritual growth."[118] Martin Laird, another contemporary Roman Catholic scholar, affirms this reality declaring, "[u]nion with God is not something that needs to be acquired but realized."[119]

Further, the Holy Spirit was central to the Puritan development and experience of spiritual marriage. Preston declares, "Christ sends his Spirit into the heart; therefore thou must consider, whether thou have

116. King, *Marriage of the Lambe*, 7.

117. Lye, *True Believer's Union*, 285–88. Flavel apparently knew Lye's work and enlarged this summary by adding this union was also immediate, efficacious, comfortable, and fruitful. *Method of Grace*, 38–42.

118. Sheldrake, *Spirituality & History*, 181; cf. Sheldrake, *Explorations in Spirituality*, 110, and Rahner, "Gradual Ascent to Perfection." McGinn observes that in Bonaventure the stages "are not successive but simultaneous and mutually interactive." *Flowering of Mysticism*, 102–3. Dupré and Wiseman assert that both Catherine of Genoa and Hadewych "describe their own experiences as starting with what would appear to be a state of union which is then followed by stages of purgation and illumination." *Light from Light*, 17.

119. Laird, *Into the Silent Land*, 10; cf. 4, 7–18.

the Spirit of thy Husband dwelling in thee or no, for except thou have the holy Ghost to dwell in thy heart, it is impossible that there should be any match."[120] He continues by affirming the Spirit's presence is critical because when we have the same Spirit of Christ we will have the same will, desires, love and hate the same things.[121] Sibbes remarks that the "Spirit of God in the hearts of his children is effectual in stirring up holy desires."[122] Goodwin affirms the same truth when he declares that the Spirit is in our hearts, preaching and persuading us of Christ's love.[123] Therefore, the Holy Spirit is not only necessary for creating God's gracious initiative in the formation of spiritual marriage, but also responsible for deepening the experiential nature of it. John Owen devotes a major portion of his trinitarian work on spiritual marriage to the Holy Spirit.[124] According to Owen, the Spirit is actively involved by being the sanctifier and comforter and bringing to remembrance what Jesus spoke. Owen recognized that spiritual marriage included the important soteriological emphasis that was so prominent in Calvin; however, both realized that this did not exhaust the understanding of it. Owen writes, "[a]s a means of retaining communion with God, whereby we sweetly ease our hearts in the bosom of the Father, and receive in refreshing tastes his love. The soul is never more raised with the love of God than when by the Spirit taken into intimate communion with him in the discharge of this duty."[125]

Significantly, while the Puritans continued to employ the language of union with Christ, they expanded Calvin's understanding of communion with Christ. Union was the necessary foundation for communion, and Preston asserts that this required "mutuall consent" among both parties.[126] Union was the initial connection while communion was the ongoing relational experience and enjoyment of that union.[127] Owen affirms the distinction: "[o]ur communion, then, with God consisteth

120. Preston, *Churches Marriage*, 17; cf. 11–12.

121. Ibid.

122. Sibbes, *Breathing After God*, 219.

123. Goodwin, *Christ Set Forth*, 107.

124. Owen, *Communion with God*, 222–74.

125. Ibid., 249.

126. Preston, *Churches Marriage*, 8–9; cf. Owen, *Communion with God*, 8.

127. On the nature and dynamics of communion with God see Packer, *Quest for Godliness*, 201–18 and Kapic, *Communion with the Triune God*, 20–46.

in *his communication of himself unto us, with our returnal unto him* of that which he requireth and accepteth, flowing from that *union* which is Jesus Christ we have with him."[128] Clearly, for Owen, spiritual marriage includes both the rich gifts of salvation and also the experience of love: "[h]ow few saints are experimentally acquainted with this privilege of holding immediate communion with the Father in love!"[129] A further reminder of the reciprocal nature of this communion is stated: "Christ having given himself to the soul, loves the soul; and the soul having given itself unto Christ, loveth him also."[130] Clearly one recognizes the important reciprocal nature of godly marriage, that it finds an echo in spiritual marriage.

King extends the awareness of spiritual marriage with Christ as he unfolds four consequences that include mutual delight between Christ and the spouse, cohabitation that is necessary to preserve the friendship, mutual bearing of one another's burdens, and mutual adhering and cleaving to one another.[131] Interestingly, he draws from Bernard's sermons on the Song of Songs.[132] King introduces a very significant theme in the first consequence of mutual delight. He observes that the satisfied soul delights in Christ by contemplation of his person and beauty as expressed in Song 5:10.[133] King is not the only Puritan that connects contemplation with spiritual marriage. Owen comments, "this is a little glimpse of some of that communion which we enjoy with Christ . . . In the contemplation of the excellencies, desirableness, love, and grace of our dear Lord Jesus."[134] Likewise, Rous captures the importance of how contemplation deepens the enjoyment of Christ in spiritual marriage:

> The highest and happiest, and sweetest harmony is, when the soule is in an unizon with her Saviour and husband: every touch and sound of the soule thus tuned to Christ Jesus, resoundeth in him, toucheth and moveth him. And as with the sound of outward musicke the spirit of God came upon the Prophet; so

128. Owen, *Communion with God*, 8; cf. Flavel, *Method of Grace*, 151.

129. Ibid., 32.

130. Ibid., 118.

131. King, *Marriage of the Lambe*, 17–26.

132. Ibid., 26. The reference is to *SCC* 31.

133. Ibid., 18. Sibbes also employs Ps 27:4 to proclaim Christ's beauty in relation to contemplation. *Breathing After God*, 237.

134. Owen, *Communion with God*, 154.

with the sound of this inward musicke (be it in contemplations, ardencies, desires, invocations, resolutions) the spirit of Christ Jesus commeth more powerfully and plentifully into the soule.[135]

Edward Pearse also recognizes how contemplation enriches spiritual marriage, "[t]hus Christ is every way acceptable, and infinitely acceptable, and as ever, Soul, thou wouldst be indeed espoused to him, dwell much in study and contemplation of his acceptableness. Labour to be possest with a deep and daily renewed sense of it, which will sweetly draw and allure thy Soul to him."[136] Both delight and enjoyment were significant experiences of being in union and communion with Jesus. Rous confesses, "[f]or the soule having tasted Christ in an heavenly communion, so loves him, that to please him is a pleasure and delight to her selfe."[137] Furthermore, Rous declares the richness that the believer can expect from this spiritual marriage, "that an heavenly joy is to the soule a restaurative medicine: and that when she enjoyth her Saviour in the contemplations and tastes of his love, then is she filled with marrow and fatnesse."[138] King asserts Peter's Transfiguration experience captures the depth of this love that soars even higher, a "doting love that carries the soule to a spiritual distraction." Peter "was so transported, so ravished with the love of Christ, that like a man spiritually distracted he knew not what hee sayd."[139] Owen recognizes the reciprocal nature of "conjugal affection, in communion between Christ and believers:—*he delights in them, and they delight in him.*"[140] Similarly Pearse rejoices as he speaks of the benefit of spiritual marriage, "[t]here is sweetness and delight in Christ." He continues by making reference to Bernard and declares, "[h]ow sweet is his presence, entercourse, and communion with Him." On the very next page Bernard is again quoted, this time from *On Loving God*, that individuals share "the joy of Communion with him."[141]

---

135. Rous, *Mysticall Marriage*, 306–7; cf. 88, 268, and 282 for other benefits of spiritual marriage.

136. Pearse, *Best Match*, 226; cf. 215 where a similar declaration is made following a reference to Bernard.

137. Rous, *Mysticall Marriage*, 73.

138. Ibid., 268–69.

139. King, *Marriage of the Lambe*, 34–35.

140. Owen, *Communion with God*, 132.

141. Pearse, *Best Match*, 222, 223, 224; cf. esp. 17, 18, 19, 25, and 262 for additional usage of Bernard to communicate the delights of being in communion with Jesus.

Clearly the intimate joys and mutual delight of spiritual marriage echo the intimacy and enjoyment of godly marriage.

Obviously this depth of joy that arises from a growing spiritual marriage does not happen automatically. Therefore, Thomas Watson declares, "[m]inisters are paranymphi, friends of the bridegroom. This day I come a wooing for your love. Love him who is so lovely."[142] Puritan preaching sought to woo and prepare the way for the Holy Spirit to work in listeners' souls.[143] Frequently they employed maternal metaphors for themselves[144] as John Cotton illustrates, "[b]rests are parts and vessels that give milk to babes of the Church, which resemble the Ministers of this Church of the Jews."[145] One source of this Puritan imagery is Jesus who spoke of being a mother hen (Matt 23:37). The Old Testament affirms the imagery of God as a mother of the faithful (e.g., Isa 42:14; 49:15–16; 66:13). Following the Restoration, when the nonconformist cause was more persecuted, Peter Sterry turned to the more peaceful maternal metaphors of Jesus as mother in his writings.[146] Of course, these examples of gender inversion of Jesus as Mother are not unique to the Puritans but common among medieval males, such as Bernard, and to a lesser extent to females such as Gertrude of Helfta and Mechtild of Hackeborn.[147] This obviously raises questions regarding contemporary gender issues, however, since they were not germane to the seventeenth century they cannot be examined here.

Contrary to Longfellow, who is misled by Scheper's limited reading of the sources on spiritual marriage, I have found that many Puritans used erotic imagery to stimulate their experience of spiritual marriage.[148]

142. Watson, *Christ's Loveliness*, 319.

143. The language of wooing is abundant. See for example Vincent, *Christ the Best Husband*, 5; Rutherford, *Christ and the Doves*, 9, 10, 14; and Pearse, *Best Match*, 2. The language can also used of Jesus, the bridegroom, who woos his bride. Hieron, *The Bridegroome*, 11.

144. See for example Dillon, "Nursing Fathers and Brides of Christ." cf. Leverenz, *Language of Puritan Feeling*, esp. 143–45 and Webster, "Gender Inversion and Canticles," 150–51.

145. Cotton, *Brief Exposition on Canticles*, 198.

146. Matar, "Devotion to Jesus as Mother."

147. Bynum, *Jesus as Mother*, 110–69, 189–90, 131n72, 211–2n132; cf. McGinn, *Flowering of Mysticism*, 169.

148. Longfellow, *Women and Religious Writing*, 29. See Williams, "Puritan Enjoyment of God," 183n123, 192n155, 195, for a critique of Scheper. On the pervasiveness of erotic language in Puritanism see Jones, "Union with Christ," 201–2; Porterfield, *Female*

More broadly, many scholars find a deep interaction between sexual love and spiritual love in the Puritan writings on spiritual marriage.[149] Richard Godbeer advances the premise that "[p]erhaps the most remarkable aspect of Puritan sexuality was not its spiritualization of the erotic but its eroticization of the spiritual."[150] Further, McGinn maintains, "the study of Christian mysticism shows that we should be scandalized not so much by the presence of such erotic elements as by their absence."[151] Thomas Hooker clearly demonstrates a daring usage of erotic language when he refers to Prov 5:18–19: "If a husband hath a loose heart, and will not content himselfe with the wife of his youth, but hath his back doores, and his goings out; this makes a breach in matrimoniall affection; but when he is satisfied with her brests, he is ravished with her love: so hope hath an expectation of mercy, and is satisfied therewith; desire longs for mercy, and is satisfied therewith; the will closeth Christ, and it is fully satisfied with him."[152] Rous employs Gen 26:8, the other favorite Puritan text for encouraging love-play within godly marriage, and counsels his readers, "*Isaac* sported with *Rebekah*, . . . So doth the mysticall wife also, she thinkes sometimes how she may please her husband by service, and not onely how she may take pleasure in him and of him."[153] Rous also encourages his readers to lust after Jesus: "[a]nd if hee come not yet into thee, stirre up thy spirituall concupiscence, and therewith let the soule lust mightily for him, and let her lusts and desires ascend up to him in strong cryes and invocations, & then by his spirit he will descend unto thee."[154] Rutherford employs similar erotic language and imagery of the Song of Songs to stimulate and encourage spiritual marriage. Often he utilizes the image of the kisses of his mouth from Song 1:2.[155] In a letter to John Gordon he wrote, "and now many a sweet, sweet, soft kiss, many

Piety in New England, esp. 26–29, 36–39, 44, 72; and Williams, "Puritan Enjoyment of God," 195–99, 202–3.

149. See for example Westerkamp, "Engendering Puritan Religious Culture," 113, 115; Porterfield, *Female Piety in New England*, esp. 72–74; Achinstein, "Romance of the Spirit," 415; Godbeer, "Love Raptures," esp. 53, 58, 62 and Godbeer, *Sexual Revolution in Early America*, esp. 57–58, 72–74, 356n68–69.

150. Godbeer, *Sexual Revolution in Early America*, 55.

151. McGinn, "Language of Love in Mysticism," 205; cf. 225.

152. Hooker, *Soules Exaltation*, 5–6.

153. Rous, *Mysticall Marriage*, 64–66.

154. Ibid., 288–89.

155. The language is prominent in Isaac Ambrose's writing on experience and will be examined in chapter 3.

perfumed, well-smelled kisses, and embracements have I received of my royal Master. He and I have had much love together."[156] Sibbes devoted a full sermon to this text.[157]

Thomas Shepard employs yet another dimension of the Puritan use of sexual imagery in sermons: "but now when laid in the bosom of Christ, when sucking the breasts of the grace of Christ, when you can go no farther, though thou wert in heaven, for there is no other happiness there, now sit still contented."[158] By the end of the seventeenth century some scholars detect a growing trend to distance one's self from the lush and erotic language of Song of Songs and spiritual marriage.[159] Winship comments that clergy "tended to focus more on the reasonableness of their version of Christianity than upon its mysteries."[160] However, Godbeer asserts that Winship is mistaken in his reading of the sources and that from approximately the midpoint of the seventeenth century into the first quarter of the eighteenth century the actual usage of erotic language increased and became more personal, intimate, and loving.[161] William Sherlock's verbal attacks on John Owen and other Puritans who emphasized the experiential centrality of union with Christ also reflect this fear. Sherlock's critique was against the subjective intimacy and emotional nature of a believers' relationship with Christ through spiritual marriage. He maintained the metaphor of spiritual marriage marginalized the importance of reason and elevated the emotions in relationship to faith.[162]

But the Puritans were careful not to elevate their earthly marriage above the spiritual marriage and cautioned couples not to enjoy sexual love more than their love for Jesus.[163] Rutherford adamantly declares, "I

156. Rutherford, *Letters*, 346. This language is abundant in Rutherford, see *Letters*, 87,164, 186, 226, 251, 336, 342, 443, 512, 572, 632, etc.

157. Sibbes, *Spouse, Her Earnest Desire*, 197–208. The use of kissing imagery saturates Puritan writings.

158. Shepard, *Parable of Ten Virgins*, 592; cf. 66.

159. Achinstein, "Romance of the Spirit", 414 in reference to Isaac Watts.

160. Winship, "Behold the Bridegroom Cometh!" 178.

161. Godbeer, *Sexual Revolution in Early America*, 56, 74, 76–77, 355n58.

162. Longfellow, *Women and Religious Writing*, 186; cf. Clarke, *Politics, Religion, and the Song of Songs*, 177–88; Dewey Wallace, *Puritans and Predestination*, 170–73; and Kapic, *Communion with God*, 153–56.

163. Williams, "Puritan Enjoyment of God," 168, 176; Moore, "Sexing the Soul," 186; and Porterfield, *Feminine Spirituality in America*, 31.

will not have Two Husbands."[164] Godbeer maintains the Puritans understood the importance of keeping the two marriages in their proper relationship. He acknowledges that within the Puritan emphasis of spiritual
marriage there was a potential to under-value human marriage.[165] Rous
is more forceful declaring that the primary marriage for the Christian is
in heaven: "[t]here is a law in heaven, that the heavenly Bride may at one
time have but one Husband."[166] Further, an almost universal warning in
most works on spiritual marriage was the potential for spiritual adultery
or unfaithfulness to Jesus. Sibbes states the issue squarely, "Christ will
allow of no bigamy or double marriage."[167] Anthony Burgess counsels,
"[i]f we desire not all things in reference to him, we are guilty of spirituall
Idolatry."[168] Hooker consistently warns others, "the end of our creation
and redemption was, that we might have communion with God; but all
of us have played the adulteresses, we have had our wicked lovers."[169]

Yet another highly significant component of spiritual marriage
was the recognition that if Jesus Christ was the divine Bridegroom then
his followers were his brides. Obviously it would not be difficult for
Puritan women to conceptualize themselves as brides of Christ since
they were females.[170] However, the same metaphor was also applied to
men. Porterfield is correct when she states that "a metaphoric change
of gender was required" for males to perceive themselves as brides of
Christ.[171] Moreover, some scholars maintain that gender flexibility or inversion[172] created anguished tension and gender gymnastics for Puritan

---

164. Rutherford, *Christ and the Doves*, 26.

165. Godbeer, "Love Raptures," 52, 63–65, and Godbeer, *Sexual Revolution in Early America*, 52, 62.

166. Rous, *Mysticall Marriage*, 18.

167. Sibbes, *Bowels Opened*, 187; cf. King, *Marriage of the Lambe*, 105, 108.

168. Burgess, *CXLV Expository Sermons*, 34. King also connects spiritual adultery to idolatry. *Marriage of the Lambe*, 105; cf. p. 108.

169. Hooker, *Soules Implantation*, 31; cf. 151, 230, 247–48, 257, 261, etc.; cf. Hooker, *Soules Preparation for Christ*, 41, 66, 86. Similar warnings can be found in other writings of Hooker.

170. Clarke acknowledges that the reverse was often a greater challenge. Husbands in godly marriage could hardly compare favorably with Jesus, the divine husband. *Politics, Religion, and the Song of Songs*, 159.

171. Porterfield, *Feminine Spirituality in America*, 27.

172. Spirituality and gender flexibility has become a very significant topic. Some of the more helpful writings on this topic include Dahill, "Genre of Gender"; Coffey, *Theology and the British Revolutions*, 104–10; Mullan, *Scottish Puritanism*, 140–70;

males.[173] Others allow too much of the twenty first-century sexual questions to be read into the seventeenth century and speak of "homosexual panic" among Puritan males or seek to apply queer theory to the Song of Songs.[174] Still others read the Puritans as if Freud lived in the seventeenth century.[175] Additionally, Longfellow warns that some well intentioned feminist scholars may actually create more harm than good in their efforts to cast early modern women writers as feminists.[176] Perhaps it would be wiser to heed the sagacious voice of Susan Juster: "[w]as early modern faith so powerful because it effectively harnessed the enormous emotional and physical satisfactions of sex for spiritual purposes, or did human relationships benefit from an infusion of the erotics of spiritual communion into the intimate lives of men and women?"[177]

Puritans of the seventeenth century lived with greater gender fluidity than the next century.[178] It is dangerous to read the contemporary uncertainty regarding gender back into the Puritan culture and wise to recognize that the Puritans were conscious of the mystery within the metaphoric language of spiritual marriage. Godbeer asserts that "Puritan

---

Moore, "Sexing the Soul"; Webster, "Gender Inversion and Canticles"; Belden Lane, "Two Schools of Desire," 393–97; cf. fn 75 and fn 144 above.

173. Westerkamp, "Engendering Puritan Religious Culture," 115. Webster acknowledges while it was a major change it did not create anxiety for Puritan males, "Gender Inversion and Canticles," 151. Moore accurately adds that this gender change was not an escape for men. "Sexing the Soul," 184.

174. Walter Hughes, "Meat Out of the Eater," 107–19; Leverenz, *Language of Puritan Feeling*, 129, 132; Rambuss, *Closet Devotions*; and Fessenden, Radel and Zaborowska, eds. *Puritan Origins of American Sex.*

175. Leverenz, *Language of Puritan Feeling*, esp. 4, 10–11, 14–15, 20–22, 107. Porterfield often veers towards a twentieth-century psychological reading of the Puritans. *Female Piety in New England*. Similar claims were made in the monastic period, see Burrows, "Foundations for Erotic Christology," 478–79.

176. Longfellow, *Women and Religious Writing*, 214–16; cf. esp. 123 for her warning of the danger of "over reading" by feminist critics.

177. Juster, "Eros and Desire in Early Modern Sexuality," 205. Dillon asserts, "What is striking about the persistent use of the eroticized Bride of Christ tropology is the extent to which this language does not seem to induce anxiety or homosexual panic, but rather serves as a dominant, culturally accepted account of masculinity among Puritans." "Nursing Fathers and Brides of Christ," 134.

178. Godbeer, *Sexual Revolution in Early America*, 55, 79–83, 357n74; Godbeer, "Performing Patriarchy," 291, 293, 301, 303, 306, 323; Moore, "Sexing the Soul," 183–84; Tom Webster, "Gender Inversion and Canticles," 149, 151, 159–61; and Longfellow, *Women and Religious Writings*, 83.

men who understood their theology had no reason to believe that their masculinity would be threatened by their union as brides to Christ: the son of God was to marry not men and women but the souls of men and women. That distinction was important since souls did not adopt the sex of the bodies they inhabited."[179] He continues by insisting "[t]he use of marital and romantic imagery in a spiritual context did not pose a problem for male New Englanders since notions of gender were in some respects remarkably fluid."[180] Additionally, it must be recalled that the Puritans followed the lead of previous generations in understanding the feminine nature of the soul.[181] Hence Puritan males did not need to be threatened by any gender gymnastics since Christ was marrying their female soul. Further, the Puritans typically understood the soul more expansively than is common today. John Robotham writes, "[t]he soule is put for all the faculties of nature, and for the uniting of all affections, whereby they goe forth most strongly . . . The soule is here by a Synechdoche put for all the Affections of the soule."[182]

None of this discussion discounts Porterfield's earlier comment regarding the "metaphoric change of gender was required" for men to become brides of Christ. Spiritually the Puritan male was required to behave as if he were a female, taking on the humility and submission that was more commonly associated with females than males in marriage. Godbeer demonstrates that males needed to learn the feminine qualities of submission and obedience, not only in their spiritual lives, but also within the political arena of life.[183] Webster's conclusion seems valid; "subordination and humility were seen as spiritually valuable and, in these eyes, they were assets more readily available to women, properly trained, than men."[184]

---

179. Ibid., 79; cf. Godbeer, "Performing Patriarchy," 302. For an opposing view see Tom Webster, "Gender Inversion and Canticles," 157–58.

180. Ibid., 82; cf. Godbeer, Overflowing of Friendship, 86.

181. Moore, "Sexing the Soul," 175; cf. Williams, "Puritan Enjoyment of God," 173–74. Occasionally the Puritans saw the soul as genderless.

182. Robotham, Exposition of Solomons Song, 126.

183. Godbeer, "Performing Patriarchy," 292–93, 296 and Godbeer, Overflowing of Friendship, 4; cf. Mack, Visionary Women, 49–50 and Longfellow, Women and Religious Writing, 118.

184. Tom Webster, "Gender Inversion and Canticles," 159.

SPIRITUAL MARRIAGE IN ISAAC AMBROSE

Isaac Ambrose employed many of the same biblical texts that inspired his fellow Puritan preachers when speaking on spiritual marriage. However, unlike the works previously explored in this chapter, Ambrose did not produce any specific work that dealt exclusively with spiritual marriage. Rather he examined the importance of union with Christ as it intersected various themes of Puritan theology. Therefore, in *Prima*, devoted to the new birth, Ambrose describes how spiritual marriage begins with a person's conversion. *Media*, his work on sanctification, demonstrates how spiritual practices guide a person to grow more fully in Christ. Most significantly, *Looking Unto Jesus* represents how contemplative delight and enjoyment of God emerges from spiritual marriage. One of his popular texts related to spiritual marriage was Hos 2:19: "[a]nd I will betroth thee unto me for ever, yea, I will betroth thee unto me in righteousness, and in judgment, and in loving-kindness, and in mercies."[185] As previously noted Ambrose also utilized Ps 45.[186] Further, he frequently employed Isa 62:5: "[f]or as a young man marrieth a virgin, so shall thy sons marry thee: and as a bridegroom rejoiceth over the bride, so shall thy God rejoice over thee."[187] The additional range of Scripture employed by Ambrose to illustrate spiritual marriage included Isa 54:8, 10; John 17:21–23; 1 Cor 6:17; 2 Cor 11:2; Eph 5:25, 27; and Rev 19:7; 21:9. Surveying his biblical passages reveals a consistency with both the more popular medieval texts and those of other Puritans. Further, numerous references to the Song of Songs were employed, but none of them ever served as the primary Scripture for his writings.

Additionally, Ambrose made full use of the biblical bridal imagery that paralleled both Bernard and his Puritan colleagues. In examining the importance of a solitary place for engaging in meditation he writes, "[t]he Bridegroom, of our Soul, The Lord Jesus Christ, is bashful (said *Bernard) and never comes to his meditating Bride in the presence of a multitude.*"[188] Ambrose also suggests how he and his congregation

---

185. Ambrose, *Prima* in *Prima, Media, & Ultima* (1654), 24; Ambrose, *Media* (1657), 293; and Ambrose, *Looking Unto Jesus*, 11, 1038. Additionally he used Hos 2:18. *Looking Unto Jesus*, 1117.

186. Ambrose used both v. 10 in *Looking Unto Jesus*, 11 and v. 13 in *Ultima* in *Prima, Media, & Ultima* (1654), 68 and *Looking Unto Jesus*, 1039.

187. Ambrose, *Looking Unto Jesus*, 98, 1117.

188. Ambrose, *Media* (1657), 218.

might envision being the bride of Christ. In *Prima* he declares, "he is not only to be thy Saviour, but thy husband; thou must love him, and serve him, and honor him, and obey him."[189] Ambrose duplicates this theme in *Ultima*: "if we are but once truly incorporated into Christ, we must take him as our Husband and Lord; we must love, honour, and serve him."[190] These words echo the wedding vows of human marriage and confirm the seriousness of this relationship between Jesus Christ and the individual believer. In this same work Ambrose draws upon the imagery of Song of Songs to speak of the believer as spouse: "[o] ravishing voice! *I charge you O daughters of Jerusalem, if you finde my well-beloved, that you tell him I am sick of love.* What else? You that are Gods servants are no lesse his spouse, your soul is the bride, and when the day is come (this day of doom) *God give you joy, the joy of heaven for ever and ever.*"[191] Further, Ambrose reaffirms that this marriage takes place between Jesus Christ and the soul: "[t]he Lord Christ marries himself to the souls of his Saints."[192] At times Ambrose recognizes that this marriage involves both the individual believer and the church.

Significantly for Ambrose, spiritual marriage was the foundation from which all spiritual life originated. The initial page of *Media* announces, "[t]he first Privilege which immediately follows our *Union with Christ is Justification.*"[193] Likewise in *Looking Unto Jesus*, Ambrose asserts the primacy of this relationship, "[t]he Lord Christ marries himself to the souls of his Saints . . . and for this cause the soul must forsake all, and cleave unto Christ, as married wives use to do, we must leave all for our husband the Lord Jesus."[194] Ambrose advances this same priority from God's perspective: "Gods purposes are without any alteration, the love of Christ after thousands of yeares is still as the love of a Bridegroom upon the wedding day."[195] Clearly according to Ambrose, God's central purpose is to be in a marital relationship with God's people. The quote that

189. Ambrose, *Prima* in *Prima, Media, & Ultima* (1654), 67.

190. Ambrose, *Ultima* in *Prima, Media, & Ultima* (1654), 194; cf. Jones, "Union with Christ," 197 for the "marriage covenant" language of Thomas Doolittle.

191. Ibid., 117; cf. 196 for a variation of this referring to Bernard in relation to the penitent thief on the cross.

192. Ambrose, *Looking Unto Jesus*, 11.

193. Ambrose, *Media* (1657), 1.

194. Ambrose, *Looking Unto Jesus*, 11.

195. Ibid., 98.

introduced this chapter is a robust description of Ambrose's understanding. Since God has taken the initiative toward humanity, humanity must respond appropriately: "[o] my soul, henceforth cling to thy Saviour, go out of thy self, and creep to him, and affect not onely union, but very unity with him; bathe thy self hereafter again and again, many and many a time in those delicious intimacies of thy Spiritual marriage."[196]

Ambrose is consistent with other Puritan writers in distinguishing between union and communion with Christ: "[u]nion is the ground of our communion with Christ; and the nearer our union, and the greater our communion."[197] This relationship begins at conversion and often was referred to as the "first espousal."[198] Conversely, it was not fully realized until the person died: "[w]hen first a soul believes, it is contracted to Christ, when the soul is sentenced to glory, then is the solemnitie, and consummation of the marriage."[199] This significant foundation created a highly relational and affective understanding of what it meant to be in communion with Jesus Christ. Ambrose asks the question, "[w]hat is this communion with Christ, but very heaven aforehand." He cites Song 2:4, "we are *brought into Christs banqueting-house*" and then continues to expand the meaning of communion with Christ, "[o]h it's an happy thing to have Christ dwell in our hearts, and for us to lodge in Christs bosome! Oh its an happy thing to maintain a reciprocal communication of affairs betwixt Christ and our souls!"[200] This reflects the mutual and dialogical nature of the covenant fellowship between Jesus Christ and the church or individual believer. Ambrose parallels all writers previously explored in this chapter by ascribing the feminine nature to the soul: "[o] my soul, my soul! what can we say of such a creature? to summe up all; she is in nature *a substance, created by God*."[201] Furthermore, Ambrose follows the lead of earlier Puritans in recognizing the challenge to continually be committed to Jesus Christ as the divine Bridegroom. He warns all

196. Ambrose, *Media* (1657), 236.

197. Ambrose, *Looking Unto Jesus*, 913. Ambrose includes a detailed summary of John Owen's *Communion with God* in his funeral sermon for Lady Margaret Houghton, *Redeeming the Time*, 11–12

198. Ambrose, *Ultima* in *Prima, Media, & Ultima* (1654), 74; cf. 62 where the same language is used with a reference to Bernard.

199. Ambrose, *Looking Unto Jesus*, 1077.

200. Ibid., 40.

201. Ambrose, *Ultima* in *Prima, Media, & Ultima* (1654), 69.

believers of the dangers of spiritual adultery and declares, "far be it from us to love thee like a harlot, and not like a wife."[202]

Central to Ambrose's theology of spiritual marriage is the role of the Holy Spirit who was active in both forming and maintaining union and communion. The Spirit is the "principal bond of our union betwixt Christ and us."[203] Ambrose shares a common feature with John Owen in asserting that our communion is not only with the Father and the Son, but also with the Holy Spirit.[204] God graciously sends the Holy Spirit to dwell within believers because apart from the Spirit's presence and power no one is able to be in Christ or follow Christ.[205] This indwelling presence of the Spirit illuminates the understanding to recognize Christ and his benefits more fully; consequently, one of the major activities of the Spirit is to assist believers in following Jesus. Therefore, it is essential for individuals to seek to be in communion with the Holy Spirit.[206] Further, Ambrose challenges his readers to be aware of the movement of the Holy Spirit. Since the Holy Spirit "lifts up our souls towards heaven" it is crucial "that Christians would be much in observation of, and in lissening to the movings, workings, hints, and intimations of that Spirit that comes from heaven."[207] Indeed, one of the necessities for followers of Jesus is to "feel the Spirit in his stirrings" so that they might "co-operate with the Spirit."[208] The benefit of such careful attentiveness to the Spirit may create "a spirit even swallowed up in communion with God."[209]

Equally important to Ambrose's theology of spiritual marriage is the role of faith. This too requires the involvement of the Holy Spirit since faith comes from the Spirit.[210] Further, within Ambrose's teaching on prayer he contends, "there is no grace but from Christ, and no communion with Christ but by faith."[211] He follows Calvin in emphasizing a

---

202. Ambrose, *Looking Unto Jesus*, 9, 447, and Ambrose, *Media* (1657), 465.

203. Ibid., 884; cf. 858, 860.

204. Ibid., 861; cf. Owen, *Communion with God*, 222–74.

205. Ibid., 857, 876. Ambrose also maintains that the Spirit continues to assist in "*growing the soul with Christ.*" *Prima* (Appendix) in *Prima, Media, & Ultima* (1654), 66–67.

206. Ibid., 444, 450, 1128, 1140.

207. Ibid., 846; cf. 815 (incorrectly numbered as 905), 1140.

208. Ibid., 1140.

209. Ibid., 815 (incorrectly numbered as 905).

210. Ibid., 788–89.

211. Ambrose, *Media* (1657), 469.

strong affective quality of faith. However, Ambrose's perception of faith as relational and affective expands beyond that of Calvin and is consistent with other Puritans of the seventeenth century. In relation to the Lord's Supper, Ambrose maintains: "So if thus it be, that Christ in the Sacrament offers himself to come to us, let our faith busily bestir itself in widening the passage, and opening our hearts to make Christ way, let us strive with might and main to stretch open our hearts to such a breadth and largeness, as a fit way may be made for the King of glory to come in, let us hasten, open, clasp, imbrace, welcome, and receive Christ offered to us."[212] Clearly Ambrose understood that faith had two natures and while it was essential for salvation it also possessed a vibrant relational and experimental dimension. When he spoke of contending against the devil in a person's "riper years" he wrote, "[f]aith hath his change of rayments for gracious souls; sometimes it acts the soul in joy and rejoycing, sometimes only in adherence and waiting."[213] Furthermore Ambrose affirms that spiritual love arises from faith and the reciprocal relationship of that experience of love refreshes a person's faith.[214] But even more, for Ambrose, faith not only has an affective quality but also a contemplative dimension for "by contemplative faith, [we] behold Christ."[215]

Contemplation is one of the significant aspects of piety in which Ambrose distinguished himself. His largest work, *Looking Unto Jesus*, is essentially a contemplative journey that experientially explores the christological spectrum of how beholding Christ can transform a person to be more like him. Only as a person is in union and communion with Jesus is this possible. This major dimension of Ambrose's theology and spiritual experience will be examined in chapter 4. However, one brief example that illustrates this is the soul's challenge to conform herself to Christ in relation to the final judgment: "[o]h then let us call upon our souls! . . . he would have us to be still arising, ascending, and mounting up in divine contemplation to his Majesty . . . Oh that every morning, and every evening, at least, our hearts would arise, ascend and go to Christ in the heavens."[216]

212. Ibid., 418; cf. 89.

213. Ambrose, *War with Devils*, 101.

214. Ambrose, *Looking Unto Jesus*, 230 and Ambrose, *Media* (1657), esp. 224; cf. 172, 285.

215. Ibid., 23.

216. Ibid., 1152.

Ambrose elevates the enjoyment and delight of God in spiritual marriage and can soar with the best of medieval writers in seeking to express the ineffable experience of mystical union with Christ. The following rhapsodic example reflects his present desire of spiritual marriage and yearns for a deepening of this union and communion of love:

> Set us on fire, burn us, make us new and transform us, that nothing besides thee may live in us. O wound very deeply our hearts with the dart of thy love . . . O that we were sick of love . . . and by an heavenly excess may be transported into an heavenly love, that we may imbrace Christ, who is the Lord from heaven, with a love like himself.—Nor do we desire onely the pleasures of love, and the joyes of thy union, but that we may become generative and fruitful, far be it from us to love thee like a harlot, and not like a wife: O let us desire union with thee, and to bring forth fruit unto thee.[217]

Clearly this validates the importance of conjugal love, desire, and joy for Ambrose and significantly expands his depiction of spiritual marriage that will be examined in detail in chapter 5. However, for now its exuberance is descriptive of the deep and burning desire to be filled only with the fire of divine love and for any impurities to be purged so as to increase both the experience of this divine love and to bear fruit that is faithful and glorifying to this spiritual marriage.

It is often difficult to grasp the depth of a person's spiritual teaching and experience when it is atomized. Since Ambrose's instruction on spiritual marriage is so dynamic it is helpful to examine it in a more integrated manner. In portraying the nature of the soul's love to Christ Ambrose proclaims, "it is the souls rest or reposal of it selfe in the bosome of Christ, with content unspeakable and glorious, being perswaded of her interest in that Song of the Spouse, I am my welbeloveds, and my wel-beloveds is mine. This, O my soul, is the nature of thy love to Christ."[218] As Ambrose continues his meditation he cites Ps 1:6–7 and declares, "[w]e return unto our rest, because the Lord hath dealt bountifully with us, when sweetly we repose our selves in the lap of our Saviour with content unspeakable, and full of glory."[219] This language is not uncommon, and Ambrose employed this imagery previously in

---

217. Ambrose, *Media* (1657), 465.

218. Ibid., 224.

219. Ibid. Cf. 208 for another example within his meditation on heaven.

describing his understanding of communion with Christ: "[o]h it's an happy thing to have Christ dwell in our hearts, and for us to lodge in Christs bosome! Oh its an happy thing to maintaine a reciprocal communication of affairs betwixt Christ and our souls!"[220] The Puritan language of reposing in Christ's bosom may sound unusual due to its medieval echoes.[221] Clearly it is reminiscent of Bernard of Clairvaux as he speaks of Jesus, "[that] he lets the soul which contemplates repose on his breast."[222] However, Scripture appears to be the primary inspiration for Ambrose's usage of this language. In his first example Ambrose cites Song 6:3 and in the *Looking Unto Jesus* reference he draws upon Song 2:4 and Peter's transfiguration experience. This suggests that people from different periods of history might use similar terms independently of each other due to the metaphoric richness of Scripture. Reposing in Christ's bosom illustrates a relationship of deep intimacy and contentment of resting in Christ's presence. Often relationships between two people reach their apogee when their voices become silent and they are united by the delight and enjoyment of each other. Ambrose reflects this pattern in his reposing with Jesus.

The above references clearly indicate the joy and delight that a person could experience in spiritual marriage. Williams asserts that the phrase, "joy unspeakable and full of glory," drawn from 1 Pet 1:8, was a common referent "used to describe ecstasy, which virtually became code-words for intense delight."[223] Chapter 1 introduced Simon Chan's assessment that Puritans who practiced greater asceticism typically experienced greater contemplation, and Ambrose's use of spiritual practices in guiding a person into communion with God certainly confirms this. He declares, "[i]n right performance of *Duties*, we come to have fuller Union with Christ, and by this coming to him, we come to, and see the Father by him."[224] Earlier in the same work he reminds his readers, "[b]ecause in *Duties* they have converses, and communion with God . . . The Saints look upon *Duties* (the Word, Sacraments, Prayers, & c.) as Bridges to give

220. Ambrose, *Looking Unto Jesus*, 40; cf. 1004.

221. Rutherford speaks of "sleeping in the bosom of the Almighty." *Letters*, 34; cf. 251, 560. Baxter invites readers to lay their hearts "to rest, as in the bosom of Christ." *Saints Everlasting Rest*, 330; cf. 85n158 above. None of these examples reach the depth of intimacy of Ambrose.

222. Bernard, *SCC* 51.10; cf. 51.5.

223. Williams, "Puritan Enjoyment of God," 116.

224. Ambrose, *Media* (1657), 74.

them a passage to God, as Boats carry them into the bosom of Christ, as means to bring them into more intimate communion with their heavenly Father, and therefore are they so much taken with them."[225] Further, these spiritual duties that were dependent upon a person's union with Christ could also be practiced in a contemplative manner and thereby deepening the experience and enjoyment of spiritual marriage between the person and Jesus. It is now possible to summarize and assess the continuities and discontinuities between Isaac Ambrose and Bernard, Calvin, and other Puritans.

CONTINUITIES AND DISCONTINUITIES IN THE STUDY OF SPIRITUAL MARRIAGE

One of the critical issues examined in this chapter is how the spiritual marriage metaphor functioned in Ambrose as well as other Puritans. For Bernard, union with God was primarily a relational experience that emphasized love. Calvin and the Puritans all shared the same theology of spiritual marriage and maintained there were two unique components. Spiritual marriage began when a person was united with Christ through the new birth of salvation through faith. However, there is more. All of the Protestant writers that have been explored in this chapter would recognize that by virtue of a person's union with Christ they would also share in all of the benefits of Christ's life, death, resurrection, ascension, and the sending of the Holy Spirit. This leads to the second aspect of spiritual marriage within the Protestant understanding of communion that was unnecessary in Bernard. While this was certainly present and essential in Calvin, it became more significant in the Puritans; Ambrose especially, elevated the importance of communion with Christ. Further, this must not be conceptualized as two stages to spiritual marriage. Reformed theologians would insist that while union is the beginning a person never loses that important connection of being engrafted into Christ. However, what does vary is the person's experiential sense of God's love and enjoyment of God. Therefore, the reciprocal nature of the Reformed perspective of communion resembles Bernard's stronger love-based experiential focus. Significantly, unlike the contemporary church, neither Bernard, Calvin, or the Puritans, limited union with Christ only

225. Ibid., 33. This significant topic will be explored in chapter 4.

to the forensic nature of being made right with God. We will return to the implications of this for us today in chapter 6.

Further, Bernard and the Puritans share a common bond in their use of the Song of Songs. While it is often very difficult to trace influences, Ambrose was deeply shaped by his knowledge of this premier biblical book of spiritual intimacy with Jesus, the divine Bridegroom, and also encouraged further through his awareness of Bernard. While Ambrose never employed the Song of Songs as his primary text, he frequently included numerous passages from this book. Significantly, Calvin stands alone at this point. Instead of relying upon the Canticles, his major theological fulcrum was the Lord's Supper. Even though Calvin would have appreciated the experiential dimension of piety held by Bernard and the Puritans, his desire was to frame this more corporately in public worship, thus guarding against the perceived excesses he found in late medieval individualized piety. Significantly, in the Lord's Supper the dynamic importance of experience and enjoyment can be seen in Calvin. He confesses, "[n]ow, if anyone should ask me how this takes place [i.e. Christ's true presence in the Supper], I shall not be ashamed to confess that it is a secret too lofty for either my mind to comprehend or my words to declare. And, to speak more plainly, I rather experience than understand it."[226] Bishop Edward Reynolds is representative of those Puritans who emphasized this teaching of spiritual marriage with the Lord's Supper.[227] The necessity of grace as the means for salvation and spiritual marriage is another common conviction of both Bernard and Calvin. Further, embedded in the above discussion, all of these writers would agree that betrothal to spiritual marriage occurs on earth and is consummated only in heaven.

The earlier examination of the importance of faith and love discovered that the gap between Bernard and Calvin was not as wide as some might initially assume. The Puritans and other Reformed and Evangelical descendants continued to develop a more affective understanding of faith as well as the more intimate dance between faith and love. The *Nadere Reformatie* of the late sixteenth- and seventeenth-century Netherlands were direct descendents of Calvin as were the Puritans of England and New England. Arie de Reuver in his excellent study on Dutch Pietism concludes, "[t]heir mysticism is one with that which is

---

226. Calvin, *Institutes*, 4.17.32.

227. Reynolds, *Meditations on the Lords Last Supper*.

drenched in the scriptural word that by means of the secret operation of the Holy Spirit brings about a gracious and highly real faith-encounter and a loving fellowship with God in Christ—both marked by hope."[228]

Another feature that must be highlighted is that some of the Puritans discussed in this chapter followed Bernard's example in using erotic metaphors for motivating others in their spiritual marriage. Neither Calvin nor Ambrose followed this approach. This prompts the question why, at least for Ambrose, he did not follow the pattern of many of his fellow Puritans in employing the metaphors of sexual stimulation? I imagine that Ambrose was so transfixed by the glorious love of beholding Jesus, his divine Bridegroom that he did not need to rely upon this imagery. Another contributing factor could have been his struggle with poor health. *Looking Unto Jesus* was written after recovering from a major illness. Possibly his soul was so saturated with gratitude that this was a sufficient motivation for him.

Even though Calvin and the Puritans were familiar with Bernard of Clairvaux, he does not appear to be the dominant influence of their understanding, practice, and experience of spiritual marriage. Rather, the biblical foundation of mystical union, processed through their own experiences of the intimacy and enjoyment of conjugal love in their godly marriages, provided greater encouragement and inspiration. Further, both Calvin and the Puritans greatly extended the inclusiveness of this spiritual experience by removing it from the cloisters and bringing it into the streets. However, this should not imply that Bernard was unimportant, as chapter 4 will clearly demonstrate. Additionally, while Ambrose reveals an awareness of the medieval writers Gerson and Bonaventure nonetheless his primary formative influence was Scripture.[229] This parallels Coffey's conclusion in relation to Rutherford, that it is difficult "to understand the ideas of Puritan writers without reference to their principal intellectual source, the Bible itself."[230] Having established the biblical and theological foundation of spiritual marriage, it is now possible to explore the spiritual experiences of Ambrose's contemplative-mystical piety that originated from his union with Christ.

228. De Reuver, *Sweet Communion*, 284.

229. For Gerson see Ambrose, *War with Devils*, 173. For Bonaventure see Ambrose, *Looking Unto Jesus*, 1000.

230. Coffey, *Theology and the British Revolutions*, 81.

Chapter Three

Contemplative Biography of Isaac Ambrose

> For the things wherein they excelled (Ambrose and his
> brother Machin), I have not known the like. Mr. Ambrose for
> his habitual course of contemplation and rare improvement
> of secret opportunities.
>
> —Henry Newcome[1]

A **contemplative biography** offers a window into the soul of another person. It attempts to reveal the spiritual dynamics as that individual gazes at God through the various dimensions of life. More specifically it endeavors to trace the contours of the soul and observe the ways in which a person has experienced God. During the seventeenth century contemplation was defined as "the action of beholding, or looking at with attention and thought."[2] Similarly, Ambrose declares, "[w]hat, shall he ascend, and shall not we in our contemplations follow after him? gaze, O my soul, on this wonderful object, thou needest not feare any check from God or Angel, so that thy contemplation be spiritual and divine."[3] In *Media* he combines the importance of contemplation with

1. Newcome, *Autobiography of Newcome*, 143.

2. *OED*, 17:811. Henry Cockeram defines it similarly, "a beholding in ones mind." *English Dictionarie*, n.p.

3. Ambrose, *Looking Unto Jesus*, 871–72.

love and the experience of God's presence and joyfully asserts: "[w]hat happinesse of a glorified Saint, but that he is always under the line of love, ever in the contemplation of, and converses with God, and shall that be thought our burthen here, which is our glory hereafter?"[4] Later Ambrose raises some questions of practical divinity and asks, "[w]hat are the signes of a sincere love to Christ?" He replies, "a contemplation of Christs love, and desires after further sense of it, Eph. 3.17, 18, 19."[5]

Over the centuries there has been a fairly consistent understanding of the meaning of contemplation.[6] Therefore, it is not surprising that contemporary voices echo the seventeenth century in the usage of this term. Thomas Merton describes contemplation as a "constant loving attention to God" and as a "simple contemplative gaze."[7] Likewise Richard Foster writes, "[p]ut simply, the contemplative life is the steady gaze of the soul upon the God who loves us."[8] The integrative thread that unites these various definitions with Ambrose's own understanding is that contemplation is a loving and sustained gaze upon God's presence in creation and God's mighty acts. It is more about noticing and admiring God's presence than it is about being able to dissect and explain the meaning of some aspect about God. Further, contemplation is an attitude and a practice that may yield the gift of a contemplative experience. Contemplation also produces increased love and knowledge. However, the gift of contemplation is always dependent upon God's grace, as Bernard continually reminded his fellow monks.[9] There is no formula or technique that guarantees that if a person prays in a certain way that it will produce a contemplative experience. Moreover, contemplation is both an attitude and activity of loving focused attention or gazing on God that provides a means for keeping company with and enjoying Jesus Christ. Therefore, the goal of this chapter is to create a contemplative biography of Ambrose's diverse experiences of God and his neighbor through the various dimensions of his life. A careful review of his writings will reveal an abundance of mystical texts, mystical vocabulary, and robust mystic experiences that all emerge from his spiritual marriage with Jesus.

4. Ambrose, Media (1657), 34.

5. Ibid., 355–56.

6. For a helpful introduction to contemplation see Aumann, New Catholic Encyclopedia, 4:203–9.

7. Merton, New Seeds of Contemplation, 217, 219; cf. von Balthasar, Prayer, 20, 104–11.

8. Foster, Streams of Living Water, 49; cf. Foster, Prayer the Heart's True Home, 158.

9. McGinn, Growth of Mysticism, 211.

NATURE AND STRUCTURE OF THE
CONTEMPLATIVE BIOGRAPHY

One of the challenges in developing a contemplative biography for Ambrose is the limited sources available. While he recognized the value of keeping a diary and is often cited as a model for engaging in this practice, his own diary is not extant.[10] It was not uncommon for Puritans to destroy their diaries at death, and this likely explains the absence of Ambrose's diary.[11] Fortunately he wove two lengthy sections of selected entries into *Media* to illustrate his practice of keeping a diary.[12] These limited resources, which cover only ten years of Ambrose's life, prevent the possibility of a developmental study of his spirituality. Charles Cohen's correctly notes, "[a]ll historical inquiries proceed at the mercy of their methods, and psychological studies of vanished minds place a premium on methodological precision."[13] Therefore, I will be employing a thematic rather than chronological framework to examine Ambrose's life. Further, I will be employing the Spiritual Movement Matrix, a tool used by some spiritual directors for observing how God is experienced as well as the contemplative movements within a person's life to guide this examination.[14] The usage of this tool reflects the importance of the social sciences in the study of Christian spirituality.

10. Ambrose, *Media* (1657), 87; cf. Sachse, *Diary of Roger Lowe*, 2 and Keeble, *Literary Culture Nonconformity*, 208. These sources rightly indicate that Ambrose suggested this in his first edition of *Media* (1650). However, Mascuch, *Origins of Individualist Self*, 113, began a trend of misleading later scholars that *Media* 1652 was the first edition in which Ambrose suggested keeping a diary. See for example, Herdt, *Putting On Virtue*, 203–4. On the importance of diary keeping for the Puritans see Hambrick-Stowe, *Practice of Piety*, esp. 176, 186–93 and Tomalin, *Samuel Pepys*, 78–89.

11. Hambrick-Stowe, *Practice of Piety*, 188–89 and Brekus, "Writing as Protestant Practice," 33.

12. These entries vary over the three editions of *Media*. The first edition contains the largest amount of diary material. The second and third editions are identical. The most significant change is the substitution of his 1651 retreat experiences in place of the much lengthier and varied experiences in the 1650 edition. Additionally he greatly reduced the number of examples provided in his section entitled "Experiences." Ambrose reports the reduction in the latter two editions was due to his assessment that not all of the material in the first edition was edifying for others. *Media* (1652), 171 and *Media* (1657), 189.

13. Cohen, *God's Caress*, 14.

14. The Spiritual Movement Matrix was developed by Andrew Dreitcer and Patricia Bulkley in 1997 for training spiritual directors at San Francisco Theological Seminary, San Anselmo, CA. See Appendix 1. Forerunners to this Matrix include the "Grid Arena" and "Experience Circle." Shea, "Spiritual Direction and Social Consciousness"; Keegan,

The Spiritual Movement Matrix consists of four arenas or dimensions:[15] Intrapersonal, Interpersonal, Structural, and Environmental. The first two categories are self-explanatory. I will be dividing the Intrapersonal dimension, which focuses upon the relationship with self, into two separate categories to include Ambrose's experience of God through his annual retreats and the struggles of his soul. The second dimension, the Interpersonal, relates to Ambrose's interaction with others. The third category is the Structural. This systemic dimension includes the whole constellation of larger relational groupings, including families, churches, communities, and organizations. Normally this focuses upon the specific roles a person engages with others within those structures. The final dimension is the Environmental. I will rename it the Geo-Environmental to examine the interactive relationship between creation and Ambrose's life. In other words, how did the uniqueness of place and specific environments shape Ambrose's experiences?

Before examining his experiences however, the strengths and limitations of the Spiritual Movement Matrix need to be considered. There are four strengths to this interpretation method. First, as previously indicated, the Matrix was developed to help spiritual directors and supervisors guide others in better understanding their experiences of God. Therefore, the Matrix offers a practical means for reviewing Ambrose's experiences and noting God's presence therein. Second, the Matrix is not rigid in categorizing experiences; the four dimensions are fluid and open-ended. The dashed lines between the four categories visually communicate the reality that one's experience of God in the Interpersonal dimension can easily overflow into the Structural and vice versa.[16] Depending upon the focus and the nature of reflection, Ambrose's experiences could indeed be placed in virtually any of the four dimensions. Third, the Matrix reminds those in spiritual direction of the importance of both the affective and interpretive levels of experience. Thus, if a person typically speaks of experiences in an affective manner, that person could be encouraged to consider how those experiences can be

"Spiritual Direction for Justice"; Cleary, "Societal Context for Supervision"; and Liebert, "Supervision as Widening Horizons." I have decided to use the Matrix because I feel it is the most flexible and descriptive instrument of all of these mentioned.

15. While the Matrix refers to these categories as "arenas" I will use the term "dimension" because it appears more expansive and open-ended.

16. Keegan, "Spiritual Direction for Justice," 8, 9, 18, and Liebert, "Supervision as Widening Horizons," 133.

deepened by also paying attention to the interpretive thread of the experience. The converse is also true; an individual who normally speaks of God at the interpretive level could be encouraged to deepen those experiences by the affective component of those experiences. Later in this chapter a specific occasion of Ambrose's participation in the Lord's Supper will demonstrate his failure to experience the expected affective level until he engaged in an interpretive reflection that yielded the desired outcome. Fourth, this tool recognizes that God is present in every dimension of life, not just the obvious Intrapersonal or spiritual dimensions.[17] Clearly John Bunyan, representative of the Puritans, reflects that awareness when he asks, "[h]ave you forgot the Close, the Milk-house, the Stable, the Barn, and the like, where God did visit your soul?"[18] This awareness encourages readers to attend to the subtler yet nonetheless important places in which Ambrose experienced God. Therefore, the goal for this meditative reading of Ambrose's life is to observe the dynamic contours of his heart and soul in relationship with God and those around him. Further, this examination of his life will help to recognize his experiences of God and to detect the degree to which they reflect a contemplative attitude and awareness.

There are also four potential limitations to employing the Spiritual Movement Matrix. First, and most obvious, this tool was designed to help spiritual directors guide individuals or groups in becoming more attentive to the presence of God. The assumption was that you were guiding persons who could interact with you and thereby further explore and deepen their respective experiences. Applying this to Ambrose, who is dead, noticeably limits its usage. Additionally, Karl Rahner remarks, "the transition from the experience itself to a recognition of it at the conceptual and reflexive level is more difficult for the actual subject undergoing the experience, so that this subject can actually prevent this transition from taking place."[19] In other words, a reader's perception of Ambrose's experience today may not have been the actual experience he had in the seventeenth century. However, once that is acknowledged the Matrix is still a helpful instrument for exploring the experiences of

17. Liebert comments, "[i]n our culture, what we think of as 'spiritual' language is typically language of the intrapersonal or interpersonal arenas." "Supervision as Widening Horizons," 133–34.

18. Bunyan, *Grace Abounding to Chief of Sinners*, preface [7].

19. Rahner, "Experience of God Today," 150.

Ambrose. A second potential caution is the manner in which Ambrose's experiences are placed within the various dimensions of the Matrix. It might be difficult to determine the placement for a specific event from his life. However, undue preoccupation with this may cause readers to miss the importance of simultaneity. This principle, first advanced by Rahner, maintains that there is a unity of experience of God and self.[20] Accordingly, a person who does not experience God at any significant depth cannot experience him or herself significantly either. By this, Rahner posits that there is an intimate connection between the experience of self or one's neighbor and experience of God. Liebert has refined Rahner's thinking and maintains, "the notion of simultaneity suggests that an experience of the Holy in one arena will 'overflow' or 'bleed into' all the other arenas of a single life."[21] Ambrose illustrates this through his annual retreat into the wilderness each May. This isolated location provided both an opportunity for prolonged meditation and communion with God as well as living with nature, hence a combination of both the Intrapersonal and Geo-Environmental dimensions. Third, and closely related, is the reminder not to compress Ambrose's experiences too tightly into any dimension. Once these categories are conceptualized as neat and tidy boxes into which everything must fit, the ability to observe how Ambrose experienced life is reduced. Fourth, the Matrix has solid lines around their outer edges that could convey a limitation to the ways in which a person might experience God.

INTRAPERSONAL DIMENSION: RETREATS

As previously mentioned, the Intrapersonal dimension will be divided into two categories, Ambrose's experience with God through his retreat practices and the struggles of his soul. However, it is first necessary to recognize McGinn's caution not to focus too hastily upon a person's experience since many people gravitate only towards the more spectacular and intense visionary accounts.[22] He downplays this, stressing that some of the better-known mystics (such as Origen, Meister Eckhart, and John of the Cross) minimized the importance of experience, especially of

---

20. Rahner, "Experience of Self and Experience of God," 122–32.

21. Liebert, "Supervision as Widening Horizons," 134; cf. 128, 129, 132, 141, 143.

22. McGinn, *Foundations of Mysticism*, xiv; cf. xvii.

the more rapturous nature.[23] More recently, McGinn has asserted that neither mystics nor scholars before the nineteenth century employed the term "mystical experience."[24] In place of the language of experience, McGinn proposes the term "consciousness," which contains both the felt nature of the experience as well as the more reflective interpretation of this experience.[25] Sheldrake has also articulated the problematic nature of defining mysticism based on experience. He cites three reasons: it frequently separates mysticism from theology, it privatizes mysticism, and it elevates certain heightened experiences that create an exclusive elitism.[26] These are critical warnings and must guide the reader of mystical texts. Nonetheless, while recognizing the importance of McGinn's and Sheldrake's concerns regarding the usage of "experience," McGinn's alternative of consciousness seems equally problematic, conveying a strong psychological theme that may also complicate the reading of these texts. Further, the Puritans were known for their experiential or, as they preferred to call it, experimental focus on faith consequently, experience is more reflective of their language. J. I. Packer maintains, "Puritanism was essentially an experimental faith, a religion of 'heart-work', a sustained practice of seeking the face of God." He continues, "[o]ur interest focuses on religious experience, as such, and on man's quest for God, whereas the Puritans were concerned with the God of whom men have experience, and in the manner of his dealings with those whom he draws to himself."[27] Therefore, with sensitivity to these concerns I will examine some of the personal experiences that Ambrose recorded.

The writings of Isaac Ambrose breathe with the inspired pulse of a person who has experienced the love and joy of God. He urges his readers, "[l]abour so to know Christ, as to have a practical and experimental knowledge of Christ in his influences, and not meerly a notional [one]." Puritans stressed this message repeatedly because they knew people could receive "some notional, speculative brain knowledge of Jesus

23. Ibid., xviii; cf. McGinn, *Flowering of Mysticism*, 18, 24 and Dupré and Wiseman, *Light from Light*, 4.

24. McGinn, "Mystical Consciousness," 45.

25. Ibid., esp. 59; cf. McGinn, *Foundations of Mysticism*, xiv.

26. Sheldrake, *Spaces for the Sacred*, 119–20; cf. Sheldrake, *Explorations in Spirituality*, 107–8.

27. Packer, *Quest for Godliness*, 215, 216.

Christ, but they are not changed, their hearts are not over-powered."[28] Ambrose was interested in changed hearts, beginning with himself. He asserts in his opening words to *Media*, "I have writ nothing, but in some measure I have, by the Lords assistance, practiced the same, and felt the comfort of it in my own heart and soul."[29] Illustrative of this, Ambrose names the experimental writers who nourished his own soul in the beginning of *Media* "Angier, Ash, Ball, Baxter, Bolton, Burroughs, Burges, Byfield, Downham, Dyke, Goodwin, Gouge, Hooker, Leigh, Mason, Rogers, Shepherd, Torshel, White, & c."[30]

Ambrose, like Christians for hundreds of years before him, sought to prepare and cultivate his heart through the use of spiritual disciplines, or duties, as he preferred to call them. While some resisted these practices due to the influence of antinomianism he stresses their importance. Further, Ambrose recognizes from studying his own heart that the intentional choices that he makes to engage them reaps rich dividends in his relationship with God. Ambrose defines spiritual duties as "[b]ridges to give them a passage to God, as Boats to carry them into the bosom of Christ." He cautions his readers that there is nothing unique about these practices, and great care must be exercised so as not to use them to bargain with God. He stresses that these disciplines are a source of delight and joy "because in *Duties* they come to see the face of God in Christ: Hence *Duties* are called *The face or presence of God*."[31] Further, practicing them brings a portion of heaven to that person, "[h]ence they who meet with God in duty, usually finde their hearts sweetly refreshed, as if Heaven were in them."[32] Puritans typically divided spiritual duties into the categories of secret, private, and public.[33] Secret duties described the individual's personal spiritual practices. Private pertains to a small group of friends invited to your house, and public described the larger gatherings in the church building for spiritual exercises. Since these

---

28. Ambrose, *War with Devils*, 87, 88.

29. Ambrose, *Media* (1657), To the Reader [8].

30. Ibid., To the Reader [7]. A comparative review indicates that Burroughs was added in the second edition and Baxter in the third edition. This reveals Ambrose's continual desire to be expanding his awareness of experimental writings.

31. Ibid., 33.

32. Ibid., 34.

33. Ibid., t.p., and 42; cf. *Westminster Directory for Family-Worship*, subtitle.

duties contained such potential, the Puritans often engaged them with great intensity.

A major component of Ambrose's spiritual duties and a primary means for his experience of God were his annual month-long retreats in May. Edmund Calamy comments upon Ambrose's pattern: "'[t]was his usual Custom once in a Year, for the space of a Month to retire into a little Hut in a Wood, and avoiding all Humane Converse to devote himself to Contemplation.'"[34] This practice appears to have been fairly unique to him.[35] One wonders whether he first began this spiritual discipline by following the practice of his biblical namesake. Genesis 24:63 records, "and Isaac went out in the fields at night to meditate."[36] The first recorded experience of these retreats was May, 1641. This coincided with the beginning of his diary.[37] The complete entry from May 20, 1646 provides both an example of the framework Ambrose followed during his retreat as well as some of the ways in which he experienced God:

> I came to *Weddicre* [i.e. one of Ambrose's places of retreat], which I did upon mature resolution, every year about that pleasant Spring time (if the Lord pleased) to retire my self, and in some solitary and silent place to practice especially the secret Duties of a Christian: In this place are sweet silent Woods, and therein this moneth, and part of the next, the Lord by his Spirit wrought in me Evangelical Repentance for sin, gave me sweet comforts, and Spiritual refreshings in my commerce, and intercourse with him, by Prayer, and Meditation, and Self-Examination, & discovered to me the causes of my many troubles and discouragements in my Ministry: whereupon I prayed more fervently, pressed the Lord with his promises, set his Power, and Wisdom, and Mercy on work; and so waited and believed, till the Lord *answered every*

---

34. Matthews, *Calamy Revised*, 9.

35. Joseph Alleine also withdrew in solitude for retreats but they were shorter in duration than those of Ambrose. Theodosia Alleine, *Life and Death*, 43–44. Additionally, John Lightfoot of Ashley "built a study in his garden, in which he devoted all his spare time to researches in Hebrew." *DNB*, 11:1108. Mary Rich spent much time in contemplation in her garden or "wilderness." Fraser, "Mary Rich, Countess of Warwick," 49. Thomas Shepard also used his garden for his meditations. McGiffert, *God's Plot*, 122, 126.

36. Elsewhere Ambrose draws upon this text to indicate that evening might be the best time for some people to practice their spiritual duties. *Media* (1657), 217.

37. Ambrose, *Media* (1657), 87. I assume that the first retreat was in 1641; though it is possible it began earlier. I believe it was closely connected with Ambrose's practice to keep a diary.

Petition, and I could not but observe his hand in it. This was a comfortable time to my soul.[38]

Through his vivid and highly descriptive language, Ambrose provides a number of insights to this particular retreat experience. He was both conscious of and dependent upon the Spirit to lead him to a greater awareness of his sins and to experience the accompanying refreshment that brought him into a deeper personal communion with God. As he broadened his use of spiritual practices, he again gained personal insight and discovered the causes for his discouragement in ministry. His spiritual intensity reflects his devotion and love for God. This renewed awareness guided him to pray boldly, waiting until God responded with an answer to each of his petitions. This retreat entry also utilizes the language of banking depicting how he exchanged his sins for the "sweet comforts" of God's presence. Clearly Ambrose recognized God's intimate presence and movement in his life. Significantly, while Ambrose could not withdraw permanently to a monastery as contemplative Christians did in the Western Catholic tradition, he modified this practice through his annual retreats for prolonged periods of communion with God.

Ambrose described other experiences of how his spiritual duties cultivated sensitivity to perceiving and enjoying God. On May 17, 1648, he writes, "[a]t several times I ran through the Duties of *Watchfulness, Self-Examination, Experiences, Meditation*, the *Life of Faith*; and many a time I felt many sweet stirrings of Christs Spirit: the Lord Jesus appeared to my soul, gave me the kisses of his mouth, especially in my Prayers to, and praises of his Majesty. *Surely thou art my Lord, and I will praise thee: Thou art my God, and I will exalt thee. Hallelujah.*"[39] While the Puritans, including Ambrose, knew Bernard of Clairvaux's Sermons on the Song of Songs, none make any reference to his teaching on the three-fold kisses. The Puritan resistance to spiritual hierarchies or exclusiveness would certainly clash with Bernard's third kiss.[40]

38. Ambrose, *Media* (1650), 74.

39. Ibid., 79.

40. Bernard introduces his teaching on the three-fold kiss in *SCC* 3. See McGinn, *Growth of Mysticism*, 166. Sibbes did speak of "degrees of his kisses" but he understood them as an encouragement through periods of struggle and not increasing levels of spiritual intensity. *Spouse, Her Earnest Desire*, 206. See also Keach, *Tropologia Key to Scripture Metaphors*, 53, 567–70 and Won, "Communion with Christ," 159, 169, 199, 340n91, 353n3.

A common theme uniting the previous retreat experiences is the use of the word sweetness. Ambrose describes his location as the "sweet silent Woods." Further, he experiences God through sweet "comforts," "communion," and "stirrings." Sweetness was a common term among the Puritans as well as earlier Christians.[41] These and other retreat entries specifically reveal that spiritual duties were both the motivation and means for Ambrose experiencing and delighting in God. Further, the depth of intimacy and enjoyment of God are revealed by employing the bridal language of Song of Songs.

In the second and third editions of *Media*, Ambrose included different examples from his retreat experience for 1651.[42] The great benefit of this variation is that we are provided with an overview of a more complete experience from the month rather than the previous scattered entries from various years. Here he provides nine specific entries for the nineteen days of his retreat that reflects the same basic pattern as the 1646 account. It appears that virtually any of the spiritual duties that Ambrose engaged had the potential to lift his soul into deeper contemplative awareness and adoration of God. For example, on May 17, 1651 he reports, "[t]his day in the morning, *I meditated on the love of Christ*, wherein Christ appeared, and melted my heart in many sweet passages. In the Evening *I meditated on Eternity*, of hell: and on eternity of Heaven, wherein the Lord both melted, and cheered, and warmed, and refreshed my soul. Surely the touches of Gods Spirit are as sensible as any outward touches. Allelujah."[43] Clearly God's Spirit made deep impressions upon Ambrose's soul. His description suggests that this was a strongly palpable experience that deeply touched and transformed his soul. The language of melting, cheering, and warming the heart has long been used by contemplative writers in their attempt to articulate their knowing and loving God. The remaining dates of this retreat produced a similar cycle of renewed awareness of sin and negligence followed by confession that in turn brought a renewed experience of God's presence

41. See Hesselink, "Calvin: Theologian of Sweetness." Cf. McGinn, *Growth of Mysticism*; McGinn, *Flowering of Mysticism*; and McGinn, *Harvest of Mysticism*, indexes.

42. Ambrose, *Media* (1652), 73–75 and Ambrose, *Media* (1657), 88–90.

43. Ambrose, *Media* (1657), 88–89. Ambrose specifically mentions the following spiritual duties in which he experienced God: watchfulness, self-tryal (i.e., self-examination), experience, evidences, meditation, life of faith, prayer, reading the Word, self-denial, and saints suffering, 73–75; cf. Ambrose, *Media* (1650), 112 for Ambrose's "consideration of Eternity."

and promises. The concluding words of his last entry for this year's retreat is a helpful summary of his experience: "[n]ow the Spirit left in my soul a sweet scent and favour behind it. Allelujah. *Amen, Amen*."[44]

There were other retreat experiences when Ambrose's soul soared to the suburbs of heaven. May 20, 1641 captures this overwhelming experience: "[t]his day in the Evening the Lord in his mercy poured into my soul the ravishing joy of his blessed Spirit. O how sweet was the Lord unto me? I never felt such a lovely taste of Heaven before: I believed this was *the joyful sound*, the *Kisses of his mouth*, the *Sweetnesses of Christ*, the *Joy of his Spirit, the new wine of his kingdom*; it continued with me about two days."[45] There are a number of significant themes from this two-day encounter. Ambrose specifically mentions he experienced each member of the Trinity. Joy is the dominant affection, mentioned three times. Sweetness is mentioned twice. Ambrose comments that he has never had an experience of this depth before. In fact, he traces this experience to the time in which he "began to see Spiritual things . . . upon which followed more desire and endeavors after grace."[46] One can understand how this contemplative experience of God's presence would inspire a person to continue to cultivate a relationship of gazing lovingly on God. There are two additional items that need to be noted. First, Ambrose again reflects the bridal desire and delight of the Song of Songs, very similar to his sample meditation on the soul's love to Christ. There he writes, "[o] let me taste how gracious thou art, by some real experiments in my own heart, smile upon me from heaven, answer me with some alluring whispers of the Spirit of Adoption; *Kiss me with the kisses of thy mouth, for thy love is better than wine.* O let me bathe my soul in the delicious intimacies of a Spiritual communion with thee my God."[47] This reflects the intimacy of spiritual marriage that has long been a theme within the contemplative-mystical tradition of Christian spirituality. Second this description captures the rich devotional language of meditating on heaven. Heavenly-mindedness was a common theme in

---

44. Ibid., 90.

45. Ambrose, *Media* (1650), 71. This event was so significant that it was recorded again in *Media* in a slightly different version. There Ambrose describes it as "Spiritual, heavenly ravishing love-trance" that was a "blessed foretaste of heaven." *Media* (1650), 111; cf. 134 for a third reference to this experience.

46. Ambrose, *Media* (1657), 214.

47. Ibid., 235 (incorrectly numbered 237).

Christian mysticism; according to McGinn contemplation was "understood as burning desire for heaven."[48] Some Puritans shared a similar desire for heavenly-mindedness.[49]

It is unfortunate that the diary entries for the remaining days of Ambrose's retreat have been lost. Nonetheless, the erotic language reminiscent of the Song of Songs is sufficient to indicate the warmth of Ambrose's relationship with God. Contemplative experiences are often ineffable, however, there is ample evidence from these numerous attempted expressions of his retreat experiences to support the reality that Ambrose was deeply transformed by his contemplative visits with God.

Contemporary readers might question Ambrose's practice of an annual month-long retreat. This is all the more surprising since unlike Bernard and earlier monastic Christians who followed this pattern as a way of life Ambrose was married and had three children.[50] However, we need to realize that many men were away for long periods of time during the seventeenth century for business or ministry. Further, Ambrose asserts that he felt called and compelled to make these annual retreats. He draws upon Jesus' account of being driven into the wilderness as a model for him to emulate. He contends,

> In this respect, I know not but the wilderness might be an advantage to Christs designe: In this solitary place, he could not but breath out more pure inspiration; heaven usually is more open, and God usually more familiar and frequent in his visits in such places. I know not what others experiences may be, but if I have found anything of God, or of his grace, I may thank a wood, a wildernesse, a desert, a solitary place, for its accommodation; and have I not a blessed pattern here before me?[51]

Earlier in a May 16, 1648 diary entry, he provides another motivation for this practice, "I came to *Weddicre*, to renew my engagements and loves

48. McGinn, *Growth of Mysticism*, 140.

49. This will be explored in depth in chapter 4.

50. Ambrose married his wife Judith probably in 1633. In 1641 when Ambrose began his annual retreats his oldest child, Rachel, would have been six and a half years old. In addition, he had two sons, Augustine and Richard. Smith, *Records of Preston Church*, 225.

51. Ambrose, *Looking Unto Jesus*, 380. Oliver Heywood, a fellow Lancashire Puritan, acknowledges the benefit of withdrawing when he counsels; " man shal best enjoy himself alone: Solitary recesses are of singular advantage, both for getting and increasing grace." *Heart Treasure*, 93.

with my Lord and my God this Spring also: *My ground is that of Cant.*
2.11,12. Come my beloved, let us go forth into the fields, etc. there will I
give thee my loves. The bridegroom of our souls (said Bernard) is bashful,
and more frequently visits his bride in the solitary places."[52] Therefore,
according to Ambrose, Christ provides a double motivation; both in his
actual practice of retreating to the wilderness and in the bridal reminder
from Song of Songs, where Jesus, the Bridegroom, offers a biblical warrant for this practice of solitude or removing one's self from the busyness
of daily life. In a fascinating comment on Ambrose's teaching on meditation, he stresses that the minister's time is not his own; rather he needs to
use it for the benefit of his people. He continues by saying, "I hear them
[i.e. the congregation] crying after me, To your closet, and there pray for
us that we perish not; study for us, that we may learn of you how to walk
in his paths: for if we perish, and you will not give warning, *then must*
our blood be required at your hands."[53] That awareness and responsibility
created a strong motivation for Ambrose to take his annual retreats. But
to comprehend the full reason for Ambrose's understanding regarding
his annual retreats one additional insight needs to be grasped.

Ambrose was not naïve and recognized that inherent within his
practice of an annual retreat was also the danger of greater temptation.
He cites Jesus' wilderness experience facing the devil's temptation and
continues by saying wilderness places

> are no freer from temptations, than they that are more publike;
> Satan hath his temptations of another sort, and especially his most
> hideous and horrible injections in such places more then publike.
> And this more resolves me than all the arguments that ever I read,
> of the errour of those Eremites and Votaries of old, who, to free
> themselves from Satans malice, and for more holiness, voluntarily
> forsook the societies of men, and lived by themselves in woods,
> and wildernesses; And yet is there no mean betwixt these two ex-
> tremes? is not society good? and is not solitariness good in their
> times and season? I dare not for a world deny either, and I think
> he is no Christian that makes not use of both.[54]

---

52. Ambrose, *Media* (1650), 78–79. Ambrose duplicates this entry as the justification for his annual retreat on May 13, 1651. *Media* (1657), 88.

53. Ambrose, *Media* (1657), 220; cf. 218 on the importance of solitary places.

54. Ambrose, *War with Devils*, 171–72.

Those are strong words. Ambrose realizes the tension between being submerged in the busyness of daily activities as well as the freedom of solitude for prolonged meditation and prayer. While this tension exists, he leaves no doubt that solitude offers a greater opportunity to "enjoy the benefits" of God.[55] Therefore, he believes his practice of an annual month-long retreat allows him to benefit from both of these necessities of the spiritual life. He continues his appeal by commenting on the proper use of solitude and discerning when it is best to avoid and when it is wise to enter it. He writes,

> Hence I say, that in the very time of the assaults, or of Satans injections, it is good to avoid solitariness, as of choice; yet if God, by virtue of our calling, shall draw or lead us into solitary places at such a time, we need not fear, *Jesus Christ was led of the Spirit into the wilderness, to be tempted of the devil.* If we are led into a wilderness by Divine Providence, and in our calling, and that we run not our selves rashly into a temptation, we may confidently expect a comfortable issue out of it.[56]

Additionally, Ambrose cautions his readers to resist "to roving, ranging thoughts" so that their time in solitude might be well spent.[57] Clearly for Ambrose, his retreats were more than a spiritual luxury or an escape from the pressures of life. Rather, in identifying with Jesus, he felt drawn into the wilderness by the Holy Spirit to prepare and refine him to be the best minister for his congregation.

In reviewing Ambrose's retreat experiences it is evident that he possessed a contemplative desire that was consciously aware of God. His experiences were renewed by his sweet enjoyment of communion with God. This deep communion of "delicate intimacies" is strongly reflective of spiritual marriage with Jesus. This was certainly one of the results of his annual retreats, deepening his contemplative joy in communion with God. Unfortunately, Ambrose's diary does not mention any of his personal "closet" times of devotion. However, his funeral sermon for Lady Houghton, *Redeeming the Time*, suggests that Ambrose would

---

55. Ambrose, *Communion with Angels*, 277.

56. Ambrose, *War with Devils*, 172; cf. Scudder, *Christians Daily Walke*, 184–87 for a discussion on the proper use of solitude. Nehemiah Wallington confesses that "solitariness" created a greater temptation towards suicide and lust for himself. Seaver, *Wallington's World*, 31, 126.

57. Ibid., 172.

have engaged in a variety of forms of meditation and prayer in both the morning and evening that could no doubt produce similar experiences.[58] Ambrose's retreats also increased his awareness of how his sins created a barrier between himself and God. Therefore, he shared a commonality with other Christians who recognized one of the fruits of contemplative prayer was an increased awareness of sin. On May 22, 1646, he detected with great sadness that, "[t]he Lord by his spirit wrought in one a depth of humiliation for sin, and yet he was troubled that he was not more troubled for it."[59] Growing in godliness and holiness was one of the major emphases of Puritan piety. They understood that this was not possible without a serious awareness of their own sins and a desire to work towards their sanctification as they lived more fully by God's grace. The retreat experience of May 19, 1648, serves as both a summary of this retreat section and creates a bridge for the next dimension of the struggles of Ambrose's soul. He writes, "[o]ne felt many strivings, and contrary workings in his spirit; sometimes in prayer ravished, and sometimes heavy; sometimes full of comfort, and sometimes exceedingly dejected; sometimes patient, and other whiles impatience. O the fickleness and uncertainty of the heart in the course of piety."[60]

INTRAPERSONAL DIMENSION: STRUGGLES OF THE SOUL

Ambrose also experienced God through the struggles of his soul. Frank Luttmer captures the Puritans' understanding of temptations when he declares: "the very experience of spiritual struggle was a sign of God's saving grace; the torment of temptation, the affliction of conscience born of an awareness of one's sins, and the consciousness of being unworthy of salvation were all symptoms of a soul engaged in 'warfare' not wallowing in 'security', a cause for hope not despair."[61] Some scholars have drawn attention to the heightened sense of anxiety and despair that marked certain Puritans. While Paul Seaver admits that Nehemiah Wallington's case was more extreme than most, he does indicate that Wallington was often suicidal.[62] Thomas Shepard's experience, while less intense, was

---

58. Ambrose, *Redeeming the Time*, 17–19.
59. Ambrose, *Media* (1650), 112; cf. 107.
60. Ibid., 115.
61. Luttmer, "Persecutors, Tempters and the Devil," 67.
62. Seaver, *Wallington's World*, 16, 21–25, 31, 76.

still often consumed with spiritual anxiety regarding his assurance; in "the final analysis, Shepard simply does not get off the treadmill."[63] John Bunyan records in his autobiography, *Grace Abounding to the Chief of Sinners*, a similar pilgrimage of doubt, despair, and fear that he had committed the unpardonable sin against the Holy Spirit. Hambrick-Stowe offers a more balanced assessment and acknowledges "anxiety was a motivating force in the daily devotional practice of New Englanders throughout their lives" but that "Puritan anxiety was not spiritually crippling" and "led to an ever-deepening relationship with the God of salvation."[64] While Ambrose recognizes that one of the tools employed by the devil is despair, he does not seem overly troubled by it in comparison with Shepard, Wallington, Bunyan, and others.[65] Nor does he seem to battle with melancholy as many Puritans did. Struggles often tend to be personalized and attack the individual at the place of greatest vulnerability. Ambrose understood this and counsels his readers that the "evils that arise from *the Devil*, are temptations of several sorts."[66] That reality reveals the wide spectrum of struggles experienced by Puritans in the seventeenth century. Henry Newcome, Ambrose's close friend, often wrestled with his use of time, bemoaning the large quantities he spent playing billiards and smoking rather than in meditation.[67] Conversely, Ralph Josselin, the Essex Puritan minister, in his idiosyncratic diary often seems preoccupied with his health, especially his navel.[68] Ambrose referred to "our special sins, our *Dalilah* sins" as those most challenging to face.[69] While he does not specifically name his Dalilah sin, his diary reveals that he was more susceptible to the temptation of pride, which will be examined later.

Traditionally, Christians have examined the struggles of the soul according to the three-fold temptations of the devil, the flesh, and the

63. Tipson, "Routinized Piety of Shepard's Diary," 74–75. See also McGiffert, *God's Plot*, 19–26 for a helpful treatment of anxiety and assurance within the Puritans.

64. Hambrick-Stowe, *Practice of Piety*, 20, 284, 89; cf. 286–87.

65. Ambrose, *War with Devils*, 178–86.

66. Ambrose, *Media* (1657), 286.

67. On playing billiards see Newcome, *Diary*, 67, 72, 75, 82, 158n. On smoking tobacco see 68, 70, 139, 166, 168, 182, 194, 196, 199, 218.

68. Macfarlane, *Diary of Ralph Josselin*, 140n1, 141.

69. Ambrose, *Media* (1657), 47, 65, 100, 454.

world.[70] Unlike some in our contemporary technological world, the Puritans believed in the reality of Satan's presence.[71] Due to the vicious, virulent, and persistent nature of the devil to deceive or destroy Christians, Ambrose writes of the importance of entering into spiritual combat and wrestling with Satan.[72] The Puritans were well aware of the long tradition of spiritual combat that can be traced back to the Bible.[73] William Gurnall's *The Christian in Complete Armour* employed the Pauline battle imagery of Eph 6 and was one of the most popular Puritan works on this subject. Gurnall cites Tertullian, Augustine, and Jerome as well as later writers such as Bernard and Gerson. Clearly the gulf between Western Catholic and Puritan writings on this subject was not as wide as some might suspect.[74] More importantly to this study is Ambrose's knowledge of some early sources on spiritual warfare. In *War with Devils* he writes, "*Athanasius* tells of an Hermite to whom God should reveal the state of the world."[75] Obviously this refers to Antony, the early desert father, whose experience of spiritual combat was recorded by Athanasius. Later in this same work, Ambrose makes a specific reference to the twenty-third scale that is pride in John Climacus's *Ladder of Divine Ascent*.[76]

Ambrose asserts that the devil is a formidable foe "and enters into Spirits; his wrestling is so close, that neither understanding, will, affections, nor any thing within can escape his fangs."[77] This should not imply that the devil could control the individual believer in Jesus. Ambrose clarifies that the Devil "cannot compel or force you to Sin." Therefore,

---

70. There appears to be no consistency how Puritan authors arranged these three headings. Ambrose employs this pattern that will be followed in examining his development of temptation. Ibid., 286–87.

71. Spurr, *English Puritanism*, 180.

72. Ambrose, *War with Devils*, 2, 3, 5, 15, 17, 19, 22, 26, 29, 163.

73. There is no adequate history that traces the Puritan awareness of this topic back to the NT. The best historiography on this subject is Russell, *Mephistopheles: Devil in the Modern World*. For Calvin's understanding see Charles Hall, *With the Spirit's Sword*. For Puritan sources see Wakefield, *Puritan Devotion*, 132–35; Bozeman, *Precisianist Strain*, esp. 110–13, 236–37; and Zacharias, *Embattled Christian*.

74. See for example Clark, "Protestant Demonology," 73, 79 and Bozeman, *Precisianist Strain*, 79

75. Ambrose, *War with Devils*, 56.

76. Ibid., 170.

77. Ibid., 15.

it is "not that Sathan imports any new thing into our minds, which he found not in our fancies before."[78] Further, as he expounds his thinking more fully Ambrose declares that Satan knows "our thoughts, as well as words and actions" but this is only true for the "outer rooms" of our life. Ambrose seeks to reassure his readers as he limits the power of the devil in the lives of Christians, "for the most inner room or privy chamber, wherein we place the understanding and will, as Sathan cannot intuitively or immediately discern it, so neither can he imperiously or efficaciously work upon it."[79]

This can be demonstrated from Ambrose's diary. While he occasionally experienced these torments being awake,[80] most temptations occurred during sleep. These nocturnal encounters with Satan powerfully illustrate how he experienced God amid these troubling attacks upon his soul. On March 6, 1647, Ambrose reports, "[t]his night in his sleep a troubled soul was by Satan tempted to sin, but the Lord stood by him, put prayers into him though asleep, whereby he overcame the temptation; then awaking, he deeply apprehended Satans approach and busie temptations: it struck him into fears, but praising God for his assistance, he received boldness, and then slept again."[81] It is significant that Ambrose's sensitivity to God cultivated through his contemplative awareness was able to experience God even during his sleep. Since dreams can originate from godly sources as well as the devil, Ambrose provides guidance in distinguishing those that come from God's angels.[82]

Doubt was another temptation that Satan often used, and twice Ambrose wrestles with it within a day of each other. The first struggle occurred on May 20, 1651: "[i]n the Morning I fell on *Reading the Word*, perused the directions, and then searched into the *Common places and uses of my corruptions in nature and practice; of my comforts against the burthens of my daily infirmities; of establishing my heart against the fear of falling away; of directions in my calling; of comforts against outward*

---

78. Ibid., 10.

79. Ibid., 49. Luttmer affirms this assessment from his broad study of the topic, "According to Puritan divines, the devil could not directly read minds, but his powers as a spirit, his unparalleled knowledge, and his long experience enabled him to know the 'very thoughts and intents of the heart.'" "Persecutors, Tempters and the Devil," 64n104.

80. Ambrose, *Media* (1650), 107.

81. Ibid., 108; cf. 107.

82. Ambrose, *Communion with Angels*, 248.

crosses; of my priviledges in Christ above all the wicked in the world." He
also describes the other occasion from the previous day: "[i]n the former
part of this day I exercised the *life of Faith*, when the Lord strengthened me to act Faith on severall Promises, both temporal, spiritual, and
eternal. I had then sweet, refreshing, and encouraging impressions on
my soul against all the fearful, sinful, and doubting dreams I had the
night or two before dreamed."[83] Ambrose provides no indication from
his earlier entries of the cause for these "doubting dreams" but does
affirm that God strengthened and removed his fears. Additionally he
confesses, mostly likely from his own experiences, that "the best cure
and remedy of doubtings, is to perfect and strengthen our assurance."[84]
Unlike Shepard and Wallington who struggled for years to attain assurance Ambrose appears to have experienced it sooner.

It is often difficult to accurately ascertain the placement of these
temptations since there is some overlap of categories. In one sense this
is reflective of the principle of simultaneity already discussed. Ambrose
realized the same challenge when he declared that the devil "hath his
aydes, these are led under the conduct of those two Captain-Generals,
the World and the Flesh."[85] Further, since the devil commonly works
through the flesh, this serves as a helpful bridge to the next category
of struggle. Once again while on retreat, Ambrose experienced the torments of the tempter. On May 25, 1646, he recorded this battle: "[t]he
Lord opened a poor creatures eye, to see in some measure the depths of
Satan, and deceitfulness of his own heart: he acted in things doubtful,
against the reluctancy of his own conscience before; no question this is
sin, because it is not faith."[86] Ambrose provides an additional commentary on this experience by adding Rom 14:22 and Gal 2:14 in the margin, which is his desired response. Both of these passages reinforce the
importance of walking according to the gospel and living before God in
a manner that is acceptable to God. In other words, when Satan tempts
you, you must remember to look at God.

The second general category of temptations originates from the
flesh. Ambrose declares that the flesh does not mean "the body and the
flesh thereof, but that corruption of nature, which hath defiled the Body

83. Ambrose, *Media* (1657), 89.

84. Ibid., 211.

85. Ambrose, *War with Devils*, 16.

86. Ambrose, *Media* (1650), 106.

and Soul."[87] Further, he states that the "evils that arise from *the flesh*, are lusts or temptations of Uncleanness."[88] Based upon the available diary entries, Ambrose reported as many experiences of the flesh as of the world and devil combined. Not surprisingly, later in *War with Devils* he observes, "[t]he Flesh is a worse enemy than the Devil himself; for never could the Devil hurt us, if this imbred enemy did not betray us: This is the root, the fountain, the origine of all other sin, *when lust have conceived, it bringeth forth sin*."[89]

More specifically, Ambrose's greatest struggles of the soul were related to the flesh. As previously indicated, his major challenge appears to have been pride.[90] The following examples reflect his honesty and struggle as well as the ways in which he experienced God amid these battles. His primary conflict appears to have been his desire to create a better public image then was justified. On May 15, 1646, "[t]his day a poor soul upon strict examination of his heart, found that formerly he had judged many sinful actions lawful and good, and had excused many actions though in themselves sinful: he felt not such a powerful operation of his corruptions before, and so through Pride and Ignorance thought better of himself than he had cause."[91] Further, on May 13, 1646, "[o]ne performed indeed a good action, but he exceedingly overprized it; which he found afterwards."[92] It is not surprising, considering the great importance spiritual duties occupied in Ambrose's life, that his greatest strength could potentially also become his greatest weakness.[93] In the 1652 edition of *Media* Ambrose added a new section entitled "Self-denial" that specifically addressed his struggle: "[t]here is nothing that a Christian is more apt to be proud of then spirituall things."[94] This

87. Ambrose, *War with Devils*, 52; cf. 16.

88. Ambrose, *Media* (1657), 286.

89. Ambrose, *War with Devils*, 57.

90. Pride was also a common temptation to both Henry Newcome and Thomas Shepard. See Newcome, *Diary*, 49, 201 and McGiffert, *God's Plot*, 25, 85, 88, 103, 108, 128; cf. Haller, *Rise of Puritanism*, 153–54, 196.

91. Ambrose, *Media* (1650), 115; cf. 114.

92. Ibid., 114.

93. Owen Watkins links the potential for pride with diary keeping and asserts "[t]he early nineteenth-century editor of Ebenezer Erskine's diary thought the practice could be dangerous because it might supply fuel for spiritual pride." *Puritan Experience*, 23.

94. Ambrose, *Media* (1657), 157.

addition of self-denial suggests a significant place of transformation in Ambrose's personal battle with pride.

Anger was another struggle that Ambrose mentions and on January 23, 1647, he records, "[t]his evening one fell into exorbitancy of passion; it was so strong in him, that it cast him into *Palpitation of heart*."[95] There is no indication of the reason for his strong response. However, he supplies some marginal references that convey the desired disposition from this event (Ps 37:8; Eph 4:31; Col 3:12, 13). Fortunately the very next day he was able to report, "[o]ne troubled in conscience for his rash anger, reconciled himself to his adversary, and immediately God spake peace to his conscience."[96] Apparently Ambrose took seriously the Pauline admonition of not letting the sun go down on your anger. In fact, this verse from Eph 4:31 was one of the marginal texts adjoined to this event.

The world constituted the third temptation, and Ambrose recognized that this included "covetousness, cares, evil company."[97] He later enlarged this to encompass on the one hand, "pleasure, honours, riches" and on the other hand, "[t]hreats, Miseries, afflictions, Poverty, Ignominy."[98] Living in Lancashire during the seventeenth century, in particular during the decade of the 1640s when the country was often ravaged by the Civil War, strained the already meager resources of many. Finances were typically inadequate for ministers. Ambrose bluntly confesses on March 27, 1647, " poor soul being mightily insnared with the world, and finding by experience its vanity and vexation, he resolved against it."[99] On the same date Ambrose conveys the severity of this struggle when he discloses he was "exceedingly troubled by the cares of this life."[100] Later that same year, on December 11, 1647, Ambrose records progress towards his goal, "[t]his day one observed GODS goodness, in supplying fully all his Temporal wants: This he construed

---

95. Ambrose, *Media* (1650), 106.

96. Ibid., 108.

97. Ambrose, *Media* (1657), 287.

98. Ambrose, *War with Devils*, 51; cf. 16 and Luttmer, "Persecutors, Tempters and the Devil," 44–45.

99. Ambrose, *Media* (1657), 186. Earlier on February 27, 1645, Ambrose records that he had received an augmentation to his salary and preys "Incline my heart unto thy testimonies, and not to covetousness." *Media* (1650), 73.

100. Ibid., 185.

as earnest both of Spiritual and Eternal favors and mercies in Christ."[101] Ambrose's response reflects gratitude rather than greed. One of the qualities of gratitude is that it increases one's ability to notice life and detect the origin of blessings, hence to have a more contemplative attitude towards life. Additionally, it is likely that this awareness of the proper use of resources enabled a transformation within him, motivating him to later write about the importance of looking off from the world so that you are able to look on to Jesus.[102] He declares, "[t]he eye cannot look upwards and downwards, at once in a direct line; we cannot seriously minde heaven and earth in one thought."[103]

Illness also reflects the temptations of the world. John Waite, in his introduction to *Media*, refers to Ambrose's weak health without any elaboration.[104] Ambrose includes a number of examples of his health in his diary. While fevers and weakness were common ailments, on August 7, 1646, he records that he suffered from a stitch in his side that troubled him throughout his sermon. His sickness grew progressively worse; when the doctor was unable to ease his pain he wrote his will. However, later he was able to declare, "[t]he Lord restored one to his health, out of a dangerous disease, and he praised God for it in the public Assemblies."[105] While his last extant diary entry was in 1651, he suffered from a "sore sickness" in 1653 that provided the inspiration for writing *Looking Unto Jesus*.[106] Ambrose's experience surrounding his health confirms Hambrick-Stowe's observation that illness could intensify personal devotion.[107] In a dream recorded on July 19, 1647, Ambrose connects his awareness that his end might be near with an increased desire for intimacy with Jesus:

> This night desiring God to sanctifie my sleep and dreams, that I sinned not in them: I dreamed, that after some troubles of life, my time limited was at an end, and that I heard the very voyce of God calling me by name into his glorious Kingdom; whither when I came, heavenly ornaments were put upon me by the hand

101. Ambrose, *Media* (1650), 105.
102. Ambrose *Looking Unto Jesus*, 6–20.
103. Ibid., 10.
104. Ambrose, *Media* (1657), To the Reader (John Waite), [1].
105. Ambrose, *Media* (1650), 105.
106. Ambrose, *Looking unto Jesus*, To the Reader, [1].
107. Hambrick-Stowe, *Practice of Piety*, 225; cf. Cohen, *God's Caress*, 214–15.

of God, and of Christ: My soul was exceedingly ravished. *The Lord grant I may make some use of this, to be more heavenly-minded, and to breathe more after Christ.*[108]

This amazing experience transformed Ambrose's desire to focus more consistently upon Christ and expand his meditation on heaven. Additionally, his method of processing this reveals the combination of an affective level experience of a dream further deepened through the interpretive level, to determine the best use of this experience.

The Puritans realized that external events in life could often be a means to awakening them to an inner awareness of truth. This discipline of applying a theological truth in a practical way also illustrates the experimental piety of the Puritans. Ambrose vividly illustrates this practice from his March 17, 1645, entry with a fascinating parable on his sickness: "[a]fter some extreme torment, one voided a Stone; and suddenly the Spirit of Christ injected this motion into his heart, That the best cure for the stone in his heart, was to look on Christ, whose heart he pierced; and to consider that Christ looks on him in every action, and therefore that he should still carry as in his presence, that his heart should be stil on *Gods* eye."[109] Ambrose appropriately includes Ezek 11:19–20, which requests God to remove the prophet's heart of stone and replace it with a heart of flesh. Ambrose's personal response parallels the advice he gave to a fellow minister who visited him for counsel during sickness; he said, "sanctifie his sickness to his Spiritual advantage."[110] It does appear from the material preserved that Ambrose's heart was softened and changed and aided him in looking unto Jesus.

Struggles of the soul typically create a sense of anxiety, and anxiety frequently raises the question of whether or not a person is living closely with God. Yet for Ambrose, those skirmishes with desolation did not draw him away from God, at least not for lengthy periods as they did for other Puritans. Further, a number of significant points of transformation within his soul have been observed: wrestling with Satan drew him closer to God, periodic doubts renewed his faith and trust in God's promises, anger was transformed into reconciliation, financial fears were converted by God's provisions into gratitude rather than greed, illness created a deeper hunger for Christ and increased his heavenly-mindedness, and

108. Ambrose, *Media* (1650), 76.

109. Ibid., 112.

110. Ibid., 76.

the persistence of pride created the discipline of self-denial. Consistently throughout, instead of focusing upon his struggles, Ambrose turned his gaze in a more contemplative way upon Jesus. Lovelace makes the significant connection that was frequently neglected by the Puritans: "[i] t is remarkable that the Puritans could so easily overlook a third biblical path to assurance that Luther had uncovered: naked reliance on the work of Christ."[111] Ambrose connects this assurance that comes from recognizing God's love in Christ with the ability to overcome the world's temptations: "[i]s a man assured of God's love in Christ? Such a one fears not any troubles, he knows all comes through his Fathers hands . . . He gets a victory against the world by his *Faith*, and *Samson*-like, breaks all bands of temptations as straw."[112] This solid christocentric foundation, that would later form the groundwork for *Looking Unto Jesus*, reduces anxiety, increases freedom and encourages Ambrose to lovingly gaze upon Jesus. Even his greatest interior struggle with pride seems to have brought renewed intimacy with Jesus.

INTERPERSONAL DIMENSION

The third dimension elucidates the ways in which Ambrose experienced God through his one-on-one relationships with other individuals. His diary includes numerous examples of how he sought to lead others to know God more deeply. This sensitivity and concern among Puritan ministers earned them the title, "physicians of the soul."[113] Haller providers a helpful summary of this form of pastoral care: "[t]heir function was to probe the conscience of the down-hearted sinner, to name and cure the malady of his soul, and then to send him out strengthened and emboldened for the continuance of his lifelong battle with the world and the devil."[114] While the soul physician's primary concern was to assist the other person in experiencing God, Ambrose's diary reveals that God often challenged him through others as well. Again it is clear that the Puritans did not exist in a vacuum. Their practice of caring for souls both

111. Lovelace, *American Pietism of Cotton Mather*, 101. Nehemiah Wallington finally discovered the same reality that assurance ultimately rests on trusting Jesus. Seaver, *Wallington's World*, 43.

112. Ambrose, *Media* (1657), 209–10.

113. See for example, Haller, *Rise of Puritanism*, 26–48.

114. Ibid., 27. For a detailed summary of the themes and methods of this soul care see Lewis, *Genius of Puritanism*, 63–135.

recognized and interacted with the long history of spiritual direction.[115] Casuistry, or cases of conscience, was a cornerstone of the Puritan physician of the soul and developed through both resistance to and reform of the large reservoir of Roman Catholic literature.[116] Richard Greenham has been acknowledged as the founding father of Puritan casuistry. He is also representative of the Puritan awareness of patristic and medieval sources on this subject.[117]

Being a physician of the soul requires the blending of contemplation and action. The contemplative attitude provides the sensitivity and the ability to observe God's presence within the life of another person. Contemplation requires patience in waiting and lingering in God's presence. The soul physician must learn the same skills to help those in need. Further, this awareness must be expanded into the action of guiding the other person who will possess varying degrees of self-awareness of God. This critical marriage between contemplation and action has had a long and venerated history throughout Christian spirituality.[118] Bernard of Clairvaux describes this interaction using Martha and Mary from Luke 10:38–42. Just as these two sisters lived under the same roof, action and contemplation need to be united not separated.[119] Thomas Hooker demonstrates a less balanced understanding between the two sisters, revealing the typical Puritan animosity towards the Church of England worship, when he "identified the busy show of activity in the liturgy with Martha and the devotional life of 'heart religion' with Mary."[120]

115. McNeill, *History of Cure of Souls*, 192–269; cf. Keller, "Puritan Resources for Biblical Counseling," 11–44 and Bozeman, *Precisianist Strain*, esp. 72–73, 129–36, 140–43, 162–63. Bozeman tends to diminish the specific nature and function of Puritan soul care by making it synonymous with the term minister.

116. See for example Bozeman, *Precisianist Strain*, 78–83. For a broader treatment of Puritan casuistry see McNeill, "Casuistry in the Puritan Age," 76–89, and Thomas, "Cases of Conscience," 29–56.

117. On Greenham in general see Parker and Carlson, "Practical Divinity," esp. 97–119; Jebb, "Richard Greenham and Troubled Souls"; and Bozeman, *Precisianist Strain*, 129–36. On patristic and medieval knowledge of the Puritans see Bozeman, *Precisianist Strain*, 77–78, 130–31, 143, 215; McNeill, *History of Cure of Souls*, 227, 265; McNeill, "Casuistry in the Puritan Age," 79, 81–82; and Tom Webster, *Godly Clergy*, 81, 170.

118. For examples of this in the first millennium plus of Christian spirituality see McGinn, *Foundations of Mysticism*, 225–26, 256–57; McGinn, *Growth of Mysticism*, 31–32, 35–36, 74–79, 184–85, 218–23; and McGinn, *Flowering of Mysticism*, 14–15,

119. Bernard, SCC 51.2; cf. McGinn, *Growth of Mysticism*, 222–23.

120. Hambrick-Stowe, *Practice of Piety*, 43.

Sensitive to the experimental emphasis upon heart religion, Ambrose declares that personal experiences with God are not to be kept silent or restricted for personal growth. Rather they are to be freely shared to encourage others in their spiritual pilgrimage. In his introduction to spiritual conferences, Ambrose declares this principle: "[t]he Christian that hath collected experiences, or found out methods, for the advancement of holiness, must not deny such knowledge to the body; Christians must drive an open and free trade, they must teach one another the mystery of godliness."[121] Later in the same work, Ambrose provides the encouragement for this spiritual sharing: "[w]ould Christians thus meet and exchange words and notions, they might build up one another, they might heat and inflame one another, they might strengthen and encourage one another, as the brethren did *Paul*: and have we not an express Command for this *Duty* of Conference?"[122]

M. M. Knappen asserts, "[c]onferences with fellow Christians on spiritual matters were a very important part of the Puritan's spiritual life."[123] While these meetings often included more than one person, they could also refer to one-on-one spiritual counsel. Ambrose used the term specifically in this manner, as did other Puritans of his day.[124] The following reference could be directed to both individuals and groups: "*[r]eading the holy Scriptures*, which is nothing else but a kinde of holy conference with God, wherein we enquire after, and he reveals unto us himself and his will."[125] Ambrose devotes a large section to this in *Media*,[126] and the variety of topics of practical divinity covered include the following: cases of conscience of humanity after the fall, signs of sincere humility, signs of a hard heart, evidence of a true and evangelical repentance, signs of a sincere love to Christ, causes why Christ might withdraw himself from us, signs of true grace, ways of handling doubt,

121. Ambrose, Media (1657), 339.

122. Ibid., 344. Tom Webster provides the best descriptive treatment of the nature and usage of conferences. *Godly Clergy*, 36–59.

123. Knappen, *Two Elizabethan Puritan Diaries*, 8; cf. vii, 84.

124. Ambrose, *Communion with Angels*, 133. For a helpful overview to conferences see Hambrick-Stowe, *Practice of Piety*, 150–55 and Schwanda, "Growing in Christ," 28–30; cf. Ash, Nalton, and Church, *Heavenly Conference Between Christ and Mary*; Seaver, *Wallington's World*, 40, 97, 148; and Flavel, *Conference Between a Minister and Doubting Christian*, 6:460–69.

125. Ambrose, Media (1657), 477.

126. Ibid., 338–77.

means towards seeking unity among Christians, and observation of the Lord's Day, etc.

Coming alongside of another person to provide spiritual counsel is challenging and requires great perceptiveness. Ambrose demonstrates the delicate balance when he asserts; "[e]xcuse me that I speak thus much to encourage sinners to come to Christ, I would be sometimes a *Boanerges*, and sometimes a *Barnabas*; a son of thunder to rouse hard hearts, and a son of consolation to cherre up drooping spirits."[127] This language was not unique to Ambrose. Simon Chan comments that among Puritan pastors "a few possessed that rare balance of " Boanerges: A Son of Thunder in preaching the Law" and a "Barnabas, a Son of Sweet Consolation" in preaching "the exceeding Riches of Divine Grace in the Lord Jesus Christ."[128] A helpful approach for tracing this in Ambrose is through his practice of spiritual guidance. Parishioners and ministers alike struggled with various "cases of conscience" or concerns of the heart that could cover practically any aspect of life. Ambrose includes a varied collection illustrative of his spiritual counsel that reflects Jesus' own ministry in the Gospels. He provided such spiritual guidance to individuals who experienced doubt in their spiritual condition, spiritual desertion, troubled conscience, sickness, and approaching death. On certain occasions he spoke the needed words of conviction, while more frequently he sought to redirect broken people back to the love of God.

These themes broaden in a March 3, 1647, diary entry. Ambrose reports, "Mr. B. a godly Minister in the North, being troubled in Conscience, came to me, and desired some Spiritual advice: After acknowledgement of my unfitness and weakness, I directed, as the Lord enabled." Five days later these two men gathered with others for a private day of humiliation. Ambrose continues, "the terror of Conscience had so worn out his Spirit, and wasted his body, that he was not able (as he said) to perform: yet desiring him to depend on God, and to cast himself on him for ability; he prayed with such fervency, humility and brokenness of heart, that he opened the fountains of all eyes about him,

---

127. Ambrose, *Looking Unto Jesus*, 746.

128. Chan, "Puritan Meditative Tradition," 151. Samuel Clarke described his father as "a Boanerges to the wicked but a Barnabas to the humble and broken in spirit." Haller, *Rise of Puritanism*, 102; cf. 110; cf. Wakefield, *Puritan Devotion*, 112; Watkins, *Puritan Experience*, 9; Heywood, *Narrative of John Angier*, 35; and Tom Webster, *Godly Clergy*, 6, 101.

Ambrose, *Looking Unto Jesus*, 746

and caused a flood of tears in my Chamber, I never saw the like day. *All the glory to God.*"[129] A number of significant points emerge from this event. First, Ambrose recognized his own inadequacy and utter weakness in assisting a struggling person. However, he was also cognizant of his need to depend upon the guidance of the Holy Spirit to direct his efforts. Second, wisely he understood that his responsibility was to help the person depend upon God, not himself. Towards that end, the physician of the soul may need to urge the person to engage in behavior that might be very painful in the short run. Finally, Ambrose realized that he is only the conduit or the means. All praise and credit is directed towards God, the source of this gracious gift of restoration. Three and a half weeks later on March 29, Ambrose received a letter from this same minister expressing his gratitude and progress in resolving his problem. In response, Ambrose declares, "[o] our Father, hallowed be thy Name in this and all things."[130]

Additionally, *Prima* and *Ultima* were instrumental in the conversion of another minister. Ambrose reports the joyous news, "[t]his day I was told by a godly Minister Mr. *C.* that Mr. *B.* residing in *Glasco*, and lighting by Providence on my Book of the *First and Last things*, it was a means (as he acknowledged) of his Conversion; at this time he was ordained Minister by the *L.* Classis, and reported to be a holy and able man. *Glory and praise to thee, O my Lord and my God.*"[131] Not only was Ambrose able to guide others through his physical presence but also through his writings.

While the previous examples exhibit Ambrose's spiritual guidance to other ministers, the following incident pertains to a woman from his congregation. On March 1, 1647, he writes, "[t]his day Mistris *C.* sent for me, expressing that my sermons of *Eternity* had struck her with fear and trembling, and that she was troubled in Conscience, and desired to be informed in Gods ways: I advised her, and prayed with her; many a tear came from her: *The Lord by his Spirit work in her a thorough and saving Conversion.*"[132] Once again the importance of the Holy Spirit is evident. Further, this occasion as well as numerous others from his diary confirms Ambrose's words regarding the importance of being a Barnabas to

129. Ambrose, *Media* (1650), 75.
130. Ibid.
131. Ibid., 77.
132. Ibid., 74–75.

those who were in distress: "Christians should not triumph over them that are on the ground, and thrown down by a temptation, but rather they should sit by them on the same flat, and mourn with them and for them, and feel some of their weight."[133] Ambrose gives witness to this contemplative practice of sitting with a person at the time of great need, watching and waiting with them for God to work within their lives: "*R. M.* sent for me again, and drawing to his end, he proclaimed *God's goodness, and sweetness, and mercy,* which were his last words; and after, in the midst of our Prayers, he gave up the ghost."[134] This practice illustrates the critical skill of patience to perceive the presence of God, whether directly or through another person.

All of the above examples reflect the attitude of Barnabas. However, there is one additional experience from Ambrose's diary that resembles the approach of Boenerges. This situation incarnates Charles Cohen's understanding of the Puritan preacher's role in conversion: "[p]reachers meant to unsettle their audiences by driving home the enormity of sin."[135] Ambrose perceptively recognized that a troubled conscience was receptive for conversion. On November 29, 1647, he reports,

> This night I was told that Mistris *E.D.* was upon my Prayer the last Fast troubled in Conscience; and that since she had much talked of me, and desired to see me, but her Companion concealing it, she now apprehended the time was past, and utterly despaired: I sent for her, and at her first entrance into my Chamber, she cryed, *O that face! I dare not look on it! Shall such a lost creature as I look upon thee?—Had I seen thee yesternight, I might have been saved; but now I am lost[,] time is past;—O terrors of the Lord are upon me,* &c. yet after she was pleased to hear me pray: And then I advised her, *to search out her sin—To submit to the Lord, to wonder at Gods mercy, that yet she lived, and was on this side Hell.*[136]

The uniqueness of this account compared with the previous examples reveals that this is the only occasion in which Ambrose requested that the person meet him in his study. Perhaps being a Barnabas prompted

133. Ambrose, *Media* (1657), 341.

134. Ambrose, *Media* (1650), 76; cf. The initial reference of Ambrose's visit to R.M. on June 26, 1647. *Media* (1650), 76. See also the July 1, 1648 visit with a woman trapped in desertion. Ambrose, *Media* (1657), 188.

135. Cohen, *God's Caress*, 169; cf. 170. The purpose of spiritual terror was to activate sinners.

136. Ambrose, *Media* (1650), 77.

the soul physician to visit the person in his or her own familiar setting, while the more challenging practice of being a Boenerges was conducted in the minister's chamber where he had more authority and advantage. The final outcome of this visit is unknown, but Ambrose offers these additional details: "[s]he spake sensibly, acknowledging God to be righteous, That she deserved the state she was in: yet promised to yield, and to be quiet under Gods hand, and to search out her sins: so for that time we parted." Unfortunately, that was the last time Ambrose saw her. He later learned that this woman suffered a "deep melancholy" and was taken by her friend to Ireland.[137] This is a reminder that a soul physician is not the only person who might influence the outcome of a conflicted relationship. Due to the lack of further details, it is difficult to determine how Ambrose experienced God through this situation. However, it does illustrate that sometimes we meet God through others, and sometimes we might miss God through the same relationships.

Whether Ambrose was offering spiritual counsel to a troubled or anxious conscience, or coming alongside one who was struggling to receive assurance of conversion, or providing the comfort of grace and peace through his prayers, he was a gifted soul physician. Clearly his effectiveness was not dependent upon his own abilities but rather his reliance upon the Holy Spirit, his blending of contemplation and action, and his ability to be a Barnabas and a Boenerges, that enabled him to guide others into experiencing God's transforming presence. Further, he wisely acknowledged, "[t]here lies many times a great deal of spiritual wealth, in some obscure and neglected Christians, which many supercilious and conceited professors do pass by and neglect."[138] This discovery comes only through consistent contemplative listening that is attentive to the unexpected and recognizes that God may speak through any one, anywhere and when God does, to give praise and thanks to God alone.

STRUCTURAL DIMENSION

While his annual retreats occupied a cornerstone in his spiritual life, Ambrose also recognized the significance of communal spiritual duties. Cohen accurately asserts "Puritan saints found their faith as much

137. Ibid., 77–78.
138. Ambrose, *Media* (1657), 337.

through social communication as through introspective wrangling."[139]
The frequent diary entries of public and private fasts with both ministers
and laity reveal the great importance of this discipline for Ambrose.[140]
Horton Davies correctly asserts that fast days were not a Puritan innova-
tion but already stipulated in 1563 in the *Elizabethan Book of Homilies*.[141]
However, the Protestant origin of this practice can be traced earlier. The
form of prayer that Grindal developed in 1563 was an adaptation of the
Genevan liturgy that in turn was derived from Leviticus 23:27–32.[142]
Additionally, the Puritans were quick to indicate the significant differences between themselves and the Roman Catholic observance of fasting. While Rome focused more on the external actions, the Puritans also
emphasized the internal movement of the soul. The Puritan practice was
also voluntary. Finally, almsgiving for the poor and needy soon became
a standard practice within Puritanism.[143]

Henry Scudder describes the purpose of these fasts as *"sanctifying a
day to the Lord by a willing abstinence from meats and drinke, and from delights & worldly labours, that the whole man may be more thorowly humbled
before God, and more fervent in prayer."*[144] According to Ambrose, there
were four important components to a fast day: fasting from sin, combining Scripture and prayer, following up with expressions of mercy, and

---

139. Cohen, *God's Caress*, 151. Sociability in Puritan piety is a central theme in
Tom Webster, *Godly Clergy*.

140. See Ambrose, *Media* (1650), 72, 73, 74, 75, 77, 79, 80, 83, 84, 101, 104, 105, 110.
The literature on fasting and fast days within Puritanism is extensive. See for example
Tom Webster, *Godly Clergy*, 60–74; Walsham, *Providence in Early Modern England*,
142–47, 164–66; Durston, "Better Humiliation of People"; Collinson, *Elizabethan
Puritan Movement*, 214–19, 437–40; Collinson, *Religion of Protestants*, 167–68, 260–63;
and the index in Hambrick-Stowe, *Practice of Piety*. For fasting in Protestant Scotland
see Schmidt, *Holy Fairs*, 19, 28, 32–33, 55, 77–78, 121, 239n10 and Mullan, *Scottish
Puritanism*, 29, 115, 275–76.

141. Horton Davies, *Worship and Theology in England*, 2: 238.

142. Winthrop Hudson, "Fast Days and Civil Religion," 12; Collinson, *Elizabethan
Puritan Movement*, 215; and Walsham, *Providence in Early Modern England*, 143.

143. On the distinction between Roman Catholic and Puritan fasting see Tom
Webster, *Godly Clergy*, 61, 64, 72, and Durston, "Better Humiliation of People," 129. On
the voluntary nature see Tom Webster, *Godly Clergy*, 63, 69, 71. On almsgiving and fasting see Tom Webster, *Godly Clergy*, 61; Walsham, *Providence in Early Modern England*,
143, 145; and Collinson, *Religion of the Protestants*, 261–62. On the Roman Catholic
practice of fasting see Bossy, *English Catholic Community*, 110–16.

144. Scudder, *Christians Daily Walke*, 69–70.

renewing the covenant with God.[145] He resolves the question of whether a private or public fast day is more important by wisely articulating that it all depends upon the person and the specific situation.[146] Preaching was also a part of fast days.[147] Additionally, fasting was frequently connected with humiliation.[148] Perhaps most illuminating and suggestive of his own experiences, Ambrose declares that "[f]asting days are soul-feeding days, and soul-curing days; some diseases, some lusts will go out no other ways."[149]

One example of a "soul-feeding" day occurred in Ambrose's own house on January 6, 1642, "[t]his day a private Fast being observed, the Lord gave some, that exercised, the very spirit & power of Prayer, to the ravishment of hearers; surely it was the Spirit spake in them."[150] This incident, with ecstatic language reminiscent of Ambrose's retreat experiences, enabled him to taste the ravishing presence of God. Its significance is heightened by a previous reference in a slightly different form: "[t]his day I observed a private Fast in my house; where by the Spirit of Prayer in some Christians, all hearts were warmed, affections moved, and Christ manifested his presence in the midst of us."[151] Another "soul-feeding" day was August 16, 1648, just one day before the Battle of Preston that would end the second Civil War. Ambrose reports,

> A Fast was upon the occasion observed in *Manchester*. In my preparation unto it (reading the Bible) I light upon *Isa.* 49.17— 51.12, 13. After the duty begun, the Lord kept my heart up as in a flame: The day was sweetly observed, but the Conclusion of it (when Mr. *Angier* prayed) was exceedingly sweet; his Prayer was so working, that I believe it melted all hearts: and for my own, it pleased the Lord so to soften it, and break it, that (so far as I can

145. Ambrose, *Media* (1657), 569–71. This treatment rather closely resembles the format provided by Lewis Bayly, *Practice of Piety*, 491–520. See also Scudder, *Christians Daily Walke*, 68–147 for a more in depth treatment of fasting.

146. Ibid., 359–60.

147. Walsham, *Providence in Early Modern England*, 283–87; Hambrick-Stowe, *Practice of Piety*, 135, 247–49; and Old, *Reading and Preaching Scriptures*, 4:296–99.

148. Durston, "Better Humiliation of People," 133–35, 140, 145 and Hambrick-Stowe, *Practice of Piety*, 100, 102–3.

149. Ambrose, *Media* (1657), 343. According to Catherine Nunn, Henry Newcome experienced similar benefits: "[h]e considered that the quiet contemplation which they encouraged was a conduit by which God could work on the soul of the individual." Henry Newcome and his Circle," 14.

150. Ibid., 184

151. Ambrose, *Media* (1650), 71.

remember) it was never in such a melting frame in any publike
Ordinance before.[152]

This same event is mentioned in John Angier's diary.[153]

However, of all of the many references that Ambrose makes to
fasting, the one that reflects the greatest experiential nature and "soul-
curing" power upon his faith occurred on October 4, 1647: "[t]his day I
was called by some discontented Brethren to a private Fast: I construed
this as good news from Heaven, was obedient unto it, and joyned with
them. Some sparkles of former love still remained in every one of us:
not withstanding former breaches, *I trust God will by degrees unite our
hearts more and more.*"[154] Assessing these experiences, fast days were
occasions for Ambrose's heart to be converted, melted, and ravished, for
his affections to be moved, to experience the presence of Christ, and to
be motivated to seek reconciliation in broken relationships.

Family worship was another significant communal discipline. On
May 3, 1648, Ambrose writes, "[w]e had sudden news of some Cavaliers
driven out of *Scotland*, and drawing towards us: At morning, in order
of our Family-duty, we read *Psal. 124.* and at night *1 Pet. 5.7.* both
which places refreshed and cheered my soul."[155] Later that same year on
August 1, Ambrose wrote, "[i]n the morning, a little while before day, I
dreamed fearfully of Satans being busie with me about my bed, and in
terror I awaked; the night was rough: Hereupon I meditated on Gods
Judgements now abroad on the earth. After in my Family-duty was read
Psal. 103. and from *ver.* 8, 9, 10, 11, 12, 13. whence I drew some Spiritual
comfort."[156] A number of themes converge with this second incident.
First, it reflects the principle of simultaneity. While this event began in
his dreams and could readily be placed in the Intrapersonal Struggles of
the Soul dimension, he found resolution and peace from God as he read
Scripture to his family. Second, this dream was just two weeks before the
Battle of Preston. Third, the means towards granting Ambrose comfort
in both of these troubling situations was the public reading and meditating on Scripture with his family.

152. Ibid., 80.
153. Heywood, *Narrative of John Angier*, 42–43.
154. Ambrose, *Media* (1650), 77.
155. Ibid., 78.
156. Ibid., 79.

Clearly, the Lord's Supper was also a significant aspect of Puritan public worship.[157] The evidence from Ambrose's diary confirms this truth for him. On May 2, 1646, he records "[t[his day (after three years want) we administered and received the Sacrament of the Lords Supper; it was the most heavenly heart-breaking day (especially at the time of the Ordinance) that of a long time we enjoyed: Many souls were raised, many hearts melted. *Blessed be God*."[158] Obviously both Ambrose and his congregation were deeply moved by this experience. The infrequency of celebration in relation to its overpowering nature appears confusing, unless we are aware of the historical context.[159] While the Church of England stipulated receiving the Lord's Supper three times a year, few congregants received it more than once a year on Easter.[160] Puritans took St. Paul's admonition in 1 Cor 11:28 very seriously and recognized the importance of proper preparation and self-examination. In his teaching on the sacrament, Ambrose states, "Christ makes offer to come into our hearts, and therefore we must open the gates."[161] "Open the gates" refers to the critical role that self-examination plays in preparation.[162] Two years later on May 7 Ambrose records his own experience while fencing the Table, "I administrated the Sacrament of the Lords Supper; wherein I found much sweetness, and blessed impressions of the Spirit of Christ, and Spiritual inlargements above my self, and a return of Prayers, in that the Lord hedged his Sacrament, that some such came not in, whom I desired to keep out. *Hallelujah. Blessed be God*."[163] Most Puritans, at least those simi-

157. For an overview to the Puritan understanding of the Lord's Supper see Wakefield, *Puritan Devotion*, 42–54; Horton Davies, *Worship of English Puritans*, esp. 22, 119, 150, 204–16; Hambrick-Stowe, *Practice of Piety*, 32–33, 123–26, 206–18; and Holifield, *Covenant Sealed*, esp. 109–38.

158. Ambrose, *Media* (1650), 76.

159. See for example Arnold Hunt, "Lord's Supper Early Modern England," 41–45, 51–57, 60–61, 74, 76, 82; Collinson, "English Conventicle," 255–58; Green, *Print and Protestantism*, 289; and Spufford, *World of Rural Dissenters*, 88–91.

160. Arnold Hunt, "Lord's Supper Early Modern England," 41, 45, and Haigh, *Plain Man's Pathways to Heaven*, 5, 80–81. For the specific practices of the Lord's Supper among nonconformist ministers and laity in Lancashire see Richardson, *Puritanism in North-West England*, 30–33, 48–49, 76–79.

161. Ambrose, *Media* (1657), 418.

162. The importance of self-examination produced numerous devotional manuals to guide Puritans in preparing for the Lord's Supper. See Green, *Print and Protestantism*, 290–91 and Hambrick-Stowe, *Practice of Piety*, 206–18.

163. Ambrose, *Media* (1650), 78. For a broader description of "excluding ungodly

lar to Ambrose, did not believe in the converting potential of the Lord's Supper.[164] Nonetheless something happened through the Lord's Supper. Ambrose believed that, through the promises of Christ that "the Bread conveys whole Christ, and the wine conveys whole Christ."[165]

In relationship to this, Ambrose's understanding of the sacraments might seem contradictory. However, if we grasp the exclusive nature of the sacrament as only for believers it was not inconsistent. Ambrose declares, "*[t[he Lords Supper* is the Sacrament of our continuance in Christ, of our confirmation in spiritual life, and the power of Grace already planted within us."[166] However, as he knew from his own experience, they "*do not always work for the present, but the efficacy may come afterwards.*"[167] On April 21, 1644, he writes, "[t]his day one received the Sacrament of the Lords Supper, but found not in it the comfortable presence of Christ as at other times; it troubled his soul, and then falling to examination and prayer, the Lord was pleased at last to give him a sweet visit, and spiritual refreshing."[168] Later on May 7, 1648 he combines sermon and sacrament and observes, "[t]his day one felt many sweet impressions of Gods Spirit in his heart, sometimes melting, and sometimes chearing his soul, in the publick Ordinances of the Word and Sacraments."[169] These last two experiences contain a number of important insights. Ambrose's initial entry reminds readers that God's presence can be missed even through the means of God's grace. Further, this illustrates how the affective and interpretive components of the Spiritual Movement Matrix interact to guide a person in experiencing God more fully. Ambrose originally missed God affectively. But when he noticed this absence he engaged in interpretive reflection and self-examination until he received the desired affective experience of God.

Ambrose's participation in sermon and sacrament also had the potential to transform his inner life. On some occasions his heart is melted

---

parishioners" from the Lord's Supper see Richardson, *Puritanism in North-West England*, 48–49.

164. For a historical summary on the debate of whether or not the Lord's Supper was a "converting ordinance" see Holifield, *Covenant Sealed*, esp. 110–25.

165. Ambrose, *Media* (1657), 175.

166. Ibid., 393–94.

167. Ibid., 426.

168. Ambrose, *Media* (1650), 111.

169. Ambrose, *Media* (1657), 187.

and his soul is cheered and renewed.[170] The following words are a fitting summary to his perception of God's presence through communion, "*Lord, I believe that through this golden pipe of the Lords Supper, I shall receive the golden oyl of Grace from Christ, now be it to me according to my faith: Lord, I believe, help thou my unbelief: O come down into my soul, and fill it full of the Lord Christ, of the body and blood of Christ.*"[171]

The previous testimony from Ambrose's diary combined the Lord's Supper with preaching. Preaching was one of the major roles of the Puritan minister.[172] Ambrose was appointed as one of the four King's Preachers in Lancashire in 1631.[173] Unfortunately he did not leave any records regarding this involvement. However, a number of entries do record his experience in the pulpit. On one occasion Ambrose required and received divine strength and encouragement to preach amid growing conflict. The 1640s were difficult for all people within England, but perhaps particularly for those ministers of the Church of England who became nonconformists. On November 15, 1642 he observes the beginning of this tension: "I was taken prisoner . . . Now began the troublesome times; and this year the Lord many a time assisted me in the Preaching of his Word boldly to the Enemy, both above ordinary, and far above my self."[174] Earlier that same year, on May 15 he provides the context for this growing problem: "I first Preached against all Superstitious vanities, and particularly against the Cross in Baptism: This was the first occasion of the peoples general discontent, ever since when some of them have been irreconcileable: Now begun the divisions of Church and State. Reformation proves an hard work. I received strong consolation afterwards out of Psal. 37. v. 32, 33,34. and out of Psal. 57. throughout."[175] With such an dramatic change of focus in his preaching it is not surprising that Ambrose frequently cites the importance of Scripture as a means of his encouragement and experience of God.

170. Ambrose, *Media* (1650), 84–85.

171. Ambrose, *Media* (1657), 422.

172. For a general introduction see Horton Davies, *Worship and Theology in England*, 2:133–77; Horton Davies, *Worship of English Puritans*, 182–203; and Hambrick-Stowe, *Practice of Piety*, 116–23.

173. Axon, "King's Preachers in Lancashire," 87.

174. Ambrose, *Media* (1650), 72.

175. Ibid., 71–72.

However, in light of the above accounts, we need to recognize that Ambrose understood the destructive nature of conflict and sought to avoid controversy. His irenic spirit desired unity and sought for the best, even with those whom he disagreed.[176] He cautions readers to avoid engaging in controversial points because they serve to "discompose our spirits, waste our zeale, our love, our delight in *Jesus*" and also work as an "interruption and diversion of our contemplations."[177] Later, in *War with Devils* he provides additional reasons for avoiding conflict: "[t]ake heed of spending, or rather mis-spending your precious time and thoughts in needless Controversies, in doubtfall disputations . . . None are more apt to fall into-errours, than they that busie themselves most with unnecessary, curious, circumstantial points."[178] Brauer maintains that tolerance is a fruit of mysticism and that Francis Rous was tolerant towards those who opposed him.[179] It is difficult to gauge if Ambrose's resistance to controversy was due to his personality, or his contemplative-mystical piety or a combination of both.

That did not mean that Ambrose compromised his values or equivocated on his theology. He preserved a number of entries that articulate the tension and turmoil related to the Civil War.[180] On October 15, 1647, he states, " Letter full of Invectives, without any Name subscribed, was in the night cast into my house: I guess the man, but desire to look up to God, to search my own heart, and to binde the Reproofs as a Crown unto my head; be the Author who he will, I much matter not, Psal. 27, 11, 12, 13, 14."[181] This statement amplified by the words of David speaks of waiting for the Lord rather than taking matters into your own hand. The next year, on January 24, 1648, Ambrose wrote, "I was troubled in minde to hear, and consider of the many oppositions I found in my Ministery;

176. Ambrose, *Communion with Angels*, Prolegomena [8–9], 199, 289. Additionally Ambrose provided a list of twenty-eight practices to encourage "Unity and Amity amongst Christians." *Media* (1657), 367–68. Dewey Wallace maintains one of the key qualities of a Puritan saint was an irenic spirit. "Image of Saintliness Puritan Hagiography," 36.

177. Ambrose, *Looking Unto Jesus*, 64, 75 (incorrectly numbered as 65), 702, 707, 1096, etc. on avoiding controversy.

178. Ambrose, *War with Devils*, 157.

179. Brauer, "Francis Rous, Puritan Mystic," 209, 233–36.

180. The literature on the Civil War is vast. The sources most directly related to Lancashire include Ormerod, *Military Proceedings in Lancashire*; Broxap, *Great Civil War in Lancashire*; and Woolrych, *Battles of English Civil War*, esp. 153–84.

181. Ambrose, *Media* (1650), 77.

at night I read a feeling passage in Rogers on Judges 13. thus:—*I have often thought it Gods mercy, to keep the knowledge of such discourage-ments from them that are to enter into the Ministery, lest they should be deterred wholly from it, till by experience they be armed against it.*"[182] It is significant to recognize his focus on God and the role of Scripture in providing comfort and strength amidst persecution.

Other diary entries record Ambrose's reflections upon the Civil War. During 1643 the town of Preston changed hands twice. In both examples Ambrose views this through the lens of God's providence.[183] Once more Preston occupied a prominent place where the decisive battle that concluded the second Civil War was fought. On August 22, 1648, days after that battle ended, Ambrose reports,

> I returned to *Preston*, and saw the wonderful works of God, and heard of many miracles of Mercies . . . That no place (whither the Enemy came) escaped Plundering, except *Preston*, which was prevented by the Armies coming in the very nick of time . . . Upon meditation of the whole business, I believed that the Lord heard *my prayers*: 1. In that my heart sympathized: 2. In that my heart was filled with joy in accomplishment: 3. In that the Mercy concerned me, in respect of my person, Family, Congregation, as much as any other.[184]

It is noteworthy that Ambrose offers thanksgiving to God for answered prayer only six weeks after he lamented during a public fast, "*[o] when will the Lord return answers!*"[185] Again he recognizes the presence of God through God's providence.

The second edition of *Media* included the new spiritual duty of the suffering of saints. Most likely Ambrose's struggles during the Civil War as a nonconformist contributed to this addition. This provides another illustration of simultaneity. The suffering that Ambrose experienced through the Civil War overlaps with the previous dimension of Intrapersonal Struggles of the Soul. Further, it will soon be clear that this also relates to the Geo-Environmental dimension since it originates in Preston. John Spurr summarizes this Puritan practice of 'sanctifying the suffering' with the "assumption that *every* event contains a divine

182. Ibid., 78.
183. Ibid., 72.
184. Ibid., 80; cf. 101.
185. Ibid., 79.

message, and the conviction that it is the saint's duty to root this out and learn from it."[186] Ambrose was among the two thousand nonconformist Puritan ministers who were ejected from their pulpits on St. Bartholomew's Day, August 24, 1662. Already in 1651 Ambrose had experienced great turmoil. During his annual retreat on May 31, he records, "I practised (as the Lord inabled) the Duty of *Saints Sufferings*; Into which condition as I was cast, so the Lord gave me to see my sin wherefore, and to bewaile it, and to pray for the contrary grace and Gods favour. The Lord was sweet to me in the preparations to, but especially in the improving of *Sufferings*. Now the Spirit left in my soul a sweet scent and favour behind it. Allelujah. *Amen, Amen.*"[187] There were abundant tensions within Preston and Lancashire to cause a sensitive, contemplative spirit to be pained. It is evident that Ambrose understood, even amid the struggles and tensions, that God's providence was present and at work in his life.

This diverse Structural dimension clearly reveals the depth and desires of Ambrose's heart. He acknowledged the difficulty of reforming people's behavior both through his preaching and restricting those who could receive the Lord's Supper. Yet even amid these troubling times Ambrose declared his renewed strength through Scripture and God's providence: "[o]n this day [Jun 24, 1643, I] understood . . . that some snares were laid for him, and by a special Providence at the same time he opened the Bible, and cast his eye on *Psa.* 37.v. 32, 33, 34 to his great incouragement and comfort."[188] God used both the heart melting humiliations of fasting and the afflictions that came through his enemies during the Civil War to strip his soul and first break and then elevate his heart to heaven. Rather than becoming bitter and attacking those who opposed him, Ambrose was cheered by the sweetness of God and lifted his heart in contemplative gratitude towards God. Significantly, through all of these experiences he discovered an inner freedom that encouraged him to continue his ministry.

186. Spurr, *English Puritanism*, 183; cf. Walsham, *Providence in Early Modern England* and Belden Lane, *Ravished By Beauty*, 134–58.

187. Ambrose, *Media* (1657), 89–90.

188. Ambrose, *Media* (1650), 110; cf. 102 for a similar event and how Ambrose received strength from Scripture.

GEO-ENVIRONMENTAL DIMENSION

Ambrose also experienced the presence of God through the Geo-Environmental dimension of life. This category is frequently ignored because many people are not conscious of how spiritual reality can be manifested in nature or through the uniqueness of place. However, Sheldrake contends, "it is appropriate to think of places as texts, layered with meaning."[189] Therefore, for Ambrose as well as for many others this is a dimension that must be considered. Gordon Rupp was an early advocate to detect a connection between environment and prayer when he asserted, "[o]ne fine day, somebody will write about the relation between spirituality and geography. There seems to be places in the world with an affinity for contemplative men, like the deserts of Libya or Goreme, or the northeastern corner of Scotland which in the seventeenth century produced Samuel Rutherford, Henry Scougal, Patrick Forbes."[190] While Rupp focuses predominantly upon the Puritans, he does not make any further connections between geography and piety. Belden Lane has explored the specific connections between the landscape of the New England Puritans and their piety, but no comparable study exists on their English counterparts.[191] Watkins comes closest in his brief treatment of five levels of how a person's inner experience may be associated with environment.[192]

Clearly every person is a product of his or her environment, and Ambrose was no exception. He was born in the Lancashire town of Ormskirk, where his father, Richard, was vicar. As a young man he went to Oxford. While Cambridge was the customary center for educating ministers who were sympathetic to Puritan theology, a strong connection existed between Lancashire and Brasenose College where Ambrose studied.[193] Roman Catholicism was strongly embedded in Lancashire, especially in the northwest, and in particular Garstang, where Ambrose spent a large part of his ministry.[194] In addition to entrenched recusancy,

189. Sheldrake, *Spaces for the Sacred*, 17; cf. Sheldrake, *Spirituality and Theology*, 165–95.

190. Rupp, "Devotion of Rapture," 115.

191. Belden Lane, *Landscapes of the Sacred*, 131–52; cf. Mark Peterson, "Practice of Piety in Contexts."

192. Watkins, *Puritan Experience*, 63–67.

193. Richardson, *Puritanism in North–West England*, 61–63.

194. Ibid., 153, 161–62.

other challenges that confronted a nonconformist minister included "folk-lore and superstitions [that] were so deeply ingrained that their overthrow was almost impossible; witchcraft was a feature of everyday life."[195] Furthermore, this region had strong Royalist ties, and George Fox and the Quakers were also present in Lancashire. Previously, the Sabbath habits of Lancashire prompted the infamous *Book of Sports*, written by Bishop Thomas Morton, who ordained Ambrose.[196] All of these divergent factors coalesced to create the unfriendly and challenging context in which Ambrose served as a minister.[197]

Using place as the locus for perceiving God opens a new horizon for observing how Ambrose experienced God. The most intimate place of any person is his or her home. Earlier, the ways that Ambrose experienced God in family worship were examined. However, there were other dangerous domestic events in which he also noticed God. On February 5, 1642, he records, "[t]he Lord wonderfully this day (as once before) delivered one from the danger of fire, which had begun in his house, but was discovered by the smoke."[198] Ambrose's marginalia of Isa 24:15 further amplifies his experience, "[w]herefore glorifie ye the Lord in the fires."

Radiating out in expanding concentric circles from Ambrose's house to the woods for his annual retreats reveals the interactive nature of how his retreats connect the Intrapersonal and Geo-Environmental dimensions of his life. One of his favorite places was Weddicre Woods, near Garstang. Presumably Ambrose first discovered this welcoming place when he served in Garstang as one of the King's Preachers. Clearly Weddicre Woods was unique for Ambrose. Belden Lane employs Yi-Fu Tuan's term *topophilia*, which describes those places that are attached with great meaning.[199] Similar to symbols, geographical places collect meaning and store memory over time. Sheldrake asserts that "[p]lace is

195. Ibid., 164; Thomas, *Religion and Decline of Magic*, 181n2, 182n2, 187–88, 188n1, 206, 214, 233, 266, 305, 451; and Paxman, "Lancashire Spiritual Culture and Magic," 223–43.

196. Richardson, "Puritanism and Ecclesiastical Authorities," 15; Tait, "Declaration of Sports for Lancashire," 561–68; and Love, *Fast and Thanksgiving Days*, 18–21.

197. Fishwick, *History of Garstang*, 166.

198. Ambrose, *Media* (1650), 104. Seaver addresses the reasons for frequent fires in homes. *Wallington's World*, 54–55; cf. Walsham, *Providence in Early Modern England*, 117–27, 137–38.

199. Belden Lane, *Landscapes of the Sacred*, 6.

space that has the capacity to be remembered and to evoke our attention and care."[200] Ambrose's diary reveals the *topophilia* of these annual retreat places: "[t]his day [May 19, 1647] I went to *Weddicre*, that in those sweet silent Woods (where I have found God many a time) I might fall upon the practice of some secret Duties, and enjoy sweet communion with my Lord and my God."[201]

There are at least two different ways in which to appropriate and appreciate nature. The first more elementary level provides a divergent setting that offers a contrast from the normal activities of a person's daily life.[202] Ambrose definitely understood Weddicre this way. He followed Jesus' example of entering the wilderness as a confirmation for his own practice. Wilderness is a term that is full of meaning in the study of Christian spirituality.[203] Ambrose recognized the inherent ambiguity that his retreats provided both a prolonged time to focus on God as well as increased pressures of Satan's temptation. Withdrawal is a necessity for entering a wilderness setting, and "one of the fundamental features of Christian monasticism is that it demands withdrawal."[204] Both the previous reference as well as the May 20, 1646, entry demonstrate that awareness: "I came to *Weddicre*, which I did upon mature resolution, every year about that pleasant Spring time (if the Lord pleased) to retire my self, and in some solitary and silent place to practice especially the secret Duties of a Christian."[205] The terms retire, solitary, and silent places all reveal that there was something very unique about these woods. It provided an unhurried atmosphere in which Ambrose could devote himself more fully to cultivating his relationship with the Triune God.

Second, Weddicre was more than just a relaxing landscape or distraction for Ambrose. On May 17, 1648, he speaks of the specific influence that nature had on his experience of God: "I went into the solitary Woods, to practice the secret Duties of a Christian: No sooner stepped

200. Sheldrake, *Spaces for the Sacred*, 154.

201. Ambrose, *Media* (1650), 76. Ambrose's retreat experiences are an example of Watkins' third level. *Puritan Experience*, 64.

202. This reflects Watkins' second level. *Puritan Experience*, 64.

203. Louth, *Wilderness of God*; cf. 131 where Louth asserts a dense forest served the same purpose as the desert for early Christians. For a Puritan discussion on the wilderness see Hambrick-Stowe, *Practice of Piety*, 243–77.

204. Sheldrake, *Spaces for the Sacred*, 91.

205. Ambrose, *Media* (1650), 74.

in, but the green Trees and Herbs, and the sweet singing of Birds, stirred up my soul to praise God."[206] This nicely reinforces Sheldrake's principle of the spiritual nature of place: "landscapes frequently have a capacity to carry us beyond ourselves and beyond the immediate. They are often our first intimations of the sacred."[207] Apparently not only the specific spiritual duties but also the distinctive location provided a space in which to experience God. Later in *War with Devils* Ambrose would reinforce this reality: "Much of my time I have spent in eminently famous and publike places, but at last weary of those hurries, jars, envies, pride, discord, and policies of men in streets and towns, I resolved to spend the remainder of my time, for the most part, in the silent gardens, fields and woods; there sometimes I was taken with the various tunes of melodious birds, and occasionally they have lifted up my heart in spiritual songs, and Psalms, and Hymns."[208] Significantly, Ambrose recognizes that nature provided far more than just a location for his retreat; it also served to directly inspire his experience of God. Not surprisingly, Halley comments that for Ambrose the woods were "his best school of theology."[209] Further, Ambrose also spent time at Houghton Towers as a guest of Lady Margaret Houghton, one of his benefactors. While there are no diary entries that record his retreats at this place he does mention his visits there during his funeral sermon for Lady Margaret.[210] Houghton Towers also became a meeting place for nonconformist ministers both before and after the Ejection of 1662.[211]

While Weddicre Woods and presumably the Darwen River at Houghton Towers had greatly enriched Ambrose's life, there were other significant places as well. William Bagshaw records the conversation he had with Ambrose in Manchester regarding his departure from his first church at Casteleton: "[a]t that time his love to *Castleton* (upon mention of it) revived, Tears shot into his Eyes, and from his Mouth fell this ingenuous Acknowledgement: It was my Sin (and is my Sorrow) that I left that place when the Lord was blessing my Ministry in it."[212] In

---

206. Ibid., 79. This reflects Watkins' third level. *Puritan Experience*, 64.

207. Sheldrake, *Spirituality and Theology*, 168.

208. Ambrose, *War with Devils*, 171.

209. Halley, *Lancashire: Puritanism and Nonconformity*, 2:200.

210. Ambrose, *Redeeming the Time*, 27.

211. Miller, *Hoghton Tower*, 123, 180.

212. Bagshaw, *De Spritualabus Pecci*, 23. It is likely that this meeting took place on

retrospect, Ambrose mourned the loss of his first congregation. It appears his premature departure caused him to limit or at least minimize his experience of God. Bagshaw then adds, "[m]ay this be a fair warning to others, that they be not hasty in removing from their People."[213] This reveals the potential vital relationship that can exist between ministers and the churches they serve.

Expanding with a greater concentric circle from Ambrose's house, yet still within Lancashire, is the development of Presbyterianism in 1646. Ambrose became part of this movement, which next to London had the best-developed form of Presbyterianism[214] though he was already active in serving on a committee to distribute relief due to pestilence and poverty. He also served as moderator of many of the Presbyterian provincial assemblies that were held in Preston.[215] There are no extant remarks from Ambrose's diary, but they do reinforce the earlier impression that he was a contemplative in action.

London provides the most distant region away from Lancashire. Ambrose was summoned there in May 1649, because he signed the document against the Agreement of the People. He records his final diary entry on May 28, 1649, because he delivered this book to the printers: "[u]pon serious consideration of the manifold miscarriages both in church and state, which I observed since my coming to *London*, I had some resolutions to spend the remainder of my uncertain days in a more retired and private way."[216] The far ranging importance of this event includes his introduction to Lady Mary Vere. Lady Mary and her husband, Horace, were well known supporters of Puritan causes.[217] While apparently this was the only occasion that they met, Lady Mary provided for the financial needs of Ambrose and he, in turn, dedicated all three editions of *Media* to her.[218] Undoubtedly the most significant outcome from

---

July 16, 1658, when Bagshaw preached before the Presbyterian ministers in Manchester. Brentnall, *Apostle of the Peak*, 31.

213. Ibid.

214. For Presbyterianism in Lancashire see Smithen, *Lancashire Presbyterianism* and Shaw, *Minutes Manchester Presbyterian Classis*.

215. Nightingale, *Isaac Ambrose, Religious Mystic*, 17–18, and Shaw, *Minutes Manchester Presbyterian Classis*, 24:406.

216. Ambrose, *Media* (1650), 85.

217. For a summary of Lady Vere's patronage of Puritan minister see Eales, "An Ancient Mother."

218. Ambrose, *Media* (1650, 1652, 1657), Epistle Dedication.

his London visit was his decision to withdraw and seek greater solitude from the commotion of the turbulence of Preston. This single transformative event eventually led to his relocation to Garstang. There were a number of factors motivating Ambrose: on the one hand, was the deep desire and conviction that he felt drawn to a place of greater solitude and silence so that he might spend more time with God in contemplation and less time embroiled in conflict and controversies. But, on the other hand, Ambrose realizes that this move includes a high price and will create a greater geographical distance between himself and his friends; therefore he declares, "I desire therefore to retire, and to go back again from a publick to a more private place, even from *Preston* to *Garstange*. And now my dear Brethren farewell."[219]

The petition from Garstang requesting Ambrose is quite revealing of their love and admiration for him, "hauving longe desired Mr. Ambrose to bee our Minister, diuers both of them and us being able to call him our spirituall father, of whose godly liffe and orthodoxt doctrine our whole Countie hath a singular and eminent esteeme, a truth (we believe) not unknown to many of yr selues."[220] As Ambrose was preparing to leave Preston, he discovered that they were deeply saddened to lose him as their minister. In response to their affection, Ambrose declares, "[c]ould you have wept more if you had brought me to my grave? Such chaines were these tears and prayers that (notwithstanding my resolutions), [you have expressed for me]."[221]

It is likely that there were other factors that weighed in Ambrose's decision to transfer to Garstang. Previously he had maintained that "there is work enough for foure or five priests who have their constant residence in that parish (Preston), what work may you imagine for one Gospel Minister."[222] His request for an assistant to help in the pastoral responsibilities was declined, apparently creating a greater sense of exhaustion. Ambrose candidly confesses, "I shall walk the silent fields and woods and hear more frequently the various tunes of melodious birds and keep consort with them, who without jarres are ever in their kind praising God."[223] This affords a fascinating admission that Ambrose

219. Ambrose, *Looking Unto Jesus*, 256.
220. Fishwick, *History of Garstang*, 168.
221. Ambrose, *Looking Unto Jesus*, 52.
222. Ibid., 1012–13.
223. Ibid., 256.

longs to join the birds in their continual praise of God. Further, it is interesting to speculate why he returned to Preston once he was ejected in 1662. Perhaps the attraction was Houghton Tower, and the opportunity to renew old friendships, and maybe even receive a continuation of support from the Houghton's.

Geopiety is a term that "covers a broad range of emotional bonds between man and his terrestrial home."[224] Ambrose developed a deep affinity for those places he withdrew to for his annual retreats. His records indicate that not only did he meditate "in" nature but also "on" it, finding the birds to be his faithful companions in praising God. Clearly his growing hunger for contemplative experiences sought a different place without all of the distractions and turmoil of his stressful context in Preston. Ambrose had tasted enough of the presence of God in Weddicre Woods and the Darwen River behind Houghton Tower to recognize that these "thin places" were essential for his parched soul. While his horizons were restricted by "hurries and discord," Ambrose still exercised his ministry with compassion to those in need and dedication to the Presbyterian cause. His enforced visit to London in 1649 was instrumental in clarifying this need for greater solitude and silence. This decision to seek a more tranquil place is a powerful confirmation of the depth of his contemplative hunger for God. Therefore, whether Ambrose was alone with God in retreats or actively involved with God and other people, he experienced ravishing joy and spiritual refreshment across the various dimensions of his life. This prepares the way for our next chapter that will examine more fully the devotional disciplines of meditation and contemplation that Isaac Ambrose practiced and taught to others.

224. Tuan, "Geopiety: Attachment to Place," 12.

Chapter Four

Isaac Ambrose's Spiritual Practices and Contemplative Experiences

It is the Lords pleasure that we should dayly come to him . . .
he would have us to be still arising, ascending, and mounting up in
divine contemplations to his Majesty. And is it not our duty,
and the Saints disposition to be thus? . . . if Christ be in heaven,
where should we be but in heaven with him? *for where your
treasure is, there will be your heart also.* Oh that every morning,
and every evening, at least, our hearts would arise, ascend,
and go to Christ in the heavens.

—Isaac Ambrose[1]

We are now ready to examine more fully Ambrose's understanding of the nature and experience of contemplation. This chapter will guide that exploration by considering the distinction between meditation and contemplation and then analyze Ambrose's teaching on meditation. An investigation into the historical sources and roots of Ambrose's meditative and contemplative practices will reveal his indebtedness to Bernard of Clairvaux and other medieval spiritual writers. The largest section of this chapter will survey Ambrose's use of contemplation in his

1. Ambrose, *Looking Unto Jesus*, 1152.

writings as well as review the benefits and effects of contemplation, as he understood them.

DISTINCTION BETWEEN MEDITATION AND CONTEMPLATION

Meditation was one of the primary spiritual practices of seventeenth-century Puritans.[2] However, some were more specific and drew a distinction between meditation and contemplation. John Downame declares, "in nature there is a small difference between Meditation and Contemplation, yet as the Schooles define it, there is some in degree; Meditation being an exercise of a lower and meaner nature, within the reach of all Christians which will put out their hand unto it; Contemplation more highly and heavenly, fit only for such as by long exercise have attained to much perfection."[3] Downame's reference to the Schooles reflects the traditional medieval understanding and not that of Protestantism. Thomas White's contrast written over thirty years later is more helpful. White maintained, "[c]ontemplation is more like the beatificall Vision which they have of God in Heaven, like the Angels beholding of the face of God; Meditation is like the kindling of fire, and Contemplation more like the flaming of it when fully kindled: The one is like the Spouses seeking of Christ, and the other like the Spouses enjoying of Christ."[4] Significantly, both Downame and White appear among the list of experimental writers that Ambrose endorses.[5] Therefore, Ambrose was likely familiar with the distinctions between these two practices.

While some were careful to distinguish between meditation and contemplation, there was also a blurring of linguistic lines in both the Roman Catholic and Puritan writings. Richard Baxter illustrates the

---

2. Horton Davies has produced the most expansive study on this topic, *Worship and Theology in England*; cf. Beeke, "Puritan Practice of Meditation"; Kaufmann, *Pilgrim's Progress and Traditions in Puritan Meditation*; Hambrick-Stowe, *Practice of Piety*, 161–68; Lewalski, *Protestant Poetics*, 147–68; Green, Print and Protestantism, 277–88; and Chan, "Puritan Meditative Tradition."

3. Downame, *Guide to Godlynesse*, 534.

4. White, *Method of Divine Meditation*, 4–5. Thomas Manton makes a similar distinction declaring, "[c]ontemplation is the fruit and perfection of meditation . . . In short, contemplation is a ravishing sight without discourse, the work of reason not discoursing, but raised and ecstasied into the highest way of apprehension." *Sermons Upon Genesis 24:63*, 293.

5. Ambrose, *Media* (1657), To the Reader, [7].

Puritan perspective asserting, "[t]he general title that I give this duty is meditation; not as it is precisely distinguished from thought, consideration, and contemplation; but as it is taken in the larger and usual sense for thinking on things spiritual, and so comprehending consideration and contemplation."[6] Ignatius of Loyola is representative of the Roman Catholic conflation of these terms.[7] Bernard could also use this language in a confusing manner. Since these words are occasionally interchanged and further because meditation is often the means towards which a person experiences God in a contemplative manner, it is important to understand Ambrose's practice of meditation.

ISAAC AMBROSE'S TEACHING ON MEDITATION

Ambrose constructs the foundation for his teaching on meditation by defining it: "[m]editation *is a stedfast bending of the mind to some spiritual matter, discoursing of it with our selves, till we bring the same to some profitable issue*."[8] This closely parallels the description of Bishop Joseph Hall in his classic, *The Arte of Divine Meditation*: "[m]editation is nothing else but a bending of the mind upon some spirituall object, through divers formes of discourse, untill our thoughts come to an issue."[9] Clearly these definitions of meditation reveal Ambrose's awareness of Hall's approach and while they emphasize the mind that was hardly the full picture. Ambrose elsewhere defines meditation "as the bellows of the soul, that doth kindle and inflame holy affections."[10] Downame reiterates this intensity of meditation asserting, "[i]t inflameth our love towards God and all spirituall and heavenly things."[11] More expansively, for meditation to accomplish its maximum good, Edmund Calamy taught that it must enter through three doors: the "*door of the understanding*," the "*door of thy heart and of thy affections*," and the "*door of thy conversations*" for

6. Baxter, *Saints' Everlasting Rest*, 296.

7. Ganss, *Ignatius of Loyola: Spiritual Exercises*, 136, 402; Martz, *Poetry of Meditation* 16–20; Keith Egan "Contemplation," 211–12; cf. 432; cf. Shannon, "Contemplation, Contemplative Prayer," 209; and McGinn, *Growth of Mysticism*, 386.

8. Ambrose, *Media* (1657), 216.

9. Joseph Hall, *Arte of Divine Meditation*, 7.

10. Ambrose, *Media* (1657), 392.

11. Downame, *Guide to Godlynesse*, 544. Thomas Hooker likewise declares, "[s]o meditation is like fire, the heart is like a vessell, the heart is made for God, and it may be made a vessell of grace here, and of glory hereafter." *Soules Preparation for Christ*, 113.

proper Christian living.[12] Further, Ambrose employs the same analogy of eating that was common among medieval monks proclaiming a person should "ruminate, and chew the cud."[13] Calamy expands the same language, declaring, "*a meditating Christian is one that chews the cud*" and that meditation "is a *digesting* of all the things of God."[14] While this nicely parallels the imagery of Guigo II, who in the twelfth century asserted, "meditation chews it [the food] and breaks it up," Calamy cites specifically Lev 11:3 on clean and unclean beasts as the inspiration for his statement.[15]

Ambrose follows the traditional teaching that differentiates between the two forms of meditation: "*[s]udden, Occasional, or Extemporal*" or "*[d]eliberate, set, or solemn*."[16] Sudden meditations are those that a person would engage during the course of a day as God brings various events, people, or things before the senses. For example, a person walking home might notice the beauty of a sunset and extemporaneously express gratitude to God. Deliberate meditations are intentional periods in which the person selects a topic, place, and method to explore and ponder something. Ambrose observes a distinction between two types of deliberate meditations, "for it is either conversant about matters of knowledge, for the finding out of some hidden truth, or about matters of affections, *for the enkindling of our love unto God*, or if you will, *for the acting of all the powers of our soul on spiritual object*. The former of these two we leave to the Schooles and Prophets, the latter we shall search after."[17] Similar to many of his fellow Puritans, Ambrose affirms Isaac's practice from Gen 24:63 of withdrawing to the fields in the evening as guidance for the best time, place, and attitude to practice meditation.[18]

Next, Ambrose examines the two types of meditation in greater detail. Following the typical Puritan pattern, occasional or sudden medita-

12. Calamy, *Art of Divine Meditation*, 28.

13. Ambrose, *Looking Unto Jesus*, 469.

14. Calamy, *Art of Divine Meditation*, 24, 114; cf. Downame, *Guide to Godlynesse*, 546.

15. Guigo II, *Ladder of Monks*, 69; cf. 80 and Calamy, *Art of Divine Meditation*, 24.

16. Ambrose, *Media* (1657), 216.

17. Ibid., 216–17.

18. Ibid., 217–19. Thomas Manton preached ten sermons on meditation based on this text. *Sermons Genesis xxiv.63*," 263–348; cf. Joseph Hall, *Arte of Divine Meditation*, 49, 57, 62; Downame, *Guide to Godlynesse*, 541; White, *Method of Divine Meditation*, 18; Calamy, *Art of Divine Meditation*, 1, 76; and Ranew, *Solitude Improved*, 343.

tions are taken up first and always dealt with more succinctly. Ambrose reminds his reader that since the content for this type of meditation comes from daily life and a person's awareness of God's providence the possibilities are endless. To illustrate, he describes a person first awaking at dawn, the sight of the morning sky, noticing the grass, flowers, or garden, and any or all events of the day. This is followed by a brief summary of how the various occupations of magistrate, minister, tradesman, farmer, and soldier can practice occasional meditation during their daily work.[19] Significantly, this confirms the Puritan understanding that meditation was the work of all God's people and not reserved for ministers alone. Hall pointedly criticizes monks who hide in their cloisters and are confined to their cells, and while they practice contemplation they eschew the active life.[20] Likewise Calamy asserts that meditation is required of young men, kings and nobles, soldiers, learned men, and women.[21] An important component of sudden meditation is ejaculatory or arrow prayers. In *Redeeming the Time*, Ambrose contends that while God sometimes calls a person "extraordinarily to such spiritual duties all day long" individuals are not to neglect their "particular calling, with which I may either mingle some actings of grace, or ejaculatory duties, as suddenly to look up to heaven, and to behold the face of God, to whom I am to approve my self in my particular calling."[22] This clearly confirms the Puritan desire to balance contemplation and action.

Ambrose then turns his attention to deliberate meditations. Once again his indebtedness to Bishop Hall is evident. Every meditation is comprised of three parts: the entrance which serves to prepare the person's heart, the proceedings which are the major portion to guide the person in processing the subject matter, and the conclusion that contains a thanksgiving and suggested singing a psalm so that the "soul close up it self with much sweetness and Spiritual contentment."[23] Significantly, Ambrose quotes Bernard as he introduces the proceedings

19. Ibid., 219–21; cf. Ambrose, *Redeeming the Time*, 17–19.

20. Joseph Hall, *Arte of Divine Meditation*, 4. White also stresses that meditation is not just for ministers. *Method of Divine Meditation*, 11.

21. Calamy, *Art of Divine Meditation*, 4–5.

22. Ambrose, *Redeeming the Time*, 19; cf. Ambrose, *Ultima* in *Prima, Media & Ultima* (1654), 40. For a summary of Cotton Mather's practice of ejaculatory prayer see Mather, *Diary of Cotton Mather*, 1:81–84. On the practice and cautions for using ejaculatory meditation see Ranew, *Solitude Improved*, 204–9, 344–47.

23. Ambrose, *Media* (1657), 222–23. This reference appears only in the 1657 edition.

section, "*[c]ontemplationis accessus duo sunt, unus in intellectu, alter in affectu, unus in lumine, alter in fevore.*" Meaning "holy contemplation has two forms of ecstasy, one in the intellect, the other in the will; one of enlightenment, the other of fervor." Ambrose summarizes this insight in declaring, "[t]he proceedings of our Meditation are in this Method. 1. To begin in the understanding, 2. To end in the affections."[24] The understanding section of proceeding includes seven steps of description, distribution, causes, effects, opposites, comparatives, and testimonies.[25] The second portion on the affections moves a person through six steps of relish, complaint, wish, confession, petition, and confidence to stir up the proper response.[26] Ambrose then provides three very detailed examples of meditations: the first of the soul's love to Christ, the second of the eternity of hell, and the third of the eternity of heaven.[27]

The purpose of these meditations is to deepen the understanding and stir up the affections so a person might experience Jesus more fully. A major component of this process is the soliloquy which Baxter defines as "a preaching to one's self."[28] Occasionally in the understanding and abundantly in the affection sections, Ambrose liberally sprinkles the phrase "[o] my soul" as a way of directing and personalizing these meditations. Significantly, his three sample meditations are replete with an abundance of Scripture, frequent reminders of God's assurance and mercy regardless of the theme, including even that of hell, but little indication of the content or style of Ignatian sensory imagination, though the passages are richly described.[29] Further, each one reflects a contemplative attitude of approaching the subject with a loving and grateful stance towards God. Specifically the meditation on the eternity of hell reminded listeners that hell was a place of loss of everything and that humanity has been created for God and must recognize the seriousness

24. Ibid., 222. The Bernard citation is *SCC* 49.4.

25. While Ambrose lists nine steps in his initial instructions, all three samples provided have only seven steps. Compare Ambrose, *Media* (1657), 222 with 223–28. Huntley appropriately notes, "even Hall in his own practice rarely followed the 'steps' he set down in *Art of Divine Meditation*." *Bishop Joseph Hall*, 7.

26. Ambrose, *Media* (1657), 223.

27. Ibid., 223–72.

28. Baxter, *Saints Everlasting Rest*, 316; cf. Sibbes, *Soul's Conflict*, 199 and Knott, *Sword of the Spirit*, 58, 71–72.

29. A more detailed comparison of the Ignatian and Puritan use of imagination will be explored later in this chapter.

of sin so that this awareness creates a "pang of love" to Jesus Christ.[30] Again Ambrose mentions Bernard, *"let us go down to hell whiles we are alive, that we may not go down to hell when we are dead."*[31] He concludes this meditation with grateful delight affirming: "[m]ethinks after all my tremblings in this meditation of *the eternity of hell*, I can now with an holy comfort, and humble triumph think upon death, judgment, hell, and those endless torments, and why? If I am but in Christ, and am guided by the Spirit of grace, and sanctification; there is no condemnation can seaze on me."[32] Clearly the reason for this confident peace is that he is in Christ, another reminder of the importance of mystical union with Christ.

As might be expected, the meditations on the love to Christ and eternity of heaven overflow with an abundance of bridal language and mystical themes. Terms such as ravishment, spiritual fire, inflamed and transported by love, and contemplation of God are common. In the first meditation Ambrose's language soars as he first confesses his deep desire for Jesus: "[o] my bleeding heart and broken spirit doth languish in a thirsty *love*, panting and gasping after thee," and then he pleads more intensely *"[k]iss me with the kisses of thy mouth, for thy love is better than wine*. O let me bathe my soul in the delicious intimacies of a spiritual communion with thee my God." His final desire is that this longing will be translated into an ineffable resting *"love of complacency"* with his "dearest Husband."[33] In the meditation on heaven Ambrose reminds us, "the Saints now dwell upon the contemplation of him [God], they have time enough to take a full view of him, even *Eternity it self.*" Central to this contemplation is the richness of joy, for the saints "enjoy God, so they enjoy themselves in God."[34] Therefore, Ambrose seeks a "spiritual eye" so that he might perceive "the visions of God, and the fruitions of God" so that this might culminate in a "stronger union betwixt God and my soul . . . yea let me enjoy God in my self, and my self in God."[35] He confesses the difficulty of restraining his desire requesting, "[n]ow begin

30. Ambrose, *Media* (1657), 249.

31. Ibid., 251; cf. Calamy, *Art of Divine Meditation*, 126.

32. Ibid., 253.

33. Ibid., 235.

34. Ibid., 260.

35. Ibid., 268–69.

that *Hallelujah* on earth."[36] Strikingly, these last two examples reveal how meditation within the context of spiritual marriage can lead to contemplative experiences of love, intimacy, and ravishing enjoyment of God.

HISTORICAL ROOTS OF AMBROSE'S UNDERSTANDING OF MEDITATION

After reading a few Puritan manuals on meditation, one soon discovers a certain commonality to them. Ambrose's dependence upon Bishop Hall's *Arte of Divine Meditation* has been previously mentioned. However, he was hardly the only one. Edward Reynolds declares no one has written on meditation in his day except our *"Christian Seneca, the learned and Reverend Bishop Hall."*[37] Ambrose employs the same appellation, calling Hall "our Divine *Seneca.*"[38] According to Knott, Hall influenced Baxter, Downame, Rogers, Ambrose, and Calamy.[39] However, none of these writers borrowed from Hall without making their own revisions. Ambrose simplified Hall's approach by reducing his ten steps to seven in the understanding section and combining two steps into six for stirring up the affections. Calamy simplified Hall's complex method even further.[40] However, it must be recognized that most of these writers, including Ambrose, understood that they were offering flexible guidelines and not rigid rules to be followed.[41] Further, Kaufmann's research has distilled "two divergent traditions in Puritan meditation."[42] The first originated with Hall and his major disciples, Ambrose and Calamy. Kaufmann characterized this stream as strongly logical and eschewing the use of imagination and the senses.[43] The second was the heavenly meditation stream, best represented by Sibbes and Baxter that recovered

36. Ibid., 272.

37. Watson, *Saints Delight*, To the Reader, [6].

38. Ambrose, *Communion with Angels*, 320; cf. Downame, *Guide to Godlynesse*, 637, who refers to him as the *"divine English Seneca."*

39. Knott, *Sword of the Spirit*, 68–70; cf. Kaufmann, *Pilgrim's Progress in Puritan Meditation*, 121. Thomas White also borrowed from Joseph Hall but Nathanael Ranew appears to have been one of the few who did not.

40. Kaufmann, *Pilgrim's Progress in Puritan Meditation*, 132.

41. Ambrose, *Media* (1657), To the Reader, [8, 6–7]; Joseph Hall, *Arte of Divine Meditation*, 90, 116; and Calamy, *Art of Divine Meditation*, 177.

42. Kaufmann, *Pilgrim's Progress in Puritan Meditation*, 118–50.

43. Ibid., 124.

the use of imagination ignored by Hall.[44] This distinction appears overly simplistic, and I concur with the critique of Knott, Beeke, and Lewalski.[45] Shortly it will be evident that Ambrose had a strong sense of imagination and meditation on heaven. Additionally, Baxter was often considered to be a strong proponent of reason.[46] Further, one scholar cites both Hall and Baxter as examples of heavenly meditation.[47] Baxter's name is also closely associated with the groundbreaking research of Louis Martz who declared *The Saints' Everlasting Rest* was "the first Puritan treatise on the art of methodical meditation to appear in England."[48] Clearly this paragraph challenges the accuracy of Martz's assessment.[49] Martz brought a predominant Medieval and Roman Catholic reading to the devotional literature of seventeenth-century England; while he was helpful in recognizing this influence, the reality is that both Roman Catholic and Protestant contributions existed side-by-side within English Puritanism.

However, this prompts the larger question of who influenced Hall in developing his popular approach. He indicates his inspiration was drawn from an unknown monk who wrote 112 years before him.[50] Scholars have identified him as John Mombaer, author of the *Rosetum exercitiorum spiritualium et sacrarum meditationum*, who in turn was influenced by Johan Wessel Gansfort. Hall was not shy about his distaste for Jesuit spirituality; therefore, attempts to find Ignatian influence are unlikely to yield any results.[51] However, the irony of history is that both Gansfort and Mombaer, members of the Brethren of the Common Life, not only inspired Hall but through Garcia de Cisneros provided significant inspiration for Ignatius as well.[52] Therefore, both Hall and the Puritan method of meditation, and Ignatius and the Roman

44. Ibid., 135–36.

45. Knott, *Sword of the Spirit*, 68; Beeke, "Puritan Practice of Meditation," 77; and Lewalski, *Protestant Poetics*, 150.

46. Baxter, *Saints' Everlasting Rest*, 306; cf. Knott, *Sword of the Spirit*, 76–77

47. Chan, *Spiritual Theology*, 99.

48. Martz, *Poetry of Meditation*, 154.

49. For a critique of Martz see Wakefield, *Puritan Devotion*, 5, 87; Hambrick-Stowe, *Practice of Piety*, viii–ix, 38; and Knott, *Sword of the Spirit*, 64–65.

50. Joseph Hall, *Arte of Divine Meditation*, Epistle Dedication, [4].

51. Booty, "Joseph Hall, Arte Divine Meditation," 203.

52. Melloni, *Exercises of St. Ignatius*, esp. 1–2, 22; McGuire, *Companion to Jean Gerson*, 375–82; and Martz, *Poetry of Meditation*, 5, 331. On Cisneros see Pourrat, *Christian Spirituality*, 3:18–22.

Catholic method, share a common root. In addition, Hall made trips to Belgium, France, and the Netherlands and would have been exposed to other Continental mystical writers. One person in particular that he cites frequently in *The Arte of Divine Meditation* is Jean Gerson,[53] who was influential in the development of *devotio moderna*.[54] This awareness has prompted a recent biographer of Hall to assert that he "served to introduce continental contemplative methods to an English protestant readership."[55] Therefore, Lovelace's assessment of the Puritans is incorrect: "[o]f mystical writers (save for Bernard and Augustine) there is no mention."[56]

Closely related is the question of continuities and discontinuities between the Roman Catholic and Puritan approaches to meditation.[57] This is a significant question, as it will guide my reading of Ambrose more accurately. A certain amount of overlap would be expected, since at least initially Puritans were dependent upon Roman Catholic sources.[58] One of the more vivid demonstrations of this is Edmund Bunny's bowdlerization of Jesuit Robert Parsons' *First Book of Christian Exercise* (1582). However, this example also illustrates that Puritan writers never borrowed Roman Catholic works wholesale.[59] Protestant theological fine-tuning was always necessary to remove offensive papist passages to Protestant theology. In fact, Bunny's changes, while somewhat restrained, demonstrated his ignorance of Parson's more nuanced Roman Catholic theology.[60] This incensed Parsons to such a degree that he devoted twenty-four pages in a later volume refuting them.[61] Further,

---

53. Joseph Hall, *Arte of Divine Meditation*, 25–26, 46, 62, 85; cf. Stoeffler, *Rise of Evangelical Pietism*, 84. Gerson is also a favorite of Baxter, *Saints' Everlasting Rest*, 263, 280, 282, 287, 296, 302, 304, 311.

54. McGuire, *Companion to Jean Gerson*, 371–75.

55. McCabe, "Joseph Hall." *ODNB*, 24:635.

56. Lovelace, "Anatomy Puritan Piety," 296.

57. While Puritans and Anglicans shared a common distaste for Roman Catholics there were numerous discontinuities between these two branches of Protestants in their practice of meditation. See McGee, "Conversion and Imitation of Christ."

58. For an opposing view minimizing the Roman Catholic influence on Puritan piety see Campbell, *Religion of the Heart*, 42–44; cf. 68 for greater receptivity to this.

59. Bozeman, *Precisianist Strain*, 76. See de Reuver, *Sweet Communion*, for Willem Teellinck's revision of à Kempis' *Imitation of Christ* to fit Reformed sensibilities (116n40).

60. Houliston, "Edmund Bunny's Theft of *Book of Resolution*," compare 169 with 163–64, 173.

61. Parsons, *Christian Directory*, Preface [4–27]. Parsons previously declared that

while both groups might employ similar components, they often approach them from very different perspectives. Therefore, the respective approaches to meditation can be summarized around nine significant areas.[62] Generalizations are always prone to distortion, and there was always some blurring of boundaries both within and between these two methods. Nonetheless, first the role of Scripture was essential in shaping Puritan meditation, though less influential for Roman Catholics. However, the influence of *devotio moderna* certainly inspired the Roman Catholic recovery of Scripture. Second, Roman Catholics usually placed a greater overall emphasis upon the passion of Jesus, lingering on his crucifixion. However, Puritan sacramental meditations tended to recover, at least in part, some of this from a Protestant perspective. Next, both groups were conscious of Ignatian imagination, but within the native soil of Roman Catholicism there tended to be a greater desire to stimulate the imagination through the senses to recreate vivid details of the Gospel events. Puritans did not stir up the senses to the same degree as Ignatius, but their meditation on heaven more strongly encouraged the use of imagination.[63] Fourth, Roman Catholics focused on the Christian year through the observances of feasts and fasts while the Puritans measured time according to the weekly cycle of Sundays. Fifth, Puritans emphasized meditation on creation, hell, and heaven. In particular, hell was meditated upon to deepen the person's love for God and not intimidation. Neither creation nor heaven occupied the same prominence for Roman Catholics as they did for Puritans, but the focus on hell was directly related to the need for penance. Closely related is the sixth theme of assurance. While Puritan manuals exuded optimism and reassurance, Roman Catholic meditations warned of the need for continual spiritual struggle and of eternal damnation, with little hope of assurance. Seventh, Roman Catholics were encouraged to recreate

Bunny "greatly perverted and corrupted" his work. *Christian Directory*, To the Reader [7]; cf. Preface [2]. For a helpful introduction to Bunny's pirating of Parsons' work see Houliston, "Edmund Bunny's Theft of *Book of Resolution*."

62. This summary composite is from the following sources plus my reading of the primary sources: Horton Davies, *Worship and Theology in England*, 2:68–132; Knott, *Sword of the Spirit*, 79–81; Lewalski, *Protestant Poetics*, 148–67; Kaufmann, *Pilgrim's Progress in Puritan Meditation*, 125–28, 206–7, 215; Lovelace, *American Pietism of Cotton Mather*, 114–23; Roston, "Donne and Meditative Tradition"; and Williams, "Puritan Enjoyment of God," 303–4, 313–14.

63. See Benedict, *Christ's Churches Purely Reformed*, 530 and Cornick, *Letting God Be God*, 106.

the actual experience, in true Ignatian form, and to savor and enjoy it. Conversely, Puritans were usually taught to explore and apply the insights to their own lives and to discover the value of that experience. Eighth, given the Puritans' later origin and focus on the priesthood of all believers, all people were expected to participate in spiritual disciplines. In practice, it was not until the seventeenth century that the majority of lay Catholics gained regular access to the same means for entering into these disciplines. Finally, in Puritanism the structure and method of the sermon was the foundation for meditation.[64] That served to both democratize meditation and to model it weekly in the sermons of public worship. This was normally absent in Roman Catholicism due to the irregularity of preaching and the lack of making this connection between sermon and meditation. However, Granada is an exception asserting, "there is no difference betweene a Sermon and Consideration."[65] Therefore, the Puritan approach to meditation is both derivative and yet distinctive in certain ways.

HISTORICAL ROOTS OF CONTEMPLATION IN THE WRITINGS OF ISAAC AMBROSE

Ambrose's frequent practice of quoting patristic, medieval, and contemporary sources has been evident throughout this book. This invites the question who may have inspired him. However, before proceeding, Gilson, writing from within the context of Bernardine research, declares the challenging nature of this task: "*[t]he influence of one work on another is not to be proved from the fact that they contain formulas that are literally similar, but of different meaning*."[66] Anthony Lane's meticulous research on Calvin's use of the church fathers provides additional cautions.[67] Nonetheless, it is apparent that Ambrose willingly draws upon Western Catholic sources. Perhaps his more conciliatory attitude that shunned controversy also created a greater receptivity to medieval writings. Two glimpses of this are evident in comparing the first and second editions of *Ultima*. In 1640 Ambrose writes, "as a Pope hath told

---

64. Lewalski, *Protestant Poetics*, 152–55; cf. 157 for Ambrose on this.

65. Granada, *Treatise of Consideration and Prayer*, 6.

66. Gilson, *Mystical Theology of Bernard*, 187; cf. 186.

67. Anthony Lane, *John Calvin: Student of Church Fathers*, esp. 1–13.

us" and in the margin reveals his identity as Gregory.[68] However, in the next edition he is simply referred to as Gregory.[69] Similarly, in his first work he names Luis de Granada and his *Meditations*.[70] But in the 1654 edition, while his name is removed, the same two quotations remain, and he is secretly identified as "saith one devoutly."[71] This reveals the nature of seventeenth-century polemics, but it also indicates that at least some Puritans, while anxious to criticize and distance themselves publicly from Western Catholics, were still quite willing to embrace their writings. However, this practice pertained only to devotional works of piety, not doctrinal writings. Granada, author of the popular *Of Prayer and Meditation*, was one of the most widely read continental mystics in seventeenth-century England.[72] Ambrose also includes two references to Ignatius, though neither one is positive. In describing Jesus' crucifixion he writes, "[l]et Jesuites and Friers in meditating of Christs sufferings, cry out against the Jewes; in this bloody sweat of Christ I see another use."[73] The other reference is to the repentant thief on the cross who was "*of the Society of Jesus . . . (though no Jesuite neither)*."[74]

Ambrose makes more direct references to Bernard's usage of contemplation than any other patristic or medieval person. Bernard's teaching on contemplation is extensive. However, space limits this synopsis to only his most salient points.[75] Casey summarizes Bernard's understanding of "contemplation [as] a penetrating moment of perception which conveys something of the beauty and attractiveness of God which has the result of distracting the mind and the heart from absolutely everything

68. Ambrose, *Ultima* in *Prima, Media & Ultima* (1640), 245.

69. Ambrose, *Ultima* in *Prima, Media & Ultima* (1654), 109. Ambrose also links Gregory and Calvin in their common interpretation of the fires of hell. *Ultima* in *Prima, Media & Ultima* (1654), 146.

70. Ambrose, *Ultima* (1640), 242, 388.

71. Ambrose, *Ultima* in *Prima, Media & Ultima* (1654), 106, 212. I have not been able to determine the specific source of these quotations.

72. Horton Davies, *Worship and Theology in England*, 2:69. On Granada see Pourrat, *Christian Spirituality*, 3:95–101. Terence Cave asserts that Erasmus also influenced Granada. *Devotional Poetry in France*, 5.

73. Ambrose, *Looking Unto Jesus*, 560.

74. Ambrose, *Ultima* in *Prima, Media & Ultima* (1654), 208.

75. Much of the following section is summarized from John Sommerfeldt's *Spiritual Teachings of Bernard*, 215–50. Other studies that specifically focus on Bernard's understanding of contemplation are Butler, *Western Mysticism*, 95–110; Casey, *Athirst for God*, 289–96; and McGinn, *Growth of Mysticism*, 211–13, 221–23.

else."[76] Even though Bernard stressed the necessity of clearly differentiating between meditation and contemplation, there were occasions when the distinction faded and terms overlapped.[77] While there was not the same emphasis upon personal experience in the twelfth as the seventeenth century Bernard speaks with passionate autobiographical detail and delight.[78] Further, these experiences are always a gift, the result of God's grace.[79] Though he communicates his own experiences, Bernard cautions his readers that times of contemplation are rare and fleeting.[80]

Love is the driving force within the contemplative experience.[81] This is hardly a surprise since it is related to spiritual marriage. In fact, as one grows into deeper intimacy in spiritual marriage with Jesus as the divine Bridegroom, one will experience the joys of contemplative love and life.[82] Bernard follows the earlier historical pattern of invoking Mary, the sister of Martha (Luke 10:39), as one of the primary models of contemplation.[83] However, Bernard realizes the wisdom of the Christian life is best lived in balance and not in dichotomy. Therefore, the healthy spiritual life combines contemplation and action. Or more accurately, the contemplative life overflows in action.[84] This signals the benefits of the contemplative experience of love and knowledge.[85] Finally, the last and perhaps the greatest benefit for many is that contemplation provides a foretaste of heaven. This glimpse of the beatific vision introduces in miniature what will be the saints' fullness of joy when they repose in Jesus' presence in heaven.[86] Ambrose's deep affection for Bernard is clear in his approbation of "devout Bernard,"[87] and since the references

76. Casey, *Athirst for God*, 295. For the semantic range of terms used by Bernard to express contemplation see McGinn, *Growth in Mysticism*, 212.

77. Sommerfeldt, *Spiritual Teachings of Bernard*, 223–24, 228n36.

78. Bernard, *SCC* 74.5–7; cf. McGinn, *Growth of Mysticism*, 496n152.

79. Sommerfeldt, *Spiritual Teachings of Bernard*, 234, 238–41.

80. Bernard, *SCC* 23.15; cf. *SCC* 85.13.

81. McGinn, *Growth of Mysticism*, 190.

82. Sommerfeldt, *Spiritual Teachings of Bernard*, 244 and Bernard, *SSC* 1.11–12, 52.6, 83, 85.12–13.

83. Casey, *Athirst for God*, 296.

84. Ibid., 265; cf. McGinn, *Growth of Mysticism*, 221–23.

85. Sommerfeldt, *Spiritual Teachings of Bernard*, 241–42, 244–45.

86. Ibid., 226–27.

87. Ambrose, *War with Devils*, 182.

to Bernard are more substantive they will appear in the specific text of Ambrose's writings for greater clarity and connection.

Ambrose in particular, and the Puritans in general, were often indebted to Bernard for their understanding of contemplation; however, Calvin did not provide the same formative influence. Nonetheless, it would be a serious error to conclude that contemplation was not present in his writings. One significant distinction between Bernard and Calvin is that for Bernard contemplation was primarily relational, while for Calvin it was essentially doxological. Bernard frequently focuses upon Jesus, the Word, while Calvin's attention to contemplation is typically directed to God the Father and the works of creation and providence.[88] Unfortunately, no detailed study of contemplation in Calvin presently exists.[89] However, there is an important link between Calvin and Ambrose and other Puritans that relates to meditation on heaven. Calvin declares, "[s]ince, therefore, believers ascribe to God's grace the fact that, illumined by his Spirit, they enjoy through faith the contemplation of heavenly life."[90] In his commentary on Colossians, he asserts this more fully, "[l]et us therefore bear in mind that *that* is the true and holy *thinking* as to Christ, which forthwith bears us up into heaven, that we may there adore him, and that our minds may dwell with Him."[91] Ronald Wallace helpfully connects "[t]he 'mystical union' with Christ which played such an important part in Calvin's theology, is union with the ascended Christ" with meditation on heaven.[92] The Ascension also figured prominently in Bernard's preaching, occupying more sermons than any other topic, including Jesus' passion.[93]

The Puritans, including Ambrose, greatly expanded the connection between heavenly-mindedness and meditation on heaven with contemplation. Calvin was not the first to engage in this as McGinn's summary

88. On Calvin see, *Institutes*, 1.14.21; 1.17.9; 2.8.55; 3.20.4; 4.14.5; and *Comm* on Ps 19.

89. Zachman, *Image and Word in John Calvin* occasionally flirts with the theme of contemplation but never defines Calvin's theology of contemplation.

90. Calvin, *Institutes*, 3.2.40.

91. Calvin, *Comm* on Col 3:1. For Calvin's meditation on the heavenly life see Ronald Wallace, *Calvin's Doctrine of Christian Life*, 87–93.

92. Ronald Wallace, *Calvin, Geneva and Reformation*, 198; cf. Ronald Wallace, *Calvin's Doctrine of Christian Life*, 92. Similarly the Ascension was significant for the Puritans. Wakefield, *Puritan Devotion*, 158–59.

93. Leclercq, *Love of Learning and Desire for God*, 56.

indicates, the "fundamental aim of monastic spirituality was not so much to strive to enjoy what later ages would call mystical experience here below as to encourage *contemplatio* understood as burning desire for heaven."[94] However, while earlier Christians, including Bernard, desired heaven, there does not appear to be the same degree of emphasis upon meditating on heaven as practiced by Calvin and the Puritans.[95] Dewey Wallace reports, "[h]eavenly mindedness was the spiritual person's foretaste of the joys of heaven through meditation."[96] Further, he maintains, "Puritan spirituality became most affectively mystical with regard to such topics as heavenly mindedness and union with Christ."[97] Likewise Lovelace maintains "Puritan 'heavenly-mindedness,' despite modern jests to the contrary, was a practical mysticism that sought communion with God among the common events of daily living."[98] Moreover, Peter Toon suggests that "meditation on heaven" was the most important theme in Puritan meditation. He suggests three reasons for the importance of meditating on heaven:

> First, because Christ is there now and our salvation consists of union through the Holy Spirit with him . . . Second, we are pilgrims and sojourners on earth, journeying in faith, hope, and love toward heaven in order to be with Christ there. Heaven is the goal of our pilgrimage. And third, because we can rightly live a Christian life in the present evil age only if we have the mind of Christ, that is, if we are genuinely heavenly minded, seeing our earth and this age in the perspective of heaven.[99]

What is significant for Isaac Ambrose is that Dewey Wallace regards heavenly-mindedness as a more prominent theme following the Act of Uniformity in 1662 with "the dashing at the Restoration of so many Puritan hopes."[100] Ambrose wrote all but his two final works before 1662. Further, Baxter's popular *Saints' Everlasting Rest*, that was essentially a guide to heavenly meditation or contemplation, was written in 1649.

94. McGinn, *Growth of Mysticism*, 140.

95. For Bernard's desire for heaven see Casey, *Athirst for God*, 208–31; cf. Leclercq, *Love of Learning and Desire for God*, 56–70.

96. Dewey Wallace, *Spirituality of Later Puritans*, xvii.

97. Ibid., xviii.

98. Lovelace, *American Pietism of Cotton Mather*, 187.

99. Toon, *From Mind to Heart*, 95–96.

100. Dewey Wallace, *Spirituality of Later Puritans*, xvii. See Rowe, *Heavenly-Mindedness* as a post-Restoration example of this.

Interestingly, both of these works were based on texts from the book of
Hebrews, which is not surprising given the focus of this biblical book.[101]

IMAGINATION IN THE WRITINGS OF ISAAC AMBROSE

Previously the comparison between Roman Catholic and Puritan approaches to meditation recognized that heavenly meditation inspired a
greater usage of the imagination in the Puritans. It is helpful to frame
this significant topic within the Puritan awareness of the faculties of the
soul.[102] Ambrose follows the typical Puritan and medieval practice that
the faculties consisted of the understanding, will, and the affections.[103]
He also included the memory as a component of the faculties.[104] While,
according to Ambrose, a person could enjoy God through both their
understanding and the will,[105] the primary purpose of meditation was to
stir up the *affections* so that the person would respond appropriately.[106]
However, since the affections could be directed either towards God or
the world they required the proper guidance through the understanding so that "the affections [would not become] disordered."[107] The senses
are also important in Ambrose's anthropology, serving as the "windows
of our soul."[108] Moreover Ambrose shared the common awareness held
by Bernard and others before him that the faculties, marred by sin,
required regeneration.[109] Ambrose recognized that contemplation and

---

101. For a helpful summary of Baxter's teaching on heavenly meditation see Packer,
"Richard Baxter on Heaven."

102. The best Puritan treatment on the faculties of the soul is Reynolds, *Passions
and Faculties of Soul*; cf. Fulcher, "Puritans and the Passions" and Kapic, *Communion
with God*, 45n49.

103. Ambrose, *Ultima* in *Prima, Media & Ultima* (1654), 21; Ambrose, *Media* (1657),
140, 259, 465; and Ambrose, *Looking Unto Jesus*, 325.

104. Ambrose, *Prima* in *Prima, Media & Ultima* (1654), 3 and Ambrose, *Ultima* in
Prima, Media & Ultima (1654), 67.

105. Ambrose, *Ultima* in *Prima, Media & Ultima* (1654), 212.

106. Ambrose, *Looking Unto Jesus*, 319.

107. Ambrose, *Ultima* in *Prima, Media & Ultima* (1654), 19. The best Puritan discussion on this subject is Fenner, *Treatise of Affections*. Fenner declares that when the
affections are "inordinate" it makes a person the "worlds spouse and the devils spouse."
Treatise of Affections, 46.

108. Ambrose, *Media* (1657), 50; cf. Ambrose, *War with Devils*, 57.

109. Ambrose, *Prima* in *Prima, Media & Ultima* (1654), 8; cf. McGinn, *Growth of
Mysticism*, 201 and Sommerfledt, *Spiritual Teachings of Bernard*, 242–45.

looking unto Jesus restored the faculties until they reached an excellency through glorification in heaven.[110]

Further, the imagination functions in relationship with the faculties of the soul and contributes to our understanding of Ambrose's practice of meditation.[111] Imagination has the potential to reconstruct passages of Scripture so that a person can relive that experience and deepen the understanding and affections of that event. Ambrose illustrates this according to Jesus' post Easter visitations to his disciples: "[m]ethinks I see *Thomas's* finger on Christ's boared hand, and *Thomas's* hand in Christs pierced side. Here's a strong argument to convince my soul that Christ is risen from the dead."[112] The imagination has the potential to convince a person's soul of some event or message. In *Ultima*, Ambrose often employs the imagination to dramatize the seriousness of an event. After guiding his readers through a meditation on the horrors of hell he declares, "I have lead you through the dungeon, let this sight serve for a terrour that you never come nearer."[113] Additionally he recognized that the "imagination [can] work a real change in nature."[114] At times he combines the power of imagination with looking at Christ and declares, "[a]nd no question but there is a kinde of spiritual imaginative of power in faith to be like to Christ by looking on Christ."[115]

Puritan teaching is in agreement that the Fall severely damaged the imagination, making it unreliable. Ambrose warns his readers of the Devil's ability and desire to work in a person's imagination.[116] Sibbes expands this reality, declaring, "[a]nd amongst all the faculties of the soul, most of the disquiet and unnecessary trouble of our lives arises from the vanity and ill government of that power of the soul which we call *imagi-*

110. Ambrose, *Looking Unto Jesus*, 1094.

111. Little has been written on this important topic. For a helpful summary see Evans, "Puritan Use of Imagination," 47–88 and La Shell, "Imagination and Idol," 305–34. While Kaufmann addresses this topic frequently in *Pilgrim's Progress in Puritan Meditation* his misreading of the Puritans mars his research. See Knott, *Sword of the Spirit*, 68; Lewalski, *Protestant Poetics*, 150; Beeke, "Puritan Practice Meditation," 77; and Chan, "Puritan Meditative Tradition," 91.

112. Ambrose, *Looking Unto Jesus*, 766. Ambrose frequently uses this formula of "methinks I see [or] imagine [or] hear." *Looking Unto Jesus*, 949, 964,1102, 1142, etc.

113. Ambrose, *Ultima* in *Prima, Media & Ultima* (1654), 137.

114. Ambrose, *Looking Unto Jesus*, 526.

115. Ibid., 668.

116. Ambrose, *War with Devils*, 109, 116.

nation . . . This imagination of ours is become the seat of vanity, and thereupon of vexation to us, because it apprehends a greater happiness in outward good things than there is."[117] He continues by summarizing four major dangers of misguided imagination: making false representations, blocking reason and wise judgments, creating impressions that lack reality, and a tendency to create vanity and mischief.[118] However, Sibbes was also fully aware of the potential benefit of harnessing the imagination for good. He asserted, "[a]s the soul receives much hurt from imagination, so it may have much good thereby . . . A sanctified fancy [i.e. imagination] will make every creature a ladder to heaven."[119] Because of the importance of imagination in Ambrose's teaching on meditation and experience of God, he questions his readers directly: "is thy imagination strong?"[120] This concern is amplified by his frequent invitation and encouragement to use one's imagination by the repeated inclusion in his writings of "imagine then," as the person meditates on a passage of Scripture.[121] Not surprisingly, given the nature of his massive work on contemplation, Ambrose often personalizes Jesus in relation to the individual through imagination. In his consideration of Jesus' work of salvation he writes, "[r]eallize Christ standing by thee."[122]

This raises the question how did Ambrose's use of imagination compare with Ignatius of Loyola? While Ambrose and the Puritans essentially continued the practice of using "composition of place" in their meditation,[123] there continues to be a significant gap between Ignatius and Ambrose in style and especially content. Therefore, Lovelace is too restrictive in his critique asserting, "[t]he Ignatian type of mysticism, which stresses Christ in his human nature and the pictorial use of sensory imagination, is also alien to Puritan communion, which would insist on going to God by a route that it would consider more direct and more spiritual."[124] More accurately it can be noted that Ignatius placed

117. Sibbes, *Soul's Conflict*, 178–79.

118. Ibid., 180.

119. Ibid., 185.

120. Ambrose, *Looking Unto Jesus*, 626.

121. Ambrose, *Ultima* in *Prima, Media & Ultima* (1654), 53, 76, 115, 140, 174, 181; Ambrose, *Media* (1657), 398; Ambrose, *Looking Unto Jesus*, 519, 659, 1035; and Ambrose, *War with Devils*, 67; etc.

122. Ambrose, *Looking Unto Jesus*, 476; cf. 1077.

123. Hambrick-Stowe, *Practice of Piety*, 31–32, 38–39.

124. Lovelace, "Anatomy Puritan Piety," 3:318; cf. 296.

much greater emphasis upon all five senses for reconstructing and experiencing the biblical text. Conversely Ambrose, while able to create vivid images of the biblical stories, is more restrained in his use of the senses, typically limiting himself to sight and sound. Toon's assessment of Baxter that "[w]hile he does not go as far as Ignatius Loyola, who invites people to use all their five senses (including taste and smell) to imagine the heavenly city, Baxter certainly is uninhibited in commending the use of imagination controlled by the images and pictures of Holy Scripture" is correct for Ambrose as well.[125] Additionally, Ambrose's negative impression of Ignatius mentioned earlier in this chapter must be recalled. Further, the more subdued principles of Granada appear far more influential on Ambrose than Ignatius. While Granada also encouraged the use of all five senses, his examples lack the striking vividness of Ignatius.[126] Further, Granada also recognizes the potential danger of imagination, especially for beginners and cautions his readers not to overuse imagination because it can "weary the head."[127]

Therefore, while Ambrose made frequent use of imagination and pushed the boundaries perhaps much farther than most Puritans, there is still a gap between himself and Ignatius of Loyola.[128] This is perhaps more stark in Baxter who asserts, "I would not have thee, as the papists, draw them in pictures, nor use such ways to represent them. This, as it is a course forbidden by God, so it would but seduce and draw down thy heart; but get the liveliest picture of them in thy mind that possibly thou canst; meditate of them as if thou wert all the while beholding them . . . till thou canst say, Methinks I see a glimpse of the glory."[129] The Second Commandment against making idols is at the root of Baxter's concern. While Ignatius also influenced Granada, the latter's style appears more muted and amenable to Ambrose.[130] In reality both Ignatius and Granada

---

125. Toon, *From Mind to Heart*, 99; cf. Beeke, "Puritan Practice of Meditation," 77.

126. Granada, *Prayer and Meditation*, 250.

127. Granada, *Spiritual Doctrine*, 117.

128. Ambrose's *Looking Unto Jesus* represents a strong Puritan usage of the imagination in the eighteenth-century Scottish controversy regarding mental images. La Shell, "Imagination and Idol," 316.

129. Baxter, *Saints' Everlasting Rest*, 320.

130. Chan agrees that Granada's use of imagination would have been more acceptable to the Puritans than Ignatius. "Puritan Meditative Tradition," 2.

were influenced by the *devotio moderna* through Cisneros.[131] This again raises the critical question of influence and continuity and discontinuity. Simply because two persons appear to use roughly the same method does not guarantee that one borrowed from the other. Further, while both Ignatius and Granada drew upon *devotio moderna* in style and content, the resulting outcomes are not identical. The roots of Ambrose's style are more reflective of Hall and Granada than Ignatius. One fascinating trajectory of Puritan imagination is that John Bunyan owned a marked copy of Ambrose's *Prima, Media & Ultima*.[132] Kaufmann posits one specific example from *Pilgrim's Progress* that resembles Ambrose's approach.[133] Therefore, one can only wonder how much influence Ambrose's writing had upon Bunyan and his own development and use of imagination.[134]

CONTEMPLATION IN THE WRITINGS OF ISAAC AMBROSE

Ambrose has little to say about contemplation in his first work, but uses the term both positively and negatively. In his sermon on the new birth he encourages his listeners, "may your contemplations (guided by the Gods Word) go into that Paradise above."[135] This is not surprising given the Puritan strong dependency upon Scripture. It also echoes Bernard's frequent refrain that the *Verbum* or Word as Spouse is essential in contemplation.[136] Later in his teaching on the Ten Commandments he warns his listeners not to delight "in the inward contemplations of evil."[137] This sort of language was fairly common among the Puritans. Later, Calamy would speak of "contemplative wickedness" and "contemplative adultery."[138] This clarifies that contemplation could be used in a general way of thinking or considering. But it also implies delighting

---

131. Pourrat, *Christian Spirituality*, 26–29, 97; McGuire, *Companion to Jean Gerson*, 379–82; and Cave, *Devotional Poetry*, 5.

132. Harrison, "John Bunyan: Record of Recent Research," 53.

133. Kaufmann, *Pilgrim's Progress in Puritan Meditation*, 230.

134. In continuing the trajectory of Ambrose's teaching on imagination see Morden's comments on Bunyan's influence on Spurgeon. *Communion with Christ*, 28–30.

135. Ambrose, *Prima* in *Prima, Media & Ultima* (1654), 7.

136. McGinn, *Growth of Mysticism*, 190–93.

137. Ambrose, *Prima* in *Prima, Media & Ultima* (1654), 59.

138. Calamy, *Art Divine Meditation*, 3, 71; cf. Scudder, *Christians Daily Walke*, 185. Lockyer distinguishes between carnal and divine contemplation. *England Faithfully Watcht*, 88.

in something, delight being good or evil, depending on the object of contemplation and the source of that delight.

Ultima was also published the same year as *Prima*. These sermons address the four last things: death, judgment, hell, and heaven. One can detect an expansion of the interaction between sight and gazing and contemplation, and Ambrose declares that in contemplation a person "behold[s] the face of your Saviour."[139] The language of beholding figures prominently in *Looking Unto Jesus*. This theme is further expanded in his discussion of the beatific vision. Ambrose introduces this theme with a reference to Granada's *Meditations* that was examined earlier in this chapter. To the question "how can our souls enjoy this *Godhead*?" Ambrose replies, "[t]he *understanding* is filled by a clear glorious sight of God, called *Beatificall vision*."[140] While he does not specifically connect the beatific vision with heavenly meditation, Ambrose nonetheless recognizes the value of gazing on God. After quoting Bernard, Ambrose immediately declares, "[a]nd yet because God in his Word doth here give us as a taste of heaven, by comparing it with the most precious things that are on earth, let us follow him so far as he hath revealed it, and no further."[141] Previously he declared, "[b]eloved, I know not how to expresse it, but let your soules in some meditation flie up from *Calvary* to Heaven."[142] This initial experience will only be complete when a person reaches heaven and can "fully contemplate the glory" of God.[143]

Contemplation in *Media*

One of the primary themes of *Media* is that a person can cultivate a contemplative attitude or experience the joyful presence of God through ascetical practices. Ambrose reminds his readers that spiritual duties are like "[b]ridges to give them a passage to God, as Boats to carry them into the bosom of Christ, as means to bring them into more intimate communion with their heavenly Father." Amazingly, these spiritual activities enable a person "to see the face of God." Further, those who meet God in spiritual duties "usually find their hearts sweetly refreshed, as if

139. Ambrose, *Ultima* in *Prima, Media & Ultima* (1654), 180.

140. Ibid., 212; cf. 203, 215.

141. Ibid., 224. The reference is to *SCC* 38.

142. Ibid., 206.

143. Ibid., 227.

Heaven were in them."[144] Ambrose acknowledges that spiritual duties were not popular in his day, hence his motivation for addressing this critical topic.[145] Based on his immediate reference to Rutherford's *Survey of the Spiritual Antichrist* and comments including, "Christ hath done all Duties for us" it is clear that he is referring to Antinomianism, which among other things was resistant to spiritual practices and was prevalent in Lancashire.[146] Ambrose also advises his readers that everything that he has written he has practiced himself. Further, as previously noted, while the steps may appear to be demanding, as one works through this massive treatise of spiritual practices, he reminds them that these are guidelines and not rigid rules.[147] There are two additional principles to understanding Ambrose's teaching on spiritual practices, the first is the importance of the Holy Spirit guiding the person, and the second is Jesus' ministry of perfecting what a person offers to God.[148]

A dynamic spiritual component of *Media* is a series of retreat days that illustrate Ambrose's own personal use of these spiritual duties and how they prepared him for contemplative experiences of ravishment and delight. Philip Sheldrake perceptively recognizes that same combination when he writes, "[a] somewhat ascetical spirituality was off-set in some people [i.e. the Puritans] with a more contemplative stance and even mystical raptures as in Isaac Ambrose."[149] Clearly the spiritual duties that Ambrose describes in *Media* are identical to the ones he practices during his retreats. He engaged them in the following order: watchfulness, self-examination, experiences, evidences, meditation, life of faith, prayer, reading the Word, self-denial, and the saint's suffering. The only variation is that self-denial was practiced near the end rather than in its placement after self-examination in *Media*. However, Ambrose indicates without any explanation that self-denial was practiced "not in course."[150] The other distinction is that he would obviously not be able to engage

144. Ambrose, *Media* (1657), 33–34.

145. Ibid., To the Reader, [5]; cf. 34.

146. Ibid., To the Reader, [5–6] and Como, *Blown by the Spirit*, 35 (resistance to spiritual duties) and esp. 315–21 (antinomianism in Lancashire).

147. Ibid., To the Reader, [8, 6–7].

148. Ibid., To the Reader, [8–9], 89, 90, 184 (on the role of the Spirit) and 17 (on Christ perfecting human offering).

149. Sheldrake, *Brief History of Spirituality*, 120

150. Ambrose, *Media* (1657), 89.

in the corporate disciplines of family duties, Christian society, and the Lord's Supper. In comparing Ambrose's order with other popular devotional manuals there is obviously overlap of practices but also uniqueness, and none seem to follow a standard structure.[151]

Chapter 3 revealed that Ambrose had a contemplative experience of ravishment and ecstatic delight that lasted two days. While he provides a number of different descriptions of this celebrated event, he nowhere suggests what spiritual practices he had employed on that day. He merely indicates that God bathed his soul with a mystical sense of love and the sweetness of heavenly joy. Elsewhere the most common disciplines that produced contemplative experiences were prayer, meditation, and self-examination.[152] But on other occasions, spiritual practices that might appear to be less likely to create a contemplative response, such as meditation on hell, the saints suffering, and the "very hard lesson" of self-denial also refreshed his soul with the flames of God's love and a "sweet scent" from the Spirit.[153] To summarize, while there are some spiritual practices that may more likely create a contemplative experience than others, there are also those that are surprising. This is a reminder that spiritual disciplines are only the means for cultivating a greater attentiveness to God. Whether Ambrose, or any one else, experiences God in a contemplative way, is always determined by God's grace and not human effort. However, that does not minimize the importance of effort in forming the pattern of receptivity and responsiveness to God. Interestingly, Ambrose's practice appears to mirror Bernard, for whom, according to Leclercq, "there can be no 'mystical' experience without prior 'ascetic' experience."[154]

While Ambrose was the only person that I have discovered in the seventeenth century to take month-long retreats, there were others who cultivated a similar intensity for shorter periods. On the continent, Theodorus à Brakel, one of the primary leaders of Dutch Pietism, was known for his intense spiritual practices that could incredibly occupy up to eight hours a day even though he was married with children.[155]

151. Compare *Media* (1657) with Bayly, *Practice of Piety*, Downame, *Guide to Godlynesse*, and Scudder, *Christian's Daily Walke*.

152. Ambrose, *Media* (1650), 76, 79 and Ambrose, *Media* (1657), 88.

153. Ambrose, *Media* (1657), 89–90.

154. Leclercq, *Bernard of Clairvaux*, 35.

155. De Reuver, *Sweet Communion*, 167–68; cf. 107, 109 for the example of Willem Teellinck.

It is little wonder that these examples, which were more the norm than the exception, inspired Packer to refer to Puritanism as "reformed monasticism."[156] Similarly, Hambrick-Stowe asserts, "[t]he contemplative [Puritan] is distinguished from the common practicing believer by the regularity, protractedness, and continuing intensity of the exercises." And further, due to the intensity of Puritan devotional practices "perhaps most of the clergy—and women . . . might be described by the phrase 'Puritan contemplative.'"[157] This should not imply that Lutherans and Roman Catholics, both ministers and laity alike, were not also disciplined in spiritual practices, but this sort of intensity may seem more unusual among the Reformed.[158] However, not every one was able to endure this intensity and the ascetical demands of Puritanism. Therefore, it is no surprise that a major backlash arose from these excessive devotional demands and expectations. Antinomianism that grew with increasing strength during the 1620s was particularly resistant to these demands since they believed Christ had already accomplished everything for them.[159] While this is an important development in the history of Puritanism it is not possible to examine it due to space.[160]

A great deal can be learned about Ambrose's understanding of contemplative language and heavenly meditation by examining two passages. First, he affirms, "[w]hat is the happinesse of a glorified Saint, but that he is always under the line of love, ever in the contemplation of, and converse with God."[161] Second, he seeks to stir up the importance of this attitude and practice when he declares, "[g]et we into our hearts an habit of more heavenly-mindednesse, by much exercise, and intercourse, and acquaintance with God, by often contemplation, and foretaste of the sweetnesse, glory, and eternity of those Mansions

---

156. Packer, *Quest for Godliness*, 28, 331.

157. Hambrick-Stowe, *Practice of Piety*, 285, 287; cf. Bozeman, *Precisianist Strain*, 103, 174, 177; Lovelace, *American Pietism Cotton Mather*, 124–26; Hinson, "Puritan Spirituality," 172, 177; Op't Hof, "Protestant Pietism," 39–45; and Williams, "Puritan Enjoyment of God," 131–33 for the monastic intensity of especially Puritan laity.

158. See Benedict, *Christ's Churches Purely Reformed*, 430, 530.

159. Bozeman, *Precisianist Strain*, 184, 193, 195, 200, 202, 208–9.

160. On Antinomianism see Bozeman, *Precisianist Strain*; Como, *Blown by the Spirit*; Dewey Wallace, *Puritans and Predestination*, 113–22; and Liu, *Towards an Evangelical Spirituality*, 43–68.

161. Ambrose, *Media* (1657), 34.

above."[162] In evaluating these two passages he highlights the relational nature of being with God in contemplation. God's love is the umbrella under which this occurs. But human love is also closely related, and it creates "a certain close walking with God, [that has] been long exercised in a Christian course, [and has] often entertained Christ Jesus at Supper in their hearts."[163] Additionally, Ambrose connects heavenly-mindedness and contemplation reflective of other Puritans. He asserts that contemplation provides a preview of heaven in offering a "foretaste of the sweetnesse, glory, and eternity of those Mansions above." Elsewhere, Ambrose more specifically soars with the language of love echoing Song of Songs that is descriptive of Bernard as he pleads for Jesus to lift his soul to heaven with his rapturous love:

> O sweet Jesu, touch our souls with thy spirit . . . give us the flag-ons of the new wine of the Kingdom, which may lift up our souls above our selves in our loves, . . . and by an heavenly excess may be transported into an heavenly love, that we may imbrace Christ, . . . O let us desire union with thee . . . O burn and consume whatso-ever would grow one with our souls besides thee; O let the fire of thy spirit so wholly turn our soules into a spiritual fire.[164]

Significantly, Ambrose also includes the importance of the Holy Spirit in this process of spiritual marriage.

These above references also emphasize the importance of repetition. One is most likely to experience the gift of contemplation through cultivating the regular "habit of more heavenly-mindednesse, by much exercise, and intercourse" with the Triune God.[165] In connection with this reminder of frequent converse with God Ambrose adds two related principles regarding time. First, he cautions his readers "[n]o time can be prescribed to all men; for neither is God bound to hours, neither doth the contrary disposition of men agree in one choice of opportunities." Here he refers to Isaac's practice recorded in Gen 24:63. The most critical factor for determining the best time is "when we find our spirits most active and fit for contemplation."[166] Second, beyond the wisdom of paying attention to a person's individual temperament, Ambrose

162. Ibid., 55.

163. Ibid., 225; cf. 402 the Lord's Supper "makes the soul heavenly-minded."

164. Ibid., 465; cf. 356, 53 for the importance of love in contemplation.

165. Ibid., 55.

166. Ibid., 217.

declares, "prosperity is the fittest season for heavenly contemplation, the less troubles lies upon our estate, the more liberty we have to think of heavenly things."[167] While that may be true, Ambrose and his fellow non-conformists often found themselves at the opposite end of prosperity in pursuing their spiritual practices. Moreover, the broader context for this statement is the Life of Faith and the Saints Suffering sections in which he asserts, "[l]et us by faith realize the glorious things of heaven to us."[168] This comment regarding prosperity sounds very elitist and suggests that a wealthy person has a distinct advantage over the poor laborer. However, elsewhere when Ambrose is speaking about the wisdom of relationships within the Christian community he counsels that one should not neglect the insights of obscure people because "heavenly mindednesse may be now and then found out and discovered in plain people, that have plain carriage and plain speech."[169] Finally, while the benefits of contemplation will be explored later in this chapter clearly the "foretaste of the sweet-nesse, glory and eternity" of heaven is one of them.

Contemplation in *Looking Unto Jesus*

Ambrose confesses his motivation for writing *Looking Unto Jesus* was gratitude for recovering from a serious illness in 1653.[170] This empha-sizes the connection between gratitude and love with contemplation. Structurally, *Looking Unto Jesus* is based upon the life of Christ divided into nine periods ranging from his heavenly existence before his birth to the Second Coming. Each of these nine categories begins with the biblical foundation, or laying down the doctrine for that aspect of Jesus' life, followed by nine movements of increasing intensity of looking at Jesus intended to stir up the affections. The nine ways of looking consist of knowing, considering, desiring, hoping, believing, loving, joying,[171] calling, and conforming to that aspect of Jesus' life. This structure re-sembles both the Puritan sermon and meditation and Bernard's practice of beginning with the intellect and moving to the affections.[172]

167. Ibid., 285.
168. Ibid., 550; cf. 285.
169. Ibid., 337.
170. Ambrose, *Looking Unto Jesus*, To the Reader, [1].
171. While "joying" is not a standard English word Ambrose employs it throughout *Looking Unto Jesus*.
172. Ambrose, *Media* (1657), 222.

Some scholars have asserted that the Puritans did not write about the humanity of Christ and more specifically his passion, as was common among Roman Catholic authors.[173] However, Charles Herle's *Contemplations and Devotions on the Severall Passages of Our Blessed Saviours Death and Passion* is an exception.[174] Ambrose specifically references Herle's work in *Looking unto Jesus*.[175] Horton Davies observes that while Puritans typically eschewed meditation on Christ's humanity and passion those writers of mystical persuasion tended to conflate the distinction between Roman Catholic and Puritan meditation.[176] Intriguingly, Wakefield conjectures the possible parallels between *Looking Unto Jesus* and Bishop Guevara's *Mount Calvary*, though Ambrose "meditates upon the whole work of Christ from Creation to the last day, and thus sets Calvary in its context of the universal purpose of God in Christ."[177] John Flavel indicates that Ambrose had addressed the subject of meditating on Jesus and "done worthily" and provided guidance for his own work.[178] While Flavel does not follow Ambrose's structure, especially in his detailed stirring up the affections, he does cover the same topics beginning with Christ's pre-existence and concluding with his final judgment.

Ambrose devotes slightly less than half of the work to the nine affective categories of knowing, considering, desiring, hoping, believing, loving, joying, calling, and conforming to Jesus' life. What is the origin of these nine ways of gazing at Jesus? One possibility is the resemblance to Rutherford's *Christ Dying*, which Ambrose quotes in his introduction declaring it is, "*[a]n act of living in Christ, and on Christ, in the acts of seeing, enjoying, embracing, loving, resting on him, is that noone-day divinity, and theology of beatifical vision.*"[179] Thomas Hooker, writing nine

173. Martz, *Poetry of Meditation*, 163–64 and Kaufmann, *Pilgrim's Progress in Puritan Meditation*, 126.

174. Green identifies other Puritan works that addressed Jesus as Saviour and Exemplar, including Perkins, Preston, Reynolds, Thomas Hooker, and Thomas Goodwin. *Print and Protestantism*, 322–25.

175. Ambrose, *Looking Unto Jesus*, 612; cf. Ambrose, *Ultima in Prima, Media & Ultima* (1654), 183. The name is unclear, but the titles match.

176. Horton Davies, *Worship and Theology in England*, 2:88. Davies lists Rous, Thomas Goodwin, and Peter Sterry as Puritans possessing mystical tendencies.

177. Wakefield, *Puritan Devotion*, 95–96.

178. Flavel, *Fountain of Life*, 23, 272.

179. Ambrose, *Looking Unto Jesus*, To the Reader, [3]. The reference is Rutherford, *Christ Dying*, To the Reader, [11].

years earlier, offers another pattern that reflects even greater similarity in his discussion of how the soul grows in union with Christ asserting, "the soule settles itselfe upon Christ, hoping, expecting, longing, desiring, loving, embracing."[180] While there is some overlap between both of these lists, it is difficult to gauge their impact upon Ambrose's format. Meanwhile, Chan claims that knowing and considering relate to the intellect, desiring, hoping, believing, loving, and joying are affections, and calling and conforming pertain to the will.[181] While there is some truth to his assessment, it is overly simplistic. For example, considering, which is "consideration" is really a combination of the intellect and affections.[182] Further, Ambrose maintains believing also has a strong component of consideration to it.[183]

The title for this book is taken from Ambrose's definition of contemplation. Early in *Looking Unto Jesus* he declares, "contemplation is soul-recreation, & recreation is kept up by variety."[184] However, this wonderful image was not original to him but borrowed from Nicholas Lockyer's commentary on Col 1:16.[185] Therefore, understanding the nature of recreation in the seventeenth century can expand our awareness of how Ambrose understood contemplation.[186] While many people consider the Puritans rigid and joyless this was hardly accurate. Downame provides a detailed treatment of recreation in his massive treatise on godliness. The introductory heading provides a clear summary of his purpose: "[r]ecreation, which are not onely lawfull, but also profitable and necessary, if wee bee exercised in them according to Gods Word." He reminds his readers that Jesus rested "to refresh himselfe and repaire his strength" and that his followers must imitate this pattern so that they are renewed to "more cheerfully return to [their] labors."[187] But Downame's most illuminating assertion is that the "exercise of contemplation . . . seemeth to have been one of *Solomons* recreations in his best

180. Hooker, *Soules Exaltation*, 5.

181. Chan, "Puritan Meditative Tradition," 183.

182. Ambrose, *Looking Unto Jesus*, 88, 319, etc.

183. Ibid., 225–29, 329.

184. Ibid., 21.

185. Lockyer *England Faithfully Watcht*, 87; cf. Ranew, *Solitude Improved*, 144.

186. For a helpful summary of recreation in early modern England see McKay, "For Refreshment and Preservinge Health."

187. Downame, *Guide to Godlynesse*, 262–63.

times."[188] Downame also provides detailed guidelines for the cautious use of recreation so as not to misuse or abuse it. He warns his readers "that wee use them [i.e. the recreations] so, as they may refresh the body, but not pamper the flesh."[189] While it is difficult to understand the specific nuances that Ambrose intended when he used Lockyer's image, it is certainly possible that he perceived it similarly to Downame, especially since he was one of the experimental writers Ambrose encouraged others to read. Shortly it will be clear that Ambrose's development of contemplation is a recreation that refreshes the soul.

Again Ambrose draws from Lockyer declaring, *"an holy soul can not tyre it self in the contemplation of Jesus"* and continues in his own words, "how much lesse can it tyre it selfe in *looking unto Jesus*, which is far more comprehensive than contemplating of Jesus."[190] This is a very important distinction for Ambrose, as he equates looking unto Jesus with the "[a]rt of Christ-contemplation."[191] It is more comprehensive because there is "more content in contemplating Christ" than in the regular process of contemplating some aspect of Jesus.[192] Therefore, in looking unto Jesus a person is actually expanding the potential for subject matter that can be contemplated, since Ambrose takes readers through a complete cycle from before Jesus' birth until the final judgment. Ambrose's strong emphasis upon looking unto Jesus as a synonym for contemplation provides another very critical insight. For Ambrose and the Puritans, contemplation had a strong relational dimension that was directed toward a specific person, Jesus or God rather than some abstract truth. Significantly, this relates to the Puritan understanding of spiritual marriage. People relate to Jesus Christ through the power of the Holy Spirit to the glory of God. Robert Webber, cognizant of that distinction, asserts that during the later medieval period, *"[s]pirituality, which was once a contemplation of God's saving acts, now contemplated the self and the interior life."*[193] Ambrose and his fellow Puritans decidedly

---

188. Ibid., 266.

189. Ibid., 269–79. Quotation at 271. Bolton's attitude is more restrictive and focuses on the shortness of time and the costly nature of recreation. *Comfortable Walking with God*, 154–80.

190. Ambrose, *Looking Unto Jesus*, To the Reader, [4], 318; cf. Lockyer, *England Faithfully Watcht*, 87.

191. Ibid., 42.

192. Ibid., 45.

193. Webber, *Divine Embrace*, 51.

altered this focus in their contemplation, since the only appropriate response to God's love was to love God in return. However, before proceeding further it must be acknowledged that Ambrose, like many other spiritual writers, did not always use the term contemplation consistently. On some occasions he simply uses the term to imply to think or ponder rather than a mystical gazing or intense loving focus upon some aspect of God or God's creation.[194]

Further, Ambrose reflects Calvin's emphasis on Jesus' Ascension and heavenly-mindedness. Accordingly, "what is heaven but to be with Christ" and "what is this communion with Christ, but very heaven aforehand."[195] Once a person was betrothed to Jesus in spiritual marriage their desire would deepen as they grew in union and communion with him until they reached the fullness of heavenly joy. Contemplation was a means of providing a glimpse of heaven. Ambrose asserts the obvious reason for hungering for heaven, "[t]hat we have our share in heaven with him; he went not up as a single person, but vertually, or mystically he carried up all the Elect with him into glory."[196] He maintains, "[c]onsider of Christs ascension into heaven . . . what shall he ascend, and shall not we in our contemplations follow after him? gaze O my soul on this wonderful object."[197] Obviously this experience awaits its consummation in heaven. Quoting Bernard, Ambrose declares, "[c]onsider that *looking unto Jesus* is the work of heaven; *it is begun in this life* (saith *Bernard*) *but it is perfected in that life to come*; not onely Angels, but the Saints in glory do ever behold the face of God and Christ."[198] Significantly, Ambrose directly connects contemplation with meditating on heaven. Earlier he bemoans that the inconsistency of this practice allows some to "get up into heaven to see their Jesus but it is not dayly."[199] Therefore, he encourages his readers to make this a daily practice and "habituate your selves to such contemplations as in the next [life] . . . O tie your souls in heavenly galleries, have you eyes continually set on Christ."[200] Even more

---

194. Ambrose, *Looking Unto Jesus*, 506 (incorrectly numbered 514), 509 (incorrectly numbered 517).

195. Ibid., 1161 (incorrectly numbered 1061), 40.

196. Ibid., 829 (incorrectly numbered 929)–30; cf. 951.

197. Ibid., 871; cf. 819–924 for Ambrose's treatment of Jesus' Ascension.

198. Ibid., 46.

199. Ibid., 28 cf. 29.

200. Ibid., 30. Ambrose directly connects heavenly–mindedness and contemplation

dramatically, he challenges his readers that Jesus "would have us to be still arising, ascending, and mounting up in divine contemplation to his Majesty . . . If Christ be in heaven, where should we be but in heaven with him? . . . Oh that every morning, and every evening, at least, our hearts would arise, ascend, and go to Christ in heaven."[201] Further, it is essential to recognize the priority of the Holy Spirit in heavenly meditation. Previously, the Holy Spirit's vital responsibility for creating the bond of spiritual marriage was noted. Now the Spirit's role is further reinforced as Ambrose declares, "it is the Spirit of God" who "make[s] us heavenly minded" and "lifts up our souls towards heaven."[202]

Returning to Jesus' Ascension, it becomes clear that this event provided his early disciples with important lessons in the art of looking or beholding. This accounts for Ambrose's emphasis on "*looking off*" the world and its many distractions so that a person could be "*looking on*" Jesus.[203] Clearly this choice is essential "[b]ecause we cannot look fixedly on Christ, and such things together, and at once; the eye cannot look upwards and downwards, at once in a direct line; we cannot seriously minde heaven and earth in one thought."[204] Further, he instructs his readers that there are two ways of looking, ocular or mental, "or the inward eye" and further, mental looking can be "either notional and theoretical; or practical and experimental."[205] The entire focus of *Looking Unto Jesus* is experimental as it "stirs up the affections."[206] Ambrose bemoans the soul's meager interest in following Jesus' example when he writes, "[c]onsider that Christ looked off heaven and heavenly things for you, how much more should you look off the earth and earthly things, the world and worldly things for him."[207]

Ambrose employs a triad of words to capture the depth of this *visio Dei*: "looking," "beholding," and "gazing." Jesus is the object of focus in every situation. Previously the centrality of the object of contemplation

---

in the example of "holy Mr. *Ward.*" *Looking Unto Jesus*, 584. (incorrectly numbered 594). Ranew speaks of "habitual heavenly-mindedness." *Solitude Improved*, 227–30.

201. Ibid., 1152.
202. Ibid., 846.
203. Ibid., 5.
204. Ibid., 10.
205. Ibid., 18–19.
206. Ibid., 22–23.
207. Ibid., 14.

was mentioned. Ambrose clarifies the reason for this discerning focus since a person becomes what he or she gazes upon: "*[l]ooking to Jesus* containes this, and is the cause of this; the sight of God will make us like to God; and the sight of Christ will make us like to Christ."[208] He does not grow weary repeating this essential principle, and as he writes of Jesus' death he again challenges his readers: "this very *look* may work on us to change us, and transforme us into the very image of Jesus Christ."[209] Further, Ambrose connects spiritual marriage with contemplative looking, "and all we have is by marriage with Jesus Christ; Christ by his union hath all good things without measure . . . if by looking on Christ we come to this likenesse, to be one with Jesus Christ, Oh what a privilege is this!"[210] Drawing upon on 2 Cor 3:18 he declares, "[l]et us look on Christ till we are like Christ . . . come now let us behold this glory of Christ till we are changed in some high measure into the same glory with Christ."[211] Ambrose describes glory as the very "essence of God" and that God's nature is a "glorious essence which is most Majestical."[212] Further, God is full of "glory, beauty and excellency."[213] The appearance of glory has both intensity and power and can vary so as not to overwhelm humanity, as well as to transform those who look upon the radiant beauty of God. Jesus, as God's Son, reflects the pure brilliance and radiance of God, and those who look unto Jesus will participate in that same glory, for their "life begun in grace [will be] ending in eternal glory."[214]

The next category of contemplative vision is beholding. 2 Corinthians 3:18, which was occasionally joined with the examples of looking at Jesus, now becomes foundational for beholding. Both this text and the principle of beholding Christ were also highly significant for Bernard, though Ambrose does not quote him directly in this regard.[215] Thomas White likewise defines contemplation as "beholding of the face of God."[216]

---

208. Ibid., 349; cf. 352. 489.
209. Ibid., 679.
210. Ibid., 355.
211. Ibid., 1157.
212. Ibid., 92.
213. Ibid., 242.
214. Ibid., 356; cf. 1089–103 for Ambrose's most sustained treatment of Jesus' glory.
215. See for example Bernard, *SCC* 12.11; 24.5; 25.5; 36.6; 57.11; 62.5, 7; 67.8; 69.7.
216. White, *Method of Divine Meditation*, 4.

Ambrose also believes that "contemplative faith behold[s] Christ."[217] He combines the themes of imitation and beholding when he asserts, "we must fix our eyes on Jesus for our imitation . . . *We are changed by beholding* . . . how should this but stirre up my soule to be like Jesus Christ?"[218] Again the magnitude of the transforming sight of Jesus' glory becomes evident as Ambrose refers to 2 Cor 3:18: "[t]he very beholding of Christ hath a mighty conforming and assimilating vertue to leave the impressions of glory upon our spirits."[219] Once again in one of the conforming sections, Ambrose invites his readers to focus their "spiritual eyes" on Jesus so that they might be transformed into his image:

> Let us look fixedly on Jesus Christ, let us keep our spiritual eyes still on the patterne, untill we feel our selves conforming to it . . . Indeed the manner of this working may be secret, and insensible, yet if we follow on, we shall feele it in the issue; the beholding of Christ is a powerful beholding; there is a changing, transforming vertue goes out of Christ . . . Sight works upon the imagination in bruit creatures . . . and imagination work[s] a real change in nature.[220]

This accentuates the reality that people are changed by beholding the object upon which they contemplate. Christ's glory, the glory of heaven is so radiant and overwhelming that it transforms a person increasingly into the likeness of Jesus. Therefore, Ambrose assures his readers, "so God receives none to contemplate his face, but he transformes them into his own likenesse by the irradiaton of his light, and Christ hath none that dive into these depths of his glorious and blessed incarnation, but they carry along with them sweet impressions of an abiding and transforming nature."[221]

Gazing is the final word used by Ambrose and receives little attention in comparison with looking and beholding. However, Ambrose reinforces the significance of the Ascension declaring, "what shall he ascend, and shall not we in our contemplations follow after him? gaze O

217. Ambrose, *Looking Unto Jesus*, 23.

218. Ibid., 121; cf. McGee, "Conversion and Imitation of Christ," 28–33, for the Puritan understanding of imitation of Christ.

219. Ibid., 815–16.

220. Ibid., 526. Chan describes this specific passage as an example of "mystical" beholding. "Puritan Meditative Tradition," 198–99.

221. Ibid., 350; cf. 526, 917 for other examples of transformation that are not directly connected with 2 Cor 3:18.

my soul on this wonderful object, thou needest not feare any check from God."[222] According to Ambrose the beatific vision was the "glorious sight of Christ as God."[223] The Puritans and earlier spiritual writers recognized that contemplation could anticipate but never fully realize the beatific vision until a person reached heaven.[224] Saint Paul was the exception, briefly experiencing this during his rapture into heaven recorded in 2 Cor 12:2.[225] Further, this experience of seeing God face to face was sometimes referred to as "the very top of heaven."[226] In the following illustration Ambrose weaves the beatific vision and both beholding and gazing together to describe Christ's holiness: "the Saints in glory now *see the face of Christ*; . . . they do nothing else but stare, and gaze, and behold his face for ages, and yet they are never satisfied with beholding; suppose they could weare out their eyes at the eye-holes in beholding Christ, they should still desire to see more. O the lovelinesse of Christ ravishes the souls of the glorified."[227] Therefore, while contemplative gazing when a person is still on earth provides both a brief glimpse of God's presence and a desire to see God more fully, that fullness is reserved for heaven.[228]

Contemplation in the Other Writings of Isaac Ambrose

Redeeming the Time and the twin 1662 works, *War with Devils* and *Communion with Angels*, are the remaining works of Ambrose. In *Redeeming the Time* Ambrose references Lady Margaret's books for contemplation without identifying them. Further, he asserts a primary way for redeeming the time was to exercise "ejaculatory Duties, as suddenly to look up to Heaven."[229] In *War with Devils* Ambrose addresses his epistolary dedication to Justice Orlando Bridgman. He praises Bridgman for his heavenly-mindedness and once again equates the "Duty of looking unto

---

222. Ibid., 871–72.

223. Ibid., 1096; cf. 1092–103, 1111–13 and Ambrose, *Media* (1657), 259–60 for a sustained treatment on this topic.

224. Ibid., 481 and Williams, "Puritan Enjoyment of God," 125, 265–66.

225. Ibid., 1093–94.

226. Ibid., 1095.

227. Ibid., 481.

228. Ambrose, *Ultima* in *Prima, Media & Ultima* (1654), 203, 214–17 and Ambrose, *Looking Unto Jesus*, 1096–99, for Ambrose on the beatific vision.

229. Ambrose, *Redeeming the Time*, 28, 19.

Jesus" with contemplation.[230] Chapter 3 demonstrated that one of the greatest barriers to contemplation was the devil's temptation. The best antidote to counter this was to "have your conversation in heaven, be much in meditation of those surpassing joys, so will you frustrate Satans hopes, and escape the worlds intanglements or snares."[231] Closely related to the devil's temptations are worldly anxieties and cares. Therefore, Ambrose maintains that "heavenly-minded Christian[s]" should "pray also for heavenly-mindedness" to protect them from being "disquieted with worldly troubles."[232] There are surprisingly few references to contemplation in *Communion with Angels*, where one might expect to find a greater emphasis upon heavenly-mindedness. However, that is not the focus of Ambrose's most controversial work that examines the origin and nature of the angels' ministry, especially how they might function across the person's lifespan, including declaring God's mind and will, protecting a person from the devil's temptations, restoring people back to health, encouraging souls, and finally welcoming the saints into heaven. One additional use of the term comes in his description of Joseph Hall as "the contemplative Bishop."[233]

BENEFITS AND EFFECTS OF CONTEMPLATION

Early in *Looking Unto Jesus* Ambrose provides two lists of motives, one of wants, indicating what a person would lose by neglecting to look at Jesus, and a second positive list, based upon the benefits gained by looking unto Jesus.[234] In the second category he states, "[h]ere is a Catalogue, an Inventory of a Christians riches; have Christ and have all; . . . If Christ be yours . . . God is yours, the Father is yours, the Son is yours, the Spirit is yours, all promises are yours, for in Christ they are all made, and for him they shall be performed."[235] Not all of these benefits are of equal weight, but the primary effects of contemplation and heavenly-mindedness according to Ambrose, are contemplative understanding

230. Ambrose, *War with Devils*, Epistle Dedication, [1, 3].

231. Ibid., 111–12.

232. Ibid., 146.

233. Ambrose, *Communion with Angels*, 290. Earlier Ambrose referred to one of Joseph Hall's writings as "a sweet contemplation of an holy Divine." *Looking Unto Jesus*, 386.

234. Ambrose, *Looking Unto Jesus*, 31–46.

235. Ibid., 39.

and love, protection from temptation and danger, growing intimacy with Jesus in spiritual marriage, being transformed into Christ's likeness, and an expanding sense of enjoyment of God. First, contemplation provides a person with a new sense of understanding and love. The very structure of *Looking Unto Jesus* introduces this pattern, first the intellect or understanding is emphasized and next the affections, in which love occupies a central role. Ambrose declares that by looking at Jesus, "we gaine more, and more knowledge of Christ" and further that this helps us to "understand those great mysteries of grace." He further clarifies that this type of contemplative knowledge is "practical and experimental."[236] Additionally, as a person meditates upon Christ considering the relationship of the "bride in the bridegroome," they experience a "flaming, burning love to Christ."[237] In return "Christ gives a sincere and inward love of himself unto their hearts."[238] With even greater integration Ambrose connects these two benefits of contemplation in his stirring meditation of a soul's love to Christ: "when sweetly we repose our selves in the lap of our Saviour with content unspeakable, and full of glory, it proceeds from the last act of faith, wherby we are actually perswaded by those welcome whispers of the Spirit of adoption, that certainly Christ is our Saviour, and that our debts are cancelled to the very last mite."[239]

A second benefit of heavenly-mindedness is strength to combat suffering and protection from temptations. Ambrose asserts, "*looking on Jesus* will strengthen patience under the crosse of Christ."[240] Further, he encourages others to "pray also for heavenly-mindedness, and thou wilt not be disquieted with worldly troubles."[241] Ambrose minimized this benefit in relation to others, but Baxter did not, declaring, "a heavenly mind is exceedingly fortified against temptations, because the affections are so thoroughly prepossessed with the high delights of another world."[242]

Third, the person who intentionally meditates and contemplates on Jesus will deepen his or her intimacy of spiritual marriage with him. One of the more significant motives is that "this communion with

236. Ibid., 33.
237. Ibid., 34.
238. Ibid., 37.
239. Ambrose, *Media* (1657), 224.
240. Ambrose, *Looking Unto Jesus*, 42.
241. Ambrose, *War with Devils*, 146; cf. 111–12.
242. Baxter, *Saints' Everlasting Rest*, 269; cf. 268–70.

Christ, [is] but very heaven aforehand" and "it's an happy thing to have Christ dwell in our hearts, and for us to lodge in Christs bosome! Oh its an happy thing to maintain a reciprocal communication of affairs betwixt Christ and our souls!"[243] Ambrose employs the same intimate imagery of resting in Christ's bosom in his meditation of the soul's love to Christ. His desired goal for this meditation is for "the souls rest or reposal of it selfe in the bosome of Christ, with content unspeakable and glorious."[244] Further, since Christ "their Husband is in heaven," this motivates those who are in communion with Christ to continually seek to be in conversation with him.[245] Ambrose elaborates on the description as well as the means of cultivating this heavenly conversation: "so in our conversings with Christ there is a communion, or mutual acting of the soul upon Christ, and of Christ upon the soul; we let out our hearts to Christ, and he lets out his heart to us."[246] He also provides suggestions of how to maintain heavenly conversations including taking advantage of heavenly exercises which includes, Scripture and prayer, being cautious to avoid performing spiritual practices by mere formality, and paying attention to the Holy Spirit.[247] Since "it is the Spirit of God that must be as the chariot of *Elijah*" to guide individuals in heavenly-mindedness Ambrose challenges his readers to "observe the drawings, and movings, and mindings of the Spirit."[248]

A fourth benefit of contemplation is being transformed into Christ's likeness. Contemplation is a looking, beholding, and gazing upon an object in a sustained loving and grateful manner. When this is directed towards Jesus as the object, a person is transformed more and more into Christ's likeness. Earlier it was noticed how frequently Ambrose connects this with Saint Paul's declaration in 2 Cor 3:18 and the formative nature of God's glory. Of the nine ways of looking at Jesus, the conforming sections were most likely to be saturated with contemplative language and images. As Ambrose develops the conforming to Jesus in his incarnation section, he significantly frames this within the context of spiritual marriage: "all we have is by marriage with Jesus Christ; . . .

243. Ambrose, *Looking Unto Jesus*, 40; cf. 1004.
244. Ambrose, *Media* (1657), 224; cf. 272.
245. Ambrose, *Looking Unto Jesus*, 920.
246. Ibid., 918.
247. Ibid., 921–24.
248. Ibid., 924.

if by looking on Christ, we come to this likenesse, to be one with Jesus Christ."[249] Previously, Ambrose's repeated reliance upon the Holy Spirit was mentioned. In drawing a parallel between Mary, the mother of Jesus, and those who seek to look unto Jesus Ambrose declares, "look we to this conformity, that as Christ was conceived in *Mary* by the holy Ghost, so, that Christ be conceived in us, in a spiritual sense by the same holy Ghost."[250] Realizing that conception is only the beginning, Ambrose asserts that "formation followes conception" and further that a "life begun in grace [will be] ending in eternal glory."[251] Therefore, the final outcome of looking to Jesus is that "the sight of God will make us like to God; and the sight of Christ will make us like to Christ."[252] Further, the full benefit of the beatific vision is that a person reclaims his or her original image and likeness of Christ.

Fifth, heavenly-mindedness yields a growing sense of enjoyment and delight in God and Jesus. Once a person reaches heaven they experience a "compleate enjoyment of God."[253] While the fullness of fruition is reserved for heaven, individuals are able to experience a proleptic prelude of that joy on earth. Every opportunity of contemplation affords the individual who has been married to Jesus as Husband to taste again the heavenly joy that awaits that consummation of marriage with Christ in heaven. The Holy Spirit once again functions significantly in providing "a drop of heavens joy" into the hearts of those who follow Jesus.[254] Further, a person may already have "tasted of the joyes of heaven in prayer" in their spiritual practices.[255] Closely connected with this sense of enjoyment of God is the resulting expression that contemplation is "to worship him in his ascension up into heaven; O admire and adore him!"[256] Admiration and adoration is a proper response to experiencing the joyful presence of Jesus.

While Ambrose does not employ the common medieval distinction between Mary's contemplation and Martha's action, he and his fellow

249. Ibid., 355; cf. 354, 356.
250. Ibid., 351.
251. Ibid., 356.
252. Ibid., 349.
253. Ibid., 1084; cf. 1085–88 and Ambrose, *Media* (1657), 260–63.
254. Ibid., 876; cf. 914–15.
255. Ibid., 480.
256. Ibid., 872.

Puritans certainly recognized its importance[257] In chapter 3 Ambrose spoke of the proper balance of solitude that always was connected with returning and engagement with the world. Further, Ambrose's funeral sermon for Lady Margaret Houghton mentioned the importance of balancing contemplative practices and active living within the world.[258]

CONCLUSION

Clearly chapters 3 and 4 have demonstrated the contemplative nature of Isaac Ambrose. His writings and experience reflect a deeply focused beholding of Jesus. A careful review of his usage of contemplation and heavenly meditation reveals no apparent change or development in his understanding. His two largest works, *Media* and *Looking Unto Jesus*, are mystical texts in the best sense of the word and came in the middle of his life. These two works reveal a much richer and more robust understanding than his earlier works of *Prima* and *Ultima*. Further, his last two works, *War with Devils* and *Communion with Angels*, completed just two years before his death, indicate a marked reduction of contemplative themes. However, that should not suggest that contemplation became less important for Ambrose. Rather it appears that the degree of contemplation was directly related to the topic and texture of his works. Therefore, the focus of *Media* on spiritual practices and *Looking Unto Jesus*, which was essentially a guide to contemplation, were more likely to emphasize contemplation than his other works. Further, Ambrose's deep appreciation for Bernard is evident. He quotes him accurately and never refers to him disapprovingly. Moreover, Ambrose followed the nascent importance of the Ascension and heavenly meditation of Calvin and expanded it throughout his works.

Relative to other Puritans, Ambrose exhibits a rich expression of contemplative-mystical piety. While the sampling of Puritans read in this chapter is limited, he is far more focused on heaven than Downame. Unlike Baxter, who is frequently acknowledged because of the popularity of his *Saints' Everlasting Rest*, Ambrose devotes more attention to the actual process and enjoyment of contemplation than Baxter's preoccupation of focusing on the hindrances to heavenly meditation. Further, Baxter appears to favor more the intellect while Ambrose seems to emphasize more the affections. While Ambrose drew heavily from Bishop

257. Hambrick-Stowe, *Practice of Piety*, xiii, 280; cf. Packer, *Quest for Godliness*, 24.
258. Ambrose, *Redeeming the Time*, 19.

Hall, his writings were more sustained and deeper in contemplative awareness and experience than the Bishop's. Following Dewey Wallace's observation, it is significant that Ambrose wrote before the Restoration hence his contemplative nature was not a withdrawal from the increased persecution that later nonconformists would face. One additional theme that has appeared frequently throughout this chapter is the great importance of the Holy Spirit in uniting believers with Jesus in spiritual marriage and the meditative practices that can prepare a person for contemplative experiences to deepen that spiritual marriage. The next chapter will continue to examine contemplative experiences. However, the focus will be greatly sharpened to explore one aspect of the language of contemplation, which is ravishment. Ravishment figures prominently in the Puritan awareness of delight and enjoyment of God; while it may strike contemporary ears as being unusual it was consistently employed by seventeenth-century Christians.

Chapter Five

The Rhetoric of Ravishment: The Language of Delight and Enjoyment

This day the Lord cast one into a spiritual, heavenly, ravishing love
trance; he tasted the goodnesse of God, the very sweetness of Christ,
and was filled with the joyes of the Spirit above measure. O it was
a good day, a blessed fore-taste of Heaven, a love-token of Christ to
the Soul, *a kisse of his mouth whose love is better then wine.*

—Isaac Ambrose[1]

Delight and enjoyment may appear to be unusual terms when speaking of the Puritans. However, they were as interested in stirring
their hearts as stretching their minds. Surprising to some, their vocabulary of enjoyment overflowed through the language of sweetness,
various expressions of love, being swallowed up, and ravishment. This
chapter will examine the nature and dynamics of ravishment as well as
the related subject of desire for God. Weaving together these threads of
thought will create an awareness of the benefits and effects on ravishment according to the writings of Ambrose.

---

1. Ambrose, *Media* (1657), 183.

DEFINITION AND USE OF RAVISHMENT IN
THE WRITINGS OF ISAAC AMBROSE

Ambrose provides his readers with a clear awareness of his usage of rav-ishment through two examples from *Looking unto Jesus*. Early in this work he articulates the necessity of ravishment to draw a person out from him or herself:

> Therefore they were willed to come forth of their doores: even so, if we will behold the great King, Jesus Christ, in his most excel-lent glory (a sight able to satisfie the eye, and to ravish the heart) we must come out of our doors, we must come out of our selves, otherwise we cannot see his glory; we are in our selves shut up in a dark dungeon, and therefore we are called upon to come forth into the clear light of faith, and with the eyes of faith to behold in daily meditation the glory of Christ Jesus.[2]

Later in describing the practice of loving Jesus for his great work of sal-vation, Ambrose writes, "[i]t pleased thee, my Lord, out of thy sweet ravishments of thy heavenly love, to say to thy poor Church, *turne away thine eyes from me, for they have overcome me*; but oh let me say to thee, *turne thine eyes to me, that they may overcome me; my Lord, I would be thus ravished, I would be overcome; I would be thus out of my selfe, that I might be all in thee.*" Significantly this citation accurately recognizes that the bridegroom is the person who is being ravished by the bride in Canticles. However, Ambrose quickly reverses the relationship and begs the bridegroom to ravish him, as the bride. Immediately Ambrose adds, this "is the language of true love to Christ."[3] Clearly for him, ravishment expresses being overcome by God's greater power that draws a person out from darkness and transforms that person's sight to perceive the glory of Jesus. But there is also a reciprocal nature that lovingly responds to Christ for his great love and freedom first shared.

Ambrose employed the negative usage of ravish only once. In de-scribing the struggles of Jacob in Gen 34 he declares "after his first entry into his owne country, his wife Rachel dyes, his daughter Dinah is rav-ished, his sonne Reuben lyes with his concubine."[4] Clearly, ravish is used here in its destructive sense of rape or overpowering a person through

---

2. Ambrose, *Looking Unto Jesus*, 12.

3. Ibid., 505 (incorrectly numbered 513).

4. Ambrose, *Ultima* in *Prima, Media & Ultima* (1654), 28.

abuse or pain. That was the common definition found in seventeenth-century dictionaries. Thomas Blount's entry is representative of this and declares that ravish "signifies in our Law an unlawful taking away, either a woman or an heir in Ward: Sometime it is used also in one signification with Rape, (viz.) the violent deflouring a Woman."[5] However, in another seventeenth-century dictionary, the spiritual meaning of ravish was conveyed through the term rapture and understood as "a snatching away by violence; also an Ecstasie, or Transportment."[6] According to the *Oxford English Dictionary*, the semantic range includes both the "mystical sense" to transport a soul and the destructive expression "to ravage, despoil, plunder."[7] Williams acknowledges the ambiguous nature and tension; while ravishment has "dangerous associations with rape or abduction," it also "expressed certain characteristics of ecstasy powerfully and effectively."[8] Thomas Vincent's sermon on spiritual marriage reveals this same negative usage as he warns young virgins, "when otherwise the Devil and Sin would ravish your Virgin affections."[9] However, it is critical to recognize that the devil and sin are violating the woman, not God. Contemporary scholarship has made much of the tension associated with this term. Accusations of God's violence as a rapist abound. John Donne's Holy Sonnet XIV, "Batter my heart three-personed God," is often a lightning rod for much of this critique, and in particular his final line which reads, "[n]or ever chaste, except you ravish me."[10] While unquestionably force is exercised in ravishing or drawing the soul toward God, it does not resemble the destructive abusive control or violence that is inherent in rape. Moreover, this extravagant use of intense erotic imagery that was

5. Blount, *Glossographia*, n.p.; cf. Cockeram, *English Dictionarie*, second part, n.p.; and Phillips, *New World of English Words*, n.p. Cawdrey, *Table Alphabeticall*, renders *ravish* as "take away by force," n.p. Wilson, *Christian Dictionarie* does not include *ravish*.

6. Phillips, *New World of English Words*, n.p. Phillips also has entries for *transport* and *ecstasie*.

7. *OED*, 13:235.

8. Williams, "Puritan Enjoyment of God," 201.

9. Vincent, *Christ the Best Husband*, 18.

10. Barbara Lewalski is rather tame in her assertion that "Christ the Bridegroom of the soul is urged to become its ravisher or rapist." *Protestant Poetics*, 104. Much less restrained is Rambuss, *Closet Devotions*, 18, 50, 53–54, 68. Barbara Newman, "Rereading Donne's Holy Sonnet 14" explores the linguistic and spiritual tension of Donne's usage of ravishment; cf. McCullough, "Ravished by Grace." In my reading and comparing of sources it is clear that literary critics are much more likely to speak of God as a "rapist" than historians and theologians.

fairly typical among the Puritans[11] was a continuation of the medieval saints and reflected the best of the contemplative-mystical tradition of historic Christian spirituality. Beyond this single negative example, Ambrose always understood ravishment as the experience of being over-come, carried away by joy, or transported into the presence of God. To be ravished is to be lifted up or out beyond oneself, not by anything one does but as a gift from God. While ravishment includes being overpowered and requires surrender, this should not create fear since it is motivated by God's love. Shortly we will return to the ambiguous nature of ravishment.

BIBLICAL AND HISTORICAL SOURCES OF RAVISHMENT IN ISAAC AMBROSE

Ambrose employs both biblical as well as patristic and contemporary sources for his use of ravishment. Further, he utilizes the traditional vocabulary of desire and delight in his writings. Unfortunately, Marius van Beek's detailed study of devotional literature in the Puritans does not include the use of ravishment, since his focus was limited to new vocabulary, rather than that which was already in common usage. The first source that Ambrose employed as any good Puritan would was Scripture and in particular the Song of Songs, which had long been the preeminent book for illustrating the spiritual life and imagery for grow-ing in intimacy with Christ.[12] While the *Geneva Bible,* first published in 1560, continued to exert great influence throughout much of the first half and, in some situations, even later parts of the seventeenth century, the *Authorized Version* or *King James Bible* became available in 1611.[13] However, the Puritan usage of the Bible was extremely fluid and could often include a mixture of the Geneva and *Authorized Versions,* and preachers trained in the original languages would occasionally translate their own passages. Another factor that contributed to this fluidity was that some pastors quoted Scripture from memory.[14] Ambrose used the

11. Coffey, *Theology and British Revolutions,* 109.

12. See McGinn, "With "the Kisses of the Mouth"; Turner, *Eros and Allegory*; Coffey, "Letters by Samuel Rutherford," 104–5; and Hambrick-Stowe, *Practice of Piety,* 28.

13. Danner reports that both Lancelot Andrewes and Joseph Hall used the *Geneva Bible* until at least 1624. "Later English Calvinists and Geneva Bible," 502. Betteridge asserts the same for John Bunyan who was writing forty years later. "Bitter Notes: Geneva Annotations," 59.

14. Gordis, *Opening Scripture,* 25–26.

Authorized Version for his translation of *leb* from Song 4:9, which is a *hapax legomenon*: "[t]hou hast ravished my heart, my sister, my spouse; thou hast ravished my heart with one of thine eyes, with one chain of thy neck." The annotations created by various ecclesiastical bodies further extend this definition.[15] The *Dutch Annotations* based upon the original translation of the Synod of Dort renders this phrase from Song 4:9 as "*[t]hou hast taken my heart from me*" and then adds this note, "[o]r, *thou hast taken mine heart*: or, *hast ravished*, or *wounded mine heart*."[16] The *Westminster Annotations* based upon the *Authorized Version* declares that the word in the Septuagint conveys, "thou hast *excordiated*, or unhearted me; which is the language of great passion."[17]

A further source of inspiration was Christian tradition. Ambrose quotes Jerome: "[h]e was fairer than the sons of men; his countenance carried in it an hidden vailed star-like brightness (saith Jerome) which being but a little revealed, it so ravished his Disciples hearts, that at the first sight thereof they left all, and followed him: and it so astonished his enemies, that they stumbled and fell to the ground."[18] He also mentions Gregory the Great and when Ambrose describes the benefits of Christ's Ascension he declares, Christ's "love was so great and vast, that for our sakes he moves up and down; this ravished the Spouse, *Behold he comes leaping upon the mountains, and skipping upon the hills*, Cant. 2:8. Gregory that measured his leaps, thus gives them; he first leaps from his Fathers mansion to his Mothers womb."[19]

Earlier chapters revealed Ambrose's deep appreciation for Bernard of Clairvaux.[20] In describing spiritual duties Ambrose reminds his readers that it is easy to miss God's presence if a person's heart is "carnal and worldly." Furthermore, even when a person does experience God these times are relatively brief. Here he quotes Bernard's popular *rara hora brevis mora* (how rare the time and how brief the stay).[21] In describing

15. For a helpful overview and history of the various annotations produced during the seventeenth century see Clarke, *Politics, Religion and the Song of Songs*, 105–28.

16. Haak, *Dutch Annotations*, n.p.

17. *Westminster Annotations*, 3, n.p.; cf. Diodoti, *Geneva Annotations*, n.p.

18. Ambrose, *Looking Unto Jesus*, 273.

19. Ibid., 905.

20. For Bernard's usage of ravishment see Petry, *Late Medieval Mysticism*, 51–54; Casey, *Athirst for God*, 227, 290–92; and Gilson, *Mystical Theology of Bernard*, 106–8.

21. Ambrose, *Media* (1657), 36. The reference is to Bernard, *SCC* 23.15 but with

deliberate meditation Ambrose cites another reference from Bernard when he asserts that there are two types of contemplations in relation to God, the mind and the affections.[22] This reference will figure significantly later in the examination of the dynamics of ravishment in Ambrose.

Turning to Protestant sources, Ambrose cites Caracciolus as an example of ravishment: "[o]h if men did not know what ravishing sweetnesse were in the ways of God, they could not but embrace them, *and esteem one dayes society with Jesus Christ* (as *Caracciolus* did) *better than all the gold in the world*."[23] While Caracciolus was a convert to Calvinism, Ambrose does not quote any of Calvin's references to ravishment even though the word was not uncommon to him.[24] Another example of ravishment was drawn from Patrick Forbes (1564–1635), Bishop of Aberdeen; the specific citation is from his commentary on the Book of Revelation (on Rev 14:3).[25] Ambrose declares thusly:

> *Forbs* tells us that the Word of God hath three degrees of operation in the hearts of his chosen, *first it falleth to mens ears as the sound of many waters, a mighty great, and confused sound, and which commonly brings neither terror nor joy, but yet a wondering and acknowledgement of a strange force, and more than humane power, this is that effect which many felt hearing Christ, when they were astonished at his doctrine, as teaching with authority; what manner of doctrine is this? never man spake like this man: the next effect is the voyce of thunder, which bringeth not only wonder, but feare also: not only filleth the eares with sound, and the heart with astonishment, but moreover shaketh and terrifieth the conscience: the third effect is the sound of harping, while the word not only ravisheth with admiration, and striketh the Conscience with terrour, but also lastly filleth it with sweet peace and joy.*[26]

---

a slight variation, *rara hora et parva mora*; cf. *SCC* 85.13. John Owen also attributes this phrase to Bernard. *Holy Spirit in Prayer*, 330, and Owen, *Glory of Christ*, 293. De Reuver reports that Bernard borrowed this phrase from John of Fécamp and that it was common among the Dutch Pietists. *Sweet Communion*, 53n147.

22. Ambrose, *Media* (1657), 222. The reference is to *SCC* 49.4.

23. Ambrose, *Looking Unto Jesus*, 481. This is likely Galeacius Caracciolus (1517–86), an Italian nobleman.

24. For Calvin's use of ravishment see *Institutes*, 3.2.41; *Comm.* Ps 5:11; 19:1; 22:9–10; 89:6; 104:3; 119:97, 119; etc. For Luther's use of ravishment see Oberman, *Dawn of the Reformation*, 126–54.

25. Forbes of Corse, *Exquisite Commentarie upon Revelation*, 131–32.

26. Ambrose, *Looking Unto Jesus*, 490.

Interestingly, Ambrose duplicates this same quotation earlier in *Prima*.[27] Moreover, this reinforces the great importance the Puritans placed upon the transforming power of Scripture. More specifically, the Puritan commentaries on the Song of Songs further strengthen this understanding of ravishment. John Cotton exegetes Song 4:9 declaring, "ravishment is a force put upon a person loving, whereby he is more for the person beloved, then for himself. And when the heart is ravished, the person is willingly and heartily taken up with affection and attendance to another more than himself."[28] James Durham's *An Exposition of the Song of Solomon* was another very popular commentary. John Owen penned the dedication, confirming his appreciation for the devotional language of love in spiritual marriage in Canticles that he had previously employed in his *Communion with God*. Durham declares that ravished describes "Christ's unspeakable love, as it were, [and] coins new words to discover itself by, it is so unexpressible." He continues to enlarge its meaning by asserting, "[t]he word is borrowed from the passionateness of love, when it seizes deeply on a man, it leaves him not master of his heart, but the object loved hath it."[29] A review of other Puritan Song of Songs commentaries further substantiates this understanding.[30]

Further, there is some debate whether the usage of ravishment, typically associated with the Song of Songs, declined in prominence in the later half of the seventeenth century and early eighteenth century. On the one hand, Godbeer asserts the "references to Christ as husband and lover became more frequent and more vividly detailed in the late seventeenth century" and into the eighteenth century.[31] Conversely Winship maintains "this imagery grew far more restrained . . . after the turn of the eighteenth century."[32] My own reading of the primary sources suggests that while the usage appears to have diminished in the writings of those who conformed to the Church of England, this is not consistent for nonconformist sources as evidenced by the popular eighteenth-

27. Ambrose, *Prima* in *Prima, Media & Ultima* (1654), 63.
28. Cotton, *Brief Exposition of Canticles*, 97.
29. Durham, *Exposition of Song of Solomon*, 225.
30. See for example Ainsworth, *Solomons Song of Songs*, n.p.
31. Godbeer *Sexual Revolution*, 56, 355n58; cf. Rambuss, *Closet Devotions*, 134–35.
32. Winship, "Behold the Bridegroom Cometh," 171; cf. Belden Lane, "Two Schools of Desire," 401. While some of this debate is specifically focused on bridal imagery of the Song of Songs this was always closely connected with the use of ravishment.

century commentaries of Matthew Henry and John Gill.[33] In summary, while the Puritans in general and Ambrose in particular were clearly indebted to Bernard and other medieval sources, these writings were read through the lens of the Protestant Reformation.[34] The types of revisions that Puritans and Dutch Pietists made to Medieval and Western Catholic sources as enumerated in the previous chapter further validate this.

DESIRE AND MOTIVATION

Ambrose understood the great importance of "befriending our desires"[35] and this topic is an integral component in his contemplative-mystical writings. Moreover, his emphasis upon yearning for God was a theme present in Bernard, Calvin, and other Puritans.[36] The previous chapter established that desire was one of the nine ways of looking at Jesus. Accordingly, Ambrose defines it as "*a passion looking after the attainment of some good which we enjoy not, and which we imagine to be fitting for us.*" Or later in the same work he declares, desire is " *a certain motion of the appetite, by which the soul darts it selfe towards the absent good, purposely to draw neare, and to unite it selfe thereunto.*"[37] Ambrose recognized the biblical foundation of desire[38] and frequently employs the apostle Paul's statement in Phil 1:21,"*I desire to be dissolved, and to be with Christ*" to illustrate the nature and goal of desire.[39]

33. Henry, *Commentary on the Whole Bible* and Gill, *Exposition of Song of Solomon* consisted of 122 sermons preached on this book; cf. Clarke, *Politics, Religion and the Song of Songs*, 187–88. Likewise across the Atlantic Ocean many of Gilbert Tennent's sermons on the Lord's Supper employed the lush language of the Song of Songs. Long, *Eucharistic Theology*, 94–95; cf. 120. Additionally, George Whitefield preached a sermon entitled, "Christ the Believer's Husband" that was also dependent upon the Song of Songs. Long, *Eucharistic Theology*, 37–38; cf. Edwards, *Personal Narrative*, esp. 793, and Edwards, *Church's Marriage to Her Son*.

34. See Williams, "Puritanism: Piety of Joy," 6n17; cf. Williams, "Puritan Enjoyment of God," 15.

35. Sheldrake, *Befriending Our Desires*, 17; cf. 47.

36. On Bernard see Casey, *Athirst for God* and McGinn, *Growth of Mysticism*, 193–223. On Calvin see Belden Lane, "Spirituality as Performance of Desire." On the Puritans see Belden Lane, "Two Schools of Desire"; Belden Lane, "Rivers of Pleasure"; and Rambuss, *Closet Devotions*, though Rambuss persistently over-reads homoerotic themes into the Puritans.

37. Ambrose, *Looking Unto Jesus*, 102, 320; cf. 769.

38. See for example Pss 42:1–2; 63:1; 73:25; 84:1–2; 143:6; Isa 26:9; Luke 6:21; Phil 3:13–14.

39. Ambrose, *Looking Unto Jesus*, 321; cf. 1113 and Ambrose, *Media* (1657), 210.

Central to any understanding of desire is the object of that desire. Ambrose is insistent that while Jesus *"is altogether desirable"* and that nothing can compare "with the beauty of Christ" because he is full of glory, nonetheless individuals must be careful to guard against the desires of the world that can lead them astray.[40] Indeed the great challenge for humanity after the Fall is to ensure that the object of desire be worthy and not distorted through disordered attachments. Therefore, Ambrose urges his readers to "rouze up, and set this blessed object [of Jesus] before thy face!"[41] The role of the Holy Spirit in Ambrose's theology is essential, "as we desire the assistance of the Holy Spirit" to encourage this process.[42] According to him the "greatest gift we can expect in this world is the Spirit of Christ," and Christ's indwelling Spirit will work in individuals to transform them into greater holiness so that they might experience "dear communion with God and Christ."[43] Further, this desire serves as a connective tissue with the larger subject of spiritual marriage. Ambrose encourages his readers to "desire union with Christ" and "communion with God" and further to desire an "interest in Christs ascension into the Heaven . . . [because] my Husband, my Lord [is] in heaven."[44] Ambrose's language soars higher as he looks ahead and desires the Second Coming of Christ. Amid the expectation of this joyful reunion the object of his desire is "Christs wedding-day" and the "Marriage-Supper of the Lamb" and hearing Jesus address God about his bride: *"Father, here behold my Bride, that I have married unto my self."*[45] As he concludes this discussion on desiring Christ's return he summarizes the richness of this longing: "[c]ome now, and run over these particulars [of all the goals of spiritual marriage]; surely every one is motive enough to desire this day; it is a day of refreshing."[46] Significantly, all that Ambrose has written about de-

Additionally Ps 42:1–2 and Song 2:5 figure prominently in Ambrose's treatment of desire. *Looking Unto Jesus*, 104, 320.

40. Ibid., 773, 485, 103.

41. Ibid., 975.

42. Ambrose, *Media* (1657), 75.

43. Ambrose, *Looking Unto Jesus*, 881.

44. Ambrose, *Media* (1657), 226; cf. 465 and Ambrose, *Looking Unto Jesus*, 213, 879–80, 977–78.

45. Ambrose, *Looking Unto Jesus*, 1113–19, especially 1117–18. The association of a person's death with Christ's wedding day was common among the Puritans. Clarke, *Politics, Religion and the Song of Songs*, 70; cf. 60, 151.

46. Ibid., 1119.

sire finds its culmination in Jesus. This is not surprising since it echoes the title of his major work *Looking unto Jesus*.

Ambrose's understanding of desire recognizes the intensity or vehemence of a deep longing for Jesus that is reflective of both his fellow Puritans and the medieval tradition before him. A type of holy violence is required to reverse the tendency of human corruption as well as to overcome the violence of temptations that besiege the soul.[47] For without "an holy kinde of *violence* [a person can not] *lay hold upon the Kingdome of heaven*, Mat. 11.12."[48] Therefore, to counter the temptations and allurement of the devil, Ambrose urges stirring up "violent affections" and being responsive to "Gods merciful violence."[49] Bernard previously employed vehement love and violence when he discussed desire.[50] His usage asserted the "forceful, powerful, even violent" nature of love.[51] Later in the same century, Richard of St. Victor wrote a brief but significant treatise entitled *The Four Degrees of Violent Charity*.[52] Further, this language was not uncommon in the Eastern Orthodox tradition and appeared in John Climacus.[53] Thomas Watson, writing during Ambrose's time, published the most sustained Puritan treatment of violence in *Heaven Taken By Storm*. Watson understood that violence could be either positive or negative since it is a zealous or fervent intentionality to act in a specific way. Therefore, he writes, "[w]ithout violent affections we shall never resist violent temptations."[54] The Puritans took seriously the great entrenchment of sin and the entropy of the divided human heart. Indeed violence was often associated with conversion, or the beginning of spiritual marriage. Thomas Hooker declares, "God doth by

47. Ibid., 369 and Ambrose, *Media* (1657), 224, 289.

48. Ibid., 1007.

49. Ambrose, *Ultima* in *Prima, Media & Ultima* (1654), 196 (incorrectly numbered 194) and Ambrose, *War with Devils*, 75.

50. McGinn, *Growth of Mysticism*, 198, 203–4, 504n271; cf. Casey, *Athirst for God*, 92–93 and Burrows, "Erotic Christology."

51. McGinn, *Growth of Mysticism*, 203.

52. Ibid., 398–400, and esp. 413, 415–18.

53. Chryssavgis, "Notion of 'Divine Eros,'" 194.

54. Watson, *Heaven Taken By Storm*, 86; cf. Rutherford, *Christ Dying*, esp. 228, 282–84, 308, 361–62. Sharon Achinstein devotes a chapter to violence and cites Watson's *Heaven Taken By Storm* as well as other sources; however, she conflates Watson's spiritual usage of violence with more physical expressions of destruction. *Literature and Dissent in Milton's England*, 84–114.

an holy kind of violence plucke the sinner from sin to himselfe."[55] John Knott accurately summarizes the Puritan understanding of holy violence: "[t]he gulf between God and man was so wide and human sinfulness so persistent that some kind of extraordinary force seemed necessary to precipitate a response."[56] But it must be recognized that God does not use this divine power indiscriminately or capriciously. Sibbes offers this valuable insight into the Puritan understanding of holy violence: "for first, he deals by gentle means always, and then after, if those will not prevail, he goes to severe means, and in severe means he takes degrees; first less, and then more violent, and then violent indeed. God would never descend to sharper courses, if milder would serve the turn."[57] All of this is in agreement with Ambrose's understanding of holy violence and clarifies that God's violent or overpowering love is always an expression of compassion and mercy.

However, a careful reading of Song 4:9 reveals a significant insight regarding the origin of ravishment, that *it is the bride who ravishes the bridegroom* by flashing her eyes. Therefore, it is Jesus the divine Bridegroom, who is ravished by the spouse, the church or individual believer, not the reverse. Moreover, there is no evidence of abuse when the relationship is reversed, and the Triune God ravishes those in spiritual marriage with delight and enjoyment. Both the language in Song of Songs and of God's desire for creation is derived from the foundations of surrender and consent. Rutherford clarifies this declaring, "[m]y Wellbeloved hath ravished me; but it is done with consent of both parties, and it is allowable enough."[58] This critical insight must not be missed. Since there is mutual consent, one person is not taking advantage of the other. Further, just as Puritan marriages recognized the importance of mutual ravishment between husband and wife, the same was experientially true for Jesus and his bride, the church or individual Christians. This reiterates the truth that ravishment for the Puritans possessed both a human and spiritual dimension. Therefore, I conclude that the Puritan usage of rav-

55. Hooker, *Soules Implantation*, 1. Hooker frequently employs the language of violence to describe the divine operation on the soul. See Hooker, *Soules Implantation*, esp. 2, 68, 204, 254, and Hooker, *Soules Vocation Effectual Calling*, 635.

56. Knott, *Sword of the Spirit*, 11. Clarke similarly asserts, [t]he subject's plight is hopeless unless Christ is prepared to use a shocking amount of force to counteract the sinful activity of his errant Bride." *Politics, Religion and the Song of Songs*, 31.

57. Sibbes, *Exposition of 2 Corinthians*, 3:490.

58. Rutherford, *Letters*, 556.

ishment was not abusive or violent, as the term would be understood to-day.[59] Rather they fully recognized the pervasiveness of sin and rebellion and the deep allure the world had on those who lived on earth. They also acknowledged the necessary power of God's love that was required to attract a person to Christ and repulse the destructive nature of worldliness.

Ambrose's yearning for God also reveals a degree of *eros*, reflective of earlier mystical writers. When demonstrating the connection between prayer and love to God, he passionately pleads, "[o] burn and consume whatsoever would grow one with our souls beside thee; O let the fire of thy spirit so wholly turn our soules into a spiritual fire that the dross of the flesh and the world being wholly consumed" and "[s]et us on fire, burn us, make us anew and transform us, that nothing besides thee may live in us; O wound very deeply our hearts with the dart of thy love."[60] My reading of Ambrose confirms Alvin Plantinga's assessment: "[e]ven (and perhaps especially) the Puritans, dour and emotionally pinched as they are often represented, are full of expressions of erotic love of God."[61] Once again Ambrose articulates the critical role of the Spirit in his theology, as he urgently longs for God and begs for the flames of God's melting love to burn off any sin and the barriers of the world that keep him from enjoying God.[62] Additionally, this wounding of the soul further increases its desire for God.

According to Ambrose, grace serves an important function in his understanding of desire. Desire originates not in the soul of the seeker but rather is initiated by God: *"thou hast given me a kiss of thy mouth, and now I pant to be united to thee in a more consummate marriage; thou hast given me a tast, but my appetite and desire is not thereby diminished, but enlarged."*[63] Obviously the desire to long "after Christ" should be guided by him "whose heart is ever panting and longing after us."[64] God's grace is revealed in Ambrose's comments on Ps 63:1: "violent affections [are those] that God puts into the hearts of those who seeke him

59. Cohen comes to the same conclusion in *God's Caress*, 239–41.

60. Ambrose, *Media* (1657), 465; cf. 491 on the benefit of wounding the soul; cf. 264 on the role of the Spirit and heavenly flames.

61. Plantinga, "Testimonial Model," 313.

62. The flame of God's love was a common image in medieval writers. McGinn, *Growth of Mysticism*, 59–61, 192, 298, 302, 309, 392–94.

63. Ambrose, *Looking Unto Jesus*, 212.

64. Ibid., 975.

in sincerity and truth."[65] Ambrose recognizes his need and inadequacy as he confessed, "[o] where be those holy fits, those pangs of *love*, those *love-trances*, those Seraphical flames of conjugal affection, which made the spouse cry out, *I am sick of love*?"[66] Aware of both his necessity for increased love and desire, and as well as the challenges and barriers that could diminish his yearning, Ambrose cries out for God's assistance, "I desire, but help thou my faint desires; blow on my dying spark, it is but little; and if I know any thing of my heart, I would have it more; oh that my spark would flame! why Lord I desire that I might desire; oh breath it into me, and I will desire after thee."[67] Related to this deep yearning for Jesus Ambrose quotes Bernard: "he that thirsts let him thirsts more and he that desires let him desire yet more abundantly."[68] Not only is it critical to seek God's assistance in stirring up desires, but also it is equally important not only to speak the words of longing but also to actually feel them deeply in your soul.[69]

Further, Ambrose recognizes the importance of *contemptus mundi* and realizes that his desires and those of all people need to be refined and that "God sends afflictions to weane us from the world."[70] Therefore, Walsh is correct when she claims, "[a]bsence inflames desire as selective memory forgets all unpleasantness and longing grows pure."[71] More specifically, Belden Lane maintains that for the Puritans, "[a]ffliction, then, far from being a sign of God's indifference or lack of covenant love, becomes a means of testing, teasing, and binding the believer to the Divine Lover more closely than ever."[72] This reinforces Ambrose's previous earnest request that God would "wound very deeply our hearts with the dart of thy love." This paradoxical nature of God's love is traced to Song 2:5, "for I am sick of love." The painful absence of the bridegroom intensifies the desire and longing of the bride for her lover.[73] De Reuver

65. Ambrose, *Prima, Media & Ultima* (1654), 35.

66. Ambrose, *Media* (1657), 233.

67. Ambrose, *Looking Unto Jesus*, 979; cf. 321–22.

68. Ibid., 217. *Bern: delect: evang: serm.* is listed as the source

69. Ibid., 635.

70. Ambrose, *Ultima* (1640), 111.

71. Walsh, *Exquisite Desire*, 22.

72. Belden Lane, "Rivers of Pleasure," 85; cf. 86–89 and Belden Lane, *Ravished By Beauty*, 134–54.

73. McGinn, *Growth of Mysticism*, 61.

affirms another paradox that lovesickness comes from meditating on Christ's *via dolorosa*.[74] These painful, often debilitating experiences of affliction, suffering, and death, transform the soul, creating greater tenderness. Additionally, they reveal a person's deepest needs, and refine their desires, and redirect them more fully towards yearning intimately for God. Ambrose confesses the specific motivation for writing *Looking Unto Jesus* was recovering from a serious illness in 1653;[75] related is the addition of the Saints Suffering section in the later editions in *Media*. He recognized that suffering as a spiritual duty could shape and further encourage a person's spiritual growth. Additionally, Ambrose includes three deathbed accounts that reveal personal experiences of ravishment. Edward Gee, a colleague of Ambrose who died in 1659, experienced spiritual ravishment and heavenly joy as a prelude to the heavenly life.[76] A second deathbed experience was Mr. Holland, who in preparation for his death asked his minister to expound Rom 8. Those words produced an experience of ravishment in his spirit.[77] A third example was an unnamed "godly woman" who was overwhelmed with spiritual desertion, but as she approached the Lord's Supper she was filled with unspeakable joy. This soul-ravishing joy continued for a fortnight after eating at the Lord's Table.[78] The fact that a person could prepare for and deepen his or her desire and love for Jesus is further reinforced by a lengthy meditation composed by Ambrose to stir up the soul to love Christ more fully. Ambrose imagines Jesus speaking to the soul and comforting her, that while the soul has mistreated and been unkind to Jesus, Jesus still remains "*thy friend, thy Lord, thy brother, thy husband, and thy head.*" Ambrose suggests that these "blessed words" of Jesus caused the person to fall at his feet and cry out, "*my Saviour and my Lord.*" In response, he continues the soliloquy; "[o] my soul rouze up, can thy heart be cold when thou thinkest of this? What? Art thou not yet transported, and ravished with *love*?"[79]

---

74. De Reuver, *Sweet Communion*, 42.

75. Ambrose, *Looking Unto Jesus*, To the Reader, [1].

76. Ambrose, *War with Devils*, 184.

77. Ambrose, *Communion with Angels*, 283–84.

78. Ibid., 263. Ambrose also connects Jesus' absence with the increase of desire in *Looking Unto Jesus*, 211.

79. Ambrose, *Media* (1657), 231.

AUTOBIOGRAPHICAL EXPERIENCES OF ISAAC AMBROSE

Bernard McGinn distinguishes between mystical language, mystical theology, and mystical experience.[80] Ravishment frequently appears throughout Ambrose's corpus and is employed in each of these categories.[81] Further, Ambrose uses the biblical examples of Peter and Mary to illustrate the richness of ravishment as well as a full range of other examples to encourage believers to desire the delight and enjoyment of spiritual marriage with Jesus.

Further, Ambrose was clearly no stranger to the delight and enjoyment of being ravished by God. Many of his personal experiences occurred during his annual retreats in May. He used these times to review his diary and pray, fast, read Scripture, and practice other spiritual duties. On May 20, 1641, he was overwhelmed by a trinitarian experience and recorded it in his diary under the caption, "*Gods love to the Saints*": "[t]his day the Lord cast one into a spiritual, heavenly, ravishing love trance; he tasted the goodnesse of God, the very sweetness of Christ, and was filled with the joyes of the Spirit above measure. O it was a good day, a blessed fore-taste of Heaven, a love-token of Christ to the Soul."[82] Significantly, here and in two additional elaborations on this specific event, Ambrose reveals some of the common characteristics of mystical experiences; tasting the goodness and sweetness of God, being filled with the joy of the Spirit, receiving the kisses of God's mouth, and experiencing the foretaste of ecstatic delight and ravishment of heaven. To further our ability of imagining how Ambrose perceived this encounter, he provides a column of texts that describe his experience as one of "*great delight*" and sweetness (Song 2:3); "*exceedingly joyfull in all our tribulation*" (2 Cor 7:4); and "*filled with joy, and with the holy Ghost*" (Acts 13:52). He further supplies another category of biblical passages that he calls dispositions. Their purpose is in "answering Gods mind in every particular *Experience* [that they] may be written in our hearts,

---

80. McGinn, *Foundations of Mysticism*, 307.

81. According to my reading, ravishment appears forty seven times in *Looking Unto Jesus*; twenty times in *Media* (1657); thirteen times in *Ultima* (1654); six times in *Communion with Angels*; four times in *Prima* (1654); and once both in *Redeeming the Time* and *War with Devils*. I did not make the same detailed accounting for the words rapt or rapture but they appear less frequently in Ambrose's writings.

82. Ambrose, *Media* (1657), 183.

and brought forth in our life afterwards."[83] In other words, these are the specific results that Ambrose wants to experience and deepen in his own life. The first text is 1 Pet 1:8 and contrasts a faith that is unseen which transitions to one of seeing that is refreshed with joy unspeakable and fullness of glory. The second passage from Rev 22:17, 20 records the interaction between the Spirit and Bride who hear, thirst, and cry out for Jesus to come quickly.

This was not the only occasion Ambrose referred to this retreat experience. In the first edition of *Media* he has styled this differently and provides additional significant details of his dramatic engagement with the triune God; "[t]his day in the Evening the Lord in his mercy poured into my soul the ravishing joy of his blessed Spirit. O how sweet was the Lord unto me? I never felt such a lovely taste of Heaven before: I believe this was the *joyful sound*, the *Kisses of his mouth*, the *Sweetnesses of Christ*, the *Joy of his Spirit, the new wine of his kingdom*; it continued with me about two days."[84] Unlike his 1657 account, Ambrose acknowledges the gift of God's mercy in declaring that this was the most "lovely taste of Heaven" he had experienced. Further, he had been touched by the "*[k]isses of his mouth*" and tasted "*the new wine of his kingdom*." More incredibly, this experience continued for two days.

Readers can gain a better perspective of the powerful nature of this retreat experience when Ambrose refers to this event yet a third time. On this occasion he is examining the evidence or assurance of his faith. He defines these "as *inherent and habitual observations of the Spirits actings in the Soul*."[85] He then instructs his readers how to gather, keep, and improve or enlarge these experiences and offers this personal evidence: "[t]he unspeakable joy of Gods Spirit, which sometimes I have felt in and after Ordinances; and especially once, when for the space of two dayes I was carried away into extasie and ravishment: This was when I began to see Spiritual things; and (that which makes it my Evidence) upon which followed more desire and endeavors after grace."[86] Once again Ambrose's method of presenting his material can expand our understanding. He

---

83. Ibid., 181.

84. Ambrose, *Media* (1650), 71.

85. Ambrose, *Media* (1657), 190.

86. Ibid., 214. While no date is provided the similarity of description between these two accounts and the repetition of the two days of experience suggest these all took place on May 20, 1641.

lists Ps 89:15; Isa 12:3; John 15:11; Rom 14:17; Gal 5:22; 1 Pet 1:8, all of which contain God's promise for experiencing joy. Additionally, "extasie" is mentioned, though this is not the only occasion that he makes use of it.[87] Ambrose follows the earlier pattern of Bernard, utilizing this term infrequently.[88] But unlike Bernard, Ambrose does not use the language of spiritual inebriation for ecstasy that Williams maintains "was often compared to intoxication.[89]

It is apparent from Ambrose's three-fold description that this was an extraordinary spiritual experience. The "Lord cast" him into this experience, that is, it came by God's grace and initiative, not his own. This does not imply that his spiritual practices did not prepare him for a greater degree of receptivity since, in fact, he maintains that "in and after Ordinances" these experiences occurred. Unlike Bernard, who spoke of the brevity of these ecstatic encounters, Ambrose is carried away by joy for two days. Extravagantly and lavishly he piles the descriptions on one atop another; it was "a spiritual, heavenly, ravishing love trance." It was also multi-sensory and involved both the more general references to sound and sight as well as those of taste and touch that were common in earlier medieval mystical experiences.[90] Further, it was trinitarian, involving the "goodnesse of God," "the very sweetness of Christ," and "the joyes of the Spirit above measure." Ambrose recognized the proleptic nature of his experience and perceived it as a "foretaste of heaven" or, as he called it, a "love-token of Christ to the Soul." It clearly created a new awareness and desire in his life that enabled him to recognize God more fully. Apparently from his description, this was the first time Ambrose had such an experience and that is the likely reason for his three-fold repetition of it. Placing these experiences within the landscape of

87. See Ambrose, *Media* (1657), 54, 261, 263; Ambrose, *Ultima* in *Prima, Media & Ultima* (1654), 221; Ambrose, *Looking Unto Jesus*, 251 (incorrectly numbered 152), 434, 800, 840, 1000; and Ambrose, *Communion with Angels*, 211. Flavel draws a distinction between "extraordinary" ecstasies where the soul is raptured out of the body as Paul in 2 Cor 12:2–3 and "ordinary" ecstasies where the person experiences the "foretastes of heaven." *Soul of Man*, 54–57.

88. McGinn, *Growth of Mysticism*, 508n325.

89. Williams, "Puritan Enjoyment of God," 119. On Bernard and spiritual inebriation see McGinn, *Growth of Mysticism*, 197, 212, 219. For Puritan examples of spiritual drunkenness see Sibbes, *Glance of Heaven*, 169 and Sibbes, *Commentary 2 Corinthians*, 480, and Rous, *Mysticall Marriage*, 349.

90. For Bernard's use of the spiritual senses see McGinn, *Growth of Mysticism*, 185–89.

Christian spirituality, it is significant that these are not the words of Teresa of Avila or Bernard of Clairvaux or Jan Ruusbroec, but of a moderate seventeenth-century Lancashire Puritan. Hearing this affective delight and desire for God only increases the misfortune that Ambrose's complete diary no longer exists, making it impossible to gain a deepening awareness of his mystical experiences. However, the evidence that does remain clearly reveals a contemplative-mystical piety that is every much as rich as that of Western and Roman Catholic devotional writers.

Additionally, Ambrose recorded an amazing nocturnal experience of ravishment dated July 19, 1647 from his diary:

> This night desiring God to sanctifie my sleep and dreams, that I sinned not in them: I dreamed, that after some troubles of life, my time limited was at an end, and that I heard the very voyce of God calling me by name into his glorious Kingdom; whither when I came, heavenly ornaments were pat upon me by the hand of God, and of Christ: My soul was exceedingly ravished. *The Lord grant I may make some use of this, to be more heavenly minded, and to breathe more after Christ.*[91]

Amazingly, Ambrose had cultivated such a spiritual awareness of God that he was conscious of God even in his dreams. On this occasion he rejoices that God calls him personally by name. Once again the result of this experience is a deepening desire to be heavenly-minded and more focused on Jesus and the kingdom of God.

DYNAMICS OF RAVISHMENT

According to Ambrose, a wide range of individuals can experience ravishment. His recipients include Jesus Christ, angels, specific biblical individuals such as Peter and Mary, Ambrose himself, as well as a number of his friends and colleagues. Further, there are numerous general references to the church or the disciples of Jesus. Consistent with Song 4:9, Jesus, as the divine Bridegroom, can be ravished by the church. Typically the cause of Jesus' ravishment is his great love for the church, or individual believers, or their faith in him, "[w]hen he [Jesus] sees the grace or acts of faith, he so approves of them, that he is ravished with wonder; he that rejoyced in the view of his creation, rejoyceth no lesse in the reformation of his creature, *behold thou art faire my love, behold thou*

91. Ambrose, *Media* (1650), 76.

art faire, there is no spot in thee, my sister, my spouse, thou hast wounded my heart, thou hast wounded my heart with one of thy eyes, Cant. 4, 7, 9."[92] This might sound surprising to some, but Christ is overwhelmed by the beauty and response of his followers. Jesus' willingness and even desire to be ravished affirmed his deep enjoyment and participation in the covenant of grace or spiritual marriage. By far the more frequent usage by Ambrose is for the church or bride to be ravished by Jesus, the Bridegroom. Nevertheless, on a number of occasions Ambrose uses ravishment in this former manner.[93] The *Geneva Bible* translates *leb* as wounded, however, even then the term was often understood as ravish. Joseph Hall paraphrases the verse as "[t]hou hast utterly rauisht me from myselfe . . . thou hast quite rauisht my heart with thy loue euen one cast of one of thine eyes of faith; and one of the ornaments of thy sanctification wherewith then art decked by my spirit, haue thus stricken mee with loue: how much more, when I shall have a full sight of thee, and all thy graces, shall I bee affected toward thee."[94]

The angels already know that believers will some day experience the fullness of joy in heaven. Ambrose envisions that these heavenly messengers "know what Christ hath done and suffered for them [the saints], *The mystery of godlinesse is seen of Angels*, it is so seen, that they take great delight to behold, yes, they are ravished in the very beholding of it."[95] Peter and Mary are the biblical figures that most frequently experience ravishment in Ambrose's writings. Before examining them, two other examples must be mentioned. One relates to the spiritual duty that Ambrose calls "Reading the Word," "[t]hat it happens sometimes such raptures may seize on a man, even while he is reading the Scriptures; as the Disciples *hearts burned within them, whist our Saviour talked with them, going to Emmaus*, and if so, then the heart opens itself to close with and draw in that ravishing object."[96] The apostle Paul illustrates the other example: "[t]hus *Paul* prayed for the *Thessalonians*, and when *Timothy* came, and brought him good tidings of *their faith and charity*, he was not only *comforted*, but in his ravishment he cryes, *What thanks can we*

---

92. Ambrose, *Looking Unto Jesus*, 414. This is the only occasion where Ambrose translates *leb* as wounded rather than ravish.

93. Ibid., 28, 504, 505, 1046 for other examples of Jesus being ravished by the church.

94. Hall, *Salomons Divine Arts*, 39–40.

95. Ambrose, *Communion with Angels*, 205.

96. Ambrose, *Media* (1657), 482.

render again to God for you?"[97] Ambrose includes 1 Thess 3:6, 7, 9 in the margin which indicate that Paul is overjoyed with the good news that he has received from Timothy regarding these believers.

Ambrose recognizes the origin of ravishment can be God, Jesus, the Holy Spirit, and Scripture, which is normally representative of the voice of Jesus. Additionally, the use of spiritual duties can ravish humanity; therefore, as previously stated, the church has the ability to ravish Jesus. Since elsewhere in this chapter many references to God and Jesus have already been examined, only the Holy Spirit, Scripture, and spiritual duties' ability to ravish will now be considered. Consistent with Calvin's strong emphasis upon the "inner witness" or testimony of the Holy Spirit, Ambrose follows that same Reformed pattern: "[t]here is a testimony of the Spirit which sometimes the Spirit may suggest and testifie to the sanctified conscience with a secret still heart-ravishing voice."[98] Not surprisingly the Holy Spirit often engages with Scripture and spiritual disciplines to create ravishment. In his discussion of hearing the Word, Ambrose declares, "*[o]h what meltings, chearings, warmings of the Spirit had such a one? and such a one? the Word was to them as honey . . . I wonder at Saints that tell of so much sweetnesse, and comfort and ravishing of heart.*"[99] Finally, the Spirit can work through spiritual practices as acknowledged by Ambrose from his personal retreat experience: "[t]he unspeakable joy of Gods Spirit, which sometimes I have felt in and after Ordinances and especially once, when for the space of two dayes I was carried away into extasie and ravishment."[100] His colleague John Angier had a similar experience, "oh how inlarged was he in those Days and Duties! he seemed to be transported into Extasies of Admiration."[101]

Additionally, while most of these experiences are mediated through spiritual duties or meditation on Scripture, some are the result of direct causality or unmediated contact with God. Peter's post-Easter experience

97. Ibid., 451.

98. Ambrose, *Looking Unto Jesus*, 889; cf. 809, 881; cf. Ambrose, *Ultima in Prima, Media & Ultima* (1654), 201; Ambrose, *Media* (1657), 10, 184, 492; and Ambrose, *War with Devils*, 184 for other examples of the Spirit's role in "ravishment." For Calvin on the inner witness of the Spirit see *Institutes*, 1.7.4–5; 3.2.34.

99. Ibid., 809; cf. 490, 773, 817 and Ambrose, *Media* (1657), 54, 233, 482, 492 for Scripture's ability to ravish.

100. Ambrose, *Media* (1657), 214; cf. 36, 162, and 256 for the use of spiritual duties in ravishment.

101. Heywood, *Narrative of John Angier*, 44.

reflects this: "Christs apparitions are ravishing sights; if he but stand on the shore, *Peter* throws himselfe over-board to come to Christ."[102] And again as he speaks of loving Jesus for his coming into the world through his incarnation, "me-thinks the very sight of Christ incarnate is enough to ravish thee with the apprehension of his infinite goodnesse: see how he calls out, or (as it were) draws out the soul to union, vision, and participation of his glory!"[103] These samples of direct causality illustrate the "ravishing" power of Jesus' glory. That is when people see Jesus in the splendor of his beauty and holiness, such as Peter at the Transfiguration, or Mary on Easter morning, or the saints in heaven they cannot resist being ravished by the overwhelming sight of Jesus' glory.

But there is much more to Ambrose's rhetoric of ravishment. Since this term is such a significant component of his understanding of delight and enjoyment of God and because ravishment has received little sustained research into its nature and dynamics, it bears further exploration. Therefore, to guide our consideration into the "excess of meaning" in Ambrose's use of ravishment, I want to read his texts more fully through four additional categories. There will be some overlap that will create additional reinforcement between some of these themes, but they provide a more nuanced hermeneutic for appreciating Ambrose's usage of ravishment. First, as previously highlighted, Ambrose follows Bernard's pattern in emphasizing the importance and interaction of the intellectual and affective development of ravishment.[104] He declares that his method of meditation is to "begin in the understanding [and] end in the affections." Here he quotes Bernard in a familiar passage related to the integration of these two approaches, "[f]or as holy contemplation has two forms of ecstasy, one in the intellect, the other in the will; one of enlightenment, the other fervor."[105] Scholars indicate while the Cistercian abbot desired a balance he often preferred the affective dimension.[106] This was likely due both to his resistance to the more intellectual approach of his rival,

---

102. Ambrose, *Looking Unto Jesus*, 769. Peter's experience is the same at Jesus' Transfiguration. *Looking Unto Jesus*, 459. On the importance of the Transfiguration see McGinn, *Foundations of Mysticism*, 67, 206–7, 222.

103. Ambrose, *Looking Unto Jesus*, 338; cf. 213, 273, 481, 505, 725, 769, 908, 990, for other examples of direct causality.

104. McGinn discusses the interplay of knowledge and love in Bernard. *Growth of Mysticism*, 200–203.

105. Ambrose, *Media* (1657), 222. This reference is to Bernard *SCC* 49.4.

106. See Casey, *Athirst for God*, 100 and Butler, *Western Mysticism*, 102.

Peter Abelard, and the less stable nature of the intellect since the Fall.[107] According to Ambrose, the intellectual forms the foundation for the affective, and a careful reading of his uses of ravishment confirms that he consistently follows this pattern. Due to Ambrose's high priority upon Scripture, if the intellect is lacking there cannot be any affective response. This is clearly revealed by those who foolishly neglect the spiritual duties that usually in some way engage Scripture and could provide a rich experience of Jesus. Ambrose bewails this sadness, "[t]hey have not that love to Christ, which Christs beholders have; they meditate not upon Christ as lovers on their love; they delight not themselves in Christ . . . Surely they have no flaming, burning love to Christ . . . O they feel not those ravishing comforts, which usually Christ speaks to the heart, when he speaks from his heart in love."[108] Further, in a revealing passage Ambrose declares, "Christs inward beauty would ravish love out of the devils, if they had but grace to see his beauty."[109] This statement is significant for two reasons. First, it reiterates that the devil cannot be ravished because it cannot possess any awareness of Christ's beauty. Secondly, it reveals ravishment is a gift from God, dependent upon grace.

In his meditation on the soul's love to Jesus, Ambrose begins by confessing, "[t]hese, O these were the blessed words, which his Spirit from his Gospel spake unto me, till he made me cast my self at his feet, yea into his armes, and to cry out, *my Saviour and my Lord*; And now, O my soul rouze up, can thy heart be cold when thou thinkest of this? What? are thou not yet transported, and ravished with *love*? is it possible that thy heart should hold, when it remembers these boundlesse compassions?"[110] The same dynamic interaction between the intellect and affection is at work when Ambrose speaks of the penitent thief from the cross. Reflecting on his experience of gazing upon Jesus he declares, "I deny not but the other joyes in Heaven are transcendent and ravishing, but they are all no better than accessories to this principal, drops to this Ocean, glimpses to this Sun. If you ask, how can our souls enjoy this *Godhead*? I answer, two ways; first, by the *understanding*; secondly, by

107. McGinn, *Growth of Mysticism*, 201.

108. Ambrose, *Looking Unto Jesus*, 34; cf. 35.

109. Ibid., 481.

110. Ambrose, *Media* (1657), 231.

the *will*."[111] This clearly reveals Ambrose's balanced usage of the interaction of affections and intellect.

However, that does not diminish the possibility that in some situations the intellect is dominant while in other occasions the affection takes the primary role. The former is reflected by Ambrose's declaration of Christ's resurrection, "[o]n these things may the soul expatiate; O it is worthy, blessed, soul-ravishing subject to think upon: and the rather if we consider that conformity which we beleeve."[112] Likewise Ambrose provides an affective dominant usage of ravishment that focuses upon the beauty of Christ's holiness: "holyness gives the soul a dear communion with God and Christ, . . . holyness admits the soul into the most intimate conferences with Jesus Christ in his bed-chamber, in his galleries of love; . . . holyness attracts the eye, and heart, and longings, and ravishments, the tender compassions, and everlasting delights of the Lord Jesus."[113] Significantly, this pattern of combining and integrating the intellectual and affective dimensions is reminiscent of the Spiritual Movement Matrix employed in chapter 3. While Ambrose consistently follows this pattern, there are modified variations when the angels or saints of heaven are ravished; they do not require the same sort of knowledge as those do on earth. However, their experiences still include a content or awareness that creates their ravishment.

Second, Ambrose illustrates how ravishment is typically experienced mentally rather than physically or bodily. Many of the previous examples reinforce this usage; however, on a few occasions there are somatic reactions to ravishment. On Easter morning Jesus reveals himself to Mary, "this one word *Mary*, lightens her eyes, dryes up her teares, cheares her heart, revives her spirits that were as good as dead . . . And hence it is that being ravished with his voyce, and impatient of delayes; she takes his talke out of his mouth, and to his first and other word *Mary*, she answers, *Rabboni*."[114] Additionally, in Ambrose's treatment some who were ravished could not eat or sleep, Peter jumped overboard

---

111. Ambrose, *Ultima* in *Prima, Media & Ultima* (1654), 212.

112. Ambrose, *Looking Unto Jesus*, 762. According to my reading Ambrose uses equally the intellect and the affective dominantly nine times.

113. Ibid., 881.

114. Ibid., 764; cf. Ambrose, *Media* (1657), 451, for another example of tears as the response to ravishment.

and swam ashore to greet Jesus, and fainting and swooning overcame others.[115]

A third category that can expand our understanding of the dynamics of ravishment is that these experiences can be either metaphorical or visual. The majority of Ambrose's uses are metaphoric or figurative, but unlike the predominant emphasis of the mental as compared with physical experiences of ravishment, there is a greater representation that is visual. On the one hand, the metaphoric is demonstrated when Ambrose refers to Patrick Forbes of Corse in his teaching on the third and deepest power of Scripture in its operation on the human heart. Ambrose quotes Forbes, declaring that *"while the word not only ravisheth with admiration, and striketh the conscience with terrour, but lastly filleth it with sweet peace and joy."*[116] Later in the same work, within the context of the Holy Spirit's illuminating power, Ambrose refers to Robert Bolton's *General Directions for A Comfortable Walking with God* and declares, "[t]here is a testimony of the Spirit which sometimes the Spirit may suggest and testifie to the sanctified conscience with secret still heart-ravishing voyce . . . *thou art the child of God.*"[117] Conversely, Christ's Transfiguration was an overpowering visual experience for Peter: "now if ever, whiles he was upon earth, was the beauty of Christ seen at height, *Peter* saw it, and was so ravished at the sight, that he talked he knew not what."[118] Yet another group who experienced the visual dynamic of ravishment were the saints in glory who "now *see the face of Christ* . . . O this lovelinesse of Christ ravishes the souls of the glorified."[119] Mary's Easter morning experience of ravishment was also tangible and visual.[120] None of Ambrose's personal experiences exhibit the visual dynamic of ravishment. However, those that do are related to the direct encounter with Christ whether here on earth with Peter, Mary, or a person facing death, or his saints in heaven who behold the radiant beauty of Jesus.

115. Ambrose, *Communion with Angels*, 263 and Ambrose, *Looking Unto Jesus*, 769, 881.

116. Ambrose, *Looking Unto Jesus*, 490.

117. Ibid., 889.

118. Ibid., 459; cf. 213.

119. Ibid., 481; cf. 908, 990.

120. Ibid., 796.

Four, Ambrose's metaphorical use of ravishment alerts readers to the importance of the spiritual senses.[121] Just as a person has five external senses to perceive life, spiritual writers from at least the time of Origen spoke of the internal spiritual counterparts to these external senses. Ambrose described the senses as the "windows of the soul," and therefore a person must be vigilant to "guard" these gates of awareness.[122] While the senses are susceptible to temptation and can lead a person astray, the "spiritual senses [are also] . . . the very way by which we must receive sweetnesse and strength from the Lord Jesus."[123] Interestingly, angels play a critical role in Ambrose's understanding of the senses, especially at the time of death. He quotes from Gregory saying, "*sometimes by heavenly inspiration they* [i.e. those facing death] *penetrate with their spiritual eyes the very secrets of heaven itself.*"[124] The stimulation of the spiritual senses can greatly deepen a person's experience.

Therefore, in surveying Ambrose's usage of the spiritual senses, he employs each one at least once, while sight is the dominant means for experiencing ravishment.[125] Peter is often captivated by the glorious presence of Jesus, but there are others who equally experience ravishment through sight, "[a] sight of Christ in his beauty and glory would ravish souls, and draw them to run after him."[126] Many of these experiences relate to the beauty or the holiness of God or Jesus. The last chapter established that there is a strong correlation between the title, *Looking Unto Jesus*, and the visual beholding of Jesus. The spiritual sense of sound, frequently associated with Mary, is also significant. According to Bernard, hearing must precede seeing due to our fallen state.[127] Mary's Easter morning experience clearly confirms this premise.[128] She didn't recognize Jesus visually until he spoke her name audibly:

121. For an introduction to the spiritual senses see Sheldrake, "Senses, Spiritual" and McGinn, *Foundations Mysticism*, 121–24. For Bernard's usage of the spiritual senses see McGinn, *Growth Mysticism*, 185–90.

122. Ambrose, *Media* (1657), 50; cf. Ambrose, *War with Devils*, 57.

123. Ambrose, *Looking Unto Jesus*, 47.

124. Ambrose, *Communion with Angels*, 277. The Gregory reference is *Dia.* I.4.c.16.

125. According to my tabulation sight is used twenty times, sound nine times, taste six times, and touch and smell once each.

126. Ambrose, *Looking Unto Jesus*, 793.

127. McGinn, *Growth of Mysticism*, 187.

128. Mary's Easter morning experience with Jesus is another common biblical text for mystical experiences in the early church. McGinn, *Foundations of Mysticism*, 67.

One word of Christ wrought so strange an alteration in her, as if she had been wholly made new, when she was only named. And hence it is that being ravished with his voice, and impatient of delayes, she takes his talk out of his mouth, and to his first and only word Mary, she answers, Rabboni, which is to say, Master, q.d. Master, is it thou? With many a salt tear have I sought thee, and art thou unexpectedly so near at hand! . . . I feel I am exceedingly transported beyond myself.[129]

The remaining three senses are used far less frequently than sight and sound. This again reveals the contrast between Ignatius and his richer usage of the senses and the more restrictive usage of Ambrose. Nonetheless, in his 1641 retreat experience Ambrose spoke of tasting God's sweetness.[130] Further, he describes how in reading Scripture people can "clearly discern the glory and beauty of those heavenly mysteries, and taste of the goodness of them, they cannot but ravish readers with admiration, yea transport them with strong and heavenly affections of love, joy and desire."[131] While Ambrose does not use the language of sweetness in relationship to ravishment as frequently as Flavel, he does use it abundantly in his writings.[132] Finally, the sense of smell and touch appear only once each.[133] Regardless of the specific sense, ravishment exerts an overwhelming power on them. According to the *Westminster Annotations*, ravishment burns "hotly in love, whose strange force it is to transvulnerate and stupifie the very soule, so as no sense nor reason is left."[134] This parallels Cuthbert Butler's conclusion that in ecstasy the mind is often separated or alienated from the body.[135] However, it is the common opinion of Puritan authors that "in ecstasies, all the senses and powers are idle, except the understanding."[136] Therefore, when believers experienced ravishment God "did not attempt to bypass the mind and affections."[137]

129. Ambrose, *Looking Unto Jesus*, 764.
130. Ambrose, *Media* (1657), 183.
131. Ibid., 482.
132. See for example Flavel, *England's Duty*, 215, 220, 223.
133. Ambrose, *Looking Unto Jesus*, 907, 34.
134. *Westminster Annotations*, Song 4:9 n.p
135. Bulter, *Western Mysticism*, 51.
136. Flavel, *Soul of Man*, 55 and Williams, "Puritan Enjoyment of God," 117–18, cites Owen and Sibbes to verify this Puritan understanding.
137. Williams, "Puritan Enjoyment of God," 118.

BENEFITS AND EFFECTS OF RAVISHMENT

My analysis of the effects of ravishment yields four general categories of benefits: a sense of knowledge or new awareness from the experience of God, assurance or confidence of some promise or blessing from God, greater desire to seek or long after God, and the delight of enjoyment of God. In *Looking Unto Jesus* Ambrose provides a vivid illustration of how ravishment can create a new sense of knowledge or awareness. Significantly the nature of this knowledge can vary and create many different expressions, from awareness of human rebellion to the amazing depth of Jesus' love and his ravishment by the church, to how to live and follow Jesus, to an awareness of the future benefits of heaven. In the conforming to Jesus section, in relation to his gift of salvation to humanity during his earthly life, Ambrose writes:

> O the sweet expressions, gracious conversation! Oh the glorious shine, blessed lustre of his divine soul! Oh the sweet countenance, sacred discourse, ravishing demenour, winning deportment of Jesus Christ! and now I reflect upon my selfe, oh alas! Oh the total, wide, vast, utter difference, distance, disproportion of mine therefrom! . . . Ah my rudenesse, grosenesse, deformity, odiousnesse, sleightnesse, contemptiblenesse . . . how clearly are these, and all other my enormities discovered, discerned, made evident, and plaine by the blessed and holy life of Jesus.[138]

Therefore, the ravishing sight of Jesus reveals the huge chasm that separates him from humanity and only heightens the awareness of a person's utter rebellion and distance from a holy God.

Occasionally Ambrose has Jesus speak the words of Song 4:9 and address his church:

> *Turne away thine eyes, for they have overcome me; thou hast ravished my heart, my sister, my spouse, with one of thine eyes:* Christ was held in the galleries, and captivated with love to his people, so that his eye was ever upon them, . . . and is Christ so tender in his love towards us, that he ever minds us, and shall our mindes be so loose to him? so fluttering, and fleeting? shall there be no more care to binde our selves in cords of love to him, who hath bound himself in such cords of love to us?[139]

---

138. Ambrose, *Looking Unto Jesus*, 522.

139. Ibid., 28; cf. 504–5 for greater expansion of this theme.

While initially Jesus is ravished by his deep love for the church, that knowledge of his compassionate love overwhelms the church and creates in them a new awareness of the love that they are invited to reciprocate to him. For Ambrose, Scripture plays a central role in ravishing and creating this new knowledge of God. It serves as a reminder of the Puritan devotion to the reading and preaching of Scripture. Additionally, ravishment can produce a new awareness of God's divine love. The specific context is of a person meditating on Jesus' suffering for those condemned because of sin: "[i]ndeed with what lesse than ravishment of spirit can I behold the Lord Jesus, . . . into what extasies may I be cast to see the Judge of all the world accused, judged, condemned? . . . Oh what raptures of spirit can be sufficient for admiration of this so infinite mercy? be thou swallowed up O my soul in the depth of divine love."[140] Ambrose also provides a list of ten different categories of biblical passages that affected his soul personally, including to "rebuke of corruption," to "comfort him against outward crosses," to the "privileges in Christ," to "sweet passages, which melted his heart," to *"[p]laces that in reading, he found sensible comfort and ravishing of heart in."*[141] The list is vast and far ranging and includes numerous specific references to fourteen different Old Testament books and eleven different New Testament books. This suggests that Ambrose could be ravished by a very broad cross section of biblical texts.

The experiences of Peter at the Transfiguration and Mary at Easter morning have already been considered, and clearly both of these situations created a deepening knowledge of Jesus' identity and mission as well as a responsive love to this new awareness.[142] Peter sees the glorified Christ and hears the voice of God and gains new insight and information about Jesus. Similarly, Mary hears the voice of Jesus and discovers the good news that he is truly alive, as the angels had declared. Mary's ravishing encounter confirmed the promise of Jesus that he would be raised to new life in three days (Matt 16:21; Mark 8:31; Luke 9:22). Therefore, in both of these experiences, Peter and Mary discovered a deepening knowing and loving of Jesus. Mary's experience further indicates that

140. Ibid., 658.

141. Ambrose, *Media* (1657), 486–88, 492.

142. See McGinn, "Love, Knowledge and *Unio Mystica*" for the history of love and knowledge as it relates to union with God.

some of these areas of new knowledge suggest the promissory nature of faith and obedience before one can experience the depth of ravishment.

The second category of assurance of God's promises also covers a range of benefits including God's love, presence, and protection, to the promise that Jesus has purged a person's sins and there is assurance of salvation, to a confident peace at the time of death, and to the promise of joy that awaits a person in heaven. Ambrose recounts his visit to his "dear and Reverend Brother M. *Edw. Gee*" during the "horrid temptations" that he faced on "his death-bed." He writes "at that time of his last sickness I went to visit him, and I found him as full of spiritual ravishings and heavenly joyes as (I thought) his heart could hold."[143] On this occasion ravishment provided a deep sense of peace and comfort during the final hours that the Puritans felt were often periods of the greatest doubt and onslaught of temptations by the devil. However, God frequently provides a deep sense of "the Spirit of Assurance" long before a person reaches this eschatological stage. In writing about the privilege of adoption as God's children, Ambrose proclaims how the "Spirit bears witness with us in every part, premises, and conclusion; onely it testifies more clearly, certainly, comfortably, sweetly, ravishing the soul with unspeakable joy, and peace in the conclusion."[144] He also uses Bernard as an illustration and then comments that the use of spiritual duties is "brim full of rare and ravishing comfort."[145]

According to Ambrose, while ravishment can create a deep peace and assurance of God's promises, he cautions his readers that ravishment itself is not always reliable. He warns that some "have *tasted the good Word of God* (have found some relish in the sweet and saving promises of the Gospel) *and the powers of the world to come* (have had some ravishing apprehensions of the joyes and glory in heaven); *and yet fall away* (by a total apostasy)."[146] Chapter 3 established the potential instability of experiences, that, regardless of its significance, it can be derived from

143. Ambrose, *War with Devils*, 184; cf. Ambrose, *Communion with Angels*, 283–84 for a similar deathbed experience involving ravishment that created an assurance of Mr. Holland's promise of being in heaven.

144. Ambrose, *Media* (1657), 10.

145. Ibid., 36. Elsewhere Ambrose asserts that ravishment speaks the word of comforting assurance to our troubled conscience. *Ultima* in *Prima, Media & Ultima* (1654), 201.

146. Ambrose, *Looking Unto Jesus*, 817. The same principle is repeated in *Media* (1657), 389, and *Ultima* in *Prima, Media & Ultima* (1654), 193.

sources other than God. In the next category of desire, it will be apparent that the previous categories of knowledge and awareness and assurance of God's promises can also function as a means toward increasing desire.

Third, Ambrose articulates that one of the primary benefits of ravishment is that it increases the desire and longing for God. This is clearly evident from his May retreat experience cited earlier in this chapter: "[t]he unspeakable joy of Gods Spirit, which sometimes I have felt in and after Ordinances; and especially once, when for the space of two dayes I was carried away into extasie and ravishment: This was when I began to see Spiritual things; and upon which followed more desire and endeavors after grace."[147] Significantly this was not a single experience, but rather a common pattern. Ambrose reinforces the same message in *Prima* when he declares, "they [God's promises] would even ravish thee, and quicken thy *desires*."[148] Likewise, earlier in *Prima* after Ambrose describes the sight of Jesus to a humbled sinner as a "most pleasant, ravishing, heavenly sight," he asserts the very next step to encourage this new birth is "an hungering desire after Christ and his merits."[149] He reiterates this again in *Looking Unto Jesus*, when he declares, "[a] sight of Christ in his beauty and glory would ravish souls, and draw them to run after him."[150] Previously in the same work Ambrose asserts the expanding and transformative nature of "spiritual desires after Christ, [that they] do neither load, nor cloy the heart, but rather open, and enlarge it for more and more."[151] Clearly for Ambrose, ravishment created a growing desire to yearn for deeper intimacy with God, and reciprocally this desire also prepared him and others for being ravished by God. It is also apparent that any aspect of Jesus' presence, whether his beauty or spiritual duties to engage with him or his promises, had the potential to stir up and enlarge a person's desires after God. In fact, the mere thought of reflecting on Jesus was enough to ravish Ambrose's soul. He confesses his inability to love Jesus properly: "[h]ad I a thousand hearts to bestow on *Christ*, they were all too little, they were never able to *love* him sufficiently."[152] Further, Ambrose declares, "[t]here is a twofold *love*,

---

147. Ambrose, *Media* (1657), 214.

148. Ambrose, *Prima* in *Prima (Appendix), Media & Ultima* (1654), 50.

149. Ambrose, *Prima* in *Prima, Media & Ultima* (1654), 34–35.

150. Ambrose, *Looking Unto Jesus*, 792–93.

151. Ibid., 321.

152. Ambrose, *Media* (1657), 229.

one of *desire*, which is an earnest longing after that which we believe would do us much good, if we could attain to it; another of *complacency*, when having attained that which we desire, we hugge and embrace it, and solace our selves in the fruition of it." The first love, which Ambrose also calls an "affectionate longing or thirsty love" is the love that has been examined.[153] The second love that matures into fruition leads to the final benefit of ravishment that is delight and enjoyment of God.

This fourth benefit once again analyzes Ambrose's May 20, 1641, seminal retreat experience to fathom more deeply his understanding of ravishment and how it can create a sense of joy and foretaste of the heavenly consummation of spiritual marriage.[154] There Ambrose effusively declares, "[t]his day the Lord cast one into a spiritual, heavenly, ravishing love trance; he tasted the goodnesse of God, the very sweetness of Christ, and was filled with the joyes of the Spirit above measure. O it was a good day, a blessed fore-taste of Heaven, a love-token of Christ to the Soul."[155] Clearly the spiritual practices of this retreat not only provided him with a future taste of the joys of heaven, they also granted him a present experience of the same joys through the Holy Spirit. Ambrose appended a series of verses that serve as an expansion of his experience. Not surprisingly, four out of the five passages are directly related to the enjoyment of God.[156] His first reference is Song 2:3, "*I sate down under his shadow with great delight, and his fruit was sweet to my taste.*" Next he cites 2 Cor 7:4, "*I am filled with comfort, I am exceedingly joyfull in all our tribulations.*" Another verse is Acts 13:52, "*And they were filled with joy, and with the holy Ghost.*" The fourth reference of 1 Pet 1:8 also reinforced the theme of joy, "[w]hom having not seen, ye love, in whom, though now ye see him not, yet believing ye rejoyce with joy unspeakable, and full of glory."

Enjoying God was a significant theme in Ambrose's lengthy meditation that was intended to awaken believers with the expectation of eternity in heaven. As he progresses through the various phases of this

153. Ibid., 224

154. On the Puritan enjoyment of God see Gwyn-Thomas, "Puritan Doctrine of Joy," 119–40, and Yuille, *Inner Sanctum of Puritan Piety*, 85–94. For spiritual enjoyment within Dutch Pietism see de Reuver, *Sweet Communion*, 190–91, 216–21, 227-28, 240–41.

155. Ambrose, *Media* (1657), 183.

156. The remaining passage is Rev 22:17, 20 and extends the heavenly invitation to come and enjoy the benefits of heaven.

meditation, Ambrose asks: "what are the effects, O my soul, of this eternity?" He replies; "[o] what ravishing of spirit will the souls of the just
be cast into, at this recalling of time past and that the memory of things
here below."[157] Later the meditation addresses the "[f]ruition of God"
which includes the "happinesse of Heaven." He continues by declaring,
"[a]nd in this kinde of love of God, and enjoyment of themselves in God,
the Saints are ravished with God and are in a kind of extasie eternally."
This expansive experience involves all of the faculties of the soul. For
"here is the pure, spiritual quintessential joyes of Heaven! the Saints are
so swallowed up in God."[158] Ambrose employs almost identical language
in a sermon entitled *Heavens Happiness*. After he introduces the theme
of fruition he asserts, "*[t]o be with God*, implies the fruition of God."
One aspect of fruition is to "enjoy God fully." Next, he speaks in a manner reminiscent of Bernard of Clairvaux and refers to three degrees of
love. The third degree "is a love of the glorified Saints; and in this kinde
of love of God, and enjoyment of our selves in him, the soul shall be
ravished with God, and be in a kinde of extasie eternally."[159] At this point
a person has passed from the earthly experience to the expectation of
the fuller experience in heaven. That focus is more clearly articulated
in *Looking Unto Jesus*. Ambrose reminds believers of their earthly relationship when Jesus "whispered to thy soul the forgiveness of thy sinnes
. . . oh what joy was then? what meltings, movings, stirrings, leapings of
heart were then in thy bosome? but was that joy any thing to this? or to
be compared with this? that was a drop, but here's an Ocean, here's fullness of joy; oh what leapings of heart, what ravishments will be within
when thou shalt see thy self in the armes of Christ."[160] Ambrose employs
another water metaphor as he reinforces that present enjoyments are
nothing in comparison to their eschatological fulfillment in heaven:
"even so all the enjoyments of God in the use of meanes, graces, blessings, ordinances are infinitely inferiour to than enjoyment of God which
shall be without all meanes; all ravishments of our spirit in prayer, hearing, reading, meditating, is but a sip of those rivers which we shall have

157. Ambrose, *Media* (1657), 256.

158. Ibid., 260–61.

159. Ambrose, *Ultima* in *Prima, Media & Ultima* (1654), 221. Ambrose begins with
Bernard's second degree of love since his focus is on loving God and not self.

160. Ambrose, *Looking Unto Jesus*, 1108.

in heaven."[161] These examples reveal Ambrose's concern that his listeners and readers would not miss the promised joy and delight that awaits those who will be consummating their "spiritual marriage" with Christ in heaven. Clearly, the enjoyment of God that begins in a very tangible manner already on earth is proleptic, and the experience of ravishment and joy will grow more fully in heaven. Using the language of covenant that often parallels that of spiritual marriage, Ambrose reiterates that enjoyment of God grows as a person lives more fully in him. He declares,

> He hath made a covenant with thee, of spiritual mercies; even a covenant of peace, and grace, and blessing, and life for evermore; God is become thy God, he is all things to thee; he hath forgiven thy sinnes, he hath given thee his Spirit, to lead thee, to sanctifie theee to uphold thee in that state wherein thou standest; and at last he will bring thee to a full enjoyment of himself in glory, where thou shalt blesse him, and rejoyce before him with joy unspeakable, and full of glory.[162]

Therefore, deepening intimacy with God in spiritual marriage and the resulting ravishment creates a growing sense of enjoyment of God. That, in turn, produces an expanding awareness or knowledge that leads a person full circle from where he or she began. Later in the same work Ambrose enlarges this fullness of God's presence and joy because he "is *All in all* to all his Saints" because "God is the very top of heavens joy."[163]

Before summarizing the insights of the ravished soul in the writings of Ambrose, it is significant to recognize that the effects of ravishment closely parallel the research of Cuthbert Butler for three early patristic and medieval spiritual giants. For example, for Augustine the benefits of ravishment were "[c]learer perception of the truth" and "full enjoyment," for Gregory, it was "self-knowledge, humility, fervour and love," and for Bernard "love, fervour, active zeal."[164]

CONCLUSION

In summary, we have discovered that ravishment was a highly charged word and that Ambrose used it to communicate being overcome by or

---

161. Ibid., 1084.

162. Ibid., 236–37.

163. Ibid., 1111.

164. Butler, *Western Mysticism*; for Augustine, 49; for Gregory, 82; for Bernard, 108.

taken out of this world by the love of the Triune God. It was a term of heavenly delight and therefore captured a sense of the intensification of desire of a person who had experienced being carried away by the divine joy of spiritual marriage. There is no evident change in Ambrose's usage of ravishment in his works. While his treatment is consistent throughout his writings, what is apparent here, as it was in our study of contemplation, is how the specific theological nature of Ambrose's writing controls the usage of ravishment. Therefore in *Media*, a work on sanctification that emphasizes the role of spiritual practices, ravishment is frequently connected with engaging spiritual exercises. In *Looking Unto Jesus*, with its strong christological focus, ravishment tends to relate to beholding or listening to Jesus. The references in *Ultima, Communion with Angels,* and *War with Devils* include a number of experiences around death. Obviously, there is a strong eschatological nature to ravishment, since a person is more likely to focus on God and meditate on heaven the closer they approach death. However, that does not minimize the very real benefits a person may experience who is still on earth.[165]

Ambrose maintains that while ravishment is a gift of God's grace, a person can prepare to be more receptive and therefore more likely to experience it through the use of spiritual practices. Reflecting Bernard, these experiences are rare and episodic rather than continuous, though on one occasion Ambrose enjoyed his experience for two days. Additionally, gender does not have any major effect upon ravishment, as Ambrose draws equally upon the examples of Peter and Mary. Again following Bernard's lead, though in a more balanced fashion, Ambrose develops his theology and experience of Christ-mysticism through the interaction of the intellect and affections. Further, most of Ambrose's uses of ravishment were metaphoric and mental rather than visual and physical, though there were exceptions in both categories. At the completion of the next chapter, when the important topic of retrieval will be introduced, I will return to this subject of ravishment and consider whether this ambiguous term is still usable today. The next chapter focuses on the twin challenges of resistance and retrieval to the contemplative-mystical piety of Ambrose.

---

165. Williams, "Puritan Enjoyment of God," 198n174; Dewey Wallace, "Saintliness in Puritan Hagiography," 36–37; and more broadly on the spiritual significance of death see Hambrick-Stowe, *Practice of Piety,* 224–41.

Chapter Six

Resistance and Retrieval

The people seemed to have a renewed taste for those old pious
and experimental writers, Mr. Hooker, Shepard, Gurnal,
William Guthrie, Joseph Allein, Isaac Ambrose, Dr. Owen, and
others; . . . The evangelical writings of these deceased authors,
as well as of others alive, both in England, Scotland, and New
England, were now read with singular pleasure; some of them
reprinted and in great numbers quickly bought and studied.

—John Gillies[1]

This book has raised the question whether a contemplative-mystical
piety existed within the moderate stream of English Puritanism.
More specifically it has been focused on Isaac Ambrose to determine
whether there is any evidence of a contemplative-mystical theology and
experience in his writings. However, there is another crucial question
that still requires attention, and that is whether the piety and practices
of Isaac Ambrose can be retrieved for the twenty-first century. Before
that can be determined, it is first necessary to recognize that Ambrose
and other Puritans were equally critical of certain spiritual practices
and their resulting mystical experiences in the seventeenth century. More

1. Gillies, *Historical Success of the Gospel*, 2:170–71. This reference pertains to the
Great Awakening in America.

197

problematic in addressing the prospects of a contemporary retrieval of a contemplative-mystical piety is the well-known resistance of Karl Barth, who once referred to mysticism as "esoteric atheism."[2] Barth's theological influence casts a very long shadow over the landscape of the contemporary academy and even to some degree the church. However, Barth does not speak for all Reformed or Protestant Christians, and his interpretation of mystical experience distorts a more balanced understanding of the contemplative-mystical piety of the Reformed and Evangelical traditions. Therefore, this chapter will first examine the seventeenth-century concerns regarding mysticism followed by an analysis of Barth's misgivings pertaining to contemplative experiences. The focus will then shift to Herman Bavinck for reconstructing a more balanced Reformed and Evangelical understanding. Finally, this chapter will conclude with a summary of contemplative-mystical principles from Ambrose that can be retrieved for the contemporary church.

SEVENTEENTH-CENTURY RESISTANCE TO MYSTICISM

While this study has been exploring the possibility of a seventeenth-century contemplative-mystical piety within Puritanism, at one level the Puritans were strongly suspicious of mysticism. Consequently Ambrose and most Puritans would have been aghast to be called mystics. McGinn reminds readers that this label would have equally confused Bernard and other medieval Christians.[3] In fact, as chapter 1 reported, mysticism was an invention of the seventeenth century in France. However, McGinn's historical construct provides a valuable means for studying the Puritans. More specifically, a primary reason for Ambrose's distrust of the term was the Quakers. Clearly, Ambrose's fears were heightened because the Quakers were particularly strong in Lancashire, and records indicate their presence in Preston during his ministry.[4] While George Fox, founder of the Quakers, was raised in a Puritan home, he had radically jettisoned those roots. Geoffrey Nuttall summarizes the outcome asserting that Fox and his fellow Quakers "disturbed this conjunction . . . between God's Word in Scripture and the Holy Spirit."[5] Ambrose

---

2. Barth, *CD* 1/2:322.

3. McGinn, *Foundations of Mysticism*, xvi; cf. Harmless, *Mystics*, 232.

4. Nightingale, *Quaker Movement in Lancashire*, 10, 36; cf. Welch, "Quakers, Ranters and Puritan Mystics," 66, and Watts, *The Dissenters*, 195–96.

5 Nuttall, *Holy Spirit in Puritan Faith*, 20–47, quotation at 26; cf. Nuttall, "Puritan and

confirms Nuttall's summary, warning his readers to be alert to the blasphemies of the "Quakers and Ranters" because they do not have "the Spirit of Christ within them."[6] Ambrose's remarks reveal one of the common themes within Quaker theology that alarmed the Puritans. Fox created a distinction and growing tension between the internal word of the Spirit from the external Word of Scripture.[7] Over time the internal word grew in importance to the diminishment and even exclusion of the external Word. Overall, Ambrose seldom mentions the Quakers in his writing. However, that should not minimize their significance due to Ambrose's irenic spirit and his desire to eschew controversies because they reduced his contemplative attitude. However, it is possible to gauge the seriousness of the Quaker threat from a different angle. In his discussion of assurance of heaven and the role of the Holy Spirit Ambrose declares that "the holy Ghost works not by enthusiasmes or dreames" instead a person can find assurance through "*the promises of the Gospel*."[8] To summarize his primary concern, Ambrose declares, "*the testimony of Gods Spirit is* ever agreeable to the Word."[9] Therefore, one of his primary reasons for rejecting the mysticism and enthusiasm of the Quakers was that they had failed to maintain the critical balance of Word and Spirit.[10] Instead, the Spirit became excessively prominent and eventually this created an even stronger inner subjectivism. John Owen also criticized Quakerism because their understanding of the "Spirit rendered the written Word of no value" not because of their teaching of direct contact with the Spirit.[11] Moreover, Ambrose condemned the Antinomians, specifically Tobias Crisp, because his theology paralleled the Quaker tendency of disrupting the proper balance between

Quaker Mysticism," 522, and Nuttall, *Puritan Spirit*, 174–75. For a helpful treatment of the issues surrounding this conflict see Adam, *Word and Spirit: Puritan-Quaker Debate*.

6. Ambrose, *Looking Unto Jesus*, 901.While there is a technical difference between Quakers, Ranters, and Seekers they were often combined due to their common heterodoxy.

7. Nuttall, *Holy Spirit in Puritan Faith*, 30.

8. Ambrose, *Ultima* in *Prima, Media & Ultima* (1654), 197. Ambrose specifically names Quakers as "dreamers." *Looking Unto Jesus*, 1157.

9. Ambrose, *Ultima* in *Prima, Media & Ultima* (1654), 199.

10. Cornick, *Letting God Be God*, 93.

11. King, "Affective Spirituality of John Owen," 226n25.

Word and Spirit.[12] While Ambrose was irenic and resisted polemics, Rutherford often engaged in them and frequently criticized Crisp.[13]

Further, Ambrose does not direct any specific criticism against Roman Catholic expressions of mysticism or contemplative prayer, though other Puritans did. John Owen wrote a detailed critique of contemplative or mental prayer in response to the Benedictine Dom Serenus de Cressy.[14] No doubt part of Owen's rebuke of Cressy was due to his conversion to Roman Catholicism.[15] Owen declares that "whatever there may be in the height of this 'contemplative prayer,' as it is called, it neither is prayer nor can on any account be so esteemed."[16] According to Owen, the primary fault of mental prayer is that it bypasses the importance of the mind or understanding.[17] Additionally, he finds no biblical support for it; further, the prayer that Jesus taught his disciples employed words.[18] Moreover, Owen associates mental prayer with the Quakers, and Ambrose's reaction to them illuminates the seriousness of this charge.[19] Surprisingly, Owen can also approve of "mental prayer, and all actings of the mind in holy meditations" provided that the mind is actively engaged.[20] Therefore, the following words of Owen actually affirms the value of contemplative prayer:

> The spiritual *intense fixation of the mind*, by contemplation on God in Christ, until the soul be as it were swallowed up in admiration and delight, and being brought unto an utter loss, through

12. Ambrose, *Media* (1657), 199–200; cf. Ambrose, *Looking Unto Jesus*, 888. On the connection between Antinomianism and Quakers see Mack, *Visionary Women*, 155, 157, 277.

13. Rutherford, *Christ Dying*, 24, 104–6, 165, 247, 257, 319–22, 499 (incorrectly numbered 463), 507–13 (incorrectly numbered 471–77), 537 (incorrectly numbered 501), 548 (incorrectly numbered 512) and *Survey of the Spiritual Anitchrist*, 193 (Part I), 234 (Part II).

14. Owen, *Holy Spirit in Prayer*, 328–38.

15. *DNB*, 5:75–76. The controversy and criticism that surrounded Cressy was at least partially due to his editing of Augustine Baker's works. See Lunn, "Augustine Baker."

16. Owen, *Holy Spirit in Prayer*, 334–35.

17. Ibid., esp. 335; cf. 328–31, 336.

18. Ibid., 330, 337.

19. Ibid., 331.

20. Ibid., 335. For mental prayer in the Puritans see Scougal, *Life of God in Soul of Man*, 121–23 (incorrectly numbered 121); Wakefield, *Puritan Devotion*, 85–89; and Horton Davies, *Worship and Theology in England*, 2:125n149. Both Wakefield and Davies specifically mention Ambrose in relation to mental prayer.

the infiniteness of those excellencies which it doth admire and adore, it returns again into its own abasements, out of a sense of its infinite distance from what it would absolutely and eternally embrace, and, withal, the inexpressible rest and satisfaction which the will and affections receive in their approaches unto the eternal Fountain of goodness, are things to be aimed at in prayer, and which, through the riches of divine condescension, are frequently enjoyed. The soul is hereby raised and ravished, not into ecstasies or unaccountable raptures, not acted into motions above the power of its own understanding and will; but in all the faculties and affections of it, through the effectual workings of the Spirit of grace and the lively impressions of divine love, with intimations of the relations and kindness of God, is filled with rest, in "joy unspeakable and full of glory."[21]

Clearly Owen was not opposed to all types of contemplative prayer, only those that ignored the mind and the other faculties of the soul. Therefore, what at first appears to be resistance to contemplation dissolves upon closer examination, and, in reality, as the previous chapters have demonstrated many Puritans eagerly embraced contemplative practices.

RECEPTION OF ISAAC AMBROSE SINCE THE SEVENTEENTH CENTURY

Before examining the contemporary resistance to a contemplative-mystical piety, it is significant to recognize the reception of Ambrose's works following his death.[22] The popularity of his writing is reflected in the numerous editions of his *Complete Works*, beginning with the first edition in 1674, followed subsequently by reprints in 1682, 1689, 1701, 1723, 1759, 1768, 1769, 1799, 1813, 1816, 1820, 1829, 1835, 1839, etc. Further, many of his individual publications went through numerous editions. John Wesley edited major portions of Ambrose's writings that filled two

21. Ibid., 329–30. For a helpful elaboration of Owen's perspective on contemplative spirituality see King "Affective Spirituality of John Owen."

22. For a broader treatment of the heritage of Puritanism see Coffey, "Puritan Legacies."

volumes in his *Christian Library*.[23] Additionally references to Ambrose appear in the eighteenth[24], nineteenth[25], and twentieth centuries.[26]

CONTEMPORARY RESISTANCE TO CONTEMPLATIVE-MYSTICAL PIETY WITHIN THE REFORMED TRADITION: KARL BARTH

There is no evidence that anyone criticized Ambrose during his own time or since for his contemplative-mystical piety. However, in traveling across the centuries since Ambrose, Karl Barth's (1886–1968) name is typically associated with resistance to a more experiential relationship with the Trinity. Barth is best known for his massive thirteen-volume *Church Dogmatics*, that unfortunately were uncompleted due to his death. I fully realize that Barth is not the only Reformed theologian who has registered concerns about a contemplative piety. In many ways there may be even more strident critics than Barth. And while Reformed theology is much broader than Barth, he does represent the most prominent Protestant theologian of the twentieth century and his influence is far ranging. Further, Barth's animosity to contemplative and mystical themes is well known and, therefore, more readily recognizable than other lesser-known writers. Indeed his misgivings and ever cautious anxiety regarding experience and contemplative piety are somewhat typical of others within the Reformed and Evangelical tradition, at least until recent years. Therefore, an examination of Barth will enable us to better understand the Reformed and Evangelical resistance and apprehensions to contemplative piety. In similar fashion, to represent the other side of the debate, I have selected the Dutch theologian Herman Bavinck (1854–1921) to serve as a corrective to the myopic vision of Barth. Bavinck was born and wrote most of his theology before Barth, but they emerged from somewhat similar family backgrounds that had been formed by a more pietistic or experiential environment. Bavinck

23. Wesley, *Christian Library*, 7:311—9:132.

24. Philip Ryken, *Thomas Boston*, 11, 16, 71, 152–53, etc; Gillies, *Historical Success of the Gospel*, 2:170–71; Oliver, *History of English Calvinistic Baptists*, 264; and Jones, "Evangelical Revival in Wales," 242.

25. Spurgeon, *Lectures to My Students*, 51 (first series) and *Treasury of David*, 1:348, 360, 436; 2:30, 399; and 3:245.

26. Griffiths, *Example of Jesus*, 7, 38, 44, 57, 87, 184. Additionally there have been numerous editions of Ambrose's works published in Dutch. See below.

too, expresses some caution regarding the type of piety that has been examined in this book; however, as we shall soon discover, he clearly resolved these issues differently than Barth. Additionally, Bavinck's *Reformed Dogmatics* has been translated into English and provides an interesting point of comparison with Barth. Therefore, I am using Barth and Bavinck solely as conversation partners in relation to the specific question of resistance and retrieval of a contemplative-mystical piety. Obviously, my reading must be selective because of the enormity of material and specialists in either of these theologians may be disappointed by what I have not included. Nonetheless, I trust my survey of both Barth and Bavinck is accurate to guide further discussions of this important topic.

In the previous chapters of this book four main themes were surveyed from the writings of Isaac Ambrose: the importance of *unio mystica* or spiritual marriage, the role of experience of God, spiritual practices and contemplative experiences, and the language of delight and enjoyment. These four central themes of Ambrose will now be used to examine the theology of Barth and Bavinck and their perception of a contemplative-mystical piety. It will soon become evident that Ambrose and others in the seventeenth century previously articulated some of Barth's criticisms waged against experience and mysticism in the twentieth century, and therefore, serve as a wise reminder for contemporary efforts of retrieval. However, it will also be clear that some of Barth's disparagement was significantly distorted by his own context and may have limited significance for today.

Unio Mystica

Exploring Barth's understanding of spiritual marriage reveals his complexity and, according to George Hunsinger, he was not always clear in his writings, "seeming to take away with one hand what he has just established with the other." This was partially due to his dialectic theology. Other factors create additional challenges for those interested in understanding him. Not surprisingly, Hunsinger declares that "Karl Barth has achieved the dubious distinction of being habitually honored but not much read."[27]

---

27. Hunsinger, *How to Read Barth*, 27.

Barth briefly defines *unio mystica* as "the presence of grace in which God can give Himself to each individual, or assume the individual into unity of life with Himself, in the Christian experience and relationship."[28] His more detailed treatment of *unio mystica* comes when he addresses "The Vocation of Man." Here he declares "the goal of vocation" is "the fellowship of Christians with Christ." Clearly Barth shares the common Reformed understanding that union enables a person to become a Christian: "[t]he union of the Christian with Christ which makes a man a Christian is their conjunction in which each has his own independence, uniqueness and activity."[29] Later he reiterates the importance that "the Christian's *unio cum Christo*" is not the "climax of Christian experience and development in the face of which the anxious question might well be raised whether we have reached the point, or will ever do so." Rather, Barth asserts that union with Christ is "what makes us Christians whatever our development or experience."[30] Returning to his description of the nature of this union with Christ, Barth recognizes it is a relationship that is "true, total and indissoluble union."[31] Clearly for Barth, Christ takes the initiative through his grace in drawing and welcoming humanity unto himself. Therefore, he asserts "Jesus Christ [i]s the Subject who initiates and acts decisively in this union."[32] Barth expands this principle declaring, "[t]he purpose for which Christians are already called here and now in their life-histories within universal history is that in the self-giving of Jesus Christ to them, and theirs to Him, they should enter into their union with Him, their *unio cum Christo*." The nature of this union with Christ is "a single totality, a fluid and differentiated but genuine and solid unity."[33] Barth proceeds to explore the New Testament foundation for this union beginning with John 15: Jesus is the vine and individual Christians are the branches that are engrafted into him, and then continuing with John 14:20, "I in you" and "Ye in me." He broadens his consideration by referring to numerous Pauline variations of "being in Christ" or "in the Lord" (e.g., Rom 8:1; 2 Cor 5:17; 12:2;

28. Barth, *CD* 4/2:55.
29. Ibid., 4/2:540.
30. Ibid., 4/3:548; cf. 2/2:601.
31. Ibid., 4/3:540.
32. Ibid., 4/3:541.
33. Ibid., 4/3:540.

Phil 2:5; Col 2:6; etc.).[34] Barth then raises the very practical question, what is the nature and meaning of the word "in"? He responds, "the 'in' must indeed indicate on both sides that the spatial distance between Christ and the Christian disappears, that Christ is spatially present where Christians are, and that Christians are spatially present where Christ is."[35] Therefore, according to Barth, the *unio mystica* provides for a deep relational intimacy between Christ and Christians.[36] Additionally, he recognizes the Old Testament bridal language that "Yahweh is always the Lover, Bridegroom and Husband."[37]

This leads Barth to a historical excursus on mystical union. He also begins to display a growing hesitation regarding this foundational concept of union with Christ. While he reviews both Luther's and Calvin's understanding of *unio mystica* accurately,[38] he previously articulated a very different message, especially in relation to the biblical foundation and that of Calvin. Earlier, in speaking of Calvin's use of the *unio mystica*, he laments that Calvin ever used the term and asserts that this type of language should never be employed "unless it is highly qualified."[39] This reflects Barth's suspicion to mysticism that will be examined in the next section. He recognizes that mystical union has often been linked with mystical experiences. In an interesting historical comment, Barth refers to A. E. Biedermann, who was the "greatest exponent of Neo-Protestantism after Schleiermacher," and in relation to his treatment of this topic declares, "the concept of the *unio mystica*, . . . has been quietly and secretly filled out in a way which we can only describe as highly questionable."[40] This provides a valuable insight into Barth's polemic, that while he does not object unilaterally to the principle of mystical union he does raise serious reservations as he battles the anxieties of his past. It also reminds readers that no one should read Barth flat-footed without some awareness of his context and audience. Therefore, Barth cautiously warns, "[u]nless we consider, safeguard and expressly state these things [i.e. in relation to *unio mystica*], we do better not to speak of 'Christ-

34. Ibid., 4/3:545–46.

35. Ibid., 4/3:547.

36. Hunsinger explores this theme in *How to Read Barth*, 173–75, 179.

37. Barth, *CD* 3/1:316; cf. 315–18.

38. Ibid., 4/3:549–54.

39. Ibid., 4/3:539–40. The Calvin reference is *Institutes*, 3.11.10.

40. Ibid., 4/2:57.

mysticism' when there is obviously no compelling reason to do so."[41] Barth affirms that it is only John and Paul who provide a biblical sanction for employing the living "in Christ" passages in the New Testament. Additionally, in commenting on these two biblical authors he mentions their "disturbing boldness" in using the language of mystical union.[42] It is one thing to challenge Calvin's use of mystical union, but it seems inappropriate to cast the same judgment upon the writers of Scripture.

Experience

Barth's name has become synonymous with challenging humanity's ability to experience God.[43] In fact, a contemporary Barthian interpreter has remarked, "[o]ne can read many pages of 'The Word of God and Experience' before realizing that Barth wants to *affirm* the necessity of 'Christian experience.'"[44] Indeed he does, for Barth declares "[e]xperience therefore, of the Word of God must at least also be experience of His presence."[45] Barth's reticence to give proper weight to experience is a radical shift from his early emphasis upon the experiential that was indebted to Schleiermacher and Wilhelm Herrmann.[46] However, the context of World War I created a personal crisis that deeply shook Barth's theological foundations. He was deeply troubled to discover that many of his liberal theological professors, including his own highly respected mentor Herrmann, supported the Kaiser's justification for Germany's participation in and further expansion of the war. In a letter to Herrmann, Barth reveals his shaken conviction that "we learned to acknowledge 'experience' as the constitutive principle of knowing and doing in the domain of religion." Further, he objects to "the fact that German Christians 'experience' their war as a holy war is supposed to bring us to silence."[47] This forced Barth to recognize the unstable and ambiguous nature of experience. McCormack accurately summarizes

41. Ibid., 4/3:540.

42. Ibid., 4/3:549.

43. Barth bemoans that fact that his critics were continually accusing him of placing "revelation and faith from the believer's standpoint up in the clouds." *CD* 1/1:239.

44. Mangina, *Barth on the Christian Life*, 49n39.

45. Barth, *CD* 1/1:235; cf. 238, 239, 256.

46. Mangina, *Barth on the Christian Life*, 21 and Busch, *Karl Barth: His Life*, 62.

47. McCormack, *Barth's Dialectical Theology*, 113; cf. 111–17 for the broader details on the war's effect upon Barth's thinking. See also Barth, "Concluding Unscientific Postscript on Schleiermacher," 263–64.

his dilemma, "[i]f religious experience could give rise to such divergent and even contradictory conclusions, perhaps it could no longer be relied upon to provide an adequate ground and starting-point for theology."[48] Additionally, this relates to Barth's strong aversion to natural theology due to its subjective origin in humanity and further connection with Nazi Germany.[49]

Katherine Sonderegger provides a nuanced summary of Barth's actual understanding of the nature and role of experience: "Barth does not *deny* human experience, its inwardness, piety, and self-certainty, but rather *unsettles* it: creaturely reality can reflect but cannot ground Christian knowledge of God. To *begin* with human experience of God, with faith, is to enter an airless room. We leave with what we took in—our own ideas, passions, and introspections."[50] These words can be understood in relation to Barth's perception of the objective and subjective dynamics of experiencing the Word of God.[51] Schleiermacher and others had made humanity the determinant for experience and truth.[52] However, Barth questions, "[c]an we say with final human certainty that this is so?"[53] Barth stresses the danger of this highly subjective approach, reminding readers that this self-determination robs humanity of any guide for discerning truth, "[i]f we hold to what we may fix and investigate as man's acknowledgment of the Word of God, to the experienceable in Christian experience—where do we get the criterion for separating this experience from others, what is genuine in it from what is not?"[54] Therefore, the only solid foundation for "having knowledge of the Word of God, [is] by our self-determination being determined by the Word of God."[55] The Holy Spirit serves a critical role in Barth's

48. McCormack, *Barth's Dialectical Theology*, 113.

49. John Webster, *Cambridge Companion to Barth*, 32–33, 229–32, 302.

50. Sonderegger, "Barth and Feminism," 262; cf. McCormack, *Barth's Dialectical Theology*, 157n129.

51. Hunsinger asserts that objectivism is one of the six major motifs for reading Barth. *How to Read Barth*, 35–39.

52. Barth's relationship to Schleiermacher extends beyond the scope of this book. For Barth's assessment, appreciation, and critique of Schleiermacher see Barth, "Schleiermacher" in *Protestant Theology in Nineteenth Century*, 411–59, and Barth, "Concluding Unscientific Postscript on Schleiermacher." See also Torrance, "Christian Experience of Schleiermacher and Barth," 83–113.

53. Barth, *CD* 1/1:246; cf. 1/1:247.

54. Ibid., 1/1:248.

55. Ibid., 1/1:256.

understanding of the experience of the Word of God, "[t]he work of the Holy Spirit is that our blind eyes are opened and that thankfully and in thankful self-surrender we recognize and acknowledge that it is so . . . He is the Spirit of the Word itself who brings to our ears the Word and nothing but the Word."[56] Therefore, for Barth this relates to the critical dimension of obedient conformity to the Word of God.

Barth reveals an additional insight into this through a very illuminating treatment of evangelical hymnody.[57] As he traces the unfolding history from the sixteenth century through the eighteenth century, he detects both a growing preoccupation with the self and a greater emotional emphasis. The tragedy of this, according to Barth, is that "confession and proclamation have given way to religious poetry" and hymns have become increasingly self-focused.[58] By the time of the nineteenth century, Barth contends that "[e]ven Reformation praise of God disappears in the gurgling gullet of modern religious self-confession."[59] Barth is alarmed by the changing landscape of increased subjectivity and romanticism in hymnody and believes this danger created two results: "[f]irst, Jesus Christ would cease to be understood unequivocally as the Lord; and second, we ourselves would consequently come to usurp the center which rightfully belongs to him."[60] This reflects one of Barth's deep fears that, left to our own resources, humanity is likely to drift into theological abstraction, and even worse, idolatry, if we are not focused on Jesus Christ, the Word of God. Before departing from this discussion it is helpful to comment briefly on the interaction between the intellect and the affect. While obviously Barth recognizes their importance, he does not appear to provide any sustained development of their interaction. However, he asserts in a lecture on Calvin given in Paris, "theology . . . moves the head and heart most fully."[61]

56. Ibid., 1/2:239; cf. 244, 246–48, 268, 271, 272, 276 for Barth's fuller understanding of the interaction between Word and Spirit; cf. Macchia, "Spirit of God and Spirit of Life."

57. Ibid., 1/2:252–57.

58. Ibid., 1/2:254.

59. Ibid., 1/2:256.

60. Hunsinger, *How to Read Barth*, 40. Barth declares, "[t]he self-satisfied man rests upon himself and has no need of God." *CD* 1/2:263.

61. Busch, *Karl Barth: His Life*, 244. For Barth on reason see Mangina, *Barth: Theologian of Christian Witness*, 49. For Barth on affectivity see Mangina, *Barth on the Christian Life*, 125–63.

Further, Barth's understanding of mysticism can serve as a case study of his theology of experience. Perhaps surprisingly to some readers, Barth acknowledges the legitimacy of a certain type of mysticism. Referring to Paul in Gal 2:20 Barth apprehensively questions, "[i]s this mysticism? Well, if and so far as it is mysticism, then Paul too was a mystic . . . If this is mysticism, then mysticism is an indispensable part of the Christian faith." Barth also reveals an appreciation for "Bernard's mysticism, with its strongly Christological character" and did not believe it should "be regarded as mysticism in the more dubious sense." Similarly he affirms the "Sabbath mysticism of Calvin."[62] In his development of experience of the Word of God, Barth declares that the person who is "claimed by the Word of God" is "a participator in the reality of the Word" and that this rightly introduces the "concept of mysticism."[63] A few pages later Barth enlarges his position, "[i]f we care to give the name of mystical thought to the thought of what is Beyond all experience and which becomes visible at that moment, it is not worth while objecting to the expression. So long as it remains clear—what is so-called mystical thinking often does not remain clear."[64]

While the previous paragraph reveals that Barth can be sympathetic to some forms of highly qualified mysticism, overall his indiscriminate usage of language and failure to qualify his specific focus has earned him his bad reputation. Therefore, according to McGinn, Barth "saw little good in mysticism."[65] Clearly his disdain for the term mysticism[66] and its comparison to agnostic philosophy[67] or "esoteric atheism"[68] did not improve his cause. Further, Barth enumerates the major errors he finds in mysticism including its tendency towards "world-renunciation,"[69] the use of human "technique and craft" that seeks to reach a union with God

62. Barth, *CD* 3/4:59. Elsewhere Barth employs Bernard only in brief illustrative ways except for a cursory comment that Luther came to the very edge of mysticism as Calvin did also "probably treading in the footsteps of Bernard." *CD* 4/3:549.

63. Ibid., 1/1:242.

64. Ibid., 1/1:254.

65. McGinn, *Foundations of Mysticism*, 269.

66. Barth, *CD* 4/2:57.

67. Ibid., 1/2:750.

68. Ibid., 1/2:322.

69. Ibid., 4/2:545.

apart from Scripture,[70] "self-surrender and ultimately of absorption,"[71] and its apophatic or "negative comprehensibility."[72] Additionally, Barth finds great disagreement with the "pious egocentricity" of the "quietistic mystical type" that includes "Madame de Guyon, Pierre Poiret and Gerhard Tersteegen."[73] He even refers to Tersteegen's piety as "reformed mysticism"[74] or "mystical Pietism."[75] Barth takes a similar negative opinion of "natural mysticism" that found one popular expression in Schleiermacher.[76]

Practices and Contemplation

While Isaac Ambrose would have had little disagreement with Barth's teaching on christocentric mysticism, that agreement would have quickly vanished with his understanding of spiritual practices and contemplation. Barth occasionally employs contemplation synonymously with to "think" or "reflect" upon something.[77] However, he has relatively nothing positive to say about contemplation. Most damaging is his assertion that contemplation has no biblical foundation and "is not especially Christian" since it is built upon "mystical technique."[78] One wonders how Barth would interpret the rich contemplative themes of Pss 27:4; 42:2; 63:1–5; 73:25; 131:2? Further, he maintains that "[c]ontemplation in itself and as such, therefore, can be only a *cul-de-sac*" and that "God withdraws from every kind of contemplation." Clearly a significant motivation for Barth's resistance is his belief that God could not be the object of contemplation.[79] Instead Barth believes the individual encounters only himself in contemplation.[80] It is a pity that Barth, who

70. Ibid., 3/4:59.

71. Ibid., 1/2:261.

72. Ibid., 2/1:193–94. This charge is revealing, since one detects a strong apophatic tendency in Barth's theology, especially in his continual warning to turn from idolatry to a more pure perception of the God of Jesus Christ as revealed in the Word of God.

73. Ibid., 4/3:568.

74. Ibid., 2/2:113.

75. Ibid., 4/3:553; cf. 1/2:255. Elsewhere Barth asserts that "Christian mysticism" is a parallel movement to Pietism. *CD* 4/2:11.

76. Ibid., 3/4:119–22.

77. See for example Ibid., 1/2:730, 3/2:98, 3/3:55.

78. Ibid., 3/4:560.

79. Ibid., 3/4:563.

80. Ibid., 3/4:562; cf. 2/1:651.

was appreciative of Hans Urs von Balthasar's work on Christology, was not equally aware of his work on prayer.[81] There von Balthasar faithfully confesses, "[t]he object of contemplation is God, and God is trinitarian life; but for us he is life in the incarnation of the Son, from which we may never withdraw our gaze in contemplating God."[82] Likewise, it is unfortunate that Barth was unaware of Isaac Ambrose or other biblical expressions of Puritan contemplative-mystical piety. How would Barth have responded to the strongly christocentric contemplative piety of Ambrose's *Looking Unto Jesus*? We will never know but clearly Ambrose has placed the focus on Christ and not on himself.

The only positive statement that I have discovered in Barth's usage of contemplation pertains to humanity's love to God: "[a]s one element in the activity which puts the love to God into effect, there may be a place for a feeling of enjoyable contemplation of God." However, Barth quickly qualifies this, "[b]ut it cannot take the place of that activity."[83] Therefore, the freedom to engage in contemplation is tempered by Barth's fear that it will reduce the greater priority of action. This is related to Barth's foundational concept of actualism. Hunsinger asserts that it is both "the most distinctive and perhaps the most difficult of [Barth's] motifs." While Barth's teaching on actualism pertains to the activity of Christ, it finds a parallel in the human vocation that is expected to follow Christ and to "be set in motion" and active in the world.[84] Therefore, God's acts are central to Barth's theology because they reveal God's identity. Smedes summarizes the implications of Barth's active theology: "to be 'in Christ' means being where the action of Christ is going on. The theologian of the 'wholly other' is not likely to be burning the mystic flame."[85] Therefore, one could say that actualism places a greater emphasis upon doing than being. This is further validated by Neder's summary of Barth's distinctive "ways in which union with Christ differs from mysticism." His one point is "[u]nion with Christ is personal, not impersonal. It does not reduce the believer to silence."[86] Barth is clear that humanity must also rest and

---

81. Ibid., 4/1:768.

82. Von Balthasar, *Prayer*, 154.

83. Barth, *CD* 4/1:104.

84. Neder, *Participation in Christ*, 75.

85. Smedes, *Union with Christ*, 63.

86. Neder, *Participation in Christ*, 78.

relax so that they can function properly in doing their work.[87] However, in Barth's theology "The Active Life" occupies a central role, and his limited comments on contemplation are subsumed under this section.[88] This overarching emphasis upon activity provides little freedom to contemplate the mighty acts of God. Moreover, he tends to equate the term "indolence" with contemplation[89] and perceives it as ultimately hiding or withdrawal from the world.[90] One wonders how Barth would read the story of Mary and Martha (Luke 10:38–42) or Jesus own practice of withdrawing early in the morning or late at night to rest in prayer with God (e.g., Mark 1:35; Luke 5:16; etc.). Barth's distorted thinking that consistently elevates action at the expense of contemplation communicates that they are not equally legitimate expressions of the Christian life.[91] While he affirms, "*[o]ra!* and therefore *Labora!*"[92] his understanding of the interaction between these two movements is illuminating: "Where theology is concerned, the rule *Ora et labora!* is valid under all circumstances-pray and work! And the gist of the rule is not merely that *orare*, although it should be the beginning, would afterward be only incidental to the execution of the *laborare*. The rule means, moreover, that *laborare* itself, and as such, is essentially an *orare*. Work must be that sort of act that has the manner and meaning of a prayer in all its dimensions, relationships, and moments."[93] Barth's emphasis on work as prayer dismantles the original Benedictine balance of prayer and work and undermines the centrality of prayer as a significant means for guiding Christian action. Barth also seems to miss the biblical precedent of this cycle of withdrawing from the pressing demands of daily life and returning to action renewed as mirrored in Jesus own life (Matt 4:1–11 and Luke 4:1–13) as well as commanding his disciples to practice the same pattern (Mark 6:31).

87. Barth, *CD* 3/4:550–52.

88. Ibid., 3/4:470–564

89. Ibid., 3/4:473–74.

90. Barth, *Evangelical Theology*, 83.

91. Barth, *CD* 3/4:500–501; cf. 473–74.

92. Ibid., 3/4:534. Barth does not indicate that this is the Benedictine motto though he does reveal some knowledge of Benedict and refers specifically to the *Rule* on a few occasions. *CD* 4/2:13, 16, 17, 18; cf. 1/2:783, 4/2:12, 14. However, Barth reveals his great displeasure with the final sentence of the *Rule*. *CD* 4/2:18.

93. Barth, *Evangelical Theology*, 160.

Further, Barth's understanding of prayer "is decisively petition" and provides little room for contemplation. The primary form of prayer becomes invocation, not interior listening. In reality, for Barth the Lord's Prayer was focused more upon ethics than the spiritual life. While obviously petition is not the only form of prayer, it is the overarching means since no one can present "himself as worthy or of presenting anything worthy to God." Therefore, petition is representative of coming before God with "empty hands."[94] Moreover, Barth's reference to Ignatius of Loyola is particularly damaging to the nature and importance of spiritual practices:

> If by devotions we mean this simple thing, then we may understand prayer as a devotional exercise. But if by devotion we mean an exercise in the cultivation of the soul or spirit, i.e., the attempt to intensify and deepen ourselves, to purify and cleanse ourselves inwardly, to attain clarity and self-control, and finally to set ourselves on a good footing and in agreement with the deity by this preparation, then it is high time we realized that not merely have we not even begun to pray or prepared ourselves for prayer, but that we have actually turned away from what is commanded us as prayer. This type of exercise, as evolved and prescribed by Ignatius Loyola for his pupils and as variously recommended in modern secular religion, can perform a useful function as a means of psychical hygiene, but it has nothing whatever to do with the prayer required of us. Prayer begins where this kind of exercise leaves off; and this exercise must leave off where the prayer begins in which neither the collected man nor the distraught, neither the deepened nor the superficial, neither the purified and cleansed nor the impure, and not even the clear and strong, has anything whatever to represent or offer to God, but everything to ask of him.[95]

Leaving aside the question as to whether this is an accurate description of Ignatius of Loyola,[96] it clearly depicts Barth's animosity to other expressions of prayer. More succinctly he declares, "wordless prayer . . . cannot

---

94. Barth, *CD* 3/4:97.

95. Ibid., 3/4:97–98.

96. It is difficult to gauge Barth's first-hand knowledge of Ignatius' *Spiritual Exercises*. However, this distorted attack suggests that either he had not read them or grossly misunderstood them. Aside from this blistering assault there are only two references to Ignatius in the *CD*. See *CD* 4/2:12 and 4/3:23.

be regarded as true prayer."[97] Isaac Ambrose would radically disagree with his very narrow assessment of "devotional exercise" since *Media* was devoted to cultivating spiritual practices to assist a person in the very process of sanctification or growing in conformity to Jesus Christ.

Language of Delight and Enjoyment

Reflective of his time, Barth read the Song of Songs in a purely literal manner. In fact, he baldly declares that this book "is not an allegory."[98] Therefore, one would not expect to find the devotional language of delight and enjoyment such as "ravishment" that was so prominent in Ambrose and other Puritans in Barth's writings. However, due to his allergic reaction to mystical experiences, Barth's assessment of the German pietistic hymns of Nicolai and Gerhardt is surprising. He asserts that it is better to have some "religious eroticism" than simply sterile dusty dogmatic correctness. Barth continues by declaring "[b]ut how arid would be our hymn-books if we were to purge out all elements of this kind! . . . If a choice has to be made, is it not better to say a little too much and occasionally to slip up with Nicolai and even with Zinzendorf and Novalis than to be rigidly correct with Kant and Ritschl and my 1921 *Römerbrief* and Bultmann."[99] Yet just a few pages earlier, Barth asserts the opposite perspective with equal force speaking of "debased religious eroticism" of pietistic hymns.[100] Therefore, a deeper consideration once again requires a tempering of Barth's initial enthusiasm for devotional language. This was demonstrated previously in the discussion on subjectivity and Barth's fear that this language could turn the focus inward and away from Christ and into theological abstraction.

To summarize, it is obvious Barth was no champion of contemplation. On the one hand, he clearly demonstrates an interest in this topic by his frequent commentary on it, and some scholars may even find a sort of internal aesthetic to his writings. Further, Barth can at times speak favorably of a highly qualified form of Christian mysticism. Yet, on the other hand, his inconsistency of expression often communicates greater confusion than clarity. It is one thing to know the sources of

97. Barth, *CD* 3/4:112.

98. Ibid., 3/1:319; cf. 3/2:294.

99. Ibid., 4/2:798.

100. Ibid., 4/2:795.

contemplative piety and adamantly disagree or even reject them, but it is entirely another thing to simply not be conversant with them. A review of the index to the *Church Dogmatics* reveals that Barth does not mention Granada or Gerson, two names that specifically influenced Isaac Ambrose. Additionally, Barth's references to Bernard are extremely meager, not to mention his absence of Sibbes, Baxter, and Owen. However, there are a few references to William Ames and one to William Perkins. Therefore, it appears at least part of his confusion towards biblical and historical contemplative piety was his lack of awareness of the primary sources. Certainly it is appropriate to challenge Calvin's interpretation of Scripture as Barth does, but it is obvious that his own selective reading of Scripture distorts the biblical witness to true Christian mysticism.

Further, Barth's perception that God cannot be the object of contemplation and that it is nothing more than a self-centered *cul-de-sac* reveals his foundational fear regarding experience. While all people have been shaped by their past, Barth's anxieties from his earlier years appear to have made him unduly apprehensive about engaging in a relationship of devotion and love to God through union and communion with Christ by the power of the Holy Spirit. Alan Torrance, a Barth scholar, perceptively observes that Barth stressed "Christian experience" over "Christian experiences"[101] and continues his judgment that "[o]ne suspects that Barth's theology would perhaps have been enriched if he had been able to appreciate equally fully the music of Beethoven or Brahms or perhaps even Rachmaninoff in addition to that of Mozart!"[102] Therefore, it is indeed unfortunate that Barth's misgivings of experience of God in general and true Christian contemplative piety in particular have created a distorted perception and fear that is still present today within some portions of the Reformed and Evangelical church. As previously stated, Barth is a complicated person to read and interpret; while it is obvious that the spiritual life was important for him, this review indicates that his theology was not supportive of the ascetical practices or contemplative-mystical piety of Isaac Ambrose.

---

101. Torrance, "Christian Experience of Schleiermacher and Barth," 112.
102. Ibid., 111.

CONTINUATION OF BARTHIAN RESISTANCE TO
CONTEMPLATIVE-MYSTICAL EXPERIENCE

Significantly, the trajectory of resistance to mystical experiences begun in Barth has continued into the twenty-first century with his disciples. Donald Bloesch is one Reformed theologian who both acknowledges his deep appreciation for Barth and continues to exhibit a similar resistance to contemplative piety.[103] Since he addresses contemplation and mysticism in a number of his writings, only his most recent work that represents his mature thinking will be used. While occasionally Bloesch can affirm that the terms "Christian" and "mysticism" can actually coexist,[104] his fundamental conviction is that "[m]ysticism has been treated in this book as a Christian aberration" and "stands in contrast to biblical, evangelical faith."[105] Bloesch works from an inflexible binary model that tends to ossify his categories. Therefore, rather than appreciating the dynamic biblical interaction between contemplation and action he tends to depict them in stark contrast to each other.[106] Similarly, following Barth, he delineates prayer as predominantly petition[107] and creates another unnecessary distinction that prayer "is not being transported into glory" but "an exchange of ideas for the purpose of doing God's will."[108] While more could be said regarding Bloesch's antipathy to contemplation and healthy biblical mysticism, Bruce Demarest, another Reformed theologian, has clearly assessed the primary weakness of this book. "[M]ystical spirituality in the soft (i.e., biblical) or relational sense is not a dangerous distortion of Christian life and mission, but is the very essence thereof."[109]

103. Bloesch, *Spirituality Old & New*, 20, and Chung, *Karl Barth and Evangelical Theology*, xv.

104. Ibid., 37, 50, 137.

105. Ibid., 143, 145; cf. 18, 50, 68, 81; cf. Houston, "Reflections on Mysticism," 167.

106. Ibid., 42, 58, 133.

107. Ibid., 94, 133.

108. Ibid., 81, 82; cf. 41.

109. Demarest, review of *Spirituality Old & New*, 113.

RETRIEVAL OF CONTEMPLATIVE-MYSTICAL PIETY WITHIN THE REFORMED TRADITION: HERMAN BAVINCK

While Barth articulates a strong resistance to contemplative-mystical piety he is not representative of all Reformed theologians. Another Reformed voice that has become increasingly more prominent in recent years is the Dutch neo-calvinist Herman Bavinck. This is directly related to the English translation of his *Reformed Dogmatics*.[110] Bavinck was older than Barth, and there is no indication that he was familiar with the *Church Dogmatics*. However, Barth did include a number of references to Bavinck's theology and, for the most part, it was appreciative.[111] Nonetheless, while Bavinck shares some of Barth's concerns regarding mysticism, he is far more receptive to a healthy and biblically balanced experience of contemplation.

Unio Mystica

Unlike Barth, who frequently qualifies and cautions against using the terminology of *unio mystica*, Bavinck approaches this topic with much greater confidence. He asserts that the origin of "the mystical union between Christ and his church, existed long before believers were personally incorporated into it—or else Christ could not have made satisfaction for them either."[112] Further, his understanding of *unio mystica* was consistent with that of Bernard, Calvin, and the Puritans. He defines it as a "most intimate union with God by the Holy Spirit, a union of persons, an unbreakable and eternal covenant between God and ourselves, which cannot be at all adequately described by the word 'ethical' and is therefore called 'mystical.'"[113] Bavinck reveals another distinction from Barth by frequently emphasizing the Holy Spirit's role in uniting the individual into union with Christ.[114] Additionally, Bavinck continues that this "union of persons, [is] not only in will and disposition but also in being and nature."[115]

---

110. This translation began in 2003 and was completed in 2008.

111. Vissers, "Karl Barth's Appreciative Use of Bavinck."

112. Bavinck, *Reformed Dogmatics*, 4:214.

113. Ibid., 3:304.

114. Ibid., 1:570; 4:89, 251, 541, 577–78, and Bavinck, *Our Reasonable Faith*, 398.

115. Ibid., 4:577.

However, Bavinck is quick to qualify and maintains that union with Christ "is not a pantheistic mingling of the two [Christ and the individual], not a 'substantial union,' as it has been viewed by the mysticism of earlier and later times, nor on the other hand is it mere agreement in disposition, will, and purpose, as rationalism understood it and Ritschl again explained it."[116] Bavinck then immediately declares that what "Scripture tells us of this mystical union goes far beyond moral agreement in will and disposition" and then lists numerous biblical grounds for union with Christ, including references that "Christ lives and dwells in believers" (John 14:23; 17:23, 26; Gal 2:20; Eph 3:17) and "that they exist in him" (John 15:1–7; Rom 8:1; 1 Cor 1:30; 2 Cor 5:17). He additionally reminds his readers that this same union is sometimes compared to a "husband and wife" (1 Cor 6:16–17; Eph 5:32) and a "cornerstone and building" (1 Cor 3:11, 16; 6:19; Eph 2:21; 1 Pet 2:4–5).[117] Later he declares that the mystical union "can only be made somewhat clear to us by the images of the vine and the branch, the head and the body, a bridegroom and his bride, the cornerstone and the building that rests on it."[118]

For Bavinck, *unio mystica* is central to his theology.[119] Within this framework, Bavinck recognizes the many benefits a person receives from his or her union with Christ. Much like Calvin, Bavinck remarks that a person's union with Christ is "strengthened in the Supper."[120] Bavinck also asserts that the mystical union is the primary means for imitating Christ.[121] Consistent with the best of Reformed theology, he perceives the parallel but not equal nature of Word and Sacrament affirming, "in the Lord's Supper we indeed do not receive any other or any more benefits than we do in the Word, but also no fewer."[122] This mystical union "transforms humans in the divine image and makes them participants in the divine nature (2 Cor. 3:18; Gal. 2:20; 2 Pet. 1:4)."[123]

116. Ibid., 4:250.

117. Ibid., 4:251.

118. Ibid., 4:567–68; cf. 576.

119. Gleason, *Herman Bavinck*, 476–77.

120. Bavinck, *Reformed Dogmatics*, 4:577–78. For a further elaboration on this topic see Gleason, "Calvin and Bavinck on Lord's Supper," 5–81.

121. Bavinck, *Imitation of Christ (1885–86)*, 21; cf. 17, 22.

122. Bavinck, *Reformed Dogmatics*, 4: 567; cf. 577.

123. Ibid., 3:304.

Further, it is through mystical union that all of Christ's benefits from justification to sanctification accrue to the individual.[124] The intimacy of *unio mystica* naturally leads to a consideration of experience. Once again it will become clear that the apprehension and anxieties of Barth have receded as Bavinck embraces a deeper appreciation for experiencing God's presence.

Experience

Bavinck also faced a major personal crisis that challenged his understanding of experience, however, unlike Barth's with his former professors, it did not cripple him. Similar to Barth, Bavinck's father was strongly experiential and pious.[125] Bavinck was raised within the Secession Church that had broken away from the National Reformed Church in 1834 due to the lack of vibrant faith and orthodox theology. This fledging denomination reflected many of the same principles and practices of the *Nadere Reformatie* and English Puritanism. In preparation for his pastoral training he first attended his denomination's seminary in Kampen. However, after his first year he transferred to the more prominent University of Leiden. This was motivated by his desire for the most progressive and modern theological teaching. His father and others were concerned about his faith due to the strong liberal nature of Leiden. While Bavinck writes in his journal of his desire to "remain standing [in the faith]" and succeeds in that desire, he looks back in retrospect commenting, "Leiden has benefited me in many ways: I hope always to acknowledge that gratefully. But it has also greatly impoverished me, robbed me, not only of much ballast (for which I am happy), but also of much that I recently, especially when I preach, recognize as vital for my own spiritual life."[126] In fact, he once described his training at Leiden as "stones for bread."[127] Before his departure from Kampen, Bavinck confessed, "I am a child of the secession, and I hope always to remain one."[128] Amid this personal struggle he successfully weathered the theological challenges

---

124. Ibid., 3:591; cf. 4:123, 578–81 and Bavinck, *Sacrifice of Praise*, 24.

125. Gleason, *Herman Bavinck*, 25, 34.

126. Editor's introduction, *Reformed Dogmatics*, 1:13.

127. Bolt, "Between Kampen and Amsterdam," 269. For an elaboration of Leiden's effect on Bavinck see Dosker, "Herman Bavinck," 450–52 and Harnick, "Something That Must Remain," 250–55.

128. Bolt, "Between Kampen and Amsterdam," 269; cf. 268.

and according to John Bolt, editor of the *Reformed Dogmatics*, Bavinck was "thus definitely shaped by strong patterns of deep pietistic Reformed spirituality."[129] However, Bavinck equally critiqued the weaknesses of his church, recognizing the potential for an other-worldliness and anti-cultural withdrawal.[130] Nonetheless, Bavinck validated his piety and orthodoxy by returning to Kampen in 1882 as professor.

However, this tension causes some to view "Bavinck as a man between two worlds."[131] Unfortunately, the most recent English biography on Bavinck does not indicate that some scholars take a dissenting view on the challenges of Bavinck's time at Leiden.[132] However, Bavinck clearly articulates some form of personal tension:

> The antithesis, therefore, is fairly sharp: on the one side, a Christian life that considers the highest goal, now and hereafter, to be the contemplation of God and fellowship with him, and for that reason (always being more or less hostile to the riches of an earthly life) is in danger of falling into monasticism and asceticism, pietism and mysticism; but on the side of Ritschl, a Christian life that considers its highest goal to be the kingdom of God, that is, the moral obligation of mankind, and for that reason (always being more or less adverse to the withdrawal into solitude and quiet communion with God), is in danger of degenerating into cold Pelagianism and an unfeeling moralism. Personally, I do not yet see any way of combining the two points of view, but I do know that there is much that is excellent in both, and that both contain undeniable truth.[133]

While some might interpret this as confusion, I perceive this as a healthy balance within Bavinck's piety and agree with Bolt's assessment "about the unity of the two streams in Bavinck" and that, unlike Barth, he both

129. Editor's introduction, *Reformed Dogmatics*, 1:12; cf. 4:24 and Veenhof, "History of Theology and Spirituality," 276.

130. Bolt, "Imitation of Christ Theme," 77.

131. Editor's introduction, *Reformed Dogmatics*, 1:13. For an expansion on this see Bolt, "Between Kampen and Amsterdam," 264–69, and Harnick, "Something that Must Remain," 249–52.

132. Gleason, *Herman Bavinck*, 45–68. In personal communication with Gleason on September 14, 2010, he asserted "Leiden created a far less radical shift for Bavinck."

133. Editor's introduction, *Reformed Dogmatics*, 1:14.

sought and was successful in being "pious, orthodox, and thoroughly contemporary."[134]

Bavinck articulates his understanding of experience most lucidly in his 1908–9 Princeton Stone Lecture "Revelation and Religious Experience." There he maintains the importance of revelation as the foundation for experience.[135] Further, "[e]xperience by itself is not sufficient. Scripture is the norm also for our emotional life and tells us what we ought to experience."[136] Bavinck clearly asserts the essential nature of experience, "that dogmatics, especially in the doctrine of the *ordo salutis*, must become more psychological, and must reckon more fully with religious experience."[137] Previously he wrote, "[o]nly through experience does one first understand the truth. Experience discovers in the words of Scripture an entirely new spiritual meaning; it shows us a truth behind the truth, not because it wants to say something else, but because we have then experienced and benefited from it in our hearts."[138] Even more forcefully he declares, "[t]hese experiences [e.g., 'longing for God, communion with God, delight in God'] do not merely exist but have a right to exist; they are inseparable from godliness, and therefore find their classic expression in the Bible as a whole, especially in the Psalms."[139] One quickly recognizes Bavinck's boldness that was absent in Barth. Nonetheless, Bavinck is critical of the psychology of religion movement that studied conversions and those who had experienced revivals because it shifted the focus of dogmatics from the "exposition of the doctrine of Scripture" to "a description of conscious religious ideas or pious emotions."[140]

Bavinck, similar at this point to Barth, understands that experience alone can never be the foundation for faith because there must be some objective truth that first invites a response.[141] As previously stated,

134. Bolt, "Between Kampen and Amsterdam," 269; cf. Harnick, "Something that Must Remain," 252.

135. Bavinck, *Philosophy of Revelation*, 208. This specific lecture was not delivered at Princeton but elsewhere during his visit in the United States.

136. Bavinck, *Reformed Dogmatics*, 1:534.

137. Bavinck, *Philosophy of Revelation*, 209.

138. Bavinck, *Certainty of Faith*, 42.

139. Bavinck, *Reformed Dogmatics*, 1:533–34.

140. Bavinck, *Essays on Religion*, 62; cf. Bavinck, *Philosophy of Revelation*, 210. Bavinck devotes an entire chapter to this topic in *Essays of Religion*, 61–80.

141. Bavinck, *Certainty of Faith*, 67, 69, 92.

Bavinck understood "Scripture is the norm also for our emotional life and tells us what we ought to experience."[142] Barth no doubt would approve of that assessment. Therefore, Bavinck, unlike Barth, does not panic when subjective experiences are mentioned because "[t]he word 'faith' . . . expresses subjective religiousness."[143] However, it must be stressed that Bavinck's subjective dimension of faith is radically different from Schleiermacher's subjectivism.[144] In *The Certainty of Faith* Bavinck reveals the essential dynamics of both truth and experience, "[t]here is a certainty that pertains to objective religious truth and a certainty that pertains to the subject's share in the benefits promised by that truth. The two kinds of certainty are doubtlessly very closely interconnected, but they should, nevertheless, be distinguished and not confused."[145] More succinctly, he summarizes his position in his Stone Lecture declaring faith is "a trustful knowledge and a knowing trust."[146] Additionally, the Holy Spirit plays a significant role in this dynamic of experience, "[h]ence the subjective activity of the Holy Spirit has to be added to the objective word."[147] Earlier, Bavinck refers to the Spirit's role in "subjective revelation" as illumination.[148] I will consider his more comprehensive understanding of the dynamic relationship between Word and Spirit and a person's experiences of God following his critique of mysticism.

Not only is Bavinck's comfort level in relation to the subjective dimension of experience greater than Barth's, he also articulates a more balanced treatment of the intellect and affections. Bavinck asserts, "[t]he heart cannot be separated from the head, nor faith as trust from faith as knowledge."[149] In his inaugural address at the Free University of Amsterdam he defines his vision for doing theology and declares it is "a service of worship, a consecration of mind and heart to the honor of His name."[150] Bavinck demonstrated this in both his writings and lifestyle. Henry Dosker, his life long friend, confirmed this balance: "[Bavinck]

---

142. Bavinck, *Reformed Dogmatics*, 1:534; cf. 3:26.

143. Bavinck, *Philosophy of Revelation*, 225; cf. *Reformed Dogmatics*, 4:130.

144. Bavinck, *Reformed Dogmatics*, 1:66–70, 521.

145. Bavinck, *Certainty of Faith*, 28; cf. 82.

146. Bavinck, *Philosophy of Revelation*, 240.

147. Bavinck, *Reformed Dogmatics*, 4:460.

148. Ibid., 1:350.

149. Bavinck, *Philosophy of Revelation*, 208; cf. Bavinck, *Essays on Religion*, 26.

150. Bavinck, *Our Reasonable Faith*, 7.

had a thoroughly disciplined mind, with the heart of a child." Later, as a summary of Bavinck's method, Dosker declared, "[t]he service of God, both with heart and intellect, is the aim of all true Christian theology."[151] Significantly, Bavinck appreciated the unique contribution of these human faculties and never sought to elevate one over the other. Therefore, he maintained the intellect and the will "are consistently interconnected and reciprocally support and promote each other."[152] Bavinck demonstrates their mutual significance in his communion meditation, *The Sacrifice of Praise*. In describing the importance of introducing children to Scripture, he claims it must "be both instruction and training, at the same time working upon mind and heart."[153] As Bavinck expands his teaching he highlights first the danger of emphasizing only the emotions, "[t]he cultivation of emotions and the awakening of affections without true and clear representations is even dangerous."[154] Likewise, he warns of the risk of ignoring the affections, "[h]e, who impresses the truth upon his mind, without having his heart in it, receives only the image of the things, while he remains a stranger unto the things themselves."[155] Clearly, Bavinck once again exhibits a greater balance than Barth on this point.

Not surprisingly, Bavinck's historical context affected his understanding of mysticism and his reservations regarding it. The balanced mystical piety of the first generation of the *Nadere Reformatie* was eclipsed by an increasing otherworldly withdrawal from society. This same pattern was repeated in Bavinck's time with the Secession.[156] Therefore, Bavinck's assessment of mysticism can be summarized in relation to three primary concerns. First, he objects to its exclusive nature. Since it is typically associated with monasticism, it limits the experience "to a small number of privileged persons."[157] Second, while not an accurate assessment, Bavinck believed that pantheistic[158] and Neoplatonic

---

151. Dosker, "Bavinck," 454, 463.

152. Bavinck, *Reformed Dogmatics*, 4:153; cf. Bavinck, *Essays on Religion*, 199–204 where he asserts the cooperative interaction of the intellect and will rather than the primacy of one over the other.

153. Bavinck, *Sacrifice of Praise*, 42.

154. Ibid., 43.

155. Ibid., 44; cf. Bavinck, *Certainty of Faith*, 76.

156. Bolt, "Imitation of Christ Theme," 55–57.

157. Bavinck, *Reformed Dogmatics*, 1:148.

158. Ibid., 2:69; cf. 4:75, 456–57 and Bavinck, *Imitation of Christ (1885–86)*, 18.

roots inspired Pseudo-Dionysius and was devoid of a biblical foundation.[159] Third, and most importantly, mysticism tended to either under-
value or, over, time marginalize the use of Scripture.[160] Bavinck's position
becomes clearer in examining his critique of "Anabaptist mysticism,"
which likely refers to the Quakers. In true irenic fashion, he praises the
early Anabaptists who had "many upright believers" who had sacrificed
"their blood for the cause of the Lord."[161] However, according to Bavinck,
their zeal eventually created two serious errors. First, people became
content "with the internal Word alone, despising Scripture and church,
office and sacrament, appealing to private revelations and becoming guilty of various excesses." This parallels Ambrose's critique of the
seventeenth-century Quakers. Second, "when the initial exuberance was
past, gradually the internal Word was robbed of its special, supernatural
character, coming to be more and more identified with the natural light
of reason and conscience." The resulting tragedy, from Bavinck's perspective, was that the Anabaptists and others who followed this pattern
"despised the Word [and] surrendered the criterion that alone enabled
them to distinguish properly between nature and grace."[162] This reflects
the central Reformed doctrine of Word and Spirit.[163] If either the Word
or Spirit loses its importance it creates an unhealthy experience. On the
contrary, Bavinck asserts, Christ "by his Word directs our faith to his
sacrifice, by his Spirit incorporates us into his fellowship, and by both
Word and Spirit prepares and preserves us for heavenly blessedness."[164]
The dynamic interaction between Word and Spirit is a familiar refrain in
Bavinck.[165] Further, and more significantly, one perceives from Bavinck's
emphasis upon the internal operation of the Holy Spirit and the "testimony of the Holy Spirit"[166] that if a healthy balance was maintained between Word and Spirit the resulting experience of mystical piety would

159. Ibid., 2:190–91

160. Ibid., 1:467, 473; 2:68; 4:102, 441.

161. Bavinck, *Saved By Grace*, 73.

162. Ibid. Cf. Bavinck, *Reformed Dogmatics*, 1:467; 3:580; 4:456–57.

163. Ibid., 73–74, 79; cf. Veenhof, "History of Theology and Spirituality," 297.

164. Bavinck, *Reformed Dogmatics*, 3:595.

165. See for example Bavinck, *Reformed Dogmatics*, 3:593; 4:332, 395, 442, 457, 459; Bavinck, *Philosophy of Revelation*, 241; Bavinck, *Sacrifice of Praise*, 38, 40; and Bavinck, *Our Reasonable Faith*, 406–7, 433, 514.

166. Bavinck, *Our Reasonable Faith*, 422–23, 511 and *Reformed Dogmatics*, 1:585.

be acceptable to him.[167] Therefore, Bavinck carefully delineates the differences between "true mysticism" and "general mysticism"[168] and between orthodox and pantheistic mysticism.[169] Further, he acknowledges that there is a mysticism "of the Reformed church"[170] and once described his father's preaching as "healthy mysticism."[171] Clearly, Bavinck did not reject all forms of mysticism and displays a more balanced perspective than Barth.

Practices and Contemplation

At first glance, it appears that Bavinck shares a number of Barth's fears regarding spiritual practices and contemplation. More specifically, Bavinck's objections are three-fold. First, he is critical that contemplation tended to "disparage knowledge" and reduce "clarity of mind."[172] Second, he frequently associates contemplation with asceticism[173] and perceives asceticism as Pelagianism, calling it "nothing other than self-willed religion."[174] Third, he adamantly rejects the Roman Catholic doctrine of superadded grace and the beatific vision that he connects with the practice of contemplation.[175] However, Bavinck does recognize that there can be an authentic or biblical asceticism.[176] Others have described him as "the man of quiet contemplation"[177] and, in his own words, he asserts, "[w]e come to the knowledge of God only by contemplating God's revelation in nature and Scripture."[178] Likewise, he maintains that "a proper Christian meditation on God's works, and words . . . is enjoined

---

167. Bavinck, *Reformed Dogmatics*, 1:467, 473, and 4:102; cf. Bavinck, *Sacrifice of Praise*, 40. This was the case in the *Nadere Reformatie*. See Beeke, "Evangelicalism and Dutch Further Reformation," 161.

168. Ibid., 3:529.

169. Ibid., 1:148.

170. Ibid., 2:191.

171. Dosker, "Bavinck," 450.

172. Bavinck, *Reformed Dogmatics*, 1:149.

173. Ibid., 3:493; 4:239, 242.

174. Ibid., 4:243; cf. Bavinck, *Imitation of Christ (1918)*, 45.

175. Ibid., 2:545; 3:529; 4:722; cf. Bavinck, *Imitation of Christ (1885–86)*, 17.

176. Ibid., 4:674; cf. 243 and Bavinck, "Catholicity of Christianity," 248.

177. Harinck, "Something that Must Remain," 250; cf. 253.

178. Bavinck, *Reformed Dogmatics*, 2:69.

by" Scripture.[179] Bavinck also claims that the task of theology is not only to guide individuals how to live life in this world and the next but "[i]t must lead us to rest in the arms of God."[180] The apparent gap between Bavinck's resistance and his more nuanced reception of contemplation can be resolved by recognizing that he accepted the common Protestant distortion that medieval Roman Catholics were Neoplatonic and taught a union of indistinction.[181] Bavinck even incorrectly associates Bernard with the theology of Pseudo-Dionysius.[182] Yet elsewhere he speaks more approvingly of Bernard's practice of mysticism.[183]

Additionally, in exploring the interaction between contemplation and action Bavinck demonstrates a radically different sensitivity than Barth. In his 1888 lecture at Kampen Bavinck acknowledges:

> The mystical life has its own legitimacy alongside activity; the busyness of work makes rest necessary. . . In this dispensation we will never achieve the full harmony and unity that we expect in the future. Some onesideness will remain in us as persons and churches. None of us has our intellect, emotions and will, our head, heart and hand, equally governed by the Gospel. However, in order to prevent the "spiritual" (*godsdienstige*), side of Christianity—that which in the good sense of the term can be called the "ascetic" side—from degenerating into an improper mysticism and monastic spirituality, it needs to be supplemented by the moral (*zedelijke*)—the truly human side.[184]

More pointedly, Bavinck continues by asserting that these two legitimate expressions of Christianity need to be integrated into one: "[f]aith appears to be great, indeed, when a person renounces all and shuts himself up in isolation. But even greater, it seems to me, is the faith of a person who, while keeping the kingdom of heaven as a treasure, at the same time brings it out into the world as a leaven, certain that He who is for us is greater than he who is against us and that He is able to preserve us

---

179. Bavinck, *Imitation of Christ (1885–86)*, 17.

180. Bavinck, *Certainty of Faith*, 17.

181. Bavinck, *Reformed Dogmatics*, 2:539; cf. 187–91.

182. Ibid., 1:148–49. Casey asserts, "that Pseudo-Dionysius had scarcely any impact at all" on Bernard. *Athirst for God*, 31.

183. Bavinck, *Imitation of Christ (1885–86)*, 14.

184. Bavinck, "Catholicity of Christianity," 248.

from evil even in the midst of the world."[185] Later in his Stone Lectures Bavinck declares, "Mary and Martha were very different in religious disposition, but Jesus loved them both."[186] He expands the interaction between contemplation and action by considering his own denomination: "[t]his tradition [i.e. the Dutch Secession movement] overestimated and overemphasized the one thing needful, which, on the other hand, is often lacking in the busyness of contemporary life. While these nineteenth century Christians forgot the world for themselves, we run the danger of losing ourselves in the world."[187] Further, the spiritual life is the foundation for every dimension of life within the world, therefore "in fellowship with God, he is strengthened for his labors and girds himself for the battle. But that mysterious life of fellowship with God is not the whole of life. The prayer chamber is the inner room, although it is not the whole house in which he lives and functions . . . Rather it is the power that enables us to faithfully fulfill our earthly calling, stamping all of life as service to God."[188] Unquestionably, Bavinck recognizes the dynamic interaction of prayer and service and once again reveals a more healthy perspective than Barth.

Language of Delight and Enjoyment

Similar to Barth, Bavinck does not employ the devotional language of ravishment and, unlike Barth, he does not appear to address the emotional nature of pietistic hymns. However, Bavinck does recognize that a "fervent, sincere faith" should produce a "little genuine enthusiasm"[189] and that maintaining the proper balance of Word and Spirit would prevent the error of "enthusiasm of the Anabaptists."[190] Likewise, to "delight in God" is an appropriate expression of spiritual hunger.[191] Conversion produces a "lively joy in God"[192] and therefore believers can enjoy communion with

---

185. Ibid.

186. Bavinck, *Philosophy of Revelation*, 234–35.

187. Bavinck, *Certainty of Faith*, 94.

188. Ibid., 95–96.

189. Ibid., 9.

190. Bavinck, *Reformed Dogmatics*, 4:326; cf. 332.

191. Ibid., 1:533.

192. Bavinck, *Philosophy of Revelation*, 237; cf. 241 and Bavinck, *Imitation of Christ (1918)*, 28.

God.[193] Bavinck's understanding of enjoyment is trinitarian, since a person may "enjoy the heartfelt joy in God through Christ."[194] Further, this joy comes through the Holy Spirit,[195] and without faith it is impossible to enjoy the benefits of God.[196] According to Bavinck, the future blessedness consists of "contemplation (*visio*), understanding (*comprehensio*), and enjoyment of God (*fruitio Dei*);[197] however, a person begins to enjoy these eschatological benefits already on earth.[198] Significantly, Bavinck believes that Jesus' invitation to the Lord's Supper offers believers the "joy of heaven" and "communion with Christ."[199]

To summarize, Bavinck noticeably demonstrates a greater receptivity than Barth to a contemplative-mystical piety. G. C. Berkouwer, who later occupied the same theological chair at the Free University as Bavinck, offers this valuable summary:

> In spite of his objections to experiential theology, Bavinck did not think that the purpose of this theology was to make subjective, pious experience the criterion of religious truth. Kuyper was more critical of experiential theology, and thought Bavinck's critique was too mild. He suspected that a pantheistic streak ran through experiential theology. Bavinck, on the other hand, was more sensitive to the dangers of dead orthodoxy, of a confession that one believed in place of a living faith that one confessed. Great theologian that he was, Bavinck certainly was aware that the Christian had to reflect about the manner in which divine revelation entered convincingly into human consciousness.[200]

Therefore, Bavinck reveals a greater flexibility to both the need for and importance of experience than Barth. While he expresses some concerns regarding mysticism, they are significantly less than Barth's. Clearly, Bavinck's theology and piety are more reflective of Isaac Ambrose's viewpoint than Barth's, and, overall Bavinck's theology is more conducive to creating the opportunity for a person to experience God more contemplatively.

193. Bavinck, *Reformed Dogmatics*, 4:91, 103, 152.

194. Ibid., 4:158; cf. 3:527.

195. Ibid., 4:257.

196. Ibid., 4:103; cf. 257, 578.

197. Ibid., 4:722.

198. Ibid., 4:721–73.

199. Ibid., 4:640; cf. 576.

200. Berkouwer, *Half Century of Theology*, 14.

Previously it was noted that the restrictive trajectory of Barth's resistance to contemplative piety has continued to the present, affecting some of his disciples, such as Bloesch. In a like manner, there is a more positive trajectory of retrieval embracing a contemplative piety extending back to the seventeenth century, connecting through Bavinck and extending to the contemporary church. The parallels between the *Nadere Reformatie* and English Puritanism have already been mentioned; significantly, they embraced the writings of Ambrose very early in their history. *Prima, Media, Ultima* was Ambrose's first work to be translated into Dutch in 1660.[201] The first Dutch translation of *Looking Unto Jesus* appeared in 1664.[202] The works of Puritanism experienced a revival of interest in mid-nineteenth-century Holland, and no less than four editions of *Looking Unto Jesus* were published in twenty-four years.[203] The second half of the twentieth century witnessed another revival of interest in the writings of Ambrose. This time seven editions of *Looking Unto Jesus* were published.[204] Willem op't Hof, an expert in Dutch Pietism and Puritanism, remarks that Lewis Bayly's *The Practice of Piety* was the number one bestseller among pietistic literature in the seventeenth century, with forty eight editions to only four to Ambrose's *Looking Unto Jesus*. However, "the appreciation of Ambrose as an edifying writer is still alive [today in contrast to that of Bayly] and perhaps more lively than ever." Op't Hof identifies Ambrose's eclipse of Bayly and contemporary popularity as due to his "reformed, experimental, mystical and especially christocentric character."[205] This popularity of Ambrose's *Looking Unto Jesus* makes it likely to be found in most "families of the experimental reformed" tradition today.[206] Interestingly, most of the publications of Ambrose's works originated in northern Holland, the same region of Bavinck's birth and early ministry, though he does not reveal any awareness of Ambrose in his writings. Apparently, Ambrose's works were only translated into Dutch.[207] In the United States, Ambrose's *Looking Unto*

---

201. Schoneveld, *Intertraffic of the Mind*, 137; Van Der Haar, *From Abbadie to Young*, 3; and Op't Hof, *Engelse Pietistische Geschriften*, 631, 633.

202. Van Der Haar, *From Abbadie to Young*, 2.

203. Op't Hof, "Dutch Reception of Ambrose," 6–7.

204. Ibid., 7.

205. Ibid., 10.

206. Ibid., 8.

207. Ibid., 9.

Jesus as well as *War with Devils*, renamed as *The Christian Warrior*, have been republished in the past few decades.[208] In summary, while Bavinck does not indicate any awareness of Isaac Ambrose, the tradition from which he came was well acquainted with him.[209]

RETRIEVAL OF ISAAC AMBROSE FOR THE CONTEMPORARY CHURCH

The examination of Barth and Bavinck revealed that there is more than one approach to Reformed theology and piety. In reviewing the contemporary landscape of the Reformed and Evangelical tradition, it becomes clear that many are still resistant to a contemplative-mystical piety. As previously articulated, Barth is not the only cause of this resistance, though his influence no doubt contributes to this. Howard Rice accurately observes that "[t]here is a particularly deeply embedded resistance to spirituality among those churches within the denominational tradition called Reformed." Rice advances a number of reasons for this resistance, including "the rigorous exercise of the intellect as a sign of obedience to God" and a highly active faith that concentrates its energy on addressing the needs of society.[210] It is illuminating that Rice does not include Barth in his survey of key Reformed leaders for recovering a renewed piety.[211] However, there are promising signs that more Reformed and Evangelical theologians are embracing a contemplative piety today.[212]

208. *Looking Unto Jesus* was published by Sprinkle Publications in 1986 and *The Christian Warrior* was published by Soli Deo Gloria in 1997.

209. However, Bavinck did know the classic *Nadere Reformatie* text of Willhelmus à Brakel, *The Christian's Reasonable Service*.

210. Rice, *Reformed Spirituality*, 9.

211. Ibid., 17.

212. See for example Moltmann, "Theology of Mystical Experience"; Ferguson, "Reformed View," 193; Postema, *Space for God*, 65–66, 130, 173, 196; Eugene Peterson, *Working the Angles*, 74–86, Eugene Peterson, *Contemplative Pastor*, and Eugene Peterson, *Eat This Book*, 109–17; Rice, *Reformed Spirituality*, 88–90, 110–17; Demarest, *Satisfy Your Soul*, 157–86; Johnson and Dreitcer, *Beyond the Ordinary*, esp. 138–43. Evangelicals are also reclaiming the richness of contemplative piety: Foster, *Prayer*, 155–66 and Foster, *Streams of Living Water*, 23–58; Huggett, *Joy of Listening to God*, esp. 32–74; Peace, *Contemplative Bible Reading*; Webber, *Divine Embrace*, 16, 20–21, 26, 37, 43–55; Houston, "Reflections on Mysticism"; Houston, *Transforming Friendship*, 115–16, 191–222, 261–68; and Houston, *Pursuit of Happiness*, 253–66.

Further, drawing upon the insights of Tracy and Sheldrake, this retrieval is a necessity so that Reformed and Evangelical Christians can be
reconnected with the fullness of their own roots and tradition. According
to Tracy, a "classic text" is of perennial value and warrants retrieval for
challenging and provoking contemporary readers. Moreover, Sheldrake
asserts the importance of retrieval because it recovers "aspects of the
past, long forgotten and even deliberately submerged"[213] and that this
task "is important for our present identity and desire to live more complete Christian lives."[214] Further, this retrieval is critical for Evangelical
and Reformed Christians because without a greater awareness of their
contemplative roots their piety will be impoverished. Directly related to
this is the bold assertion of James Houston that Puritanism collapsed,
at least in part, because it did not give greater and sustained attention
to contemplation. He contends that Puritan spirituality "might have
been a richer, more sustained spirituality if the contemplative life had"
been more fully considered.[215] Tracy also warns of the potential "temptation to domesticate all reality" yet "any classic text[s] will resist" this.[216]
Therefore, the proper posture for reading any classic text, such as Isaac
Ambrose's writings, is one of "critique and suspicion."[217] Within this hermeneutic of suspicion, it is also important to be sensitive to the originat-
ing and receiving contexts. Much has occurred since the seventeenth
century and the purpose of this book is not to transplant or create a neo-
Puritan culture in the twenty-first century. However, as we approach
the respective cultures with sensitivity, are there principles and themes
that emerge from the writings of Isaac Ambrose that can address similar
concerns and needs today? Or, to borrow William Harmless' language,
"why mystics matter,"[218] why does Isaac Ambrose matter? One factor
that assists in this hermeneutical process is the common tradition and
continuity in theological foundation between Ambrose and contemporary Reformed and Evangelical believers.

Therefore, the challenge is to retrieve the contemplative-mystical
piety of Isaac Ambrose that has the qualities of a "classic text." In reality

213. Sheldrake, *Spirituality & History*, 31.

214. Ibid., 108.

215. Houston, "Spirituality," 1050.

216. Tracy, *Plurality and Ambiguity*, 15.

217. Ibid., 79; cf. 111, 112; Sheldrake, *Spirituality & History*, 183–84.

218. Harmless, *Mystics*, 264.

this is a two-step process. Many readers may not need to take the first step, which is to read these texts with an open and inquiring mind, but some members of the Evangelical and Reformed tradition may respond similarly to Charles Hodge (1797–1878), who when asked to review John Williamson Nevin's (1803–66) *The Mystical Presence: A Vindication of the Calvinistic Doctrine of the Eucharist*, resisted for two years.[219] Hodge was shocked that his former student's theology was so divergent from Calvin. However, many Reformed theologians would now agree that Nevin's theology was more representative of Calvin than Hodge, who was more Zwinglian in his understanding. Possibly some readers may approach the contemplative-mystical piety of Ambrose with a hermeneutic of suspicion, fearing it to be unreformed. Yet no one has ever challenged Ambrose's theology or piety. Moreover, if it strikes readers as being unreformed, that fear probably says more about them than it does about the integrity of Ambrose's theology. Further, a careful reading of Ambrose will reveal a faithful confirmation of all of the major tenants of Reformed theology, including a belief in a Triune God who is powerful and transcendent and personal and immanent. Reformed theology perceives God as one who is worthy to be worshiped and also seeks friendship and fellowship with humanity. Additionally, Reformed theology is sensitive to the reality of human brokenness through sin, to God's gracious initiative to redeem and restore all of creation, to the centrality of union with Christ, to a balanced reliance upon Word and Spirit, to the importance of integrating head and heart, and to a ministry of compassion and social justice to those in need.

The second step of the retrieval process recognizes that by retrieving Ambrose's piety a person is also retrieving his sources. This may be problematic for some readers, since Ambrose made frequent use of Western Catholic writings. However, the previous chapters confirmed that Calvin, Ambrose, and his fellow Puritans were willing to embrace and even strongly endorse medieval sources, especially those of Bernard of Clairvaux. David Cornick accurately affirms a central characteristic of Reformed piety, maintaining its "continuity" with the early church and that "[to] be Reformed was to be Catholic,"[220] and Richard Muller asserts that "Reformed orthodox theology" gives witness to "a conscious

---

219. Cornick, *Letting God Be God*, 134–35; cf. Hageman, "Reformed Spirituality," 74–75.

220. Ibid., 131; cf. 132–33.

catholicity."[221] This should not imply a homogeneous theology or an indiscriminate reception of all Western Catholic spiritual writings. Chapter 4 illustrated that Reformed authors always filtered these writings through their own theology.[222] Additionally, the same chapter revealed that Ambrose and other Puritans developed a strong resistance to the post-Tridentine writers, such as Ignatius of Loyola. However, moving into the eighteenth and the early portion of the nineteenth century, a sharper cleavage of discontinuity emerges. This is a complex matter to sort out, and obviously there are numerous factors involved. While space does not permit a detailed treatment of the causes of this unfortunate gap, a few brief comments are in order. The demise of scholasticism and the expanding pervasiveness of the Enlightenment certainly contributed to this discontinuity. The decline of scholasticism encouraged less emphasis upon patristic and medieval texts, the very sources most widely used by the Puritans. Additionally, the Enlightenment increased the priority of rationalism while marginalizing enthusiasm, thus decreasing the importance of mystery. Interestingly, Wesley did not include Bernard in his *Christian Library*. Significantly, as a result of rationalism both Roman Catholic and Protestant historians disapproved of Bernard.[223] With the turn of the century and the advance of romanticism there was "an idolizing of the Middle Ages" and an "interest in this medieval saint [i.e. Bernard] was rekindled."[224] This coincides with the renewed receptivity among nineteenth-century Reformed writers of Western Catholic sources.

Therefore, just as there are theological principles to guide readers in being able to retrieve Ambrose's piety, there are also theological principles to retrieve his sources as well. This is a significant step and ultimately achieves two important outcomes: the concerned reader can be assured of maintaining faithfulness to a Reformed and Evangelical identity, and also a hermeneutics of consent allows the interested persons to benefit from the robust nature of Ambrose's contemplative-mystical piety. This can be demonstrated by using Bernard, though these theological principles are also applicable to other medieval sources. Mark

221. Muller, *After Calvin*, 47; cf. 51, 53, 54.

222. See for example Hambrick-Stowe, *Early New England Meditative Poetry*, 13, 18–20, 61, and B. R. White "Echoes of Medieval Christendom," 84.

223. Bredero, *Bernard of Clairvaux*, 176–79.

224. Ibid., 180.

Noll summarizes Bernard's popularity, declaring that he was a "defender of orthodoxy."[225] Significantly, Bernard's solid exegetical foundation elevates the importance of Scripture, and a strong Pauline theme is evident throughout his writings. This is manifested in two specific ways; first, Bernard is very fond of St. Paul's metaphor of union with Christ. This is understood as a union of wills (1 Cor 6:17) and never becomes the union of essence or indistinction that created confusion and suspicion among later observers in both Catholic and Reformed traditions regarding mysticism. Second, Bernard's Pauline dependency reflects an Augustinian piety that is attentive to sin, grace, and experiencing God. Bernard valued both the intellect and affect in relationship to one's experience of God and also recognized the importance of both love and faith. This, combined with his strong christocentric emphasis made him very appealing to Reformed Christians. Additionally, while he was a monastic, Bernard was still active in traveling beyond his monastery to engage in ministry.

Therefore, by asking the question why Isaac Ambrose matters today, seven principles emerge that can inspire and guide Evangelical and Reformed theology and piety. The first three themes provide a theological foundation from which the remaining four principles of spiritual practice can emerge. First, *unio mystica* is central to Ambrose's theology and parallels the Reformed principle of God's nature and covenant making. Although the Reformed tradition has always emphasized the importance of union with Christ, as the beginning of a person's relationship with God, it is rarely understood today as fully as in Ambrose's writings. Frequently, the contemporary Reformed and Evangelical tradition focuses upon the forensic theme of justification with little regard for the relational dimension and fellowship with God.[226] This perception neglects Ambrose's theology of union and communion with Christ that he often called spiritual marriage. Not only does Jesus save and forgive a person's sins, he also draws that individual into a deepening intimacy with the Trinity. Therefore Ambrose declares, "[u]nion is the ground of our communion with Christ; and the nearer our union, and the greater our communion."[227] For Ambrose this is both personal and corporate

225. Noll, *Turning Points*, 102.

226. While Andrew Purves emphasizes union with Christ in his writings his focus is essentially forensic. See for example, *Reconstructing Pastoral Theology*.

227. Ambrose, *Looking Unto Jesus*, 913.

and resolves Bavinck's concern of a highly individualized communion with Christ. The contemporary Reformed and Evangelical tradition would greatly benefit from expanding its understanding of *unio mystica* to include the full doctrine of communion or spiritual marriage with Christ. This could likely create a greater awareness of enjoying the relational intimacy that Jesus offers to all who will embrace it and further create a deepening desire to grow in this spiritual marriage. That would then enable people to join with Ambrose in declaring, "[o]h it's an happy thing to have Christ dwell in our hearts, and for us to lodge in Christs bosome! Oh its an happy thing to maintain a reciprocal communication of affairs betwixt Christ and our souls!"[228]

Second, Ambrose challenges the contemporary church to integrate and maintain the critical balance between Word and Spirit. An immediate benefit of this interaction forms a more biblical theology of experience that avoids the all too common contemporary expressions of fragmentation and compartmentalization. Therefore, Ambrose challenges us, "*if the Spirit of Christ come along with the Word, it will rouze hearts, raise spirits, work wonders.*"[229] Clearly, Ambrose would be alarmed to discover the growing tendency among his Reformed and Evangelical descendants to reduce or ignore the importance of Scripture, as well as over-emphasizing either the intellect or the affections to the neglect of the other. Further, his method of meditation to "first lay down the Object [i.e., the biblical theme], and then direct you how to *look* upon it [i.e., stir up the affections to experience it]"[230] would calm the fears of Bavinck, who felt many Anabaptist mystics discounted Scripture. A close corollary is the development of a sanctified imagination for reading Scripture. While there is a growing receptivity to spiritual reading today through *lectio divina* and other methods, this has not always been well received in some sections of the Evangelical and Reformed tradition. To fashion healthy and biblically balanced disciples of Jesus, the overly academic reading of Scripture that can strip away the spiritual vitality of God's life must be transformed into a welcome dependency upon the Word and Spirit. Our reading of Scripture must be further enriched through a sanctified imagination to experience the fullness of God, including contemplative experiences of God.

228. Ibid., 40.
229. Ibid., 723.
230. Ibid., 129, 259, 365, 539, etc.; cf. Ambrose, *Media* (1657), 222.

Next, Ambrose has much to teach Reformed and Evangelical Christians about a theology of intentionality. This forms a critical component of Ambrose's theological structure from which he intentionally engaged in the cultivation of solitude and spiritual practices. Though he withdrew for his annual May retreats, he was cognizant of the subtle temptations of these prolonged periods of isolation. Ambrose recognized that the Holy Spirit and good angels were not the only ones to inhabit the spiritual realm. He was personally aware of spiritual combat with the powers of darkness and realized that one should carefully discern if God was calling a person to withdraw into solitude. Richard Foster articulates a similar caution: "[i]n the silent contemplation of God we are entering deeply into the spiritual realm, and there is such a thing as supernatural guidance that is not divine guidance."[231] Ambrose's wisdom, drawn from Scripture, that "[i]f we are led into a wilderness by Divine Providence, and in our calling, and that we run not our selves rashly into a temptation, we may confidently expect a comfortable issue out of it,"[232] can be extended today to the increased popularity of spiritual practices, including that of retreats. Anyone who engages in these disciplines would greatly benefit from Ambrose's wisdom on the nature of spiritual reality, the discernment of motivation, and seeking God's guidance before embarking upon such disciplines. Perhaps even further, the uniqueness of Ambrose's annual retreats demonstrates the importance of spiritual reality and eternal value to a contemporary culture consumed by the externals of physical beauty and polished self-image. A deepening awareness of intentionality that properly values the fullness of life and dependency upon grace would greatly enhance our relationships with both God and humanity.

The next four spiritual practices are all derived from the previous theological foundations. Fourth, Ambrose can wisely encourage contemporary Protestant Christians in communal spiritual practices that were part of their earlier heritage. Many have criticized spirituality as being strongly individualized and disconnected from daily life. This parallels both Barth's and Bavinck's concern about the privatized nature of asceticism and pietism. While annually Ambrose spent one month a year in isolation, he did not neglect the public means of grace. Many of his contemplative experiences were communal in nature; meeting with others,

231. Foster, *Prayer*, 157.
232. Ambrose, *War with Devils*, 172.

public fasts, and the celebration of the Lord's Supper. Additionally, he emphasized the Puritan practice of conferences. While this resembles the contemporary interest in small groups for Bible study and prayer, the unfortunate reality is that many small groups today devote more time to sharing and fellowship than cultivating spiritual maturity. One specific first step would be to follow Ambrose's counsel to encourage people to communicate their experiences to others: "for the advancement of holiness, must not deny such knowledge to the body; Christians must drive an open and free trade, they must teach one another the mystery of godliness."[233] This is closely related to the unhealthy pattern of the American church, to practice "dishonest fellowship" or to communicate only that we have no spiritual needs or struggles. Efforts to reclaim more honest and interactive relationships could begin to reduce the inordinate amount of individualized and isolated spirituality and encourage others to recognize that they are not the only ones who have struggled or conversely have had unique spiritual experiences with God.

Recovering a contemplative piety and attitude is the fifth insight from Ambrose. According to him contemplation is "soul recreation" and, therefore, one of the significant ways in which a person can enjoy God. Ambrose refutes Barth's criticism of the elite nature of contemplation by democratizing it for all people. Recovering Ambrose's conviction that heavenly meditation was one of the primary spiritual practices for cultivating one's relationship with God would be valuable again today. *Looking Unto Jesus* confirms the obvious importance of this for Ambrose, and perhaps its popularity was due in part to people's hunger to learn how to meditate on heaven. Additionally, it is critical to recognize that the overall contemplative focus of Ambrose was constructed upon the premise of looking or beholding Jesus, which captures a central theme of contemplation. Clearly, Ambrose's desire for heaven was not an escape from the many dangers the English nonconformists faced in the seventeenth century. Rather they were motivated by love; since they had entered into spiritual marriage with Jesus, they longed for the consummation of what they had already tasted in part on earth. Therefore, the practice of looking unto Jesus or heavenly meditation was a contemplative-mystical expression of love and grateful gazing upon Jesus. One wonders how Barth would have responded to Ambrose's *Looking Unto Jesus*? Clearly, Ambrose's practice of contemplation was not a *cul-de-sac*,

233. Ambrose, *Media* (1657), 339.

and God was obviously the object of it. Further, it was Word-centered, Christ-focused, Spirit-empowered, and God-glorified. Perhaps the recovery of Ambrose's "contemplative-mystical piety" today faces its greatest challenge in the Western world where people are so attached to their earthly possessions that the prospects of heaven are not that attractive. Contented consumers might well question, why should one bother to look ahead to heaven when all their earthly goods already satisfy their needs? However, Reformed and Evangelical theologian Bruce Demarest persuasively argues the necessity of recovering mysticism and contemplation because they are "not a perilous aberration of Christian faith, but the promise of a rewarding life with and for Christ."[234] Therefore, Ambrose can direct others to "[g]et we into our hearts an habit of more heavenly-mindednesse, by much exercise, and intercourse, and acquaintance with God, by often contemplation, and foretaste of the sweetnesse, glory, and eternity of those Mansions above."[235]

Sixth, and an important corollary of cultivating a contemplative piety, is the biblical integration of contemplation and action. Indeed, it is unfortunate that Barth was constrained by his anxieties and failed to see the possibility and strengths that Bavinck understood in integrating these two approaches. Habitually, Reformed and Evangelical Christians have tended to emphasize the active engagement with the world more than refreshing the soul in prayer. While service is necessary, over time it frequently creates depleted and demoralized followers of Jesus. One tangible means for addressing this was sudden meditation or ejaculatory prayer. Ambrose wisely encouraged the inclusion of this and other spiritual duties throughout the day asserting, that a "particular calling, with which I may either mingle some actings of grace, or ejaculatory duties, as suddenly to look up to heaven, and to behold the face of God, to whom I am to approve my self in my particular calling."[236] A contemporary adaptation of this approach could correct the fragmented division of sacred and secular and assist Christians in recognizing God's presence throughout the day, regardless of their tasks. It could also bring a renewed focus of contemplative gratitude to whatever activity we are involved in, since the actions would be renewed through prayer, and the prayers would motivate new action and engagement.

234. Demarest, "Mysticism: Peril or Promise?" 17.

235. Ambrose, *Media* (1657), 55.

236. Ambrose, *Redeeming the Time*, 19.

Seventh, Ambrose challenges us to discover and develop a language of delight and enjoyment in our experiences of God. This principle summarizes many of the previous themes and reflects numerous theological principles of Ambrose. A person is able to perceive God because of God's gracious invitation. When a person responds to God's Spirit and lives in spiritual marriage with Jesus, he or she can grow in deeper contemplative delight and love through spiritual practices. As in any growing relationship of intimacy, desire and enjoyment are important elements. Maturing relationships can challenge individuals to find adequate language to express the depth and passion of their love. Ambrose's usage of the erotic language of the Song of Songs shaped him to speak of both being ravished by the love of Jesus and ravishing Jesus with his love. To illustrate the former he asserts, "[a]nd in this kinde of love of God, and enjoyment of themselves in God, the Saints are ravished with God and are in a kind of extasie eternally."[237] While the language of ravishment could be problematic in our contemporary over-sexed culture, it could also perhaps begin to transform the world with a purer and nobler understanding of desire and love. Significantly, Ambrose's usage of this language of delight and enjoyment could serve another important function in distinguishing between a person's intense desires for Jesus experientially, rather than the all too common contemporary focus of seeking Jesus merely for his gifts and benefits. While some critics might perceive this principle as unrealistic, given the contours of the contemporary culture, it must be recognized that this process of recapturing the intensity of contemplative desire for Jesus and the language of ravishment is already growing within some circles of the Church. Therefore, I would encourage further exploration and wise usage of the language of ravishment.[238]

In summary, it is clear that Isaac Ambrose matters today, just as he did in the seventeenth century, because he can guide the way to a more robust and experiential faith that emphasizes both the intellect and affect

237. Ambrose, *Media* (1657), 260–61.

238. Mike Bickle of the Kansas City IHOP has written an allegorical study guide for the Song of Songs with a chapter entitled "The Ravished Heart of God" and the priests of St. Aldate's Anglican Church in Oxford, England, preached thirteen sermons on the Song of Songs from 2003–7. Further, two Reformed theologians have recently written books that focus on ravishment. Lane, *Ravished By Beauty* and Long, *Eucharistic Theology*. Additionally, most current versions of the Bible continue to use the word ravish when translating Song 4:9.

and creates a relationship of intimacy that takes great delight and enjoyment in God. Significantly, contemporary Dutch Reformed Pietists have already discovered the great benefit and wisdom of Ambrose for today. It is now time for his influence to expand and become better known. Isaac Ambrose matters because he charts a path that invites people to examine the dynamics of contemplative-mystical theology, language, and experience, and to engage and enjoy a vital "soul recreation" with God.

Conclusion

This study began by asking two questions: was Isaac Ambrose a Puritan mystic and can the contemporary church retrieve any wisdom from his writings? Jean Williams' detailed analysis of Puritan sermons, commentaries, diaries, letters, and other literature has persuasively argued and clearly established that Puritan mysticism was not uncommon, nor was it an aberration, as many scholars have previously thought, but rather a common reality among many moderate Puritans. However, I have been greatly indebted to the ongoing research of Bernard McGinn. He articulates that a broader definition of the mystical element of Christian spirituality is more helpful for studying the possibility of true Christian mysticism. For not only does this open up the possibilities of discovering mystical elements within the more traditional field of the Western and Roman Catholic tradition, in which one is more likely to find them, but it also is very suggestive for that within Protestantism in general, and more particularly, within Puritanism. This book has renamed McGinn's concept of the mystical element as contemplative-mystical piety. This terminology is more conducive to Reformed and Evangelical theology and experience and hopefully begins and continues to removes the residual fears and gross exaggerations that may still exert influence in certain sections of the Protestant community.

Unlike William's research that covered a broad spectrum of seventeenth-century Puritans, this present work focuses primarily on Isaac Ambrose. Ambrose was a moderate Lancashire Puritan minister who was ejected in 1662 for nonconformity. Writers from previous generations have called him "the most meditative Puritan of Lancashire," "of a contemplative disposition," and even a "religious mystic." However, the reality is that no one has actually made a detailed study of his theology and piety. While there have been a few studies that have briefly considered Ambrose, no one has made him the primary subject of their research and writing. Therefore, in one sense, this book is distinctive and fills a gap by providing a careful examination of Ambrose's theology and particularly his contemplative-mystical piety. Further, this book can strongly confirm that Ambrose was indeed a contemplative. Therefore, I offer five specific conclusions to this study of Ambrose's piety.

First, Isaac Ambrose possessed a rich contemplative-mystical piety. That prompts the necessary question, what was the shape of his contemplative-mystical piety? McGinn expands his understanding of the mystical element of Christianity by speaking of mystical theology, mystical texts, mystical experiences, mystical practices, and mystical vocabulary. A careful reading of Ambrose's mystical texts, especially those of *Media* and *Looking Unto Jesus*, revealed that all of these categories were present within his understanding of Christianity and provided a window into his soul that traced the contours of his life. It became clear that Ambrose experienced God across a full spectrum of means: his annual month-long retreats in which he intentionally engaged in a variety of spiritual practices as well as regularly facing the personal struggles and temptations of his soul; his active ministry of being a physician of the soul to both clergy and laity; and his times of fasting and celebrating the Lord's Supper. He also experienced the transformative role of place, whether in the woods during his retreats or in villages and cities such as Preston or London. Moreover, there were some significant practices that undergirded his life. Ambrose always combined a deep study of Scripture without neglecting an affective praying of Scripture. Further, and reflective of many Puritans, he was a student of the Communion of Saints. Ambrose was not ignorant of the roots of Christian mysticism and demonstrated not only an awareness of the patristic and medieval representatives, but also some of the Eastern Orthodox tradition as well. Additionally, Ambrose recognized the great importance, indeed, the necessity of the Holy Spirit to guide his theology and direct his life. One further aspect of his contemplative-mystical piety was the importance of spiritual marriage with Jesus, and how living in that conscious relationship with gratitude awakened him to know and love God more fully. Briefly, that summarizes the nature of Isaac Ambrose's contemplative-mystical piety.

Second, this book has revised Simon Chan's conclusion of placing Ambrose within the ascetical stream of Puritan meditation. Clearly,
Ambrose displayed a strong ascetical theme within his theology and piety. However, where Chan misreads and distorts Ambrose is by minimizing the equal importance of the Holy Spirit in his theology and practice of
meditation. Chan's two categories are not intended to be exclusive or binary, and one is likely to find varying degrees of dependence upon asceticism or the Holy Spirit in different Puritans. Nonetheless, the weakness of
this approach is that it tends to create an unhealthy dichotomy that drives
a wedge between one of the most fundamental foundations of Reformed
and Evangelical theology of Word and Spirit. This critical theme emerged
at various points throughout this study; whenever it became unbalanced,
it produced distorted expressions of mysticism. However, whenever the
unity of Word and Spirit was maintained, as it was in Ambrose's theology and piety, it produced a healthy biblical contemplative-mystical piety.
Therefore, it is essential in casting Ambrose as ascetical, that we do not
miss the equally present importance of the Holy Spirit throughout his
writings. Additionally, this Reformed principle of Word and Spirit nicely
echoes Bernard of Clairvaux's teaching that contemplation is of both the
intellect and the affect. This study has also emphasized that Ambrose's
method of meditation was built on this principle, to begin by laying down
the understanding of Scripture and then stirring up the affections of the
soul to deepen a person's experience of that Scripture.

Third, while mystical experience is essentially ineffable, a tremen-
dous amount of words have been written and spoken over the centuries
attempting to describe it. The Puritans read the Song of Songs allegorically and turned to it not only for a biblical theology of spiritual marriage and intimacy, but also for an erotic vocabulary to express their
desire and delight in Jesus, the divine Bridegroom. Ambrose made full
usage of this language of delight and enjoyment. Ravishment, in particular, was a favorite word used to describe a person's experience with God.
Significantly, Ambrose used this term autobiographically to express his
own relationship of spiritual marriage with Jesus. He also employed it in
his writings to encourage others to delight and enjoy God. While many
scholars have commented on the frequency of the word ravish throughout the history of Christian spirituality, I am not aware of anyone who
has devoted a serious and sustained examination of the nature, dynamics, and benefits of ravishment within Puritan piety as I have. Further,

this research has confirmed the assertion of other writers of the strong continuity between the language of Puritan piety and that of Bernard and other medieval Christians. Additionally, this study encourages the exploration of reclaiming the use of the term ravishment for the contemporary church. Perhaps, the awareness and proper usage of ravishment and other love-language reminiscent of the Song of Songs might encourage a greater desire and hunger for God today. Further, in a culture that has in many ways lost an appreciation for the importance of language, it invites more careful reflection on how we might explore and express our intimacy with the Triune God.

Fourth, this book has examined specifically the contemplative-mystical piety of Isaac Ambrose. Ambrose used the metaphor of "soul recreation" as one of his primary images of contemplation. In one sense, all of his writings are a commentary on how the soul might engage in recreation with God. Again, while there has been some very helpful research on the nature of contemplation within Puritan piety, I have not discovered anyone who has followed Dewey Wallace's observation of a detailed study on the importance of heavenly meditation within Puritanism.[1] I have sought to be attentive to Ambrose's teaching and practice of heavenly meditation. Therefore, I accept Wallace's challenge and also take it as a motivation for future research. But much more needs to be done in this area. How did heavenly meditation develop within Puritanism? What common patterns exist as well as unique features in the various writers? What are the points of continuity and discontinuity with writers from the Western Catholic tradition? Is it accurate to affirm that Puritan writers following the Restoration privileged this more than before 1662? These are all important questions that invite serious research.

Frequently Ambrose spoke of beholding or gazing at God, and his massive and popular *Looking Unto Jesus* is a sustained meditation of looking at Jesus in love and gratitude. We discovered that one of the primary benefits of looking at Jesus in a contemplative manner is that the person is transformed to become more like Jesus. The biblical foundation for this transformative looking is 2 Cor 3:18, which has been a favorite text in the history of Christian mysticism. Further, this figured significantly among the seven principles of retrieval from Isaac Ambrose for the contemporary church that was outlined in the conclusion of the last chapter.

---

1. J. I. Packer's chapter on heavenly meditation in Baxter is the exception. "Richard Baxter on Heaven."

Fifth, as was previously stated, this book asked *two* questions. The first four conclusions all reinforce that Isaac Ambrose's understanding of basic Christianity reflected a strong contemplative-mystical piety. In many ways, the second question is even more critical. If Ambrose's ministry was motivated and sustained by his contemplative-mystical piety, what, if anything, can the Reformed and Evangelical traditions learn from him today? A typical pattern for many Protestants who become interested in the practice and study of Christian spirituality is to bemoan the lack of models and resources within their own heritage. It is not uncommon to find Reformed and Evangelical Christians searching the lives and writings of the spiritual giants of the Roman Catholic tradition because of its rich spiritual reservoir of resources. While, on the one hand, there is nothing wrong with this, yet, on the other hand, there is often a feeling of embarrassment that certain Protestant traditions are devoid of similar resources and that there appears to be an emphasis on the overly intellectual or cognitive without any great sensitivity to the affective. However, this book has demonstrated that contemplative-mystical piety, while richly present within the Western and Roman Catholic tradition, is not absent from the Reformed and Evangelical traditions. Therefore, the challenge is to recover the lost heritage of piety within Reformed theology that itself is certainly not exclusive of patristic and even medieval piety. Not only does the Reformed and Evangelical tradition include many historical examples of contemplative-mystical piety, as Isaac Ambrose and his fellow Puritans demonstrate, but also, perhaps more importantly, this theology supports and actually encourages the cultivation of "soul recreation" that delights and enjoys God with both head and heart. It is my desire that this work might provide some impetus to, and help in, retrieving and nourishing the holistic Christianity that so characterized the earlier historic faith of the Reformed tradition.

Chronology of Isaac Ambrose

1604: Ambrose was born (date unknown) and baptized at Ormskirk, Lancashire (May 29, 1604). He was the third son and youngest of six children of Rev. Richard Ambrose, vicar of Ormskirk (1572–1612). Ambrose was born and lived most of his life in the northwest region of Lancashire. This part of the country was a stronghold for Roman Catholics and during the later part of the 1640s and 1650s of George Fox and the Quakers.

February 25, 1624: Ambrose received a B.A. degree in arts and holy orders from Brasenose College, Oxford University.

1627: Bishop Thomas Morton (1564–1659), Bishop of Coventry and Lichfield, known as the author of *The Book of Sports*, ordained Ambrose as a Church of England minister. Ambrose served the parish of Castleton, Derbyshire (1627–29) and then Clapham, Yorkshire (1629–31).

1631: Ambrose was made one of the four king's preachers in Lancashire and took up residence in Garstang. The king's preachers were itinerates who were established originally for advancing the doctrines of the Protestant Reformation, especially in the more strongly Roman Catholic regions of the country.

1633: Ambrose married Judith (d. 1668, her last name is unknown). Ambrose had one daughter, Rachel (baptized January 25, 1635), and two sons, Augustine (baptized February 11, 1638) and Richard (baptized July 13, 1640).

ca. 1640: Lady Margaret Houghton, a religious woman of some prominence, took an interest in Ambrose and obtained for him the vicarage of St. John's Preston Church.

The church records assert that Ambrose was "Perhaps the most famous of the post-Reformation Vicars" of Preston.

1640: *Prima and Ultima* published.

ca. 1641: Ambrose began his annual practice of taking a month-long retreat each May in the woods. He employed this time to review his diary and engage in spiritual practices to deepen his relationship with God and renew himself for his public ministry.

ca. 1640s: Ambrose was instrumental in the establishment of Presbyterianism in Lancashire. Preston played a significant role and Ambrose often served as moderator of these meetings.

August 17–18, 1648: Battle of Preston that ended the second Civil War was fought in Preston.

1650: *Media* published. A second revised edition (1652) and a third revised and enlarged edition followed (1657).

Spring 1653: Ambrose became seriously ill with an undisclosed illness. His successful recovery motivated his writing *Looking Unto Jesus* (1658).

ca. 1654: The residual tensions surrounding the war and the religious conflict pertaining to conformity to the Church of England within Preston encouraged Ambrose to relocate to Garstang. Ambrose served as the minister of Garstang from 1654–62. However, he apparently did not renounce all claims to the vicarage of Preston until 1657.

January 4, 1657: Ambrose preaches the funeral sermon of Lady Margaret Houghton,

1658: *Looking unto Jesus* published. This was Ambrose's most significant and popular work both during his life as well as today.

Redeeming the Time (funeral sermon for Lady Margaret Houghton) published.

1660: Restoration of the monarchy.

1662: *War with Devils* and *Communion with Angels* published.

1662: Act of Uniformity. Ambrose was among the 2,000 nonconformist ministers and schoolteachers who were ejected from their positions. Nonconformity was typically defined as refusing to pray certain portions of the *Book of Common Prayer*, making the sign of the cross in baptism, kneeling for the Lord's Supper, etc.

1662: Ambrose retired to Preston.

January 23, 1664: Ambrose died suddenly at his house in Preston. He was buried two days later. There is no record of Ambrose's funeral sermon or his will or his library catalogs.

1674: First edition of the *Compleat Works of Isaac Ambrose*.

SPIRITUAL MOVEMENT MATRIX

ARENAS OF HUMAN EXPERIENCES

DIMENSIONS OF SPIRITUAL EXPERIENCE

God

Ineffable touch of the Holy
"flood of newness"
"new word spoken"
"Sighs too deep for words"
inexpressible attraction
silence, tears

Interpretive dimension
Description, words
concepts, names
rules, insight
doctrine, theology
interpretations
understandings
metaphor, images

Affective dimension
metaphor, images
affective awareness
felt attraction/pull
kinesthetic/bodily
sensations
fantasy, feelings

"Sighs too deep for words"
inexpressible attraction
silence, tears
Ineffable touch of the Holy
"flood of newness"
"new word spoken"

God

©A. Dreitcer and P. Bulkley 1997

God

Ineffable Touch of the Holy - - - - - · · · · - Ineffable Touch of the Holy

"sighs too deep for words"

"sighs too deep for words"

"sighs too deep for words"

Ineffable Touch of the Holy - - - - - · · · · · Ineffable Touch of the Holy

"sighs too deep for words"

God

- God is simultaneously present in every arena of human experience.
- God initiates a "flood of newness", "a new word spoken".
- The experience of the touch of the Holy leads to transformation.
- Both interpretive and affective dimensions are vital for the fullness of the transformative experience.

Drawing from the entire direction session place words or brief phrases on the matrix.
Trace the movement of the conversation.
Notice difficulties and openings.
Describe "new word spoken", if any. (Notice simultaneity of transformation)

250

Bibliography

PRIMARY SOURCES

Ainsworth, Henry. *Annotations upon the Five Books of Moses, Psalms and the Song of Songs.* London, 1627.

———. *Solomons Song of Songs in English Metre.* London, 1626.

Alleine, Theodosia. *The Life and Death of Mr. Joseph Alleine.* London, 1672.

Ambrose, Isaac. *The Christian Warrior: Wrestling with Sin, Satan, the World, and the Flesh.* 1662, incorrectly cited as 1660. Reprint. Morgan, PA: Soli Deo Gloria, 1997.

———. *The Compleat Works of that Eminent Minister of God's Word Mr. Isaac Ambrose, Consisting of These Treatises, viz. Prima, Media, & Ultima, or, The First, Middle, and Last Things . . . with a Sermon Added Concerning Redeeming the Time: Looking Unto Jesus as Carrying on the Great Works of Mans Salvation: War with Devils, Ministration of, and Communion with Angels.* London, 1682.

———. *The Compleat Works of Isaac Ambrose, Consisting of These . . . Treatises, Prima, Media, et. Ultima; or. The First, Middle, and Last Things . . . with a Sermon Added Concerning Redeeming the Time. Looking Unto Jesus . . . War with Devils. Ministration of, and Communion with Angels.* London, 1674.

———. *Looking Unto Jesus: A View of the Everlasting Gospel; or, The Soul's Eying of Jesus, As Carrying on the Great Work of Mans Salvation from First to Last.* London, 1658.

———. *Looking Unto Jesus: A View of the Everlasting Gospel; or, The Soul's Eying of Jesus, As Carrying on the Great Work of Mans Salvation from First to Last.* London, 1674.

———. *Looking Unto Jesus: A View of the Everlasting Gospel; or, The Souls Eying of Jesus, As Carrying on the Great Work of Mans Salvation from First to Last.* London, 1680.

———. *Looking Unto Jesus: A View of the Everlasting Gospel; or, The Soul's Eyeing of Jesus.* Reprint. Harrisonburg, VA: Sprinkle, 1986.

———. *Media, The Middle Things, in Reference to the First and Last Things: or, The Means, Duties, Ordinances, Both Secret, Private and Publike, for the Continuance and Increase of a Godly Life, Once Begun, Till We Come to Heaven.* London, 1650.

———. *Media: The Middle Things, in Reference to the First and Last Things: or, The Means, Duties, Ordinances, both Secret, Private and Publike, for the Continuance and Increase of a Godly Life, (Once Begun,) Till We Come to Heaven.* 2nd ed. London, 1652.

————. *Media: The Middle Things, in Reference to the First and Last Things: or, The Means, Duties, Ordinances, both Secret, Private and Publike, for the Continuance and Increase of a Godly Life, (Once Begun,) Till We Come to Heaven.* 3rd ed. London, 1657.

————. *Prima, The First Things or Regeneration Sermons.* London, 1640.

————. *Prima, Media & Ultima. The First, Middle and Last Things: in Three Treatises. Wherein is Set Forth, I. The Doctrine of Regeneration or the New Birth. II. The Practice of Sanctification, in the Means, Duties, Ordinances, Both Secret, Private and Publike, for the Continuance and Increase of a Godly Life. III. Mans Misery, in His Life, Death & Judgement. Gods Mercy, in Our Redemption & Salvation.* London, 1650.

————. *Prima, Media, & Ultima: The First, Middle and Last Things: in Three Treatises. Wherein is Set Forth, I. The Doctrine of Regeneration or the New Birth. II. The Practice of Sanctification, in the Means, Duties, Ordinances, Both Secret, Private and Publike, for the Continuance and Increase of a Godly Life. III. Mans Misery, in His Life, Death, Judgement & Execution. Gods Mercy, in Our Redemption & Salvation.* London, 1654.

————. *Prima, Media, & Ultima: The First, Middle and Last Things: in Three Treatises. Wherein is Set Forth, I. The Doctrine of Regeneration or the New Birth. II. The Practice of Sanctification, in the Means, Duties, Ordinances, Both Secret, Private and Publike, for the Continuance and Increase of a Godly Life. III. Certain Meditations: Mans Misery, in His Life, Death, Judgement & Execution. Gods Mercy, in Our Redemption & Salvation.* London, 1659.

————. *Redeeming the Time, A Sermon Preached at Preston in Lancashire, January 4th, 1657 at the Funerall of the Honourable Lady, the Lady Margaret Houghton.* London, 1658.

————. *Three Great Ordinances of Jesus Christ. War with Devils, Ministration of, and Communion with Angels, Looking Unto Jesus.* London, 1662.

————. *Ultima, The Last Things. In Reference to the First and Middle Things: or Certain Meditations on Life, Death, Judgement, Hell, Right Purgatory, and Heaven.* London, 1650.

————. *Ultima, The Last Things or Meditation Sermons.* London, 1640.

————. *The Works of Isaac Ambrose, Sometime Minister of Garstang, in Lancashire. To Which is Prefixed Some Account of His Life.* New ed. 4th ed. 2 vols. Edited by John Wesley. Manchester, UK: Gleave, 1813.

Angier, John. *An Helpe to Better Hearts, for Better Times.* London, 1647.

————. *Lancashires Valley of Achor is Englands Doore of Hope Set Wide Open in a Brief History of the Wise, Good, and Powerfull Hand of Divine Providence Ordering and Managing the Militia of Lancashire.* London, 1643.

Annesley, Samuel. *Communion with God. In Two Sermons Preach'd at Pauls.* London, 1655.

Ash, Simeon, James Nalton, and Joseph Church. *A Heavenly Conference Between Christ and Mary After His Resurrection.* London, 1654.

Ashwood, Bartholomew. *The Heavenly Trade, or the Best Merchandizing: The Only Way to Live Well in Impoverishing Times.* London, 1678.

Bagshaw, William. *De Spiritualibus Pecci Notes, (or Notices) Concerning the Work of God.* London, 1702.

Baillie, James. *Spiritual Marriage: or, The Union Betweene Christ and His Church.* London, 1627.

Baker, Augustine. *Holy Wisdom or Directions for the Prayer of Contemplation* [1657]. Edited by Serenus Cressy, re-edited by Abbot Sweeney. London: Burns and Oates, 1876.

Barker, Matthew. *Jesus Christ the Great Wonder. Discovered for the Amazement of the Saints.* London, 1651.

Baxter, Richard. *Christian Directory.* London, 1673.

———. *Saints Everlasting Rest.* 1649. Vol. 3 of *The Practical Works of Richard Baxter.* Reprint. Morgan, PA: Soli Deo Gloria, 2000.

Bayly, Lewis. *The Practice of Pietie Directing a Christian How to Walk, that He May Please God. Amplified by the author.* London, 1623.

Bernard of Clairvaux. *On the Song of Songs I–IV*, 4 vols. Translated by Kilian Walsh and Irene M. Edmonds. Kalamazoo, MI: Cistercian, 1971–80.

Blount, Thomas. *Glossographia: or A Dictionary Interpreting All Such Hard Words.* London, 1656.

Bolton, Robert. *Some Generall Directions for a Comfortable Walking with God.* London, 1626.

Brinsley, John. *Mystical Implantation: or The Great Gospel Mystery of the Christian's Union, & Communion with, and Conformity to Jesus Christ.* London, 1652.

Brooks, Thomas. *Heaven on Earth: A Work on Assurance.* London, 1654.

Bunyan, John. *Grace Abounding to the Chief of Sinners.* London, 1666.

Burgess, Anthony. *CXLV Expository Sermons Upon the Whole 17th Chapter of the Gospel According to St. John: or Christs Prayer.* London, 1656.

Burroughs, Jeremiah. *The Glorious Enjoyment of Heavenly Things by Faith.* In *The Saints Treasury (5 Sermons).* London, 1654.

———. *Two Treatises, First: Of Earthly Mindedness, Second: Of Conversing in Heaven, and Walking with God.* London, 1649.

Cabasilas, Nicholas. *The Life in Christ.* Translated by Carmino J. deCatanzaro. Crestwood, NY: St. Vladimir's Seminary Press, 1974.

Calamy, Edmund. *The Art of Divine Meditation.* London, 1680.

———. *The Nonconformist's Memorial; Being an Account of the Lives. Sufferings, and Printed Works, of the Two Thousand Ministers Ejected from the Church of England, Chiefly by the Act of Uniformity, Aug. 24, 166[2].* Abridged and corrected by Samuel Palmer. 2nd ed. 3 vols. London: Button and Son, and Hurst, 1802.

Calvin, John. *Commentary on the Book of Psalms.* Vol. 4–6. Translated by James Anderson. Reprint. Grand Rapids: Baker, 1999.

———. *Commentary on the Epistle of Paul to the Colossians.* Vol. 21. Translated by John Pringle. Reprint. Grand Rapids: Baker, 1999.

———. *Commentary on the Harmony of the Evangelists, Matthew Mark, and Luke.* Vol. 16. Translated by William Pringle. Reprint. Grand Rapids: Baker, 1999.

———. *Commentary on the Twelve Minor Prophets, Hosea.* Vol. 13. Translated by John Owen. Reprint. Grand Rapids: Baker, 1999.

———. *Institutes of the Christian Religion.* 1559. 2 vols. Edited by John T. McNeill. Translated by Ford Lewis Battles. Reprint. Philadelphia: Westminster, 1960.

Cawdrey, Daniel. *Family Reformation Promoted.* London, 1656.

Cawdrey, Robert. *A Table Alphabetical, Contayning and Teaching the True Writing and Understanding of Hard Usuall English Words.* 3rd ed. London, 1613.

Clarke, Samuel. *The Lives of Sundry Eminent Persons in This Later Age. In Two Parts.* London, 1683.

Cleaver, Robert. *A Godly Form of Householde Government*. London, 1592.

Cockeram, Henry. *The English Dictionarie: or, An Interpreter of Hard English Words*. London, 1623.

Conjugal Duty: Set Forth in a Collection of Ingenious and Delightful Wedding Sermons. 4 vols. Dr. Williams's Library. London, 1732–40.

Cotton, John. *A Brief Exposition with Practical Observations upon the Whole Book of Canticles*. London, 1655.

Culverwell, Ezekiel. *Time Well Spent in Sacred Meditations*. London, 1635.

De Granada, Lewis. *An Excellent Treatise of Consideration and Prayer (published with Of Prayer and Meditation, separate page numbering for both works. An Excellent Treatise follows Of Prayer and Meditation)*. London, 1599.

———. *Of Prayer and Meditation*. London, 1599.

———. *A Spiritual Doctrine*. Lovan, 1599.

De Guevara, Antonio. *Mount Calvarie*, 2nd part. *The Seven Last Words of Christ*. London, 1597.

Diodoti, John. *Pious and Learned Annotations Upon the Holy Bible: Plainly Expounding the Most Difficult Places Thereof [also known as The Geneva Annotations]*. 3rd ed. London, 1651.

Downame, John. *A Guide to Godlynesse*. London, 1629.

Durham, James. *The Song of Solomon*. 1840. Reprint. Edinburgh: Banner of Truth, 1997.

Edwards, Jonathan. *The Church's Marriage to Her Sons, and to Her God*. Vol. 25 of *The Works of Jonathan Edwards*, edited by Wilson H. Kimnach, 167–97. New Haven, CT: Yale University Press, 2006.

———. *Personal Narrative in Letters and Personal Writings*. Vol. 16 of *The Works of Jonathan Edwards*, edited by George S. Claghorn, 790–804. New Haven, CT: Yale University Press, 1998.

———. *Notes on Scripture*. Vol. 15 of *The Works of Jonathan Edwards*, edited by Stephen J. Stein. 1998. Reprint. New Haven, CT: Yale University Press, 2006.

Fenner, William. *A Treatise of the Affections: or The Soules Pulse, Whereby a Christian May Know Whether He Be Living or Dying*. London, 1642.

[Finch, H.] *An Exposition of the Song of Solomon Called Canticles Together with Profitable Observations, collected Out of the Same*. London, 1615.

Flavel, John. *England's Duty, Under the Present Gospel Liberty*. In *The Works of John Flavel*. Vol. 4, 3–268. Edinburgh: Banner of Truth, 1997.

———. *Method Grace in the Gospel-Redemption*. In *The Works of John Flavel*. Vol. 2, 3–474. Edinburgh: Banner of Truth, 1997.

———. *Pneumatologia. A Treatise of the Soul of Man*. In *The Works of John Flavel*. Vol. 2, 475–Vol. 3, 238. Edinburgh: Banner of Truth, 1997.

———. *The Works of John Flavel*. 6 vols. 1820. Reprint. Edinburgh: Banner of Truth, 1997.

Forbes of Course, Patrick. *An Equisite Commentarie upon the Revelation of Saint John*. London, 1613.

Gataker, Thomas. *A Good Wife Gods Gift: and A Wife Indeed. Two Marriage Sermons*. London, 1624.

Gataker. *Certaine Sermons. Part II [on Marriage]*. London, 1637.

Gee, Edward. *A Treatise of Prayer and Divine Providence*. London, 1653.

Geree, John. *The Character of an Old English Puritan or Nonconformist*. London, 1659.

Gill, John. *An Exposition of the Song of Solomon*. 1728. Reprint. Marshallton, DE: National Foundation for Christian Education, 1854.

Gillies, John. *Historical Collections Relating to Remarkable Periods of The Success of the Gospel and Eminent Instruments Employed in Promoting It.* 2 vols. Glasgow: Robert and Foulis, 1754.

Goodwin, Thomas. *Christ Set Forth.* 1642. Vol. 4 of *The Works of Thomas Goodwin*, 1–91. Edinburgh: Nichol, 1842.

Gouge, William. *Of Domesticall Duties, Eight Treatises.* 2nd ed. London, 1627.

———. *Of Domesticall Duties, Eight Treatises.* 3rd ed. London, 1634.

Guigo II. *The Ladder of Monks: A Letter on Contemplation and Twelve Meditations.* Translated, with an Introduction by Edmund Colledge and James Walsh. Kalamazoo, MI: Cistercian, 1979.

Gurnall, William. *The Christian in Compleat Armour, or, A Treatise of the Saints War Against the Devil, Wherein a Discovery is Made of the Great Enemy of God and His People, in His Policies, Power, Seat of His Empire, Wickednesse, and the Chief Design He Hath Against the Saints.* London, 1656.

Haak, Theodore. *The Dutch Annotations.* London, 1657.

Hall, Joseph. *The Art of Divine Meditation.* London, 1606.

———. *Breathings of the Devout Soul.* London, 1648.

———. *Christ Mysticall; or, The Blessed Union of Christ and His Members. Also, An Holy Rapture: Or, A Patheticall Meditation of the Love of Christ.* London, 1647.

———. *Contemplations, The Fifth Volume (Contemplations Upon the Old Testament and Contemplations Upon the History of the New Testament).* London, 1620.

———. *The Devout Soul. or, Rules of Heavenly Devotion.* London, 1644.

———. *Salomons Divine Arts, . . . An Open and Plaine Paraphrase, Upon the Song of Songs which is Salomon.* London, 1609.

Harrison, Michael. *The Best Match: Or, The Believer's Marriage with Christ.* London, 1691.

Henry, Matthew. *Exposition of the Old and New Testament Commentary on the Whole Bible.* Vol. 3. 1706. Reprint. New York: Revell, n.d.

Herbert, George. "The Country Parson." In *George Herbert: The Country Parson and The Temple*, edited by John N. Wall, Jr., 53–115. Mahwah, NJ: Paulist, 1981.

Herle, Charles. *Contemplations and Devotions on the Severall Passages of Our Blessed Saviors Death and Passion.* London, 1631.

Heywood, Oliver. *Heart Treasure: or, An Essay Tending to Fil and Furnish the Head and Heart of Every Christian, with a Soul-Inriching Treasure of Truths, Graces, Experiences, and Comforts to Help Him in Meditation, Conference, Religious Performances, Spiritual Actions, Enduring Afflictions, and to Fit Him for All Conditions, That He May Live Holily, Dye Happily, and Go To Heaven Triumphantly.* London, 1667.

———. *His Autobiography, Diaries, Antedote and Event Books; Illustrating the General and Family History of Yorkshire and Lancashire.* Vol. 2. Edited by J. Horsfall Turner. Brighouse, UK: Bayes, 1881.

———. *His Autobiography, Diaries, Antedote and Event Books; Illustrating the General and Family History of Yorkshire and Lancashire.* Vol. 4. Edited by J. Horsfall Turner. Bingley, UK: Harrison, 1885.

———. *Life of John Angier of Denton: Together with Angier's Diary, and Extracts from His "An Helpe to Better Hearts": Also Samuel Angier's Diary.* 1685. Reprint. Introduction by Ernest Axon. Manchester: Chetham Society, 1937.

———. *Meetness for Heaven Promoted in Some Brief Meditation upon Colos. 1.12. Designed for a Funeral Legacy.* London, n.d.

————. *A Narrative of the Holy Life, and Happy Death of That Reverend, Faithful and Zealous Man of God, and Minister of the Gospel of Jesus Christ, Mr. John Angier.* London, 1683.

Hilder, Thomas. *Conjugall Counsel: or, Seasonable Advise, Both to Unmarried, and Married Persons.* London, 1653.

Hieron, Samuel. *Bridegroome.* London, 1613.

Hooker, Thomas. *The Soules Exaltation, A Treatise Containing The Soules Union with Christ, The Soules Benefit from Union with Christ, The Soules Justification.* London, 1638.

————. *The Soules Humiliation.* 2nd ed. London, 1638.

————. *Soules Implantation, A Treatise Containing The Broken Heart, The Preparation of the Heart, The Soules Ingrafting into Christ, Spirituall Love and Joy.* London, 1637.

————. *The Soules Preparation for Christ, or a Treatise of Contrition.* London, 1632.

————. *The Soules Vocation Or Effectual Calling to Christ.* London, 1638.

Howe, John. *A Treatise of Delighting in God.* London, 1674.

Ignatius of Loyola. *A Manual of Devout Meditations and Exercises, Drawn for the Most Part, Out of the Spiritual Exercises.* Saint Omer, France: English College, 1624.

Keach, Benjamin. *Tropologia: A Key to Open Scripture Metaphors in Four Books.* London, 1682.

King, Benjamin. *The Marriage of the Lambe.* London, 1640.

Knappen, M. M. ed. *Two Elizabethan Puritan Diaries by Richard Rogers and Samuel Ward.* Chicago: American Society of Church History, 1933.

Knight, William. *A Concordance Axiomaticall Containing A Survey of Theologicall Propositions.* London, 1610.

Leigh, Edward. *Annotations on Five Poetical Books of the Old Testament.* London, 1657.

————. *Annotations Upon All the New Testament Philologicall and Theological.* London, 1650.

Lockyer, Nicholas. *England Faithfully Watcht with In Her Wounds . . . Lectures on Colossians 1.* London, 1646.

Lye, Thomas. *The True Believer's Union with Christ Jesus.* Vol. 5 of *Puritan Sermons 1659–1689: Being the Morning Exercises at Cripplegate.* 6 vols. Translated by James Nichols, 284–303. Reprint. Wheaton, IL: Roberts, 1981.

MacFarlane, Alan, ed. *The Diary of Ralph Josselin 1616–1683.* London: Oxford University Press, 1976.

Manton, Thomas. *Sermons Upon Genesis xxiv.63.* Vol. 17 of *The Complete Works of Thomas Manton.* Reprint. Worthington, PA: Maranatha, n.d.

Mather, Cotton. *Diary of Cotton Mather.* Edited by Worthington C. Ford. 2 vols. New York: Frederick Ungar, 1957.

Matthews, A. G. *Calamy Revised: Being a Revision of Edmund Calamy's Account of the Ministers and Others Ejected and Silenced, 1660–2.* Oxford: Clarendon, 1988.

McGiffert, Michael, ed. *God's Plot: Puritan Spirituality in Thomas Shepard's Cambridge.* Rev. expanded ed. Amherst, MA: University of Massachusetts Press, 1994.

Newcome, Henry. *The Autobiography of Henry Newcome, M.A.* 2 vols. Edited by Richard Parkinson. Manchester: Chetham Society, 1852.

————. *The Diary of the Rev. Henry Newcome, from September 30, 1661, to September 29, 1663.* Edited by Thomas Heywood. Manchester: Chetham Society, 1849.

————. *A Faithful Narrative of the Life and Death of that Holy and Laborious Preacher Mr. John Machin, Late of Astbury in the County of Chester.* London, 1671.

———. *The Sinner's Hope: As His Privilege, and Duty, In His Worst Condition, Stated, Cleared, and Improved*. London, 1659.

———. *Usurpation Defeated and David Restored: Being an Exact Parallel Between David and Our Most Gracious Sovereign King Charles II*. London, 1660.

Niccholes, Alexander. *A Discourse of Marriage and Wiving: And of the Great Mystery therein Contained: How to Choose a Good Wife from a Bad*. London, 1615.

Owen, John. *A Discourse of The Work of the Holy Spirit in Prayer*. In *Works of John Owen*, 4:235–354.

———. *The Grace and Duty of Being Spiritually Minded*. In *The Works of John Owen*, vol. 7, edited by William H. Goold, 261–497. Edinburgh: Banner of Truth, 1965.

———. *Meditations and Discourses on the Glory of Christ, in His Person, Office, and Grace*. In *The Works of John Owen*, vol. 1, edited by William H. Goold, 273–415. Edinburgh: Banner of Truth, 1965.

———. *Of Communion with God the Father, Son, and Holy Ghost*. In *The Works of John Owen*, vol. 2, edited by William H. Goold, 1–274. Edinburgh: Banner of Truth, 1965.

———. *The Works of John Owen*. 1850–53. 23 vols. Edited by William H. Goold. Reprint. Edinburgh: Banner of Truth, 1965.

The Paper Called the Agreement of the People Taken into Consideration, and the Lawfulness of Subscription to it Examined, and Resolved in the Negative, by the Ministers of Christ in the Province of Lancaster. London, 1649.

[Parsons, Robert.] *The Christian Directory, Guiding Men to Eternall Salvation*. n.l., 1607.

Pearse, Edward. *The Best Match or the Souls Espousal to Christ*. London, 1673.

Perkins, William. *The Art of Prophecying: or A Treatise Concerning the Sacred and Onely True Manner and Method of Preaching*. London, 1607.

———. *Christian Oeconomie or, a Short Survey of the Right Manner of Erecting and Ordering a Familie, According to the Scriptures*. London, 1609.

Peters, Hugh. *A Dying Fathers Last Legacy to An Onely Child: or Mr. Hugh Peters Advice to His Daughter*. London, 1651.

Phillips, Edward. *The New World of English Words: or, A General Dictionary*. London, 1658.

Preston, John. *The Churches Marriage or Dignitie*. London, 1638.

———. *Mount Ebal, or A Heavenly Treatise of Divine Love*. London, 1638.

———. *The Onely Love of the Chiefest of Ten Thousands: or A Heavenly Treatise of the Divine Love*. London, 1640.

Ranew, Nathanael. *Solitude Improved by Divine Meditation; or, A Treatise Proving the Duty, and Demonstrating the Necessity, Excellency, Usefulness, Natures, Kinds, and Requisites of Divine Meditation*. London, 1670.

Reynolds, Edward. *The Joy in the Lord: Opened in a Sermon*. London, 1655.

———. *Meditations on the Holy Sacrament of the Lords Last Supper*. 2nd ed. London, 1639.

———. *A Treatise on the Passions and Faculties of the Soule of Man*. London, 1640.

Robotham, John. *An Exposition on the Whole Book of Solomons Song; Commonly Called the Canticles*. London, 1652.

Rogers, Daniel. *Matrimoniall Honour: Or the Mutuall Crowne and Comfort of Godly, Loyall, and Chaste Marriage*. London, 1642.

Rous, Francis. *The Heavenly Academie*. London, 1638.

———. *The Mysticall Marriage. Experimentall Discoveries of the Heavenly Marriage betweene a Soule and Her Saviour*. London, 1631.

Rowe, John. *Heavenly-Mindedness, and Earthly Mindedness*. London, 1672.

Rutherford, Samuel. *Christ and the Doves, Heavenly Salutations, with Their Pleasant Conference Together: or A Sermon Before the Communion in Anwoth.* London, 1630.

———. *Christ Dying and Drawing Sinners to Himself.* London, 1647.

———. *Letters of Samuel Rutherford.* Edited by Andrew A. Bonar. 1664. Reprint. Edinburgh: Banner of Truth, 2006.

———. *A Survey of Spiritual Antichrist, Opening the Secrets of Familisme and Antinomianisme in the Antichristian Doctrine of John Saltmarsh, and Will. Del, Present Preachers in the Army Now in England, and, Robert Town, Tob. Crisp, H. Denne, Eaton, and Others.* 2 parts. London, 1648.

Sachse, William L., ed. *The Diary of Roger Lowe of Ashton-in-Makerfield, Lancashire 1663–74.* London: Longman, Green & Co., 1938.

Scougal, Henry. *The Life of God in the Soul of Man, or The Nature & Excellency of the Christian Religion.* London, 1677.

Scudder, Henry. *The Christians Daily Walke in Holy Securitie and Peace.* 4th ed. London, 1631.

Shepard, Thomas. *The Parable of the Ten Virgins.* 1659. Reprint. Orlando, FL: Soli Deo Gloria, 1990.

Sibbes, Richard. *Bowels Opened, Being Expository Sermons on Cant. IV.16, V., VI.* In *Works of Richard Sibbes*, vol. 2, edited by Alexander B. Grosar, 1–195. Edinburgh: Banner of Truth, 1979–82.

———. *A Breathing After God.* In *Works of Richard Sibbes*, vol. 2, edited by Alexander B. Grosar, 209–48. Edinburgh: Banner of Truth, 1979–82.

———. *Divine Meditations and Holy Contemplations.* In *Works of Richard Sibbes*, vol. 7, edited by Alexander B. Grosar, 179–228. Edinburgh: Banner of Truth, 1979–82.

———. *An Exposition of 2nd Corinthians, Chapter One or, A Learned Commentary or Exposition Upon the First Chapter of the Second Epistle of S. Paul to the Corinthians.* In *Works of Richard Sibbes*, vol. 3, edited by Alexander B. Grosar, 1–537. Edinburgh: Banner of Truth, 1979–82.

———. *A Glance of Heaven; Or, A Precious Taste of a Glorious Feast.* In *Works of Richard Sibbes*, vol. 4, edited by Alexander B. Grosar, 151–200. Edinburgh: Banner of Truth, 1979–82.

———. *The Spouse, Her Earnest Desire After Christ.* In *Works of Richard Sibbes*, vol. 2, edited by Alexander B. Grosar, 197–208. Edinburgh: Banner of Truth, 1979–82.

———. *The Soul's Conflict with Itself, and Victory Over Itself by Faith.* In *Works of Richard Sibbes*, vol. 1, edited by Alexander B. Grosar, 119–294. Edinburgh: Banner of Truth, 1979–82.

———. *Works of Richard Sibbes.* 1862–64. 7 vols. Edited by Alexander B. Grosart. Reprint. Edinburgh: Banner of Truth, 1979–82.

Smith, Henry. *Sermons.* London, 1628.

Spurgeon, Charles. *Lectures to My Students: A Selection from Addresses Delivered to the Students of The Pastors' College, Metropolitan Tabernacle.* 1875. Reprint. Grand Rapids: Baker, 1977.

———. *Treasury of David.* 5 vols. London: Marshall, 1869.

Spurstow, William. *The Wiles of the Devil in a Discourse on 2 Corinthians 2:11.* London, 1666.

Stedman, Rowland. *The Mystical Union of Believers with Christ.* London, 1668.

Steele, Richard. *What are the Duties of Husbands and Wives Toward Each Other?* Vol. 2 of *Puritan Sermons 1659–1689: Being the Morning Exercises at Cripplegate*, 6 vols., translated by James Nichols, 272–303. Reprint. Wheaton, IL: Roberts, 1981.

Taylor, Jeremy. *The Rules and Exercises of Holy Living*. London, 1650.

Taylor, Thomas. *A Good Husband and a Good Wife*. London, 1625.

Thomas, William. *Christian and Conjugal Counsell: or Christian Counsell Applyed Unto the Maried Estate*. London, 1661.

Vincent, Thomas. *Christ the Best Husband: or An Invitation of Young Women Unto Christ*. London, 1672.

Wallace, Dewey D., Jr., ed. *The Spirituality of the Later English Puritans: An Anthology*. Macon, GA: Mercer University Press, 1987.

Ward, Samuel. *The Life of Faith*. 3rd ed. London, 1622.

Watson, Thomas. *A Christian on Earth Still in Heaven*. London, 1657.

———. *Christ's Loveliness In Sermons and Select Discourses on Important Subjects*. Vol. 1. Glasgow: Shaw, 1798.

———. *Heaven Taken By Storm*. London, 1669.

———. *The Saints Delight*. London, 1657.

———. *Shewing the Mystical Union Between Christ and the Saints*. In *Discourses on Important and Interesting Subjects Being the Select Works of the Rev. Thomas Watson*. Vol. 1. Reprint. Ligonier, PA: Soli Deo Gloria, 1990.

Webbe, George. *The Bride Royall or Spiritual Marriage Between Christ and His Church*. London, 1613.

Webster, Tom, and Kenneth Schipps, eds. *The Diary of Samuel Rogers 1634–1638*. Suffolk, UK: Boydell, 2004.

Wesley, John. *Christian Library: Consisting of Extracts from and Abridgments of the Choicest Pieces of Practical Divinity Which Have Been Published in the English Tongue*. 2nd ed. 30 vols. [7:311—9:132 contains the Complete [abridged] Works of Isaac Ambrose]. Manchester: Gleave, 1812.

Westminster Annotations: *The Second Volume of Annotations Upon All of the Books of the Old and New Testament*. 3rd ed. London, 1657.

Westminster Assembly, *The Directory for Family-Worship*. 1647. Reprint. Edinburgh: Publications Committee of the Free Presbyterian Church of Scotland 1967.

Westminster Assembly. *Westminster Confession of Faith: The Larger and Shorter Catechisms*. 1647. Reprint. Edinburgh: Publications Committee of the Free Presbyterian Church of Scotland, 1967.

Whatley, William. *A Bride-Bush or, A Direction for Married Persons*. London, 1623.

———. *A Bride-Bush or, A Wedding Sermon*. London, 1617.

White, Thomas. *A Method and Instructions for the Art of Divine Meditation*. London, 1655.

———. *Power of Godlinesse*. London, 1658.

Wilson, Thomas. *A Christian Dictionary, Opening the Signification of the Chiefe Wordes Dispersed Generally through Holie Scripture of the Old and New Testament*. 4th ed. London, 1612.

Zanchi, Girolamo. *An Excellent and Learned Treatise, of the Spiritual Marriage Betweene Christ and the Church, and Every Faithful Man*. London, 1592.

SECONDARY SOURCES

Achinstein, Sharon. *Literature and Dissent in Milton's England*. Cambridge: Cambridge University Press, 2003.

———. "Romance of the Spirit: Female Sexuality and Religious Desire in Early Modern England." *ELH* 69.2 (2002) 413–38.

Adam, Peter. *Word and Spirit: The Puritan-Quaker Debate*. London: Barnard & Westwood, 2001.

Alblas, J. B. H. *Johannes Boekholt (1656–1693) The First Dutch Publisher of John Bunyan and Other English Authors*. Nieuwkoop, Nethelands: De Graaf, 1987.

Armstrong, Brian. "Puritan Spirituality: The Tension of Bible and Experience." In *The Roots of the Modern Christian Tradition*, edited by E. Rozanne Elder, 229–48, 327–30. Kalamazoo, MI: Cistercian, 1984.

Astell, Ann W. *The Song of Songs in the Middle Ages*. Ithaca, NY: Cornell University Press, 1990.

Aumann, Jordan. "Contemplation." Vol. 4 of *New Catholic Encyclopedia*. 2nd ed., 203–9. Detroit: Gale, 2003.

———. *Spiritual Theology*. London: Sheed & Ward, 1980.

Axon, Ernest. "The King's Preachers in Lancashire, 1599–1845." *Transactions of the Lancashire and Cheshire Antiquarian Society* 56 (1941–42) 67–104.

Bagley, J. J. *Lancashire Diarists: Three Centuries of Lancashire Lives*. London: Phillimore, 1975.

Bainton, Roland H. "The Bible in the Reformation." In *The Cambridge History of the Bible: The West from the Reformation to the Present Day*. Vol. 3, edited by S. L. Greenslade, 1–37. Cambridge: Cambridge University Press, 1963.

Bartel, Roland. "The Story of Public Fast Days in England." *Anglican Theological Review* 37.3 (1955) 190–200.

Barth, Karl. *Church Dogmatics*. 13 vols. 1932–67. Edited by G. W. Bromiley and T. F. Torrance, Translated by G. W. Bromiley, et al. Edinburgh: T. & T. Clark, 1936–75.

———. "Concluding Unscientific Postscript on Schleiermacher." In *Karl Barth, The Theology of Schleiermacher: Lectures at Göttingen, Winter Semester of 1923/24*, edited by Dietrich Ritschl and translated by Geoffrey W. Bromiley, 261–79. Grand Rapids: Eerdmans, 1982.

———. *Evangelical Theology: An Introduction*. Translated by Grover Foley. Grand Rapids: Eerdmans, 1963.

———. "Schleiermacher." In *Protestant Theology in the Nineteenth Century: Its Background and History*, 2nd ed., translated by Brian Cozens and John Bowden, 411–59. Grand Rapids: Eerdmans, 1959.

Bavinck, Herman. "The Catholicity of Christianity and the Church." Translated by John Bolt. *Calvin Theological Journal* 27.2 (1992) 220–51.

———. *The Certainty of Faith*. 1901. Translated by Harry der Nederlanden. St. Catharines, Ontario: Paideia, 1980.

———. *Essays on Religion, Science, and Society*. 1921. Edited by John Bolt. Translated by Harry Boonstra and Gerrit Sheeres. Grand Rapids: Baker Academic, 2008.

———. *Imitation of Christ (1885–86)*. Translated by John Bolt. Unpublished 1982.

———. *Imitation of Christ (1918)*. Translated by John Bolt. Unpublished 1982.

———. *Our Reasonable Faith*. 1909. Translated by Henry Zylstra. Grand Rapids: Baker, 1977.

———. The Philosophy of Revelation. 1909. Translated Henry E. Dosker, et al. Grand Rapids: Baker, 1979.

———. *Reformed Dogmatics*. 1895–1911. 4 vols. Edited by John Bolt. Translated by John Vriend. Grand Rapids: Baker Academic, 2003–8.

———. *The Sacrifice of Praise: Meditations Before and After Receiving Access to the Table of the Lord*. 1908. 2nd ed. Translated by John Dolfin. Grand Rapids: Kregel, 1922.

———— *Saved By Grace: The Holy Spirit's Work in Calling and Regeneration.* 1903. Edited by J. Mark Beach. Translated by Nelson D. Kloosterman. Grand Rapids, MI: Reformation Heritage, 2008.

Beeke, Joel. R. "Evangelicalism and the Dutch Further Reformation." In *Advent of Evangelicalism: Exploring Historical Continuities,* edited by Michael A. G. Haykin and Kenneth J. Stewart, 146–68. Nashville: B & H Academic, 2008.

————. "The Puritan Practice of Meditation." In *Puritan Reformed Spirituality,* 73–100. Grand Rapids: Reformation Heritage, 2004.

————. *The Quest for Full Assurance: The Legacy of Calvin and His Successors.* Edinburgh: Banner of Truth, 1999.

Beeke, Joel R., and Randall Pederson. *Meet The Puritans: With a Guide to Modern Reprints.* Grand Rapids: Reformation Heritage, 2006.

Benedict, Philip. *Christ's Churches Purely Reformed: A Social History of Calvinism.* New Haven, CT: Yale University Press, 2002.

Berkouwer, G. C. *A Half Century of Theology: Movements and Motives.* Grand Rapids: Eerdmans, 1977.

Betteridge, Maurice S. "The Bitter Notes: The Geneva Bible and its Annotations." *Sixteenth Century Journal* 14.1 (1983) 4–62.

Bialas, A. A. "Mystical Marriage." Vol. 10 of *New Catholic Encyclopedia.* 2nd ed., edited by Bernard L. Marthaler et al., 105. Detroit: Gale, 2003.

Bickle, Mike. *Song of Songs: The Ravished Heart of God.* Grandview, MO: Friends of the Bridegroom, 1999.

Billings, J. Todd. *Calvin, Participation, and the Gift: The Activity of Believers in Union with Christ.* Oxford: Oxford University Press, 2007.

Bloesch, Donald G. *Spirituality Old & New.* Downers Grove, IL: InterVarsity, 2007.

————. *The Struggle of Prayer.* San Francisco: Harper & Row, 1980.

Bolt, John. "Grand Rapids Between Kampen and Amsterdam: Herman Bavinck's Reception and Influence in North America." *Calvin Theological Journal* 38 (2003) 263–80.

————. "The Imitation of Christ Theme in the Cultural-Ethical Ideal of Herman Bavinck." PhD diss., University of St. Michaels, Toronto, 1982.

Booty. "Joseph Hall, The Arte of Divine Meditation, and Anglican Spirituality." In *The Roots of the Modern Christian Tradition,* edited by E. Rozanne Elder, 200–228, 323–27. Kalamazoo, MI: Cistercian, 1984.

Bossy, John. *The English Catholic Community 1570–1850.* Oxford: Oxford University Press, 1976.

Bouyer, Louis. "Mysticism: An Essay on the History of the Word." In *Understanding Mysticism,* edited by Richard Woods, 42–55. Garden City, NY: Image, 1980.

————. *Orthodox Spirituality and Protestant and Anglican Spirituality.* Vol. 3 of *A History of Christian Spirituality.* 1969. Reprint. New York: Seabury, 1982.

Bozeman. Theodore. *The Precisianist Strain: Disciplinary Religion and Antinomian Backlash in Puritanism to 1638.* Chapel Hill, NC: University of North Carolina Press, 2004.

Braaten, Carl E., and Robert W. Jenson, eds. *Union with Christ: The New Finnish Interpretation of Luther.* Grand Rapids: Eerdmans, 1998.

Brauer, Jerald C. "Francis Rous, Puritan Mystic, 1579–1659: An Introduction to the Study of the Mystical Element in Puritanism." Ph.D. diss., University of Chicago, 1948..

————. "The Nature of English Puritanism: Three Interpretations. I. Reflections on the Nature of English Puritanism." *Church History* 23 (1954) 99–108.

————. "Puritan Mysticism and the Development of Liberalism." *Church History* 19.3 (1950) 151–70.

————. "Types of Puritan Piety." *Church History* 56.1 (1987) 39–58.

Bredero, Adriaan H. *Bernard of Clairvaux: Between Cult and History*. Grand Rapids: Eerdmans, 1996.

Brekus, Catherine A. "Writing as a Protestant Practice: Devotional Diaries in Early New England." In *Practicing Protestants: Histories of Christian Life in America, 1630–1965*, edited by Laurie P. Maffly-Kipp, Leigh E. Schmidt, and Mark Valeri, 19–34. Baltimore: Johns Hopkins University Press, 2006.

Bremer, Francis J. *Puritanism: A Very Short Introduction*. Oxford: Oxford University Press, 2009.

Brentnall, John M. *William Bagshaw: The Apostle of the Peak*. Edinburgh: Banner of Truth, 1970.

Bronkema, Ralph. *The Essence of Puritanism*. Goes, Netherlands: Oosterbaan and Le-Cointre, 1929.

Bromiley, Geoffrey W. *An Introduction to the Theology of Karl Barth*. Grand Rapids: Eerdmans, 1979.

Broxap, Ernest. *The Great Civil War in Lancashire (1642–1651)*. 2nd ed. Edited by R. N. Dore. Manchester: Manchester University Press, 1973.

Brumm, Ursula. "Faith and Imagery in Puritan Meditation Literature." *Religion and Philosophy in the United States of America* 1 (1987) 61–75.

Buckley, Michael J. "Seventeenth-Century French Spirituality: Three Figures." Vol. 3 of *Christian Spirituality: Post-Reformation and Modern*, edited by Louis Dupré and Donald E. Saliers, 28–68. New York: Crossroad, 1989.

Burrows, Mark S. "Foundations for an Erotic Christology: Bernard of Clairvaux on Jesus as 'Tender Lover.'" *Anglican Theological Review* 80.4 (1998) 477–93.

Busch, Eberhard. *Karl Barth: His Life from Letters and Autobiographical Texts*. Translated by John Bowden. 1976. Reprint. Grand Rapids: Eerdmans, 1994.

Butler, Cuthbert. *Western Mysticism*. 2nd ed. London: Dutton, 1922.

Bynum, Caroline Walker. *Jesus as Mother: Studies in the Spirituality of the High Middle Ages*. Berkeley, CA: University of California Press, 1982.

Campbell, Ted A. *The Religion of the Heart: A Study of European Religious Life in the Seventeenth and Eighteenth Centuries*. Columbia, SC: University of South Carolina Press, 1991.

Casey, Michael. *Athirst for God: Spiritual Desire in Bernard of Clairvaux's Sermons on the Song of Songs*. Kalamazoo, MI: Cistercian, 1988.

Cave, Terrance C. *Devotional Poetry in France c. 1570–1613*. Cambridge: Cambridge University Press, 1969.

Chan, Simon. "The Puritan Meditative Tradition, 1599–1691: A Study of Ascetical Piety." PhD diss., Cambridge University, 1986.

Cheney, Jessie S. "A Troubled Union: Marriage and Metaphor in Puritan Early America." PhD diss., Columbia University, 2002.

Childs, Brevard S. "The Sensus Literalis of Scripture: An Ancient and Modern Problem." In *Beiträge zur Alttestamentlichen Theologie: Festrschrift für Walter Zimmerli*, edited by Herbert Donner, Robert Hanhart, and Rudolf Smend, 80–93. Göttingen: Vandenhoeck & Ruprect, 1977.

Chin, Clive S. "Calvin, Mystical Union, and Spirituality." *Torch Trinity Journal* 6.1 (2003) 184–210.

————. "Unio Mystica and Imitatio Christi: The Two-Dimensional Nature of John Calvin's Spirituality." PhD diss., Dallas Theological Seminary, 2002.

Christensen, Michael J., and Jeffrey A. Wittung, eds. *Partakers of the Divine Nature: The History and Development of Deification in the Christian Traditions*. Grand Rapids: Baker Academic, 2007.

Chryssavgis, John. "The Notion of 'Divine Eros' in the Ladder of St. John Climacus." *St. Vladimir's Theological Quarterly* 29.3 (2006) 191–200.

Chung, Sung Wook, ed. *Karl Barth and Evangelical Theology: Convergences and Divergences*. Grand Rapids: Baker Academic, 2006.

Clark, Stuart. "Protestant Demonology: Sin, Superstition, and Society (c.1520–c.1630)." In *Early Modern European Witchcraft: Centres and Peripheries*, edited by Bengt Ankarloo and Gustav Henningsen, 49–81. Oxford: Clarendon, 1993.

Clarke, Elizabeth. "'A Heart Terrifying Sorrow': The Deaths of Children in Seventeenth-Century Women's Manuscript Journals." In *Representations of Childhood Death*, edited by Gillian Avery and Kimberley Reynolds, 65–86. London: Macmillan, 2000.

———. "The Legacy of Mothers and Others: Women's Theological Writing, 1640–60." In *Religion in Revolutionary England*, edited by Christopher Durston and Judith Maltby, 69–90. Manchester: Manchester University Press, 2006.

———. *Politics, Religion and the Song of Songs in Seventeenth-Century England*. Basingstoke, UK: Palgrave Macmillan, 2011.

Clary, Ian Hugh. "Hot Protestants: A Taxonomy of English Puritans." *Puritan Reformed Journal* 2.1 (2010) 41–66.

Cleary, Miriam. "A Societal Context for Supervision." *Presence: An International Journal of Spiritual Direction* 4.2 (1998) 26–31.

Clemesha, H. W. *A History of Preston in Amounderness*. Manchester: Manchester University Press, 1912.

Coffey, John. "Letters by Samuel Rutherford (1600–1661)." In *The Devoted Life: An Invitation to the Puritan Classics*, edited by Kelly M. Kapic and Randall C. Gleason, 92–107. Downers Grove, IL: InterVarsity, 2004.

———. *Politics, Religion and the British Revolutions: The Mind of Samuel Rutherford*. Cambridge: Cambridge University Press, 1997.

———. "Puritanism, Evangelicalism and the Evangelical Protestant Tradition." In *Advent of Evangelicalism: Exploring Historical Continuities*, edited by Michael A. G. Haykin and Kenneth J. Stewart, 255–61. Nashville: B & H Academic, 2008.

———. "Puritan Legacies." In *The Cambridge Companion to Puritanism*, edited by John Coffey and Paul C. H. Lim, 327–45. Cambridge: Cambridge University Press, 2008.

———. "A Ticklish Business: Defining Heresy and Orthodoxy in the Puritan Revolution," in *Heresy, Literature, and Politics in Early Modern English Culture*, edited by David Loewenstein and John Marshall, 108–36. Cambridge: Cambridge University Press, 2006.

Coffey, John, and Paul C. H. Lim., eds. *The Cambridge Companion to Puritanism*. Cambridge: Cambridge University Press, 2008.

———. "Introduction." In *The Cambridge Companion to Puritanism*, edited by John Coffey and Paul C. H. Lim, 1–15. Cambridge: Cambridge University Press, 2008.

Cohen, Charles Lloyd. *God's Caress: The Psychology of Puritan Religious Experience*. Oxford: Oxford University Press, 1986.

Collinson, Patrick. *The Elizabethan Puritan Movement*. London: Cape, 1967.

———. "The English Conventicle." In *Voluntary Religion*, edited by W. J. Sheils and Diana Wood, 223–59. London: Blackwell, 1986.

————. *Godly People: Essays on English Protestantism and Puritanism*. London: Hambledon, 1983.

————. "Puritans." In Vol. 3 of *The Oxford Encyclopedia of the Reformation*, edited by Hans J. Hillerbrand, 364–70. Oxford: Oxford University Press, 1996.

————. *The Religion of Protestants: The Church in English Society 1559–1625*. Oxford: Clarendon, 1982.

Como, David R. *Blown by the Spirit: Puritanism and the Emergence of an Antinomian Underground in Pre-Civil-War England*. Stanford, CA: Stanford University Press, 2004.

————. "Radical Puritanism, c. 1558–1660." In *The Cambridge Companion to Puritanism*, edited by John Coffey and Paul C. H. Lim, 24–58. Cambridge: Cambridge University Press, 2008.

Cook, Paul E. G. "Thomas Goodwin-Mystic?" In *Diversities of Gifts*, 45–56. London: Westminster Conference, 1980.

Corduan, Winfried. *Mysticism: An Evangelical Option?* Grand Rapids: Zondervan, 1991.

Cornick, David. *Letting God Be God: The Reformed Tradition*. Maryknoll, NY: Orbis, 2008.

Cousins, Ewert. "The Fourfold Sense of Scripture in Christian Mysticism." In *Mysticism and Sacred Scripture*, edited by Steven T. Katz, 118–37. Oxford: Oxford University Press, 2000.

Crawford, Patricia. "The Challenges to Patriarchalism: How Did the Revolution Affect Women?" In *Revolution and Restoration: England in the 1650s*, edited by John Morrill, 112–28. London: Collins & Brown, 1992.

————. *Women and Religion in England 1500–1720*. London: Routledge, 1993.

Cunningham, Lawrence S. "Theological Table Talk: On Reading Spiritual Texts." *Theology Today* 56.1 (1999) 98–104.

Dahill, Lisa E. "The Genre of Gender: Gender and the Academic Study of Christian Spirituality." In *Exploring Christian Spirituality: Essays in Honor of Sandra M. Schneiders*, edited by Bruce H. Lescher and Elizabeth Liebert, 98–118. Mahwah, NJ: Paulist, 2006.

Daniels, Richard W. "'Great is the Mystery of Godliness': The Christology of John Owen." PhD diss., Westminster Theological Seminary, 1990.

Danner, Dan G. "The Later English Calvinists and the Geneva Bible." In *Later Calvinism: International Perspectives*, edited by W. Fred Graham, 489–504. Kirksville, MO: Sixteenth Century Journal, 1994.

Davies, Andrew A. "The Holy Spirit in Puritan Experience." In *Faith and Ferment*, 18–31. London: Westminster Conference, 1982.

Davies, Horton. *The Worship of the English Puritans*. Morgan, PA: Soli Deo Gloria, 1997.

————. *Worship and Theology in England: From Cranmer to Hooker 1534–1603*, Vol. 1. Princeton: Princeton University Press, 1970.

————. *Worship and Theology in England: From Andrewes to Baxter and Fox, 1603–1690*, Vol. 2. Princeton: Princeton University Press, 1975.

Davies, Stevie. *Unbridled Spirits: Women of the English Revolution: 1640–1660*. London: Women's, 1998.

Davis, Joe Lee. "Mystical Versus Enthusiastic Sensibility." *Journal of the History of Ideas* 4.3 (1943) 301–19.

De Certeau, Michel. *The Mystic Fable*. Vol. 1, *The Sixteenth and Seventeenth Centuries*. Translated by Michael B. Smith. Chicago: University of Chicago Press, 1992.

De Lubac, Henri. *Medieval Exegesis*. Vol. 1, *The Four Senses of Scripture*. Translated by Mark Sebanc. Grand Rapids: Eerdmans, 1998.

Demarest, Bruce. "Mysticism: Peril or Promise?" *Conversations* 6.1 (2008) 12–17.

———. Review of *Spirituality Old & New*, by Donald G. Bloesch. *Journal of Spiritual Formation & Soul Care* 1.1 (2008) 113.

———. *Satisfy Your Soul: Restoring the Heart of Christian Spirituality*. Colorado Springs, CO: NavPress, 1999.

De Reuver, Arie. *Sweet Communion: Trajectories of Spirituality from the Middle Ages through the Further Reformation*. Translated by James A. De Jong. Grand Rapids: Baker Academic, 2007.

Dever, Mark E. *Richard Sibbes: Puritanism and Calvinism in Late Elizabethan and Early Stuart England*. Macon, GA: Mercer University Press, 2000.

Dillon, Elizabeth Maddock. "Nursing Fathers and Brides of Christ: The Feminized Body of the Puritan Convert." In *A Centre of Wonders: The Body in Early America*, edited by Janet Moore Lindman and Michele Lise, 129–43. Ithaca, NY: Cornel University Press, 2001.

Doriani, Daniel. "The Puritans, Sex, and Pleasure." *Westminster Theological Journal* 53.1 (1991) 125–43.

Dosker, Henry E. "Herman Bavinck." *Princeton Theological Review* 20.3 (1922) 448–64.

Downey, Michael. *Understanding Christian Spirituality*. Mahwah, NJ: Paulist, 1997.

Dreyer, Elizabeth A. "Whose Story Is It?—The Appropriation of Medieval Mysticism." *Spiritus* 4.2 (2004) 151–72.

Dreyer, Elizabeth A., and Mark S. Burrows. *Minding the Spirit: The Study of Christian Spirituality*. Baltimore: Johns Hopkins University Press, 2005.

Drysdale, A. H. *The English Presbyterians: A Historical Handbook of Their Rise, Decline, and Revival*. London: Presbyterian Church of England, 1891.

Duffy, Eamon. "The Reformed Pastor in English Puritanism." In *The Pastor Bonus: Papers Read at the British-Dutch Colloquium at Utrecht, 18–21 September 2002*, edited by Theo Clemens and Wim Janse, 216–34. Leiden: Brill, 2004.

Dupré, Louis. "Unio Mystica: The State and the Experience." In *Mystical Union in Judaism, Christianity, and Islam: An Ecumenical Dialogue*, edited by Moshe Idel and Bernard McGinn, 3–23, 195–96. 1989. Reprint. New York: Continuum, 1996.

Dupré, Louis, and James A. Wiseman, eds. *Light from Light: An Anthology of Christian Mysticism*. 2nd ed. Mahwek, NJ: Paulist, 2001.

Durston, Christopher. "'For the Better Humiliation of the People': Public Days of Fasting and Thanksgiving during the English Revolution." *Seventeenth Century* 7.2 (1992) 129–49.

Durston, Christopher, and Jacqueline Eales, eds. *The Culture of English Puritanism, 1560–1700*. New York: St. Martin's, 1996.

Eales, Jacqueline. "'An Ancient Mother in Our Israel': Mary, Lady Vere." In *The Intellectual Culture of Puritan Women, 1558–1680*, edited by Johanna Harris and Elizabeth Scott-Baumann, 84–95. Basingstoke, UK: Palgrave Macmillan, 2011.

Egan, Harvey D. "Christian Apophatic and Kataphatic Mysticisms." *Theological Studies* 39.3 (1978) 399–426.

Egan, Keith J. "Contemplation." In *The New Westminster Dictionary of Christian Spirituality*, edited by Philip Sheldrake, 211–12. Louisville, KY: Westminster John Knox, 2005.

Elliott, Dyan. "The Physiology of Rapture and Female Spirituality." In *Medieval Theology and the Natural Body*, edited by Peter Biller and A. J. Minnis, 141–73. York, UK: York Medieval, 1997.

Evans, Eifion. "The Puritan Use of Imagination." *Reformation & Revival* 10.1 (2001) 47–88.

Ferguson, Sinclair. "The Reformed View." In *Christian Spirituality: Five Views of Sanctification*, edited by Donald L. Alexander, 47–76. Downers Grove, IL: InterVarsity, 1988.

Fessenden, Tracy, Nicholas F. Radel, and Magdalena J. Zaborowska, eds. *The Puritan Origins of American Sex*. London: Routledge, 2001.

Finlayson, Michael. "Puritanism and Puritans: Labels or Libels?" *Canadian Journal of History* 8.3 (1973) 201–23.

Fishwick, Henry. *The History of the Parish of Garstang in the County of Lancaster*. Manchester: Chetham Society, Part I, 1878; Part II, 1879.

Fletcher, Anthony. "The Protestant Idea of Marriage in Early Modern England." In *Religion, Culture and Society in Early Modern Britain*, edited by Anthony Fletcher and Peter Roberts, 161–81. Cambridge: Cambridge University Press, 1994.

Flinker, Noam. *The Song of Songs in English Renaissance Literature: Kisses of Their Mouths*. Suffolk, UK: Brewer, 2000.

Foster, Richard J. *Prayer Finding the Heart's True Home*. San Francisco: HarperSanFrancisco, 1992.

———. *Streams of Living Water*. San Francisco: HarperSanFrancisco, 1998.

Fraser, Antonia, "Mary Rich Countess of Warwick." *History Today* 31.6 (1981) 48–51.

Frohlich, Mary. "Spiritual Discipline, Discipline of Spirituality: Revisiting Questions of Definition and Method." *Spiritus* 1.1 (2001) 65–78.

Frost, Ronald N. "The Bruised Reed by Richard Sibbes (1577–1635)." In *The Devoted Life: An Invitation to the Puritan Classics*, edited by Kelly M. Kapic and Randall C. Gleason, 79–91. Downers Grove, IL: InterVarsity, 2004.

———. "Richard Sibbes' Theology of Grace and the Division of English Reformed Theology." PhD diss., University of London, 1996.

Frye, Roland. "The Teachings of Classical Puritanism on Conjugal Love." *Studies in the Renaissance* 2 (1955) 148–59.

Fulcher, Rodney J. "Puritans and the Passions: The Faculty Psychology in American Puritanism." *Journal of the History of the Behavioral Sciences* 9 (1973) 123–39.

Gadamer, Hans-Georg. *Truth and Method*. New York: Seabury, 1975.

Ganss, George E. ed. *Ignatius of Loyola: Spiritual Exercises and Selected Works*. New York: Paulist, 1991.

Gildrie, Richard P. "The Ceremonial Puritan Days of Humiliation and Thanksgiving." *New England Historical and Genealogical Register* 136 (1982) 2–16.

Gilson, Etienne. *The Mystical Theology of St. Bernard*. Translated by A. H. C. Downes. Kalamazoo, MI: Cistercian, 1990.

Gleason, Ronald C. "The Parable of the Ten Virgins by Thomas Shepard (1605–1649)." In *The Devoted Life: An Invitation to the Puritan Classics*, edited by Kelly M. Kapic and Randall C. Gleason, 123–37. Downers Grove, IL: InterVarsity, 2004.

Gleason, Ronald. N. "The Centrality of the *unio mystica* in the Theology of Herman Bavinck." PhD diss., Westminster Theological Seminary, 2001.

Gleason, R[on]. N. "Calvin and Bavinck on the Lord's Supper." *Westminster Theological Journal* 45 (1983) 273–303.

———. *Herman Bavinck: Pastor, Churchman, Statesman, and Theologian*. Phillipsburg, NJ: Presbyterian and Reformed, 2010.

Godbeer, Richard. "'Love Raptures': Marital, Romantic, and Erotic Images of Jesus Christ in Puritan New England, 1670–1730." In *A Shared Experience: Men, Women, and the History of Gender*, edited by Laura McCall and Donald Yacovone, 51–77. New York: New York University Press, 1998.

———. *The Overflowing of Friendship: Love Between Men and the Creation of the American Republic*. Baltimore: Johns Hopkins University Press, 2009.

———. "Performing Patriarchy: Gendered Roles and Hierarchies in Early Modern England and Seventeenth-Century New England." In *The World of John Winthrop: Essays on England and New England 1588–1649*, edited by Francis J. Bremer and Lynn A. Botelho, 290–333. Boston: Massachusetts Historical Society, 2005.

———. *Sexual Revolution in Early America*. Baltimore and London: Johns Hopkins University Press, 2002.

Gordis, Lisa M. *Opening Scripture: Bible Reading and Interpretative Authority in Puritan New England*. Chicago: University of Chicago Press, 2003.

Grabo, Norman S. "The Art of Puritan Devotion." *Seventeenth Century News* 26.1 (1968) 7–9.

Graval, Kathryn. *Ravishing Maidens: Writing Rape in Medieval French Literature and Law*. Philadelphia: University of Pennsylvania Press, 1991.

Green, Ian. *Print and Protestantism in Early Modern England*. Oxford: Oxford University Press, 2000.

Greven, Philip. *The Protestant Temperament: Patterns of Child-Rearing, Religious Experience, and the Self in Early America*. New York: Knopf, 1980.

Gribben, Crawford. *God's Irishmen: Theological Debates in Cromwellian Ireland*. Oxford: Oxford University Press, 2007.

Griffiths, Michael. *The Example of Jesus*. Downers Grove, IL: InterVarsity, 1985.

Gründler, Otto. "Justification and Sanctification in John Calvin and Bernard of Clairvaux." In *Truth as Gift: Studies in Medieval Cistercian History in honor of John R. Sommerfeldt*, edited by Marsha L. Dutton, Daniel M. La Corte and Paul Lockey, 517–35. Kalamazoo, MI: Cistercian, 2004.

Gwyn-Thomas, J. "The Puritan Doctrine of Christian Joy." In *Puritan Papers*. Vol. 2., edited by J. I. Packer, 119–40. Phillipsburg, NJ: Presbyterian and Reformed, 2001.

Hageman, Howard G. "Reformed Spirituality." In *Protestant Spiritual Traditions*. edited by Frank C. Senn, 55–79. Mahwah, NJ: Paulist, 1986.

Haigh, Christopher. *The Plain Man's Pathways to Heaven: Kinds of Christianity in Post-Reformation England*. Oxford: Oxford University Press, 2007.

Hall, Charles A. M. *With the Spirit's Sword: The Drama of Spiritual Warfare in the Theology of John Calvin*. Richmond, VA: John Knox, 1968.

Hall, David D. "Narrating Puritanism." In *New Directions in American Religious History*, edited by Harry S. Stout and D. G. Hart, 51–83. Oxford: Oxford University Press, 1997.

Hall, T. Hartley. "The Shape of Reformed Piety." In *Spiritual Traditions for the Contemporary Church*, edited by Robin Maas & Gabriel O'Donnell, 202–21. Nashville: Abingdon, 1990.

Haller, William and Malleville Haller. "The Puritan Art of Love." *Huntington Library Quarterly* 5 (1941–42) 235–72.

———. *The Rise of Puritanism*. New York: Harper, 1957.

Halley, Robert. *Lancashire: Its Puritanism and Nonconformity*, 2 vols. Manchester: Tubbs and Brook, 1869.

Hambrick-Stowe, Charles E. "Christ the Fountaine of Life by John Cotton (1584–1652)." In *The Devoted Life: An Invitation to the Puritan Classics*, edited by Kelly M. Kapic and Randall C. Gleason, 66–78. Downers Grove, IL: InterVarsity, 2004.

———. *Early New England Meditative Poetry: Anne Bradstreet and Edward Taylor*. Mahwah, NJ: Paulist, 1988.

———. "Practical Divinity and Spirituality." In *The Cambridge Companion to Puritanism*, edited by John Coffey and Paul C. H. Lim, 191–205. Cambridge: Cambridge University Press, 2008.

———. *The Practice of Piety: Puritan Devotional Disciplines in Seventeenth-Century New England*. Chapel Hill, NC: University of North Carolina Press, 1982.

———. "Puritan Spirituality in American." In *Christian Spirituality: Post-Reformation and Modern*, edited by Louis Dupré and Don Saliers, vol. 3, 338–53. New York: Crossroad, 1989.

———. "The Spirit of the Old Writers: The Great Awakening and the Persistence of Puritan Piety." In *Puritanism: Transatlantic Perspectives on a Seventeenth-Century Anglo-American Faith*, edited by Francis J. Bremer, 277–91. Boston: Massachusetts Historical Society, 1993.

Hanson, R. P. C. "Biblical Exegesis in the Early Church." In *The Cambridge History of the Bible*. Vol. 1 *From the Beginnings to Jerome*, edited by P. R. Ackroyd and C. F. Evans, 412–53. Cambridge: Cambridge University Press, 1970.

Harmless, William. *Mystics*. Oxford: Oxford University Press, 2008.

Harnick, George. "'Something That Must Remain, If the Truth Is to Be Sweet and Precious to Us': The Reformed Spirituality of Herman Bavinck." *Calvin Theological Journal* 38 (2003) 248–62.

Harris, Johanna, and Elizabeth Scott-Baumann, eds. *The Intellectual Culture of Puritan Women, 1558–1680*. Basingstoke, UK: Palgrave Macmillan, 2011.

Harrison, Frank Mott. *John Bunyan: A Record of Recent Research* (MS in Frank Mott Harrison Collection). Bedford, UK: Bedford Central Library, 1940.

Herdt, Jennifer A. *Putting On Virtue: The Legacy of the Splendid Vices*. Chicago: University of Chicago Press, 2008.

Hesselink, I. John. "Calvin: Theologian of Sweetness." *Calvin Theological Journal* 37.2 (2002) 318–32.

Hessel-Robinson, Timothy. "'Be Thou My Onely Well Belov'd': Exegesis and Spirituality in Edward Taylor's Preparatory Meditations." PhD diss., Graduate Theological Union, 2006.

Hinson, E. Glenn. "Baptist and Quaker Spirituality." In *Christian Spirituality: Post-Reformation and Modern*, vol. 3, edited by Louis Dupré and Donald E. Saliers, 324–38. New York: Crossroad, 1989.

———. "Puritan Spirituality." In *Protestant Spiritual Traditions*, edited by Frank C. Senn, 165–82. Mahwah, NJ: Paulist, 1986.

Holifield, E. Brooks. *The Covenant Sealed: The Development of Puritan Sacramental Theology in Old and New England, 1570–1720*. New Haven, CT: Yale University Press, 1974.

Houliston, Victor. "Why Robert Persons Would Not Be Pacified: Edmund Bunny's Theft of The Book of Resolution." In *The Reckoned Expense: Edmund Campion and the Early English Jesuits*, edited by Thomas M. McCoog, 159–77. Woodbridge, UK: Boydell, 1996.

Houston, James M. *In Pursuit of Happiness: Finding Genuine Fulfillment in Life*. Colorado Springs, CO: NavPress, 1996.

————. "Reflections on Mysticism: How Valid is Evangelical Anti-Mysticism?" In *Loving God and Keeping His Commandments*, edited by Markus Bockmuehl and Helmut Burkhardt, 163–181. Giessen, Basel: Brunnen, 1991.

————. "Spirituality." In *Evangelical Dictionary of Theology*, edited by Walter A. Elwell, 1046–51. Grand Rapids: Baker, 1984.

————. *The Transforming Friendship: A Guide to Prayer*. Oxford: Lion, 1989.

Hudson, Elizabeth K. "The Catholic Challenge to Puritan Piety, 1580–1620." *Catholic Historical Review* 77.1 (1991) 1–20.

Hudson, Winthrop S. "Fast Days and Civil Religion." In *Theology in Sixteenth-and Seventeenth-Century England*, 3–24. Los Angeles: University of California, 1971.

————. "Mystical Religion in the Puritan Commonwealth." *Journal of Religion* 28.1 (1948) 51–56.

Huggett, Joyce. *The Joy of Listening to God*. Downers Grove, IL: InterVarsity, 1986.

Hughes, Ann. "The Frustrations of the Godly." In *Revolution and Restoration: England in the 1650s*, edited by John Morrill, 70–90. London: Collins & Brown, 1992.

————. "Puritans and Gender" In *The Cambridge Companion to Puritanism*, edited by John Coffey and Paul C. H. Lim, 294–308. Cambridge: Cambridge University Press, 2008.

Hughes, Ann, and Richard Cust, eds. *The English Civil War*. London: Arnold, 1997.

Hughes, Walter. "'Meat Out of the Eater': Panic and Desire in American Puritan Poetry." In *Engendering Men: The Question of Male Feminist Criticism*, edited by Joseph A. Boone & Michael Cadden, 107–19. London: Routledge, 1990.

Hunsinger, George. *How to Read Barth: The Shape of His Theology*. New York: Oxford University Press, 1991.

Hunt, Arnold. "The Lord's Supper in Early Modern England." *Past & Present* 161 (1998) 39–83.

Hunt, David. *A History of Preston*. Preston, UK: Carnegie, 1992.

Hunter, Joseph. *The Rise of the Old Dissent, Exemplified in the Life of Oliver Heywood, One of the Founders of the Presbyterian Congregations in the County of York*. London: Longman, Brown, Green, and Longmans, 1842.

Huntley, Frank L. *Bishop Joseph Hall and the Protestant Meditation in Seventeenth-Century England*. Binghamton, NY: Center for Medieval & Early Renaissance Studies, 1981.

Inge, William R. *Christian Mysticism*. New York: Scribner's Sons, 1899.

Jebb, Stanley. "Richard Greenham and the Counselling of Troubled Souls." In *Puritans and Spiritual Life*, 81–101. London: Westminster Conference, 2001.

Johnson, Ben Campbell and Andrew Dreitcer, *Beyond the Ordinary: Spirituality for Church Leaders*. Grand Rapids: Eerdmans, 2001.

Johnson, George. "From Seeker to Finder: A Study in the Seventeenth Century English Spiritualism Before the Quakers." *Church History* 17.4 (1948) 299–315.

Johnson, James T. "English Puritan Thought on the Ends of Marriage." *Church History* 38.4 (1969) 429–36.

Jones, R. Tudur. "The Evangelical Revival in Wales: A Study in Spirituality." In *An Introduction to Celtic Christianity*, edited by James P. Mackey, 237–67. Edinburgh: T. & T. Clark, 1989.

————. "Union with Christ: The Existential Nerve of Puritan Piety." *Tyndale Bulletin* 41.2 (1990) 186–208.

Jung, Joanne J. "Conference: Rediscovering a Communal Tradition of Puritan Piety." PhD diss., Fuller Theological Seminary, 2007.

————. *Godly Conversation: Rediscovering the Puritan Practice of Conference.* Grand Rapids: Reformation Heritage, 2011.

Juster, Susan. "Eros and Desire in Early Modern Sexuality." *The William and Mary Quarterly.* Third series. 60.1 (2003) 203–6.

Kapic, Kelly M. *Communion with God: The Divine and the Human in the Theology of John Owen.* Grand Rapids: Baker Academic, 2007.

————. "Communion with God by John Owen (1616–1683)." In *The Devoted Life: An Invitation to the Puritan Classics,* edited by Kelly M. Kapic and Randall C. Gleason, 167–82. Downers Grove, IL: InterVarsity, 2004.

————. "Introduction: Worshiping the Triune God: The Shape of John Owen's Trinitarian Spirituality." In *Communion with the Triune God,* edited by Kelly M. Kapic and Justin Taylor, 17–46. Wheaton, IL: Crossway, 2007.

Kapic, Kelly M., and Randall C. Gleason., eds. *The Devoted Life: An Invitation to the Puritan Classics.* Downers Grove, IL: InterVarsity, 2004.

————. "Who Were the Puritans?" In *The Devoted Life: An Invitation to the Puritan Classics,* edited by Kelly M. Kapic and Randall C. Gleason, 15–37. Downers Grove, IL: InterVarsity, 2004.

Kärkkäinen, Veli-Matti. *One with God: Salvation as Deification and Justification.* Collegeville, MN: Liturgical, 2004.

Katz, Steven T. "Mysticism and the Interpretation of Sacred Scripture." In *Mysticism and Sacred Scripture,* edited by Steven T. Katz, 7–67. Oxford: Oxford University Press, 2000.

Kay, Brian K. *Trinitarian Spirituality: John Owen and the Doctrine of God in Western Devotion.* Milton Keynes, UK: Paternoster, 2007.

Kaufmann, U. Milo. *The Pilgrim's Progress and Traditions in Puritan Meditation.* New Haven, CT: Yale University Press, 1966.

Keeble, N. H. *The Literary Culture of Nonconformity in Later Seventeenth-Century England.* Leicester, UK: Leicester University Press, 1987.

Keegan, James M. "To Bring All Things Together: Spiritual Direction as Action for Justice." *Presence: An International Journal of Spiritual Direction* 1.1 (1995) 4–19.

Keller, Timothy J. "Puritan Resources for Biblical Counseling." *Journal of Pastoral Practice* 9.3 (1988) 11–44.

Kendall, R. T. *Calvin and English Calvinism to 1649.* 1979. Reprint. Milton Keynes, UK: Paternoster, 1997.

Kevan. Ernest F. *The Grace of Law: A Study in Puritan Theology.* 1976. Reprint. Ligonier, PA: Soli Deo Gloria, 1993.

King, David M. "The Affective Spirituality of John Owen." *Evangelical Quarterly* 68.3 (1996) 223–33.

————. "Grace & Duty: The Interaction of the Divine and the Human in the Theology of John Owen." PhD diss., Coventry University, 1993.

Kitching, C. J. "'Prayers Fit for the Time': Fasting and Prayers in Response to National Crises in the Reign of Elizabeth I." In *Monks, Hermits and the Ascetic Tradition,* edited by W. J. Sheils, 241–50. Oxford: Blackwell, 1985.

Kling, David W. *The Bible in History: How the Texts Have Shaped the Times.* Oxford: Oxford University Press, 2004.

Knapp, Henry M. "Understanding the Mind of God: John Owen and Seventeenth-Century Exegetical Methodology." PhD diss., Calvin Theological Seminary 2002.

Knight, Janice. *Orthodoxies in Massachusetts: Rereading American Puritanism.* Cambridge: Harvard University Press, 1994.

Knott, J. R. *The Sword of the Spirit: Puritan Responses to the Bible.* Chicago: University of Chicago Press, 1980.

Knowles, David. *The English Mystical Tradition.* New York: Harper & Row, 1961.

Krahmer, Shawn M. "The Virile Bride of Bernard of Clairvaux." *Church History* 69.2 (2000) 304–27.

Ladell, A. R. *Richard Baxter: Puritan and Mystic.* London: SPCK, 1925.

Laird, Martin. *Into the Silent Land: A Guide to the Christian Practice of Contemplation.* Oxford: Oxford University Press, 2006.

Lake, Peter. "Defining Puritanism—Again?" In *Puritanism: Transatlantic Perspectives on a Seventeenth-Century Anglo-American Faith,* edited by Francis J. Bremer, 3–29. Boston: Massachusetts Historical Society, 1993.

———. "Feminine Piety and Personal Potency: The 'Emancipation' of Mrs. Jane Ratcliffe." *Seventeenth Century* 2.2 (1987) 143–65.

———. "The Historiography of Puritanism." In *The Cambridge Companion to Puritanism,* edited by John Coffey and Paul C. H. Lim, 346–71. Cambridge: Cambridge University Press, 2008.

Lane, Anthony N. S. *John Calvin Student of the Church Fathers.* Grand Rapids: Baker, 1999.

Lane, Belden C. *Landscapes of the Sacred: Geography and Narrative in American Spirituality.* 2nd ed. Baltimore: Johns Hopkins University Press, 2001.

———. *Ravished By Beauty: The Surprising Legacy of Reformed Spirituality.* Oxford: Oxford University Press, 2011.

———. "Rivers of Pleasure, Waters of Affliction: Covenant and Desire in Puritan Spirituality." In *Yet More Light and Truth . . . Congregationalism, Covenant and Community,* edited by Steven A. Peay, 72–92. Milwaukee: Congregational, 2003.

———. "Spirituality as the Performance of Desire: Calvin on the World as a Theatre of God's Glory." *Spiritus* 1.1 (2001) 1–30.

———. "Two Schools of Desire: Nature and Marriage in Seventeenth-Century Puritanism." *Church History* 69.2 (2000) 372–402.

Lash, Nicholas. *Theology on the Way to Emmaus.* 1986. Reprint. Eugene, OR: Wipf & Stock, 2005.

La Shell, John K. "Imagination and Idol: A Puritan Tension." *Westminster Theological Journal* 49 (1987) 305–34.

Lea, Thomas D. "The Hermeneutics of the Puritans." *Journal of Evangelical Theology* 39.2 (1996) 271–85.

Leclercq, Jean. "Introduction." In *Bernard of Clairvaux: Selected Works.* Mahwah, NJ: Paulist, 1987.

———. *The Love of Learning and the Desire for God: A Study of Monastic Culture.* 1961. Reprint. New York: Fordham University Press, 1982.

———. "Ways of Prayer and Contemplation II. Western." In *Christian Spirituality: Origins to the Twelfth Century,* vol. 1, edited by Bernard McGinn, John Meyendorff, and Jean Leclercq, 415–26. New York: Crossroad, 1985.

Leites, Edmund. "The Duty to Desire: Love, Friendship, and Sexuality in Some Puritan Theories of Marriage." *Journal of Social History* 15 (1981/82) 383–408.

Leverenz, David. *The Language of Puritan Feeling: An Exploration in Literature, Psychology, and Social History.* New Brunswick, NJ: Rutgers University Press, 1980.

Lewalski, Barbara Kiefer. *Protestant Poetics and the Seventeenth-Century Religious Lyric.* Princeton: Princeton University Press, 1979.

Lewis, Peter. *Genius of Puritanism.* Haywards Heath, UK: Carey, 1977.

Liebert, Elizabeth. " Supervision as Widening Horizons." In *Supervision of Spiritual Directors: Engaging in Holy Mystery*, edited by Rebecca Bradburn Langer and Mary Rose Bumpus, 125–45. Harrisburg, PA: Morehouse, 2005.

Liu, Herrick Ping-tong. *Towards an Evangelical Spirituality: A Practical-Theological Study of Richard Baxter's Teaching and Practice of Spiritual Disciplines with Special Reference to the Chinese Cultural Context*. Hong Kong: Alliance Bible Seminary, 2000.

Lonergan, Bernard J. F. *Method in Theology*. 2nd ed. 1972. Reprint. New York: Seabury, 1979.

Long, Kimberly Bracken. *The Eucharistic Theology of the American Fairs*. Louisville, KY: Westminster John Knox, 2011.

Longfellow, Erica. *Women and Religious Writing in Early Modern England*. Cambridge: Cambridge University Press, 2004.

Louth, Andrew. *The Wilderness of God*. Nashville: Abingdon, 1991.

Love, William DeLoss. *The Fast and Thanksgiving Days of New England*. Boston: Houghton, Mifflin, 1895.

Lovelace, Richard F. *The American Pietism of Cotton Mather: Origins of American Evangelicalism*. Washington, DC: Christian University Press, 1979.

———. "The Anatomy of Puritan Piety: English Puritan Devotional Literature, 1600–1640." In *Christian Spirituality: Post-Reformation and Modern*, vol. 3, edited by Louis Dupré and Donald E. Saliers, 294–323. New York: Crossroad, 1989.

———. "Afterword: The Puritans and Spiritual Renewal." In *The Devoted Life: An Invitation to the Puritan Classics*, edited by Kelly M. Kapic and Randall C. Gleason, 298–309. Downers Grove, IL: InterVarsity, 2004.

Lowance, M. I. *The Language of Canaan: Metaphor and Symbol in New England from the Puritans to the Transcendentalists*. Cambridge, MA: Harvard University Press, 1980.

Lunn, David. "Augustine Baker (1575–1641) and the English Mystical Tradition." *Journal of Ecclesiastical History* 26.3 (1975) 267–77.

Luria, Keith P. "The Counter-Reformation and Popular Spirituality." In *Christian Spirituality: Post-Reformation and Modern*, vol. 3, edited by Louis Dupré and Donald E. Saliers, 93–120. New York: Crossroad, 1989.

Luttmer, Frank. "Persecutors, Tempters and Vassals of the Devil: The Unregenerate in Puritan Practical Divinity." *Journal of Ecclesiastical History* 51.1 (2000) 37–68.

Macchia, Frank D. "The Spirit of God and the Spirit of Life: An Evangelical Response to Karl Barth's Pneumatology." In *Karl Barth and Evangelical Theology: Convergences and Divergences*, edited by Sung Wook Chung, 149–71. Grand Rapids: Baker Academic, 2006.

Mack, Phyllis. *Visionary Women: Ecstatic Prophecy in Seventeenth-Century England*. Berkeley, CA: University of California Press, 1992.

Maclear, James Fulton. "The Heart of New England Rent: The Mystical Element in Early Puritan History." *Mississippi Valley Historical Review* 42.4 (1956) 621–52.

Mangina, Joseph L. *Karl Barth on the Christian Life: The Practical Knowledge of God*. New York: Lang, 2001.

———. *Karl Barth: Theologian of Christian Witness*. Louisville, KY: Westminster John Knox, 2004.

Marcoulesco, Ileana. "Mystical Union." In *The Encyclopedia of Religion*, vol. 10, edited by Mircea Eliade, 239–45. New York: Macmillan, 1987.

Martin, Robert P. *A Guide to the Puritans: A Topical and Textual Index to Writings of the Puritans and Some of Their Successors Recently in Print*. Edinburgh: Banner of Truth, 1997.

Martone, John Philip. "The Map of Heaven: A Generic Study of Traherne's Poetry." PhD diss., Brown University, 1981.

Martz, Louis L. *The Poetry of Meditation: A Study of English Religious Literature of the Seventeenth Century*. New Haven, CT: Yale University Press, 1954.

Mascuch, Michael. *Origins of the Individualist Self: Autobiography and Self-Identity in England 1591–1791*. Stanford, CA: Stanford University Press, 1996.

Masson, Margaret W. "The Typology of the Female as a Model for the Regenerate: Puritan Preaching, 1690–1730." *Signs; Journal of Women in Culture and Society* 2.2 (1976) 304–15.

Matar, N.I. "A Devotion to Jesus as Mother in Restoration Puritanism." *Journal United Reformed Church History Society* 4 (1989) 304–14.

————. "Mysticism and Sectarianism in Mid-17th Century England." *Studia Mystica* 11 (1988) 55–65.

Matter, E. Ann. *The Voice of My Beloved: The Song of Songs in Western Medieval Christianity*. Philadelphia: University of Pennsylvania Press, 1990.

Mayor, Stephen. *The Lord's Supper in Early English Dissent*. London: Epworth, 1972.

McCormack, Bruce L. *Karl Barth's Critically Dialectical Theology: Its Genesis and Development 1909–1936*. New York: Oxford University Press, 1995.

McCullough, Eleanor. "Ravished by Grace: Donne's Use of the Word 'Ravish' as an Illustration of the Movement of the Soul from Contrition to Compunction." *Crux* 43.4 (2007) 32–38.

McKay, Elaine. "'For Refreshment and Preservinge Health': The Definition and Function of Recreation in Early Modern England." *Historical Research* 81.211 (2008) 52–74.

McGee, J. Sears. "Conversion and the Imitation of Christ in Anglican and Puritan Writing." *The Journal of British Studies* 15.2 (1976) 21–39.

McGiffert, Michael. "God's Controversy with Jacobean England." *American Historical Review* 88.5 (1983) 1151–74.

McGinn, Bernard. "The Changing Shape of Late Medieval Mysticism." *Church History* 65.2 (1996) 197–219.

————. *The Flowering of Mysticism: Men and Women in the New Mysticism—1200–1350*. Vol. 3 of *The Presence of God: A History of Western Christian Mysticism*. New York: Crossroad, 1998.

————. *The Foundations of Mysticism: Origins to the Fifth Century*. Vol. 1 of *The Presence of God: A History of Western Christian Mysticism*. New York: Crossroad, 1991.

————. "God as Eros: Metaphysical Foundations of Christian Mysticism." In *New Perspectives on Historical Theology: Essays in Memory of John Meyendorff*, edited by Bradley Nassif, 189–209. Grand Rapids: Eerdmans, 1996.

————. *The Growth of Mysticism: Gregory the Great through the 12th Century*. Vol. 2 of *The Presence of God: A History of Western Christian Mysticism*. New York: Crossroad, 1994.

————. *The Harvest of Mysticism in Medieval Germany (1300–1500)*. Vol. 4 of *The Presence of God: A History of Western Christian Mysticism*. New York: Crossroad, 2005.

————. "The Human Person as Image of God: II. Western Christianity." In *Christian Spirituality: Origins to the Twelfth Century*, vol. 1, edited by Bernard McGinn, John Meyendorff, and Jean Leclercq, 312–30. New York: Crossroad, 1985.

————. "The Language of Inner Experience in Christian Mysticism." *Spiritus* 1.2 (2001) 156–71.

————. "The Language of Love in Christian and Jewish Mysticism." In *Mysticism and Language*, edited by Steven T. Katz, 202–35. Oxford: Oxford University Press, 1992.

————. "Love, Knowledge and Unio Mystica in the Western Christian Tradition." In *Mystical Union in Judaism, Christianity, and Islam: An Ecumenical Dialogue*, edited by Moshe Idel and Bernard McGinn, 59–86. 1989. Reprint. New York: Continuum, 1996.

————. "Mystical Consciousness: A Modest Proposal." *Spiritus* 8.1 (2008) 44–63.

————. "Mystical Union in Judaism, Christianity, and Islam." In *The Encyclopedia of Religion*, vol. 9, 2nd ed., edited by Lindsay Jones, 6334–41. Detroit: Gale, 2005.

————. "Mysticism." In *The Oxford Encyclopedia of the Reformation*, vol. 3, edited by Hans J. Hillerbrand, 119–24. Oxford: Oxford University Press, 1996.

————. "Mysticism and Sexuality." *The Way Supplement* 77 (1993) 46–53.

————. "Tropics of Desire: Mystical Interpretation of the Song of Songs." In *That Others May Know and Love: Essays in Honor of Zachary Hayes, OFM*, edited by Michael F. Cusato and F. Edward Coughlin, 133–58. St. Bonaventure, NY: St. Bonaventure University Press, 1997.

————. "With 'the Kisses of the Mouth': Recent Works on the Song of Songs." *The Journal of Religion* 72.2 (1992) 269–75.

McGrath, Alister E. *Christian Spirituality*. Oxford: Blackwell, 1999.

————. "Justification." In *The Oxford Encyclopedia of Reformation*, vol. 2, edited by Hans J. Hillerbrand, 360–68. Oxford: Oxford University Press, 1996.

McGuire, Brian Patrick, ed. *A Companion to Jean Gerson*. Leiden: Brill, 2006.

McIntosh, Mark. "Humanity in God: On Reading Karl Barth in Relation to Mystical Theology." *Heythrop Journal* 34 (1993) 22–40.

McNeill, John T. "Casuistry in the Puritan Age." *Religion in Life* 12.1 (1942–43) 76–89.

————. *A History of the Cure of Souls*. New York: Harper & Row, 1951.

Melloni, Javier. *The Exercises of St Ignatius Loyola in the Western Tradition*. Leominster, UK: Gracewing, 2000.

Merton, Thomas. *New Seeds of Contemplation*. New York: New Direction, 1961.

Miller, George C. *Hoghton Tower: The History of the Manor, the Hereditary Lords and the Ancient Manor-house of Hoghton in Lancashire*. Preston, UK: Guardian, 1948.

Moltmann, Jürgen. "Teresa of Avila and Martin Luther: The Turn to the Mysticism of the Cross." *Studies in Religion* 13.3 (1984) 265–78.

————. "Theology of Mystical Experience." *Scottish Journal of Theology* 32.6 (1979) 501–20.

Moore Susan Hardman. "Sexing the Soul: Gender and the Rhetoric of Puritan Piety." In *Gender and Christian Religion*, edited by R. N. Swanson, 175–86. Woodbridge, UK: Boydell, 1998.

Morden, Peter J. *"Communion with Christ and His People": The Spirituality of C. H. Spurgeon*. Oxford: Regent Park College, 2010.

Morgan, Edmund S. *The Puritan Family: Religion & Domestic Relations in Seventeenth-Century New England*. Rev ed. 1944. Reprint. New York: Harper & Row, 1966.

————. "The Puritan's Marriage with God." *South Atlantic Quarterly* 48.1 (1949) 107–12.

Mullan, David George. *Scottish Puritanism 1590–1638*. Oxford: Oxford University Press, 2000.

Muller, Richard A. *After Calvin: Studies in the Development of a Theological Tradition*. Oxford: Oxford University Press, 2003.

————. "Biblical Interpretation in the Era of the Reformation: The View from the Middle Ages." In *Biblical Interpretation in the Era of the Reformation: Essays Presented to*

David C. Steinmetz in Honor of His Sixtieth Birthday, edited by Richard A. Muller and John L. Thompson, 3–16. Grand Rapids: Eerdmans, 1996.

———. *Dictionary of Latin and Greek Theological Terms: Drawn Principally from Protestant Scholastic Theology.* Grand Rapids: Baker, 1985.

———. *Post-Reformation Reformed Dogmatics.* Vol. 2, *Holy Scripture.* 2nd ed. Grand Rapids: Baker, 2003.

Murphy, Roland E. "History of Exegesis As A Hermeneutical Tool: The Song of Songs." *Biblical Theology Bulletin* 16.3 (1986) 87–91.

Murray, Iain H. *The Puritan Hope: A Study in Revival and the Interpretation of Prophecy.* Edinburgh: Banner of Truth, 1971.

Mursell, Gordon. *English Spirituality From Earliest Times to 1700.* Louisville, KY: Westminster John Knox, 2001.

———. *English Spirituality From 1700 to the Present Day.* Louisville, KY: Westminster John Knox, 2001.

———., ed. *The Story of Christian Spirituality: Two Thousand Years, from East to West.* Minneapolis: Fortress, 2001.

Newman, Barbara. *From Virile Woman to WomanChrist: Studies in Medieval Religion and Literature.* Philadelphia: University of Pennsylvania Press, 1995.

———. "Rereading John Donne's Holy Sonnet 14." *Spiritus* 4.1 (2004) 84–90.

Nightingale, Benjamin. *Early Stages of the Quaker Movement in Lancashire.* London: Congregational Union of England and Wales, 1921.

———. *The Ejected of 1662 in Cumberland & Westmorland.* 2 vols. Manchester: Manchester University Press, 1911.

———. *Ejection Worthies of 1662 I. Isaac Ambrose, Of Garstang and Preston: King's Preacher and Religious Mystic.* Preston, UK: Toulmin, 1912.

———. *Lancashire Nonconformity; or, Sketches, Historical & Descriptive, of the Churches of the Congregational and Old Presbyterian Churches in the County. The Churches of Preston, North Lancashire, and Westmorland.* Manchester: Heywood, 1890.

Noll, Mark A. "The Poetry of Anne Bradstreet (1612–1672) and Edward Taylor (1642–1729)." In *The Devoted Life: An Invitation to the Puritan Classics*, edited by Kelly M. Kapic and Randall C. Gleason, 251–69. Downers Grove, IL: InterVarsity, 2004.

———. *Turning Points: Decisive Moments in the History of Christianity.* Grand Rapids: Baker, 1997.

Nunn, Catherine. "Henry Newcome and His Circle: Presbyterianism in South-East Cheshire in the 1650s." *Transactions of the Historical Society of Lancashire & Cheshire* 150 (2003 for 2000) 7–31.

Nuttall, Geoffrey F. *The Holy Spirit in Puritan Faith and Experience.* 1946. Reprint. Chicago: University of Chicago Press, 1992.

———. "Puritan and Quaker Mysticism." *Theology* 78.664 (1975) 518–31.

———. *The Puritan Spirit: Essays and Addresses.* London: Epworth, 1967.

Oberman, Heiko A. "The Meaning of Mysticism From Meister Eckhart to Martin Luther." In *The Reformation: Roots and Ramifications*, translated by Andrew Colin Gow, 77–90. Grand Rapids: Eerdmans, 1994.

———. "Simul Gemitus et Raptus: Luther and Mysticism." In *The Dawn of the Reformation: Essays in Late Medieval and Early Reformation Thought*, 126–54. Grand Rapids: Eerdmans, 1992.

Old, Hughes Oliphant. *The Reading and Preaching of the Scriptures in the Worship of the Christian Church.* Vol. 4. *The Age of Reformation.* Grand Rapids: Eerdmans, 2002.

Oliver, Robert W. *History of the English Calvinistic Baptists 1771–1892: From John Gill to C. H. Spurgeon.* Edinburgh: Banner of Truth, 2006.

Op't Hof, Willem J. "The Dutch Reception of Isaac Ambrose." unpublished article, forthcoming.

———. *Engelse Pietistische Geschriften in het Nederlands, 1598–1622.* Rotterdam: Lindenberg Boeken & Muziek, 1987.

———. "Protestant Pietism and Medieval Monasticism." In *Confessionalism and Pietism: Religious Reform in Early Modern Europe,* edited by Fred van Lieburg, 31–50. Mainz: Von Zabern, 2006.

O'Reilly, Terrance. "The Spiritual Exercises and the Crisis of Medieval Piety." *The Way Supplement* 70 (1991) 101–13.

Ormerod, George, ed. *Tracts Relating to Military Proceedings in Lancashire During the Great Civil War,* Vol. 2 Manchester: Richards, 1844.

Ozment, Steven. *The Age of Reform 1250–1550: An Intellectual and Religious History of Late Medieval and Reformation Europe.* New Haven, CT: Yale University Press, 1980.

Packer, J. I. "The Puritan Idea of Communion with God." In *Puritan Papers,* vol. 2, edited by J. I. Packer, 103–18. Phillipsburg, NJ: Presbyterian and Reformed, 2001.

———. *A Quest for Godliness: The Puritan Vision of the Christian Life.* Wheaton, IL: Crossway, 1990.

———. "Richard Baxter on Heaven, Hope, and Holiness." In *Alive to God: Studies in Spirituality,* edited by J. I. Packer & Loren Wilkerson, 161–75. Downers Grove, IL: InterVarsity, 1992.

Parish, Helen L. "'By This Mark You Shall Known Him': Clerical Celibacy and Antichrist in English Reformation Polemic." *Studies in Church History* 33 (1997) 253–66.

Parker, Kenneth L. and Eric J. Carlson. *"Practical Divinity": The Works and Life of Revd Richard Greenham.* Aldershot, UK: Ashgate, 1998.

Partee, Charles. "Calvin's Central Dogma Again." *Sixteenth Century Journal* 18.2 (1987) 191–99.

Paxman, David. "Lancashire Spiritual Culture and the Question of Magic." In *Studies in Eighteenth-Century Culture,* edited by Timothy Erwin and Ourida Mostefai, 223–43. Baltimore: Johns Hopkins University Press, 2001.

Peace, Richard. *Contemplative Bible Reading: Experiencing God through Scripture.* Colorado Springs, CO: NavPress, 1996.

Perrin, David B. "Mysticism." In *The Blackwell Companion to Christian Spirituality,* edited by Arthur Holder, 442–58. Oxford: Blackwell, 2005.

Peters, Christine. *Patterns of Piety: Women, Gender and Religion in Late Medieval and Reformation England.* Cambridge: Cambridge University Press, 2003.

Peterson, Eugene H. *The Contemplative Pastor: Returning to the Art of Spiritual Direction.* 1989. Reprint. Grand Rapids: Eerdmans, 1993.

———. *Eat This Book: A Conversation in the Art of Spiritual Reading.* Grand Rapids: Eerdmans, 2006.

———. *Working the Angles: The Shape of Pastoral Integrity.* Grand Rapids: Eerdmans, 1987.

Peterson, Mark A. "The Practice of Piety in Puritan New England: Contexts and Consequences." In *The World of John Winthrop: Essays on England and New England 1588–1649,* edited by Francis J. Bremer and Lynn A. Botelho, 75–110. Boston: Massachusetts Historical Society, 2005.

Petry, Ray C., ed. *Late Medieval Mysticism.* London: SCM, 1957.

Pettit, Norman. *The Heart Prepared: Grace and Conversion in Puritan Spiritual Life*. New Haven, CT: Yale University Press, 1966.

———. Review of *Orthodoxies in Massachusetts: Rereading American Puritanism*, by Janice Knight. *New England Quarterly* 68.1 (1995) 145–50.

Pike, Nelson. *Mystic Union: An Essay on the Phenomenology of Mysticism*. Ithaca, NY: Cornell University Press, 1992.

Plantinga, Alvin. "The Testimonial Model: Sealed Upon Our Hearts." In *Warranted Christian Belief*, 290–323. Oxford: Oxford University Press, 2000.

Poole, Robert, ed. *The Lancashire Witches: Histories and Stories*. Manchester: Manchester University Press, 2002.

Porterfield, Amanda. *Female Piety in Puritan New England: Emergence of Religious Humanism*. Oxford: Oxford University Press, 1992.

———. *Feminine Spirituality in America: From Sarah Edwards to Martha Graham*. Philadelphia: Temple University Press, 1980.

———. "Women's Attraction to Puritanism." *Church History* 60.2 (1991) 196–209.

Postema, Don. *Space for God: The Study and Practice of Prayer and Spirituality*. Grand Rapids: CRC, 1983.

Pourrat, R. *Christian Spirituality*. Vol. 3. *Later Developments, Part I, From the Renaissance to Jansenism*. London: Burns Oates and Washbourne, 1927.

Purves, Andrew. *Reconstructing Pastoral Theology: A Christological Foundation*. Louisville, KY: Westminster John Knox, 2004.

Rahner, Karl. "Experience of God Today." In *Theological Investigations*, vol. 11, translated by David Bourke, 149–65. New York: Crossroad, 1974.

———. "Experience of Self and Experience of God." In *Theological Investigations*, vol. 13, *Theology, Anthropology, Christology*, translated by David Bourke, 122–32. New York: Crossroad, 1975.

———. "Reflections on the Problem of the Gradual Ascent to Christian Perfection." In *Theological Investigations*, vol. 3, *Theology of the Spiritual Life*, translated by Karl-H. and Boniface Kruger, 3–23. London: Darton, Longman & Todd, 1974.

Rambuss, Richard. *Closet Devotions*. Durham, NC: Duke University Press, 1998.

Ranft, Patricia. *A Woman's Way: The Forgotten History of Women Spiritual Directors*. New York: Palgrave, 2000.

Rice, Howard L. *Reformed Spirituality*. Louisville, KY: Westminster John Knox, 1991.

Richardson, R. C. "Puritanism and the Ecclesiastical Authorities: The Case of the Diocese of Chester." In *Politics, Religion and The English Civil War*, edited by Brian Manning, 3–33. New York: St. Martin's, 1973.

———. *Puritanism in North-West England: A Regional Study of the Diocese of Chester to 1642*. Manchester: Manchester University Press, 1972.

Ricoeur, Paul. "The Nuptial Metaphor." In *André LaCocque and Paul Ricoeur. Thinking Biblically: Exegetical and Hermeneutical Studies*, translated by David Pellauer, 265–303. Chicago: University of Chicago Press, 1998.

Rivers, Isabel. *Reason, Grace, and Sentiment: A Study of Language of Religion and Ethics in England, 1660–1780*. Vol. 1 *Whichcote to Wesley*. Cambridge: Cambridge University Press, 1991.

Roberts, Maurice. "Samuel Rutherford: The Comings and Goings of the Heavenly Bridegroom." In *The Trials of Puritanism*, 119–34. London: Westminster Conference, 1993.

Roston, Murray "Donne and the Meditative Tradition." *Religion & Literature* 37.1 (2005) 45–68.

Rupp, Gordon. "A Rapture of Devotion in English Puritanism." In *Reformation, Conformity, and Dissent: Essays in Honour of Geoffrey Nuttall*, edited by R. Buick Knox, 115–31. London: Epworth, 1977.

Russell, Jeffrey Burton. *Mephistopheles: The Devil in the Modern World*. Ithaca, NY: Cornell University Press, 1986.

Ryken, Leland. *Worldly Saints: The Puritans As They Really Were*. Grand Rapids: Zondervan, 1986.

Ryken, Philip Graham. *Thomas Boston as Preacher of the Fourfold State*. Edinburgh: Rutherford House, 1999.

Scheper, George L. "Reformation Attitudes toward Allegory and the Song of Songs." *Modern Language Association of American Publications* 89 (1974) 551–62.

Schmidt, Leigh Eric. *Holy Fairs: Scottish Communions and American Revivals in the Early Modern Period*. Princeton: Princeton University Press, 1989.

Schneiders, Sandra M. "Scripture and Spirituality." In *Christian Spirituality: Origins to the Twelfth Century*, vol. 2, edited by Bernard McGinn, John Meyendorff, and Jean Leclercq, 1–20. New York: Crossroad, 1992.

Schoneveld, Cornelis W. *Intertraffic of the Mind: Studies in Seventeenth-Century Anglo-Dutch Translation with a Checklist of Books Translated from English into Dutch, 1600–1700*. Leiden: Brill, 1983.

Schuringa, Gregory D. "Embracing Leer and Leven: The Theology of Simon Oomius in the Context of Nadere Reformatie Orthodoxy." PhD diss., Calvin Theological Seminary, 2003.

Schwanda, Tom. "Gazing at God: Some Preliminary Observations on Contemplative Reformed Spirituality." *Reformed Review* 56.2 (2002/2003) 101–21.

———. "Growing in Christ: Glorifying and Enjoying God through Reformed Spiritual Disciplines." *Reformation & Revival* 10.1 (2001) 19–45.

———. "'Hearts Sweetly Refreshed': Puritan Spiritual Practices Then and Now." *Journal of Spiritual Formation and Soul Care* 3.1 (2010) 21–41.

Seaver, Paul S. *Wallington's World: A Puritan Artisan in Seventeenth-Century London*. Stanford, CA: Stanford University Press, 1985.

Shannon, William H. "Contemplation, Contemplative Prayer." In *The New Dictionary of Catholic Spirituality*, edited by Michael Downey, 209–14. Collegeville, MN: Liturgical, 1993.

Shaw, William A., ed. *Minutes of the Manchester Presbyterian Classis*. Part I. Vol. 20 New Series. Manchester: Chetham Society, 1890.

———. *Minutes of the Manchester Presbyterian Classis, 1646–1660*. Part II. Vol. 22 New Series. Manchester: Chetham Society, 1891.

———. *Minutes of the Manchester Presbyterian Classis, 1646–1660*. Part III. Vol. 24 New Series. Manchester: Chetham Society, 1891.

Shea, Elinor. "Spiritual Direction and Social Consciousness." *The Way Supplement* 54 (1985) 30–42.

Sheldrake, Philip. *Befriending Our Desires*. Notre Dame, IN: Ave Maria, 1994.

———. *A Brief History of Spirituality*. Oxford: Blackwell, 2007.

———. *Explorations in Spirituality: History, Theology, and Social Practice*. Mahwah, NJ: Paulist, 2010.

———. "Interpretation." In *The Blackwell Companion to Christian Spirituality*, edited by Arthur Holder, 459–77. Oxford: Blackwell, 2005.

———. "Interpreting Texts and Traditions." *Sewanee Theological Review* 46.1 (2002) 48–68.

————, ed. *New Westminster Dictionary of Christian Spirituality*. Louisville, KY: Westminster John Knox, 2005.

————. "Senses, Spiritual." In *New Westminster Dictionary of Christian Spirituality*, edited by Philip Sheldrake, 573–74. Louisville, KY: Westminster John Knox, 2005.

————. *Spaces for the Sacred: Place, Memory, and Identity*. Baltimore: Johns Hopkins University Press, 2001.

————. "Spirituality and Its Critical Methodology." In *Exploring Christian Spirituality: Essays in Honor of Sandra M. Schneiders*, edited by Bruce H. Lescher and Elizabeth Liebert, 15–34. Mahwah, NJ: Paulist, 2006.

————. *Spirituality & History: Questions of Interpretation and Method*. 2nd ed. 1991. Reprint. Maryknoll, NY: Orbis, 1995.

————. *Spirituality and Theology: Christian Living and the Doctrine of God*. Maryknoll, NY: Orbis, 1998.

Slok, Johannes. *Devotional Language*. Translated by Henrik Mossin. Berlin: de Gruyter, 1996.

Smedes, Lewis B. *Union with Christ*. Rev ed. Grand Rapids: Eerdmans, 1983.

Smith, Nigel. *Perfection Proclaimed: Language and Literature in English Radical Religion 1640–1660*. Oxford: Clarendon, 1989.

Smith, Tom C. *Records of the Parish Church of Preston in Amounderness*. London: Gray, 1892.

Smithen, F. J. *Lancashire Presbyterianism Three Hundred Years Ago (1640–1660)*. Manchester: Aikman, 1949.

Sommerfledt John R. "Bernard as Contemplative." In *Bernardus Magister: Papers Presented at the Nonacentenary Celebration of the Birth of Saint Bernard of Clairvaux, Kalamazoo, Michigan*, edited by John R. Sommerfeldt, 73–84. Kalamazoo, MI: Cistercian, 1992.

————. *The Spiritual Teachings of Bernard of Clairvaux: An Intellectual History of the Early Cistercian Order*. Kalamazoo, MI: Cistercian, 1991.

Sommerville, C. John. *Popular Religion in Restoration England*. Gainesville, FL: University Presses of Florida, 1977.

Sonderegger, Katherine. "Barth and Feminism." In *The Cambridge Companion to Karl Barth*, edited by John Webster, 258–73. Cambridge: Cambridge University Press, 2000.

Spufford, Margaret, ed. *The World of Rural Dissenters, 1520–1725*. Cambridge: Cambridge University Press, 1995.

Spurr, John. *English Puritanism, 1603–1689*. New York: St. Martin's, 1998.

Steinmetz, David C. "Superiority of Pre-Critical Exegesis." *Theology Today* 37.1 (1980) 27–38.

Stoeffler, Fred Ernest. *The Rise of Evangelical Pietism*. Leiden: Brill, 1971.

Sutherland, Martin. "A Treatise of Delighting in God by John Howe (1630–1705)." In *The Devoted Life: An Invitation to the Puritan Classics*, edited by Kelly M. Kapic and Randall C. Gleason, 225–37. Downers Grove, IL: InterVarsity, 2004.

Tait, James. "The Declaration of Sports for Lancashire (1617)." *English Historical Review* 32 (1917) 561–68.

Tamburello, Dennis E. *Bernard of Clairvaux: Essential Writings*. New York: Crossroad, 2000.

————. "John Calvin's Mysticism And the Treatise Against the Libertines." In *Truth as Gift: Studies in Medieval Cistercian History in honor of John R. Sommerfeldt*, edited by Marsha L. Dutton, Daniel M. La Corte and Paul Lockey, 503–16. Kalamazoo, MI: Cistercian, 2004.

———. *Ordinary Mysticism*. Mahwah, NJ: Paulist, 1996.

———. *Union with Christ: John Calvin and the Mysticism of St. Bernard*. Louisville, KY: Westminster John Knox, 1994.

Tipson, Baird. "The Routinized Piety of Thomas Shepard's Diary." *Early American Literature* 13.1 (1978) 64–80.

Tomalin, Claire. *Samuel Pepys: The Unequalled Self*. New York: Vintage, 2002.

Thomas, Keith. "Cases of Conscience in Seventeenth-Century England." In *Public Duty and Private Conscience in Seventeenth-Century England: Essays Presented to G. E. Aylmer*, edited by John Morrill, Paul Slack, and Daniel Woolf, 29–56. Oxford: Clarendon, 1993.

———. *Religion and the Decline of Magic*. New York: Scribner's Sons, 1971.

Todd, Margo. "The Spiritualized Household." in *Christian Humanism and the Puritan Social Order*, 96–117. Cambridge: Cambridge University Press, 1987.

Toon, Peter. *From Mind to Heart: Christian Meditation Today*. Grand Rapids: Baker, 1987.

Torrance, Alan. "Christian Experience and Divine Revelation in the Theologies of Friedrich Schleiermacher and Karl Barth." In *Christian Experience in Theology and Life*, edited by I. Howard Marshall, 83–113. Edinburgh: Rutherford House Books, 1988.

Tracy, David. *The Analogical Imagination: Christian Theology and the Culture of Pluralism*. New York: Crossroad, 1981.

———. *On Naming the Present: God, Hermeneutics, and Church*. Maryknoll, NY: Orbis, 1994.

———. *Plurality and Ambiguity: Hermeneutics, Religion, Hope*. San Francisco: Harper & Row, 1987.

Trevor-Roper, Hugh. *Catholics, Anglicans and Puritans: Seventeenth Century Essays*. Chicago: University of Chicago Press, 1987.

Trinterud, Leonard J. "The Origins of Puritanism." *Church History* 20.1 (1951) 37–57.

Trueman, Carl R. "Puritan Theology as Historical Event: A Linguistic Approach to the Ecumenical Context." In *Reformation and Scholasticism: An Ecumenical Enterprise*, edited by Willem J. van Asselt and Eef Dekker, 253–75. Grand Rapids: Baker Academic, 2001.

Tuan, Yi-Fu. "Geopiety: A Theme in Man's Attachment to Nature and to Place." In *Geographies of the Mind: Essays in Historical Geosophy: In Honor of John Kirtland Wright*, edited by David Lowenthal and Martyn J. Bowden, 11–39. New York: Oxford University Press, 1976.

———. *Topophilia: A Study of Environmental Perception, Attitudes, and Values*. Englewoods Cliffs, NJ: Prentice-Hall, 1974.

Turner, Denys. *Eros and Allegory: Medieval Exegesis of the Song of Songs*. Kalamazoo, MI: Cistercian, 1995.

———. "Mysticism." In *The Oxford Companion to Christian Thought*, edited by Adrian Hastings, Alistair Mason, and Hugh Pyper, 460–62. Oxford: Oxford University Press, 2000.

van Beek, Marius. *An Enquiry into Puritan Vocabulary*. Groningen, Netherlands: Wolters-Noordhoff, 1969.

van den Belt, Hank. *The Authority of Scripture in Reformed Theology: Truth and Trust*. Leiden: Brill, 2008.

van den Berg, Jan. "The English Puritan Francis Rous and the Influence of His works in the Netherlands." In *Johannes van den Berg Religious Currents and Cross-Currents: Essays on Early Modern Protestantism and the Protestant Enlightenment*, edited by Jan De Bruijn, Pieter Holtrop, and Ernestine Van Der Wall, 25–42. Leiden: Brill, 1999.

van Der Haar, J. *From Abbadie to Young: A Bibliography of English, Most Puritan Works, Translated I/T Dutch Language.* Vol. 1. Veenendaal, Netherlands: Uitgeverij B. V., 1980.

Veenhof, Jan. "A History of Theology and Spirituality in the Dutch Reformed Churches (Gereformeeerde Kerken), 1892–1992." *Calvin Theological Journal* 28 (1993) 266–97.

Verduin, Kathleen. "'Our Cursed Natures': Sexuality and the Puritan Conscience." *New England Quarterly* 56.2 (1983) 220–37.

Vissers, John. "Karl Barth's Appreciative Use of Herman Bavinck's 'Reformed Dogmatics'" Presentation at "A Pearl and a Leaven: Herman Bavinck for the Twenty-first Century" Conference on September 19, 2008, Calvin Theological Seminary, Grand Rapids, Michigan.

Von Balthasar, Hans Urs. *Prayer.* Translated by A. V. Littledale. New York: Sheed & Ward, 1961.

Von Hügel, Frederich. *The Mystical Element of Religion as Studied in Saint Catherine of Genoa and Her Friends.* 2 vols. New York: Dutton, 1923.

Wack, Mary Frances. *Lovesickness in the Middle Ages: The Viaticum and Its Commentaries.* Philadelphia: University of Pennsylvania Press, 1990.

Wakefield, Gordon S. "Mysticism and its Puritan Types." *London Quarterly and Holborn Review* 191 (1966) 34–45.

———. *Puritan Devotion: Its Place in the Development of Puritan Piety.* London: Epworth, 1957.

———. "The Puritans." In *The Study of Spirituality*, edited by Cheslyn Jones, Geoffrey Wainwright, and Edward Yarnold, 437–45. Oxford: Oxford University Press, 1986.

Wallace, Dewey D., Jr. "The Image of Saintliness in Puritan Hagiography 1650–1700." In *The Divine Drama in History and Liturgy.* Allison Park, PA: Pickwick, 1984.

———. *Puritans and Predestination: Grace in English Protestant Theology, 1525–1695.* 1984. Reprint. Eugene, OR: Wipf & Stock, 2004.

———. *Shapers of English Calvinism, 1660–1714: Variety, Persistence, and Transformation.* Oxford: Oxford University Press, 2011.

Wallace, Ronald S. *Calvin, Geneva and the Reformation: A Study of Calvin as Social Reformer, Churchman, Pastor and Theologian.* Grand Rapids: Baker, 1990.

———. *Calvin's Doctrine of the Christian Life.* Tyler, TX: Geneva Divinity School Press, 1959, 1982.

Walsh, Carey Ellen. *Exquisite Desire: Religion, the Erotic, and the Song of Songs.* Minneapolis: Fortress, 2000.

Walsham, Alexandra. *Providence in Early Modern England.* Oxford: Oxford University Press, 1999.

Watkin, E. I. *Poets and Mystics.* Freeport, NY: Books for Libraries, 1953.

Watkins, O. C. *The Puritan Experience: Studies in Spiritual Autobiography.* New York: Schocken, 1972.

Walton, Brad. *Jonathan Edwards, Religious Affections and the Puritan Analysis of True Piety, Spiritual Sensation and Heart Religion.* Lewiston and Queenston and Lampeter: Mellon, 2002.

Ward, W. R. *Early Evangelicalism: A Global Intellectual History, 1670–1789*. Cambridge: Cambridge University Press, 2006.

Watts, Michael R. *The Dissenters: From the Reformation to the French Revolution*. Oxford: Oxford University Press, 1978.

Webber, Robert E. *The Divine Embrace: Recovering the Passionate Life*. Grand Rapids: Baker, 2006.

Webster, John. *Barth's Ethics of Reconciliation*. Cambridge: Cambridge University Press, 1995.

———, ed. *The Cambridge Companion to Karl Barth*. Cambridge: Cambridge University Press, 2000.

Webster, Tom. *Godly Clergy in Early Stuart England: The Caroline Puritan Movement, c. 1620–1643*. Cambridge: Cambridge University Press, 1997.

———. "'Kiss Me with the Kisses of His Mouth': Gender Inversion and Canticles in Godly Spirituality." In *Sodomy in Early Modern Europe*, edited by Tom Betteridge, 148–63. Manchester: Manchester University Press, 2002.

———. "Writing to Redundancy: Approaches to Spiritual Journals and Early Modern Spirituality." *Historical Journal* 39.1 (1996) 33–56.

Wehr, Gerhard. *The Mystical Marriage: Symbol and Meaning of the Human Experience*. Translated by Jill Sutcliffe. Northamptonshire, UK: Crucible (Aquarian), 1990.

Welch, Roger W. "Quakers, Ranters and Puritan Mystics." In *Faith and Ferment*, 50–69. London: Westminster Conference, 1982.

Wenger, Thomas L. "The New Perspective on Calvin: Responding to Recent Calvin Interpretations." *Journal of Evangelical Theology Society* 50.2 (2007) 311–28.

Westerkamp, Marilyn. "Engendering Puritan Religious Culture in Old and New England." *Pennsylvania History* 64 (1997) 105–22.

White, B. R. "Echoes of Medieval Christendom in Puritan Spirituality." *One In Christ: A Catholic Evangelical Quarterly* 16.1–2 (1980) 78–90.

White, Helen C. *English Devotional Literature [Prose] 1600–1640*. Madison: University of Wisconsin Press, 1931.

Wiles, M. F. "Origen as Biblical Scholar." In *The Cambridge History of the Bible, Vol. 1 From the Beginnings to Jerome*, edited by P. R. Ackroyd and C. F. Evans, 454–88. Cambridge: Cambridge University Press, 1970.

Willen, Diane. "Communion of the Saints: Spiritual Reciprocity in the Godly Community in Early Modern England." *Albion* 27 (1995) 19–41.

———. "Godly Women in Early Modern England: Puritanism and Gender." *Journal of Ecclesiastical History* 43.4 (1992) 561–80.

———. "Religion and the Construction of the Feminine." In *A Companion to Early Modern Women's Writing*, edited by Anita Pacheco, 22–39. Oxford: Blackwell, 2002.

Williams, D. H. *Retrieving the Tradition & Renewing Evangelicalism: A Primer for Suspicious Protestants*. Grand Rapids: Eerdmans, 1999.

Williams, Jean. "The Puritan Quest for Enjoyment of God: An Analysis of the Theological and Devotional Writings of Puritans in Seventeenth Century England." PhD diss., University of Melbourne, 1997.

———. "Puritanism: A Piety of Joy." *Kategoria* 10 (1998) 4–14.

Wilson, Paul Scott. *God Sense: Reading the Bible Preaching*. Nashville: Abingdon, 2001.

Winship, Michael P. "Behold the Bridegroom Cometh! Marital Imagery in Massachusetts Preaching, 1630–1730." *Early American Literature* 27.3 (1992) 170–84.

Wiseman, James A. "Mysticism." In *The New Dictionary of Catholic Spirituality*, edited by Michael Downey, 681–92. Collegeville, MN: Liturgical, 1993.

Won, Jonathan Jong-Chun. "Communion with Christ: An Exposition and Comparison of the Doctrine of Union and Communion with Christ in Calvin and the English Puritans." PhD diss., Westminster Theological Seminary, 1989.

Woolrych, Austin. *The Battles of the English Civil War*. 1961. Reprint. London: Phoenix, 2000.

Yeoman, Louise A. "Heart-Work: Emotion, Empowerment and Authority in Covenanting Times." PhD diss., St. Andrews University, 1991.

Yost, J. K. "The Reformation Defense of Clerical Marriage in the Reigns of Henry VIII and Edward VI." *Church History* 50.2 (1981) 152–64.

Young, B. W. "The Anglican Origin of Newman's Celibacy." *Church History* 65.1 (1996) 15–27.

Yuille, J. Stephen. *The Inner Sanctum of Puritan Piety*. Grand Rapids: Reformation Heritage, 2007.

————. *Puritan Spirituality: The Fear of God in the Affective Theology of George Swinnock*. Milton Keynes, UK: Paternoster, 2007.

Zacharias, Brian G. *The Embattled Christian: William Gurnall and the Puritan View of Spiritual Warfare*. Edinburgh: Banner of Truth, 1995.

Zachman, Randall C. *Image and Word in the Theology of John Calvin*. Notre Dame, IN: University of Notre Dame Press, 2007.

————. *John Calvin as Teacher, Pastor, and Theologian: The Shape of His Writings and Thought*. Grand Rapids: Baker Academic, 2006.

General Index

and Puritans, 26–27, 55–60, 137, 199, 243

Hooker, Thomas, 9, 26, 36n8, 37n9, 54, 60, 62, 82, 100, 124n11, 149–50, 172–73

and Isaac Ambrose, 197

Houghton, Lady Margaret/Houghton Tower

and Isaac Ambrose, 29, 67n197, 89, 118, 121, 161, 248

Houston, James, 230n212, 231

Hunsinger, George, 203, 205n36, 207n51, 208n60, 211

Ignatius of Loyola, 124, 130, 132, 134, 213

and Isaac Ambrose, 28, 127, 134, 140–42, 188, 233

imagination

and Ignatius of Loyola, 140–42

and Isaac Ambrose and Puritans, 138–42

interpretation. *See* hermeneutics

Jesus

as divine bridegroom. *See* bridal imagery and Jesus as bridegroom

and feminine image of, 59

as husband. *See* bridal imagery and Jesus as husband

Jones, R. Tudor, 59n148, 66n190

and Isaac Ambrose, 202n24

joy/enjoyment of God

and Isaac Ambrose use of, 65, 66, 69–72, 76, 81, 84–86, 89, 117, 128, 143, 148, 160–63, 166, 174, 177–79, 184, 192–95, 239, 243

and Puritan use of, 20, 32, 38, 41, 45, 56–58, 73, 123, 137, 149, 176, 191, 193n154

Kapic, Kelly, 8n34, 22n114, 56n127, 61n162, 138n102

Kaufmann, Milo, 123n2, 129, 132, 139n111

and Isaac Ambrose, 23–24, 129, 142

King, Benjamin, 36n8, 54–55, 57–58, 62n168

Knott, John, 127n28, 129, 130, 132n62, 139n111, 173

Lancashire, 112, 114–16, 119, 144

Lane, Belden, 11n55, 53, 115, 116, 170n36, 175, 239

Leclercq, Jean, 137n95, 145

Leverenz, David, 59n144, 63nn174, 175

Lewalski, Barbara, 43n41, 123n2, 130, 133n64, 165n10

and Isaac Ambrose, 24, 133n64

Liebert, Elizabeth, 78n14, 79n17, 80

Longfellow, Erica, 46, 47n68, 48n75, 54n109, 59, 63

and Isaac Ambrose, 24

Lord's Supper, 42, 73, 109, 170n33, 218, 228, 249

and Isaac Ambrose, 69, 79, 109–11, 114, 147, 176, 242, 249

Lovelace, Richard, 11n55, 15, 22n114, 99, 131, 132n62, 137, 140

Lowance, M. I., 43nn41, 42, 44n47

Luttmer, Frank, 90, 93n79, 96n98

marriage, earthly or godly of Puritans

compared with spiritual marriage, 45–46, 49

and erotic language, 50–52, 60

and intimacy and enjoyment of sex, 51–54

and Isaac Ambrose, 46, 48–49

and patriarchy in marriage, 47–49

and purpose of marriage, 49–51

marriage, spiritual

biblical foundation of, 26–38

and Bernard of Clairvaux, 38–39, 40–42, 65

compared with godly marriage in Puritans, 45–46, 49, 59–60

comparison of Bernard, Calvin, and the Puritans on, 72–74

and contemplation, 57–58, 69

enjoyment and delight of God in, 56–58, 65, 70–72, 160, 193–95

and erotic language, 37, 45–46, 59–61, 63, 74, 87, 165–65, 174, 214, 239, 243

and gender dynamics, 62–64